CULTURAL RESOURCE
LAWS & PRACTICE

Heritage Resources Management Series

Sponsored by the Heritage Resources Management Program
Division of Continuing Education, University of Nevada, Reno

Books in this series are practical guides designed to help those who work in cultural resource management, environmental management, heritage preservation, and related areas. The books are replete with examples, checklists, worksheets, and worldly advice offered by experienced practitioners in the field.

Volumes in the series:

CULTURAL RESOURCE LAWS & PRACTICE

Thomas F. King

ALTAMIRA
PRESS

A Division of Rowman & Littlefield Publishers, Inc.
Lanham • New York • Toronto • Plymouth, UK

AltaMira Press
A division of Rowman & Littlefield Publishers, Inc.
A wholly owned subsidiary of The Rowman & Littlefield Publishing Group, Inc.
4501 Forbes Boulevard, Suite 200
Lanham, MD 20706
www.altamirapress.com

Estover Road
Plymouth PL6 7PY
United Kingdom

British Library Cataloguing in Publication Information Available

Library of Congress Cataloguing-in-Publication Data

King, Thomas F.
  Cultural resource laws & practice / Thomas F. King.—3rd ed.
    p. cm.
  Cover title: Cultural resource laws and practice
  Includes bibliographical references and index.
  ISBN-13: 978-0-7591-1188-2 (cloth: alk. paper)
  ISBN-10: 0-7591-1188-X (cloth: alk. paper)
  ISBN-13: 978-0-7591-1189-9 (pbk.: alk. paper)
  ISBN-10: 0-7591-1189-8 (pbk.: alk. paper)
  1. Historic preservation—Law and legislation—United States. 2. Cultural property—Protection—Law and legislation—United States. I. Title. II. Title: Cultural resource laws and practice.

  KF4310.K56 2008
  344.73'094—dc22   2008005937

Printed in the United States of America

∞™ The paper used in this publication meets the minimum requirements of American National Standard for Information Sciences—Permanence of Paper for Printed Library Materials, ANSI/NISO Z39.48–1992.

To the memory of Robert R. Garvey Jr.,
who taught me that preservation is about live people.

Contents

Acknowledgments

I'm grateful to Jack Meinhardt of Rowman & Littlefield for encouraging me to work up this third edition of *Cultural Resource Laws and Practice*, and to all whose purchases of prior editions have justified this one. I'm thankful to Michele Aubry, Ryan Howell, Sara Palmer, Morgan Rieder, and David Siegel for suggestions about how to make this edition better than the last, and seek their forgiveness for failing to follow some of them. I reiterate the gratitude I expressed in earlier editions for the support and help provided by Mitch Allen, R. Joe Brandon, Denise DeJoseph, Nick Del Cioppo, Don Fowler, Dell Greek, Pam Lucas, Brian Kenny, Kathy Nickerson, Claudia Nissley, Mary Pierce, Lee Pye, Constance Ramirez, James Robertson, David Rotenstein, David Snyder, and Darby Stapp.

In addition, I'm grateful to all those who've worked with me over the years in developing and presenting courses in historic preservation, environmental review, and related topics, to all those who've taken my classes, and especially to all those who've challenged me and my premises in negotiations, consultations, conversations, publications, and Internet debates. For better or worse, without you all, this book would not have come to be. No one but me, however, is responsible for its faults.

Tom King
Silver Spring, Maryland
January 2008

Preface to the Third Edition

In 2003 I ended the preface to the second edition of this book—after a brief recitation of what I thought had changed since the first edition in 1998—as follows:

> And yet, much remains profoundly, and discouragingly, the same. CRM is still viewed by many—maybe most—of its self-conscious practitioners as a form of archeological research, albeit constrained by a lot of pesky though barely understood regulatory requirements and client concerns.[1] Section 106 review is still understood by many as getting a state historic preservation officer's blessing on a report. Experts continue to peer earnestly into their navels to ponder the abstractions of eligibility for the National Register of Historic Places. People still rely mindlessly on census data to find environmental justice populations. "Cultural Resource Management (CRM) Plans," even when ostensibly "integrated," continue to comprise mostly ponderous volumes of turgid historical and archeological data with vapid and often misleading recitations of standard historic preservation procedures tacked on at the end. The public is still, on the whole, closed out of CRM practice. The extensive provisions for early public participation that appear in the 1999–2000 version of the section 106 regulations continue to be ignored. It still comes as a surprise to people when I tell them that under the regulations you initiate the process by figuring out who you ought to consult and starting to consult them, not by sending out your archeologists to begin doing their standardized surveys of project areas.[2] Meanwhile, the

big issues of conflict between the modern and traditional worlds go unaddressed, or get addressed by others who are—perhaps—less equipped by background and temperament to deal with them than are CRM experts.

To me this is very sad, and frustrating, since back in 1998—and, of course, both before and since—I called as ringingly as I could for a different kind of CRM—more inclusive, comprehensive, flexible, and responsive to the voice of the people. It is hard not to wonder where I went wrong. Certainly nobody's told me I'm wrong; there's been no organized written defense of the status quo. Are people just being sensitive about my feelings? Am I just completely out to lunch?

Well, maybe, or maybe the time just hasn't been ripe for change to occur. Change takes time; change can be hard. It's so much easier to do things the way we've always done them and to use the skills we were taught in graduate school even though we never learned anything there about CRM. And everyone's overworked, many are underpaid, and—perhaps here's the crux—more and more of us are looking with hope toward retirement.

The first generation of CRM practitioners is on its way out. The members of my age cohort are leaving their cubicles to go fish or watch TV or play with grandchildren or look for Amelia Earhart. And in that, perhaps, there's hope. Maybe the up-and-coming generation will rethink what we're about in this business. And maybe a lot of them will have read *Cultural Resource Laws and Practice*.

Hope springs eternal. But like everything else, it depends. . . .

In 2008 I can't see that anything has changed—except we've gotten older and, if anything, more set in our ways. The retirement of many of my age-mates has not helped; the new kids seem to come into the field quite satisfied to just keep doing what their elders have done, in the same ways their elders have done them. Every now and then I run into someone who wants to change things, who wants to shake things up, and the encounter brightens my day. But such encounters are few and far between. Maybe I'm missing some great tidal movement that's taking place beneath the surface. I hope so.

Tom King
Silver Spring, Maryland
January 2008

Notes

1. See Tom King, "What is Section 106 Review Anyhow? Two Views," in Thinking about *Cultural Resource Management: Essays From the Edge* (Walnut Creek, CA: AltaMira Press, 2002), 38–47.

2. See 36 CFR 800.3, "Initiation of the Section 106 Process," especially 800.3(e), "plan to involve the public" and 800.3(f), "Identify other consulting parties."

The historical and cultural foundations of the Nation should be preserved as a living part of our community life and development in order to give a sense of orientation to the American people.

—National Historic Preservation Act (16 USC 470 et seq.)
Section 1(b)(2)

1

Cultural Resource Management: Why Is It? What Is It? Who Does It?

The Voice of the People

Chitaro's house sat on a rocky ledge overlooking Pou Bay on Wene Island. Midden—dark soil charged with marine shells and animal bones, detritus of meals consumed over generations, the stuff archeologists excavate—streamed down the slope. Chitaro was the political chief of Mechchitiw Village; his green, tin-roofed plywood bungalow, visible from much of the village, reflected his place in the community. With my wife—cultural anthropologist Patricia Parker—I had come to pay respects to him and to Teruio, Mechchitiw's high chief and senior elder. It was 1979. We were leaving the islands of Chuuk[1], in Micronesia, after two eventful years.

Pat had completed her dissertation fieldwork in nearby Iras Village. I had finished my contract as "Consultant to the High Commissioner of the Trust Territory of the Pacific Islands: Archeology and Historic Preservation"—a contract the HiCom would happily have terminated a year earlier had not the National Park Service and Congress of Micronesia caused him to reconsider. Pat and I had mediated a dispute between the Trust Territory Government and the villages of Iras and Mechchitiw over construction of an airport on the fringe of their tradition-haunted mountain, Tonaachaw. Now we were leaving, great with child, experience, and data, to face new challenges back on the mainland.

We chatted over instant coffee laced with sweetened canned milk—a contemporary Chuukese tradition. Then Teruio reached into a dusty corner and pulled out a magnificent conch shell. Conches, in Micronesia as throughout the Pacific, are used as trumpets. The chief blows into the conch, producing a piercing, wailing moan that summons the people to the *wuut*—the meetinghouse—to ponder issues or respond to threats, to mobilize for war.

With trembling hands (he drank a lot of coffee), Teruio presented the conch to me. Pat translated: "When you are back in Washington, in that White House, keep this to remember the voice of the people."

I've not made it to the White House, except on tours and to a reception or two, but I keep the conch in a prominent place, still specked with Chitaro's green house paint, to remind me of what I'm about. Sometimes I pick it up and think about Teruio's words. It provides a measure of focus.

Over the decades—particularly since the 1960s—the United States Congress has enacted laws aimed at controlling the federal government's impacts on aspects of the environment. Among these are laws dealing with what have come to be called "cultural resources"—variously defined, but certainly having something to do with human culture. In analyzing impacts on such "resources," and in considering what to do with them, it should go without saying (but doesn't) that we must listen to, and try to understand, "the voice of the people" whose cultural values give them meaning.

This book is about the cultural resource laws of the United States, and the regulations, standards, and guidelines that flow from them. It is about practice under those laws, regulations, standards, and guidelines, as I understand it.

Sounds boring? It can be, but not necessarily, and not always. The laws have made a difference, and they continue to. They have stopped projects that would have destroyed places people hold dear. They have caused changes in such projects, to mitigate their damage. They have been the subjects of lawsuits and congressional hearings, and they have affected the careers of civil servants, military personnel, and political leaders. On some happy occasions they have worked so that cultural concerns are integrated into project planning, allowing contemporary needs to be fulfilled while treasured aspects of the cultural environment are respected. One of the purposes of this book is to help people, organizations, and agencies achieve such "win-win" solutions.

Many people today specialize in working with the "cultural resource" laws—as attorneys, as government, Indian tribal, and corporate officials, as consultants, as field researchers. Such work can be professionally challenging and satisfying. It can also be frustrating—in large part because the laws, regulations, standards, and guidelines have been developed with little reference to any overall vision and with little coordination. They can appear to contradict one another, and they can be interpreted in many ways, some of them weird. They have spawned institutions whose goals do not always coincide with one another or, I believe, with the purposes of the laws, and whose procedures sometimes crosscut and conflict with one another.

So, another thing this book will do is reflect on some of these problems—as I see them—and, where I can, suggest ways to fix them.

What Are "Cultural Resources"?

You might think that "cultural resources" are "resources"—things that can be used, says the dictionary—that are somehow related to "culture"—this word usually taken to mean something like the beliefs, values, and ways of life that a group of people passes from generation to generation. I think that's what the term *should* mean. "Cultural resources" should be understood as those aspects of the environment—both physical and intangible, both natural and built—that have cultural value of some kind to a group of people. The group can be a community, a neighborhood, a tribe, or any of the scholarly and not-so-scholarly disciplines that document and study cultural things—archeologists, architectural historians, folklorists, cultural anthropologists. The definition should include those nonmaterial human social institutions that help make up the environment in our heads—our social institutions, our beliefs, our accustomed practices, and our perceptions of what makes the environment culturally comfortable. "Cultural resource management" (CRM) ought to mean managing all these sociocultural aspects of the environment, and all the contemporary world's impacts on them.

That ought to be how the term is understood not only because it's what the words mean, but because collectively, the laws we'll discuss in this book address all those resource types, albeit in uneven, uncoordinated ways. Unfortunately, Congress has never gotten around to enacting a comprehensive cultural resource law. Instead we have a hodgepodge of laws, regulations, and executive orders, each dealing with a particular kind of cultural resource. Figure 1 is an effort to diagram the relationships among the resource types to which the laws apply, and table 1 roughly outlines the legal authorities that relate to each such type.

In the competition for federal agency attention and funding, legal authorities that aren't the subjects of binding regulations lose out, and the resource types to which they refer get ignored. Although the regulations implementing the National Environmental Policy Act (NEPA) theoretically require attention to all aspects of the human environment, including its sociocultural aspects, those

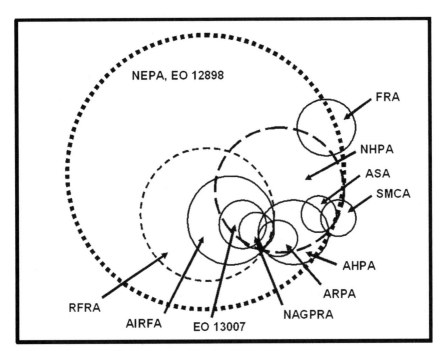

Figure 1.   Resource Types Embraced by the U.S. CRM Laws

Table 1.1. Cultural Resource Types and Relevant Legal Authorities

Resource Type	Legal Authority That May Be Relevant
Historic places in general	NEPA, NHPA
Spiritual places	NEPA, NHPA, AIRFA, RFRA, EO 13007
Cultural landscapes, rivers, etc.	NEPA, NHPA
Culturally important plants, animals	NEPA, NHPA if specific place involved
Culturally important water, air, wind patterns, etc.	NEPA, NHPA if related to identifiable place
Archeological sites	NEPA, NHPA, AHPA, ARPA if federal/ tribal land
Shipwrecks, submerged aircraft	NEPA, NHPA, ASA, SMCA if military
Native American graves, cultural items	NEPA, NHPA, NAGPRA, ARPA if federal/tribal land
Religious practices	RFRA, AIRFA, NEPA, NHPA if place-related
Traditional subsistence practices	NEPA, EO 12898 if EJ population, NHPA if place-related
Other social institutions, ways of life	NEPA, EO 12898 if EJ population, NHPA if place-related.
Songs, stories, dances	NHPA if place-related, perhaps NEPA
Historical documents	FRA, NHPA if place-related, perhaps NEPA
Artifacts	NHPA if historic place-related, perhaps ARPA, NAGPRA, NEPA, agency policies, international treaties

Key:
AHPA: Archaeological and Historic Preservation Act
AIRFA: American Indian Religious Freedom Act
ARPA: Archaeological Resources Protection Act
ASA: Abandoned Shipwrecks Act
Executive Order 12898: Environmental Justice
Executive Order 13007: Indian Sacred Sites
FRA: Federal Records Act
NAGPRA: Native American Graves Protection and Repatriation Act
NEPA: National Environmental Policy Act
NHPA: National Historic Preservation Act
RFRA: Religious Freedom Restoration Act

regulations are so broad, so general, and frankly so obtuse that they don't provide much direction. So only "historic properties," "archeological sites," and "native American graves and cultural items"—each the subject of its own special-purpose laws and regulations—get more or less routine attention, and most CRM practitioners act as though these are the *only* cultural resources.

This is too bad. Culture is a big, complex part of our world. Its "resources" are many and diverse; they are interrelated and subjective. And culture deeply affects what we do and how we relate to one another. Flying airplanes into buildings on September 11, 2001, was an act of terrorism, but it was also a cultural act, as were the attacks on Afghanistan and Iraq that it precipitated. Unrest in China, ferment in the Islamic world, acceptance and rejection of economic globalization all reflect the fact that people look at the world and life and each other through cultural lenses. Policy disrespects culture at its peril. But in planning and carrying out government programs and projects, we do precisely that—we ignore culture except to the extent it is haphazardly considered by individual members of Congress and federal agency decision makers. Or to the extent we are forced to consider it by irate citizens and social crises.

We ought to have a thoughtful, sensitive, comprehensive way of planning and carrying out government operations with respect for all parts of the sociocultural environment. But we don't. We have fairly organized ways of considering the impacts of plans and actions on historic places, archeological sites, and Native American graves and cultural items—overlapping resource types that mostly comprise discrete chunks of real estate. The rest of the sociocultural environment—in the United States and other nations—we more or less ignore.

In this book we will, like everybody else, spend most of our time dealing with historic places, archeological sites, and Native American graves and cultural items. But let no one think that this is as it should be, or as it must be, or even as the laws, collectively, make it be. Perhaps someday wise and influential political leaders will recognize that it would be sensible to attend to the impacts of government actions on the whole cultural environment, and they will clarify the law accordingly. Until that happens, we can only work with what we have.

An Exemplary Catastrophe: The African Burial Ground

A classic example of how our narrow-minded handling of cultural resources can lead to disaster is the case of the African Burial Ground in New York City.

In the late seventeenth and early eighteenth centuries, the African Burial Ground was a low area among the sand dunes of Manhattan Island, a short distance outside the walls of New Amsterdam. Enslaved Africans—yes, there were slaves in New York then—and their equally enslaved descendants buried their dead there. Later the area was buried as the dunes were leveled and New York spread north. The street called Broadway was built over one side of the cemetery, which had been more or less forgotten.

In the 1980s, Congress directed the U.S. General Services Administration (GSA) to build a new federal office building on the Broadway Block, a parcel of land just east of Broadway. GSA did an environmental assessment, during which an old map was found showing the eighteenth century "Negro burial ground."

The environmental assessment was prepared by a planning firm, which was under contract to the design and development firm that was under contract to GSA to design and build the new facility. This firm in turn subcontracted with an archeological company to do the cultural resource work. The resource—the burial ground—was perceived to be an archeological site, something buried in the ground that could be excavated. Archeologists could be hired to dig it up, remove its contents to a laboratory, study and report on it, and that would be that. No one seems to have felt the need to find out how New York's African American community might feel about the place.

When the Burial Ground was actually encountered—and turned out to be bigger and more intact than anyone expected—all hell broke loose. African Americans in New York and across the country—and around the world—vehemently protested the desecration of their ancestors' remains. Congress intervened, and the project had to be redesigned to preserve some of the bodies while the remaining were subjected to extensive and expensive excavation and analysis preparatory to reburial. The construction contractor was awarded massive penalty payments because of the delay. The last time I checked, the cost of this fiasco to the U.S. taxpayer had been upwards of $80 million. Today a monument stands on the site in belated recognition of the people buried there.[2]

There were lots of things that caused the African Burial Ground to bite GSA so hard, but one of the most important was that the site was misperceived at the outset. The moment the map was found with "Negro Burial Ground" on it, somebody should have recognized that the place would have emotional, cultural importance to African Americans. Intensive consultation should have been undertaken, a cooperative program should have been developed with the African American community, as was successfully done in a similar case in Philadelphia.[3] Dealing with the burial ground would still have been expensive, but it would have cost a lot less than $80 million, and it could have been done in a calmer, more orderly, less contentious manner. But the cultural value of the site was instead equated with archeological research value, and it was assumed that archeologists by themselves could preserve that value. The notion of what a "cultural resource" is was too narrowly construed, and the results were costly.

My point is a simple one. Cultural resources comprise a big, complex, intricate mosaic of things and institutions and values, beliefs and perceptions, customs and traditions, symbols and social structures. And it's integral to what makes people people and communities communities, so it's charged with a great deal of emotion. As a result, cultural resource management should involve a great deal more than archeology or architectural history or folklife or historic preservation. It needs to deal with management of the *whole cultural environment* and the effects of contemporary plans and decisions on that environment in all its aspects. To make it do this, however, we have to be creative, and there is nothing in laws, regulations, or the traditions of most government agencies that encourages creativity.

Cultural Resources, Cultural Heritage

In some other countries, notably the United Kingdom, and in some international contexts, the term "cultural heritage" is used to mean roughly the same range of things that we in the United States call "cultural resources."[4] I think "heritage" is a better word than "resource" to refer to such things—it seems less loutishly materialistic—but we seem to have stuck ourselves with "resource," so in the interests of communication with my probable readers, I've stuck with it too. But those familiar with laws and practices in other parts of the world should understand that to me, at least, the terms "cultural resource" and "cultural heritage" mean about the same thing.

Cultural Resources and Social Impacts

CRM as defined here is closely related to, and overlaps, another acronymous body of practice—"Social impact assessment," or SIA. SIA means:

> analyzing, monitoring, and managing the intended and unintended social consequences, both positive and negative, of planned interventions [policies, programs, plans, projects] and any social change processes invoked by those interventions.[5]

SIA is sometimes cast as "socioeconomic impact assessment," whereupon it takes on the dismal characteristics of economics and ignores the sociocultural factors that are the subjects of this book. SIA has its own interesting history and its own rules of practice; we'll discuss some of these in the chapters to come.

Cultural Resources and Historic Preservation

Like "cultural resource," the term "historic preservation" has a range of meanings, but I'll follow Congress and the National Historic Preservation Act (NHPA) in defining it to include:

> identification, evaluation, recordation, documentation, curation, acquisition, protection, management, rehabilitation restoration, stabilization, maintenance, research, interpretation, [and] conservation [of historic properties], and education and training regarding the foregoing activities or any combination of the foregoing activities.[6]

Nobody ever accused Congress of elegant wordsmithery. "Historic property," by the way, is defined in the same statute as:

> any prehistoric or historic district, site, building, structure or object included in, or eligible for inclusion on the National Register [of Historic Places], including artifacts, records, and material remains related to such a property.[7]

Historic preservation deals with one kind of cultural resource— the "historic property." Historic preservation has a highly developed (perhaps overdeveloped) body of procedure, operating at the federal and local levels, and in international, regional, state, and Indian tribal contexts. Because this corpus of law and regulation is so well developed, and sometimes so obscure, much of this book is devoted to discussing it. This shouldn't blind us, however, to the fact that historic preservation is only *one part* of CRM, and not necessarily the most important part.

"Compliance" and Beyond

"Compliance" is another word with multiple, usually implicit, definitions. To an environmental engineer, "compliance" means compliance with the Comprehensive Environmental Response, Compensation and Liability Act (CERCLA) and a few other laws that seek to control or clean up toxic and hazardous wastes. It's not unrecognized that other laws must be "complied with," too, but it's only CERCLA and its toxic-tinted kin that are seen as "real" compliance subjects. This is probably because only these laws, as opposed to those that will be discussed in this book, impose jail terms and fines on individual violators.[8]

In historic preservation and other areas of cultural resource management, "compliance" is taken to mean doing what the laws—notably Section 106 of NHPA—require to manage a project's impacts. If one does some kind of positive management, one goes "beyond compliance," which is always applauded.

I think this distinction is silly and rather sad.

Silly because positive management is the reason for compliance. Congress did not enact section 106 and its ilk just to cause agencies to pass papers around. Compliance with the law ought to result in thoughtful, balanced management of cultural resources and impacts on them. Compliance ought not to be a minimalist sort of thing; if it doesn't result in positive management, what good is it?

Silly too because an agency that's encouraged to think that it's going "beyond compliance" when it manages a cultural resource well—that is, that it's doing more than the law requires—isn't going to keep doing it when faced with conflicting demands. Stuff that's "nice to do" but not required by law won't get done when budgets shrink or demands grow. Those who turn up their noses at compliance and pat themselves on the back for getting their employers or clients to go "beyond" it live in a fool's paradise.

And it's sad because it reflects acceptance of a notion of compliance-driven cultural resource work as not entirely relevant to real management, and hence to the public interest. If widely accepted, this notion would mean that most of the multimillion dollar business of CRM—which like it or not is compliance driven—is of no real worth. I don't think that's true, but if it is, and we want to be responsible citizens, we'd all better look for new careers.

I believe that compliance and good management are essentially the same. Certainly compliance requires that we dot certain procedural i's and cross certain procedural t's, but this no more makes it poor management than good architectural draftsmanship means bad building design. Properly done compliance should result in good management, and good management should put an agency in compliance with the law.

That said, I'll cheerfully acknowledge that this book is about procedural process matters. The *substance* of CRM—how, in a hands-on way, one manages an archeological site or a book or an old building or impacts on a lifeway—is a many-splendored thing; there are so many possibilities that I wouldn't even know where to begin. *Process*, the subject of this book, is how possibilities get explored, selected, and implemented; to me this is a fascinating subject, and I hope it can be to the reader as well. In any event, it's something that a cultural resource manager must know, if she or he is to be effective.

"It Depends"

Two of the most common words you'll find in this book are "it depends." However much people might want things to be otherwise, there are few, if any, hard and fast rules in cultural resource management. How do we identify cultural resources? It depends on the law with which we're trying to comply, the kinds of resources that may exist, the kinds of things that may affect them, and other factors. How do we determine what's significant? It depends on the kind of resource, the values that people load on it, and so forth. How do we determine how to manage a resource? It depends on the resource, the management challenges, the public or private interests we're seeking to achieve or accommodate, and so on.

Some people are frustrated by this sort of ambiguity; they want a cookbook. For such people I'd suggest culinary school rather than CRM, though I think you'll find that even the temperature at which water boils depends on the altitude.

Everything in life, and certainly in CRM, depends on something else. There aren't any absolutes; everything is contingent. Absolutes are nice for lazy thinkers, but they have no place in creative management.

So I'll use "it depends" a lot. I'll try to explain what it is that specific things depend *on*, and why, and how to get along without absolutes, but I won't apologize for their nonexistence. Actually, I think CRM would be a pretty dull enterprise if there were a lot of absolutes on which to rely. And CRM is not a dull enterprise.

Who Should Read This Book?

This book is designed for use in college, university, and continuing education classes in historic preservation, environmental studies, social impact assessment, and cultural resource management. It's intended to help students understand CRM principles, policies, and procedures. It's meant to supplement and be supplemented by texts dealing with more specific topics, and with more general subjects like environmental impact assessment, with which CRM interacts. Much of it is derived from syllabi that others and I have developed for short courses in historic preservation and CRM sponsored by the National Preservation Institute (NPI), Advisory Council on Historic Preservation (ACHP), National Park Service (NPS), SWCA Environmental Consultants, and others. Thus another presumed readership comprises people who frequent such courses or would if they could afford to—typically, environmental and historic preservation people in federal and state agencies, local governments, Indian tribes, and Native Hawaiian organizations, and consultants in environmental and historic preservation work.

Finally, parts of this book are designed for colleagues who have flattered me by suggesting that I have something to contribute to their understanding of the laws and regulations, and to debating the principles that underlie them. My knowledge of the legal authorities varies. I know a good deal about some of them, though, and can speculate about a good deal more. I have speculated freely in the following chapters and have expressed my opinions liberally, in the hope of stimulating discussion.

A Word to Applicants for Federal Assistance and Permits

Some—maybe many—readers are or work for land developers, regulated utilities, and others who apply for federal assistance or permits to do their work—and hence are affected by the federal cultural resource laws even though technically they don't have to comply with them. These readers or their employers foot the bill for much if not most cultural resource management work. But few of the laws or regulations speak to them directly.

If an applicant wants to get his or her federal grant or permit, it's going to be necessary to pay to help the granting or permitting agency to fulfill its regulatory obligations. An applicant may not like this, but it really is only fair. Why should the taxpayer pay to determine what impacts an applicant's project will have? Well, one might argue, because the taxpayer is going to benefit from the project or from minimizing its impacts. Sure, one might rejoin, but it's the applicant who's going to benefit most directly from the project and the public that's going to suffer the impacts.

However we may feel about it, though, the bottom line is that in general, it's the applicant who pays for the legwork of compliance. But it's the permitting or assistance agency that actually has to comply, so they're the ones who have to make sure the work meets legal muster, and they're the ones who are supposed to interact with the other players in the project review process (see below). Sometimes they won't even let the applicant communicate with the other players, or those players don't want to communicate with the applicant. There are reasons for this. The assistance-permitting agencies don't want to lose control of what are, after all, their obligations. The external players don't want to be driven crazy by applicants hammering on their doors; they'd rather deal with the more or less known quantity represented by federal agencies. This is not always the case, though; some state historic preservation officers (SHPOs), for example, would rather deal with applicants directly. They find it simpler, and think the applicants tend to be more knowledgeable and reasonable than the agencies.

True story: I once had as a client a power company that wanted to build a transmission line, all of whose feasible alternative routes crossed both federal and nonfederal land. The SHPO said (and I think he was right) that in order for the land managing agency to consider the effects of issuing a right-of-way, it had to consider the entire project, including all its impacts on nonfederal land. My client, who felt they had to do this anyway, both because of other legal obligations and simply as good business, was willing to do what the SHPO wanted. But the land managing agency wouldn't buy it; its policy was to restrict attention to the lands under its own control. With the SHPO and agency locked in combat over what the agency was required to do, my client was left twiddling its corporate thumbs while the bills mounted. Eventually the project was abandoned.

So how do you avoid this kind of thing?

You need expertise, and it's probably not cost-effective for you to maintain it in-house. So you contract for it. Fair enough, but be careful. There are CRM consulting firms whose people know the laws and regulations and can envision creative, cost-effective, responsible ways of complying with them. But there are a lot more who only know there's some kind of law that requires you to pay them to do what they understand to be "compliance" work, and they know only one or maybe two ways to do it. These ways—typically featuring standard field surveys and digging up archeological sites—really have little to do with what the laws require, but many consulting firms are comfortable doing them and don't know how to do anything else. They can give you very costly bad advice.

So you need to know something yourself about how the laws work, which is probably why you're looking at this book. My introductory suggestion to you is that you *do* look at it, try not to get frustrated by the fact that it—like the laws and regulations it interprets—doesn't speak directly to you, think about what it *does* mean to you in real world terms. I'll try to offer pertinent suggestions where I can, to help you think about ways to relate creatively to what agencies may require you to do.

A Word to NIMBYs

Project proponents and regulatory agencies huff and puff a lot about "NIMBYs"—people who say "not in my backyard" to development. But NIMBYs want to keep things out of their backyards because they really like their backyards as they are, and often that's because their backyards have deep cultural meaning to them. They are, in fact, cultural resources. So NIMBYs, I hope this book will be helpful to you in using the cultural resource laws to promote respect for your values, your treasured cultural resources. It will give you an idea of what federal agencies should do under NEPA, NHPA, and other laws; it's up to you to insist that they do it.[9]

Laws, Regulations, and Alphabet Soup

Some readers of earlier editions have complained that they "get lost in the alphabet soup of government agencies." I don't know anything to do about that, other than to assure you that you're not alone. We all get confused when the acronyms and phrase fragments start flying. I'll try to make things as clear as I can, and some help is provided in the back of the book. Terms of art and acronyms are listed for quick reference in appendix 1 and where necessary defined in appendix 2. The laws we'll be discussing are summarized in appendix 3. Complete texts of laws, regulations, guidelines, and other relevant documents are available at a number of Web sites; my recommendations appear at the end of the bibliography.

A Bit of History

Where did cultural resource management in the United States come from? A real discussion of the field's history would take another book, but let's summarize.

In the Beginning . . .

The U.S. government began managing cultural resources in 1800, when Congress appropriated $5,000 to purchase books and create the Library of Congress. Around the same time, France seems to have come up with the idea of listing old buildings that the government thought ought to be preserved, in a cooling of revolutionary passions that threatened destruction of everything associated with the ancien régime.[10] This idea would be taken up by other European countries and eventually by the United States.

After the Civil War, the Smithsonian Institution and the Department of the Interior began to do ethnographic and archeological research, and the War Department started to acquire and preserve battlefields. Private parties and local governments began acquiring and preserving historic buildings and structures, but this was not seen as a function of the federal government. Management of impacts on the less tangible elements of the cultural environment was not even a gleam in anyone's eye.

In the late nineteenth century, driven by a rather chauvinistic concern about removal of antiquities from federal land, Congress enacted the Antiquities Act of 1906.[11] This law prohibited the excavation of antiquities from public lands without a permit from the secretary of the interior.

In 1916 the National Park Service (NPS) was created, giving the nation an agency with conservation of natural and cultural resources as part of its mission. Management of historic battlefields was transferred to NPS from the War Department.

The Depression Years

Some of the "make work" programs created to pull the country out of the Great Depression had implications for cultural resource management. Out-of-work historians were paid to write local and regional histories. Out-of-work architects were deployed to make measured drawings of historic buildings. All manner of people were hired to work on archeological projects, mostly salvaging material and data in advance of construction by the Tennessee Valley Authority and other agencies. NPS gathered some of these programs under its wing, giving them continuing life. Authority to do this came in 1935, when the Historic Sites Act[12] authorized a continuing program of recording, documenting, acquiring, and managing places important in the interpretation and commemoration of the nation's history. These places came to be called "National Historic Landmarks," and the French concept of an official register of historic places became embedded in the consciousness of the U.S. government.

Local governments pioneered the idea that what should be preserved was not just isolated great buildings, but whole neighborhoods. Thus the Old and Historic District in Charleston, South Carolina, and the Vieux Carre in New Orleans were recognized as "historic districts." This represented an important departure for historic preservation, relating the idea of preservation to urban planning and making "every citizen's house, environment, and neighborhood the prime focus of concern and action."[13]

World War II and Beyond

Contact with other cultures during World War II certainly affected Americans' perception of themselves and their own cultural resources. The rapid pace of socioeconomic change after the war caused Americans to begin worrying about what they were losing. At war's end the Corps of Engineers went to work building dams and reservoirs, while in the 1950s President Eisenhower launched construction of the Interstate Highway System. Both these programs did alarming damage to historic neighborhoods, buildings, structures, and archeological sites, and the government responded—albeit rather haltingly. NPS and the Smithsonian Institution organized the River Basin Survey program to salvage archeological sites threatened by Corps reservoirs, and in 1960 Congress passed the Reservoir Salvage Act,[14] authorizing appropriations to NPS for the program. NPS also helped spawn a nonprofit organization to promote historic preservation. The National Trust for Historic Preservation, originally conceived largely by NPS historians and architectural historians, was chartered in 1949. An increasing number of historic preservation practitioners began to emphasize preserving buildings in their social and architectural contexts, rather than as isolated artifacts. A number of conferences explored the relationships of historic preservation to urban planning. New international bodies like the United Nations

Educational, Scientific, and Cultural Organization (UNESCO) began to adopt policies and recommendations calling attention to historic landmarks, fine architecture, and archeological sites.[15] The notion of preservation as a quality of life issue for all citizens achieved widespread acceptance.

Postwar progress in cultural resource management was not limited to historic preservation and archeology. The environmental movement was stirring in response to some of the same challenges that alarmed archeologists and architectural historians. While focused initially on nature to the near-exclusion of the cultural environment, environmentalism, like preservation, soon expanded beyond preoccupation with the greatest most pristine places and became something that all people could claim as their own. In this context the human-affected environment achieved a new level of interest.

At the same time, the burgeoning of the federal government and its paperwork had created the need for a more orderly approach to records management. The Federal Records Act[16] became law in 1950, creating the basis for today's methods of archiving historical government documents.

Urban Renewal, the Great Society, and NHPA

The Kennedy administration accelerated natural and cultural resource destruction by launching urban renewal, laying waste to historic "slums" with the expectation that cities of the future would rise on their ruins. Reaction to urban renewal was not limited to "mainstream" historic preservation. Communities began to object to what the program was doing to the architectural and cultural fabric that reflected their identity.[17]

The Johnson administration, as part of the beautification program overseen by the late Lady Bird Johnson, gave its blessing to a study whose 1965 comprehensive report, *With Heritage So Rich*,[18] recommended creation of a national historic preservation program and sketched its broad outlines. This recommendation was transformed into legislation with lightning speed and enacted as the National Historic Preservation Act (NHPA) in 1966. The same Congress enacted the Department of Transportation Act, including its conservationist section 4(f).

NHPA created most of the institutions that are central to the historic preservation part of CRM today. It authorized NPS to "expand and maintain" a "National Register of Historic Places" including properties of local, state, and national historical, cultural, archeological, and architectural significance. It created an Advisory Council on Historic Preservation (ACHP) to advise the president and Congress on historic preservation. It authorized grants to states to assist them in historic preservation, to be administered by state liaison officers who later came to be known as state historic preservation officers (SHPOs). And it included, at section 106, a requirement that agencies consider the effects of their actions on places included in the Park Service's National Register.

The 1960s were also the heyday of the civil rights movement, including what came to be known as the Indian civil rights movement. During the 1950s, the government had gone through one of its periodic infatuations with the termination of Indian tribes and the absorption of Indian people into the great American melting pot. In reaction, the Indian civil rights movement included a strong element of traditional heritage—a desire to reclaim and assert the legitimacy of tribal roots. Two decades later, this was to bring tribes into the cultural resource management picture as major players. With shallower roots in North America, African Americans and other minority groups didn't have the same kinds of connections with the physical environment that Native Americans did and so have not as groups been as integrally involved in historic preservation (though there are exceptions[19]). During the 1960s, however, virtually all minority groups began to insist, with increasing intensity, on respect for their cultural traditions. The resulting perception of diversity as a positive thing has had profound impacts on cultural resource management.

Institution-Building in the 1970s

In response to NHPA, NPS reorganized its archeological and historic preservation programs into a new Office of Archeology and Historic Preservation (OAHP). The National Register and the ACHP were made parts of OAHP, with Earnest A. Connally of the University of Illinois School of Architecture at its head. Robert R. Garvey Jr. and William J. Murtagh of the National Trust were wooed away by NPS to head the ACHP and National Register respectively. Both were important in relating historic preservation to the broader cultural environment. Garvey was a grassroots preservationist without academic credentials, who saw preservation as something that should benefit ordinary people. Murtagh had (and has) a keen sense of the need for historic properties to be living parts of the contemporary environment.

While NPS was organizing OAHP, the environmental movement was gaining increasing congressional attention. With the publication and widespread popularity of Rachel Carson's *Silent Spring*, [20] the need for government action to protect the environment came to be widely recognized. One result was enactment of the National Environmental Policy Act (NEPA) in 1969. NEPA articulated national policy favoring environmental protection, created the Council on Environmental Quality (CEQ), and required agencies to consider the effects of their actions on the "quality of the human environment."

The new law was especially important for CRM because considering environmental impacts required agency infrastructure. Each federal agency—more or less—began to develop some kind of environmental staff and environmental impact assessment (EIA) procedures to ensure—more or less—that its actions were viewed through environmentally sensitive eyes. Because NEPA explicitly focused on the human environment, and called for interdisciplinary analyses involving the social sciences, social impact assessment (SIA) soon became part of the EIA mix and began to develop an identity of its own.[21] SIA addressed the relationships between sociocultural systems and the natural and built environments. And it considered the impacts of proposed actions on aspects of the environment that are purely social—such as lifeways and value systems.

It took awhile for a relationship to develop between historic preservation and environmental impact review—although one of the first cases reviewed under NHPA's section 106, involving a proposed nuclear power plant across the river from Saratoga Battlefield, raised such core environmental issues as indirect and visual impacts. Historic preservation remained peripheral to EIA practice under NEPA because NHPA's section 106, as enacted, required agencies to concern themselves only with impacts on places *included in* the National Register. These, of course, were few in number since the Register had barely been created. All an agency had to do to avoid dealing with impacts on historic properties was to keep anyone from nominating them.

This problem was alleviated in 1972 when President Nixon issued Executive Order 11593. In effect, this executive order directed agencies to treat *eligible* properties as though they were listed in the Register, and ordered NPS to establish procedures for determining eligibility. The executive order, together with court cases and other historic preservation tussles in the early 1970s, got the agencies' attention, and they began to incorporate preservation expertise and procedures into their environmental programs.

The Three Executeers and the Hegemony of Archeology

This process was hastened and given direction when NPS sent three executive order consultants to proselytize the agencies. Larry Aten, Jon Young, and Roy Reeves were very effective in their roles as knights errant, jawboning agencies into hiring preservation specialists and creating programs for executive order compliance. All three were archeologists, and the agencies they targeted for attention were those with the greatest impacts on archeological sites— construction agencies like the Corps of Engineers and land managing agencies like the Forest Service and Bureau of Land Management. Partly as a result, these agencies came to equate historic preservation with archeology and to hire archeologists to run their preservation programs. The perception of historic preservation as something done by and for archeologists, using archeological sites, remains common in the construction and land management agencies to this day.

Another reason for this perception was that the archeological community, under the leadership of Arkansas' Robert McGimsey, undertook in the late 1960s to expand the scope of the 1960 Reservoir Salvage Act. The aim of McGimsey's campaign was to require all agencies to identify archeological sites threatened by their actions and to fund recovery of the data they contained. Although this initiative was undertaken without reference to NHPA and Executive Order 11593, Aten of NPS in particular took pains to build bridges between OAHP and the archeological agitators. McGimsey had meanwhile formed a liaison with Richard Leverty, head of the

Corps of Engineers environmental program. As a result, when the desired amendment was enacted as the Moss-Bennett Act in 1974,[22] things were in place to ensure that its implementation would be integrated into OAHP's programs and that the Corps would provide a model of how the whole business of archeology and historic preservation could be done.[23]

The Birth of CRM

Archeologists were not entirely sanguine about hopping into bed with historic preservation. Some feared that the National Register would be a catalog of archeological sites ripe for looting. Some objected to the rubric "historic preservation" because their primary interests were in prehistory. Some regarded preservationists as rather effete, parts of an eastern establishment which they, as rough-tough westerners, viewed with disdain. At the same time, there was interest in relating what was coming to be called "conservation archeology"—that is, the practice of archeology under the environmental and preservation laws—to the rapidly coagulating body of policy and relatively well-funded practice called "natural resource management." So in the early 1970s archeologists in the southwestern United States began calling what they did "cultural resource management."[24]

The unfortunate results of this terminological appropriation remain with us today. Equating CRM with archeology at worst, and with historic preservation at best, has allowed the rest of the cultural environment to be ignored by federal planners and decision makers—indeed it has encouraged them to do so. When archeologists invented cultural resource management, they didn't bring the full range of cultural resources into the mix; they brought archeology. But natural resource managers, project planners, and agency officials didn't and don't know that, so they assume that when they fund CRM they're taking care of cultural resources.[25] Of course, they are not.

Tribes and Folklife

There were other forces at work during the 1970s that would to some extent counteract the narrow vision of CRM's creators. Native American groups were one such force. With enactment of the Indian Self-Determination and Education Act[26] in 1975, tribes attained a new level of authority. Tribes and intertribal organizations soon began to press for, among other things, more governmental attention to their traditional cultural values. These included protection of ancestral sites that were often of interest to archeologists, but it also included concern for spiritual places that were not archeological sites, subsistence and ceremonial use of natural resources, and the integrity of cultural and religious practices themselves. It also included a deep concern for ancestral bones and artifacts, which would become a major issue in the 1980s. Tribes and their representatives forced increased governmental attention to their cultural concerns and effected passage of legislation like the American Indian Religious Freedom Act (AIRFA) in 1978.[27]

Another important development was the growth of public interest in American traditional culture generally, expressed in the 1976 enactment of the American Folklife Preservation Act.[28] The act indicated government interest in folk culture and created the American Folklife Center (AFC) in the Library of Congress. The Center has undertaken a wide range of folklife documentation and encouragement projects, some of them in cooperation with historic preservationists in NPS, state historic preservation offices, and elsewhere. The same set of interests spawned the Festival of American Folklife in Washington, D.C., as an annual event, and folklife festivals and documentation programs at the state and local levels across the country.

Land Management and ARPA

Meanwhile, land-managing agencies that had struggled for generations with uncertain legal mandates had their missions clarified by Congress in laws like the Federal Land Policy Management Act of 1976 (FLPMA)[29] and the National Forest Management Act (NFMA) of the same year.[30] These laws, and particularly the implementing regulations drafted by the agencies to which they related—which by now had embedded environmental programs—often alluded to the management of cultural resources.

In 1974, in *United States v. Diaz*[31] the Ninth Circuit Court of Appeals found the Antiquities Act of 1906 to be unconstitutionally vague because it failed to indicate the age an object had to be in order to be an object of antiquity. This provided an opportunity for archeologists who had long seen the 1906 law as grossly out of date. The result was enactment of the Archeological Resources Protection Act (ARPA)[32] in 1979, clarifying requirements for managing the disturbance of archeological sites, features, and objects on federal and Indian tribal lands.

The PANE Decision and CEQ's Regulations

The 1970s were a period of great activity on the litigation front under NEPA, section 106, and other authorities. One particularly important Supreme Court decision had a chilling effect on the practice of social impact assessment. The Court in *Metropolitan Edison Co. v. People Against Nuclear Energy*[33]—commonly and pointedly called the "PANE decision"—declared that social and psychological effects were not by themselves sufficient to require preparation of an environmental impact statement. This followed issuance of NEPA regulations by the Council on Environmental Quality (CEQ) that included similar language about social and economic effects. Some agencies as a result concluded that social effects didn't have to be considered at all in EIA—an inaccurate reading of both PANE and the regulations, but one that has sometimes been hard to overcome.

The Rise of SHPOs, Local Governments, and Amendments to NHPA

Another important development in the 1970s was the growth in power, effectiveness, and organization among the state historic preservation officers (SHPOs). Originally provided for in NHPA as state liaison officers to administer NPS historic preservation matching grants, the SHPOs became increasingly consolidated and professionalized during the 1970s and gradually clarified their relationships with NPS. They formed the National Conference of State Historic Preservation Officers (NCSHPO) to represent their interests in Washington.

In 1978, President Carter issued a Presidential Memorandum on Environmental Quality and Water Resources Management that included direction for the Advisory Council on Historic Preservation to issue binding section 106 regulations. Under NHPA itself the ACHP had lacked rulemaking authority and had only been able to issue procedural guidance. In response to Carter's memorandum, in 1979 the ACHP reissued its procedures as true regulations, legally binding on all agencies. One important thing the regulations did was create an explicit role for SHPOs. Since most agencies did not have much historic preservation expertise, while SHPOs increasingly did, the regulations prescribed that agencies should turn to the SHPOs for consultative assistance at every step in the section 106 review process. This prescription remains with us today, with mixed effects.

NPS grants to the SHPOs also hit a high point during the Carter years, at almost $60 million divided among the fifty-seven entities that then qualified for such grants. This largesse was not to last.

Local governments had long led the way in some aspects of historic preservation—since the nineteenth century, when they were in the forefront of government involvement in preserving landmark buildings, and since the 1930s, when they pioneered the idea of historic districts as urban planning tools. In the 1970s, the federal historic preservation system began to pay more attention to them. In part, this resulted from the evolution of highly centralized Kennedy-era programs in the Department of Housing and Urban Development (HUD) into more flexible "block grant" programs that emphasized local initiative. The 1974 Community Development Act[34] allowed HUD to delegate its NEPA and section 106 responsibilities to local government recipients of block grants. Some preservationists viewed this allowance with alarm, fearing it would lead to widespread noncompliance with section 106. It may have, but it also led many local governments to beef up their environmental and historic preservation staffs and procedures, or to create them de novo. This created a ripple effect that had positive impacts on local preservation in general—and created a good many jobs for preservation specialists—while it positioned local governments for participation in the developing national preservation system.

During the 1970s, NHPA itself was amended several times. Importantly, the requirement of Executive Order 11593 to address places *eligible for* but not yet *listed in* the National Register was integrated into the law itself, by amending section 106 to refer both to registered and eligible properties. The ACHP, whose staff had been lodged in NPS, was given independent agency status after conflicts of interest with NPS project planning became apparent.

Finally, in 1980, Ohio Congressman John Seiberling—which is to say, his preservationist staffer Loretta Neumann—led Congress to make sweeping changes in almost every section of the law. In a new section 110, the 1980 amendments specified responsibilities for federal agencies; in an expanded section 101 they identified the responsibilities of state historic preservation officers. The amendments recognized local government participation in a number of ways, notably by creating a role for "certified local governments" and by mandating local participation in National Register nominations. They also included a couple of provisions relating to the cultural environment beyond historic properties. One provision directed NPS and the AFC to conduct a study of how to preserve "intangible aspects of our cultural heritage."[35] Another established a program of grants to Indian tribes and minority groups to support "the preservation of their cultural heritage."[36]

The Reagan Revolution

The ink was hardly dry on the 1980 amendments when the Reagan administration took office with a very different take on environmental matters and government activism. The 1980s were a time of struggle, retrenchment, cutbacks, and a great deal of head-ducking on the part of the federal environmental and historic preservation establishments. It was also a time when a good deal of initiative devolved to the state and local levels. Although NPS grants to the SHPOs were cut drastically (the administration was unsuccessful in doing away with them altogether), some SHPOs were able to exercise a good deal of initiative and develop their programs in new and positive directions. Many states had established "little NEPAs" (or "SEPAs") during the 1970s, and more did so during the decade. The Certified Local Government program developed, and many local governments qualified for historic preservation grants and technical assistance from NPS through the SHPOs. The Reagan administration emphasized encouraging historic preservation through the tax laws, and for awhile, federal income tax credits became a tremendous impetus for the rehabilitation of income-producing historic buildings. NEPA and CEQ survived by keeping low profiles, and the ACHP survived a major assault on the section 106 process. The section 106 regulations were revised, but actually (in my view) came out rather better than their 1979 iteration—despite the best efforts of the administration. This does not mean that they were particularly good, however; they were the product of some very difficult compromise, and while there's nothing wrong with compromise, it can produce a very lumpy sort of regulation.

The Rising of the Tribes

The 1980s also saw a dramatic rise in Indian tribal participation in governmental cultural resource management. Several tribes created historic preservation programs or built on programs that already existed. Some of the larger tribes and intertribal organizations like the National Congress of American Indians, the Native American Rights Fund, and American Indians Against Desecration (an offshoot of the American Indian Movement) were active influences on the ACHP in revising its section 106 regulations. Tribes and intertribal groups became major players in NEPA and section 106 litigation, and they began agitating for the return and reburial of ancestral remains and cultural items. This agitation led to enactment of the Native American Graves Protection and Repatriation Act (NAGPRA)[37] in 1990. The Supreme Court's 1988 decision in *Lyng v. Northwest Indian Cemetery Protective Association*[38] had a chilling effect on tribal efforts to protect spiritual places under the First Amendment to the U.S. Constitution, but this tended to cause tribes to pay more attention to alternative tools to use in protecting such sites—such as section 106. In 1989, Congress directed NPS to study tribal historic preservation needs.[39] This study, carried out in consultation with many tribes and intertribal organizations, resulted in a report titled *Keepers of the Treasures*.[40] *Keepers* reflected the tribes' interests in historic preservation as part of a broader management of cultural resources. Congress began appropriating, and NPS began granting, funds under NHPA section 101(e)(3)(B)—an obscure section providing for grants to tribes and minority groups to support preservation of cultural heritage. This grants program for a time supported projects not only in historic preservation per se but in language transmission, lifeway documentation, education, skills retention, and other aspects of cultural resource management.

Partly in response to the 1980 NHPA amendments, though more as a result of some particularly unfortunate section 106 cases, Pat Parker (now with NPS) and I spent part of the 1980s writing what became a rather controversial National Register Bulletin—number 38—on traditional cultural properties (TCPs), which NPS published in 1990. This bulletin, and the attention given to it over the years by tribes and the courts, has to some extent caused agencies to pay attention to the values that living communities invest in historic places.[41]

Deep Waters

CRM sank beneath the waves in the 1980s, too, as oil and gas exploration expanded on the ocean floor and the technology developed to permit archeologists and others to find and recover things there. Underwater archeology had developed as a research discipline and a recreational pursuit with the spreading availability of SCUBA technology in the 1960s, and by the 1980s archeological surveys, usually involving remote sensing technology, were being fairly routinely done in advance of development projects affecting submerged lands. At the same time conflicts developed between archeological interests and those of maritime salvage. Salvage firms were accustomed to operating under admiralty law, which encourages the recovery of abandoned wrecks; archeologists, of course, wanted historic wrecks either left alone or excavated only by archeologists, using archeological methods. This conflict led in 1987 to enactment of the Abandoned Shipwrecks Act (ASA),[42] which asserted federal ownership of wrecks in U.S. waters and assigned management responsibility to the states. Many coastal states had already placed controls on the excavation of shipwrecks, and others followed suit once ASA was in place. The same sorts of conflicts in the international arena would lead in the early twenty-first century to a UNESCO convention[43] on the subject.

The 1990s: Normalizing Practice

In 1992 NHPA was amended again, this time expanding federal agency responsibilities and providing formal roles and procedures in support of tribal historic preservation programs. Under these provisions, tribes could take over SHPO responsibilities under agreements with NPS[44] and substitute their own procedures for the ACHP's in section 106 review under agreements with the ACHP. In response to these amendments, the ACHP began a lengthy and contentious process of regulatory revision.

Around the same time the environmental justice (EJ) movement breathed new life into social impact assessment by emphasizing the need to involve diverse minority and low-income communities in decision making about environmental impacts. EJ found its federal expression in 1994 in Executive Order 12898[45] and an accompanying presidential memorandum directing agencies to consider environmental justice matters in their environmental impact work. President Clinton continued on a roll, from a CRM point of view, by issuing Executive Orders 13006 and 13007[46] in 1996. These executive orders deal respectively with use of historic districts and buildings in center cities and with protection of Indian sacred sites.

On the whole, however, the 1990s were a time in which practice under the CRM and EIA laws came to be standardized and embedded in governmental and private-sector operations. Academic institutions largely abandoned the field to private profit-making consulting firms. Practice became increasingly professionalized, employing procedures and jargon that were increasingly impenetrable by the general public. And as the first generation of self-identified cultural resource managers began to die and retire, a new generation took over that for the most part seems satisfied with the status quo.

Into the Twenty-First Century

At this writing—the beginnning of 2008—the twenty-first century has at best seen the continued routinization of CRM as it was practiced at the end of the twentieth. Most practitioners continue to equate cultural resources with historic properties and/or archeological sites. As a result, most cultural aspects of the environment—social institutions, cultural use of plants, animals, and land, religious practices—are acknowledged only haphazardly in planning and EIA. EIA under NEPA and project review under section 106 of NHPA have devolved into fairly rote exercises carried out by for-profit consulting firms that unabashedly see themselves as members of project proponents' development teams. Their willingness to mischaracterize environmental impacts to advance their clients' agendas varies, but even the most honorable are unable to escape the bureaucratic and economic forces that select for formulistic, lowest-common-denominator performance. CEQ and the ACHP have generally emasculated themselves in order to survive in the punishing political climate of contemporary Washington, D.C.; SHPOs have often either followed suit or seized the opportunity to become petty despots. Litigation alone promotes responsible CRM and EIA, and few extra-governmental watchdogs have the money to undertake it. Federal agencies, following the lead of the chief executive, are more arrogant and less responsive than ever to the public interest.

Substantive accomplishments have been few and faltering. In 1999 the ACHP unveiled the revised section 106 regulations on which it had labored since the 1992 NHPA amendments became law. Much fought over during their development, the regulations purported to streamline the review process. Oddly, they were rather longer and more complicated than the 1986 regulations they replaced; we'll address them in chapter 4.[47] Several large federal agencies, notably the U.S. Army and the Bureau of Land Management (BLM), undertook their own "streamlining" efforts with, at best, mixed results.[48]

In 2003, President George W. Bush put his imprimatur on historic preservation by issuing Executive Order 13287, "Preserve America."[49] This directed agencies to evaluate and report on their progress in complying with some of the requirements of NHPA (notably not section 106, but rather the broader and more "proactive" requirements of section 110), to give high-level attention to preservation in each agency's organization and to cooperate with others in programs to use and reuse historic properties for economic purposes, specifically including heritage tourism. An awards program was also created. Consistent with its overall philosophy of governance, however, the Bush administration on the whole ratcheted down compliance with cultural resource and environmental laws, and reduced funding for most CRM programs. Bush issued another executive order—EO 13352[50]— in 2004, promoting "cooperative conservation" activities by government, property owners, and other interest groups, with little evident impact on government operations.

Things appear a bit brighter outside the United States, though my perception of this condition may reflect only the illusion of greener grass on the other side of the fence. It appears that EIA is performed more honorably and with greater creativity in the European Union; social impact assessment seems to be alive and well in Canada and Australia, in contrast with its moribund condition in the United States. UNESCO has issued a convention calling for attention to "intangible cultural heritage,"[51] and the United Nations General Assembly (over U.S. objections) has affirmed the rights of indigenous people.[52] Perhaps some of all this will rub off on the United States when—and if—this country reengages the rest of the world on the basis of mutual respect. Much remains to be seen.

This thumbnail sketch brings us to the "present" as of the time this book is written (early 2008). I've left a great deal out, and except in these last few paragraphs I have resisted the temptation to editorialize. I've also emphasized the historic preservation aspects of CRM, because these are the ones I know best and, I believe, the ones that have the most established body of practice, most thoroughly grounded in law.

Players in the Field

The history of CRM in the United States has produced a number of institutional participants in its practice with whom we need to be acquainted.

Advisory Council on Historic Preservation[53]

Created by NHPA, the ACHP has two parts. The Council itself is a twenty-member board made up of a presidentially appointed chair, presidentially appointed "citizen" and "expert" members, the heads of several federal agencies, presidentially appointed representatives of local governments, state governments, and Native American interests, and two outside organizations specified in the statute—the National Trust for Historic Preservation and the National Conference of Historic Preservation Officers. Three agency members are permanent—the secretaries of the interior and agriculture and the architect of the Capitol—while other agency members are appointed by the president. The twenty meet only a few times a year; their work is done by a staff of about forty, based in Washington, D.C. The staff is headed by an executive director and is responsible for overseeing section 106 review, poking into agency programs to see how they're dealing with historic properties, doing special studies, reporting annually to the president and Congress, doing training, and otherwise serving the members, the Congress, and the president. Most CRM practitioners come into contact primarily with ACHP staff members—architectural historians, archeologists, planners, for the most part—who handle section 106 oversight and occasionally get involved in casework.

Council on Environmental Quality[54]

Created by NEPA, the Council on Environmental Quality (CEQ) is lodged in the executive office of the president. This has certain advantages compared with the ACHP, an independent agency—CEQ is closer to the president's ear. On the other hand, CEQ is more vulnerable to presidential whim than is the ACHP. Like the ACHP, CEQ consists of a council and a staff, but both are smaller than their ACHP counterparts. The council in CEQ's case has only three members, but unlike the ACHP's magnificent twenty, most of whom are paid only when they meet, CEQ's members serve full time for their tenure. The members are served by a small staff, based in Washington. CEQ oversees NEPA, provides an annual report to the president and Congress, occasionally helps resolve cases with national policy implications, and develops government-wide policy on environmental matters.

Environmental Protection Agency[55]

The Environmental Protection Agency (EPA) is a large independent agency with many responsibilities for both environmental regulation and the conduct of projects to protect or clean up the environment. EPA's primary areas of expertise and authority are in air and water pollution, but it also promotes implementation of Executive Order 12898 on environmental justice. In this context it can become involved in CRM matters on behalf of minority groups and low-income communities whose cultural environments may be disproportionately damaged by federal actions. EPA also receives and reviews all *Environmental Impact Statements* (EIS) prepared under NEPA, and an adverse EPA comment can stop an agency project cold in its tracks until the deficiency EPA has identified is repaired. EPA also funds the cleanup of pollution sources and construction of things like wastewater disposal systems. Under the Comprehensive Environmental Response, Compensation, and Liability Act (CERCLA),[56] EPA sometimes argues that it has been relieved of some NEPA and section 106 responsibilities when cleaning up "Superfund" sites, but, in fact, the statute only provides some protection from lawsuits.[57]

Institute for Environmental Conflict Resolution[58]

Created by Congress in 1998, the Institute for Environmental Conflict Resolution (IECR) is part of the Morris K. Udall Foundation, an independent federal agency based in Tucson, Arizona. As its name implies, its business is helping agencies, communities, and citizens resolve conflicts over environmental matters. It is a very small-scale operation at this writing, but has certainly done some good works in its short career, including providing assistance with some cases involving historic places and other cultural resources. In its *Citizen's Guide to the NEPA*,[59] published in December 2007, CEQ identifies the IECR as one of the three federal agencies overseeing implementation of NEPA, placing it on the same level as EPA and CEQ itself, and encourages citizens to contact it with their problems. It will be interesting to see how the IECR develops; it is certainly a resource that practitioners should know exists.

Other Federal Agencies

While the ACHP, CEQ, EPA, and IECR oversee section 106, NEPA, and related project review processes, the rest of the agencies making up the federal establishment are actually responsible for implementing the cultural resource and environmental laws. And, of course, they are also responsible for doing everything else the federal government does.

There are several types of federal agencies. Agencies like the Bureau of Land Management (BLM) and the Forest Service manage land. The Federal Highway Administration (FHWA) and Department of Housing and Urban Development (HUD) provide financial assistance to states, local governments, and others for things like highways and housing. The Corps of Engineers and Bureau of Reclamation build things. The Federal Energy Regulatory Commission (FERC) and Federal Communications Commission (FCC) issue permits and licenses. Some agencies do multiple things; the Corps of Engineers, for example, manages land around its reservoirs, constructs flood control facilities, *and* issues permits to fill waterways and wetlands.

Land Management Agencies

Land management agencies have the most elaborate responsibilities under cultural resource laws, because they actually control land on which people do cultural things and have left cultural things (artifacts, buildings) lying and standing around. They're often said to have stewardship responsibility for such things, as well as project review responsibilities.

Assistance Agencies

Agencies that provide financial assistance to others tend to work closely with, and often through, those who use their money. FHWA, for instance, works in close concert with state departments of transportation, and HUD delegates many of its environmental review responsibilities to local governments that receive its assistance.

Construction Agencies

Agencies that build things have the clearest project review responsibilities, since they themselves plan and construct projects. There are fewer and fewer simple, one-agency projects these days, however; more and more is done through assistance and partnerships.

Permitting and Licensing Agencies

These agencies—FERC, for example—typically require those who apply for their permits and licenses to do the legwork required for environmental impact review, though they hold the ace of being able to issue the permit or not. Some permitting programs, such as those under the Coastal Zone Management Act and the Clean Air Act, are delegated to state, local, and regional agencies.

Central and Regional Offices

Most agencies are organized into central and regional offices, but different agencies call their organizational levels different things, and the boundaries of regions defined by different agencies don't always correspond with one another. There are "standard" federal regions, but not all agencies have regional offices in all regions, so regions are combined and split depending on the agency's needs. Some agencies—like the Corps of Engineers, which is organized with reference to river basins—don't use the standard regions at all. Other agencies, like the Bureau of Land Management, have state offices. However they're organized, there is always tension between the field and Washington. People from Washington are regarded by the field as autocratic and out of touch; people from the field are regarded by Washington as loose cannons who don't understand policy. Some agencies have subregional field offices, which typically are in some conflict with both regional and central offices.

Federal Preservation Officers

Under NHPA, each agency is supposed to have an official who oversees its compliance with the law. This official is referred to as the federal preservation officer or FPO. The statute says that the FPO is to be "qualified," but no one has ever established what this means. Most agencies have FPOs, but their locations in the agency's organizational system, their authorities, and their expertise vary widely. Executive Order 13287, issued in 2003, directed agencies to "designate a senior policy level official to have policy oversight responsibility for the agency's historic preservation program."[60] This does not seem to have had much effect on FPO qualifications and authorities. The ACHP, to its credit, has begun reviewing agency programs under the authority of the executive order,[61] and this may eventually have useful results.

Agency NEPA and NHPA Procedures

CEQ's regulations require that each agency has its own procedures for implementing the procedural elements of NEPA, and section 110(a)(2) of NHPA imposes similar responsibilities on agencies with regard to historic preservation, including section 106 review. CEQ has to approve agency NEPA programs, and ACHP must approve those dealing with section 106. Most agencies have NEPA procedures, which vary greatly in their terms, content, and structure. A few agencies have approved NHPA procedures. Some other laws and executive orders—for example, Executive 13007 regarding Indian sacred sites—also require agencies to develop or improve administrative procedures. Executive Order 13287 directed agencies to report periodically to the ACHP and NPS on their programs under NHPA section 110. The ACHP, to its credit, has begun reviewing agency programs under this authority,[62] which may have useful results.

National Park Service[63]

NPS plays an important role in CRM, particularly in its historic preservation aspects. It's a somewhat schizophrenic role, since NPS is both a land management agency and an agency that does—well, other things.

NPS as a Land Manager

Most people know NPS as the manager of national parks, monuments, recreation areas, seashores, and other places designated for the protection and public enjoyment of natural and cultural resources. In this role, NPS is a land and resource manager much like the Forest Service, Bureau of Land Management, or Tennessee Valley Authority. As such it has responsibilities under NEPA, section 106 of NHPA, the Native American Graves Protection and Repatriation Act, and other authorities just like any other agency. CRM practitioners come into contact with it fairly frequently as it exercises these responsibilities. Having preservation and public interpretation as parts of its mission, NPS also does CRM work in and around the units of the National Park System, and CRM practitioners often interact with it as contractors on things like historic context studies, historic property surveys, preparation of historic structures reports, historic structure rehabilitation and restoration projects, and Native American coordination projects.

NPS External Programs

The other things NPS does are often referred to as its "external" or "outhouse" functions. These involve it in interactions with other agencies, states, tribes, local governments, and the public on matters having nothing to do with the National Park System. The external CRM programs include:

- The *National Register*, both a list of properties and a staff unit that manages the list, processes nominations, and so on.
- The *Archeology* program, which provides an annual report to Congress on the national archeology program and publishes a magazine called *Common Ground* that's loaded with good news about archeological and Native American matters.
- The *National NAGPRA Program*, which carries out the secretary of the interior's functions under the Native American Graves Protection and Repatriation Act (NAGPRA)—rulemaking, overseeing implementation of NAGPRA nationwide, servicing the NAGPRA Review Committee that is the statute's policy-making and dispute resolution body.
- The *Heritage Documentation* or *HABS/HAER/HALS* program[64] —the acronyms stand for Historic American Buildings Survey, Historic American Engineering Record, and Historic American Landmarks Survey—which oversees the documentation of historic architecture, engineering, and landscapes.
- *Architectural preservation* programs that promote the proper treatment and rehabilitation of historic buildings and structures under the tax code, through participation in section 106 review, and through moral suasion.

- *Grants programs* that provide grants to state historic preservation officers, Indian tribes, local governments, preservation technology researchers and educators, and, occasionally, to others to carry out historic preservation and some other CRM activities. Its grant-giving role gets NPS involved pretty directly in state and tribal historic preservation program development and oversight; NPS routinely audits its grantees and has in the past provided pretty directive advice about how they ought to do their businesses.

The titles I've given the various programs above are not necessarily those by which they will be known when you read this, nor are the programs necessarily divided up precisely as I've divided them. NPS, like most agencies, reorganizes with the phases of the moon, and you can never be sure who's going to be who next week. The external programs are particularly vulnerable to reorganization, renaming, reconfiguration, and redirection because they are forever trying to sort out their relationships with the much more powerful, higher-profile internal programs. So sometimes the external programs have distinct separate identities, and other times they flow together with various internal programs. The situation is complicated by NPS's more or less decentralized organization, which features regional offices, various kinds of support offices, centers, parks, and park clusters—all in more or less continuous power flux. Generally speaking, though, the functional areas I've noted above tend to be represented by nodes of people, money, and responsibilities, and it's with these that the average CRM practitioner will most likely come into contact. There are also several special-purpose NPS CRM programs, like the American Battlefield Preservation Program[65] (which promotes the protection of battlefields) and a staff that puts out the *CRM Journal*,[66] a biennial magazine that publishes articles on historic preservation topics.

American Folklife Center[67]

The AFC, part of the Library of Congress, is responsible for collecting and maintaining data on folklife resources. The AFC sponsors and cooperates in fieldwork to document traditional lifeways, arts, crafts, expressive culture, and oral history.

National Trust for Historic Preservation[68]

Modeled on the like-named organization in Great Britain, the National Trust was granted a federal charter in 1949 (which means little except that the government officially recognizes and approves of its existence). The Trust was instrumental in promoting enactment of NHPA and has remained an influential voice in preservation circles. A not-for-profit membership organization, the Trust maintains a number of historic properties, assists others in doing the same, provides advice and assistance to local preservation groups, and performs a range of other good works. Its chairman is a member of the ACHP. One of the most useful things the Trust does these days (I think) is litigation; it has an active, if pitifully small and undersupported, legal department that does what it can to promote agency compliance with the historic preservation laws through selective litigation.

State Historic Preservation Officers[69]

There are fifty-nine SHPOs, because, in addition to the fifty honest-to-gosh states, the District of Columbia, Puerto Rico, American Samoa, the Virgin Islands, Guam, the Commonwealth of the Northern Mariana Islands, the Republic of Palau, the Republic of the Marshall Islands, and the Federated States of Micronesia are "states" for the purposes of NHPA. The SHPO's basic function under NHPA is to coordinate historic preservation activities supported by federal grant funds in his or her state. Each SHPO receives an annual program grant from NPS—size dependent on appropriation and whatever allocation formula is currently in use. The SHPO uses this grant to carry out a wide range of functions set forth in section 101(b)(3) of NHPA, such as:

- conducting a statewide inventory of historic properties;
- nominating properties to the National Register;
- maintaining a statewide preservation plan;
- providing assistance to others;

- advising local governments, federal and state agencies, and the public;
- participating in section 106 and other reviews;
- helping local governments with program development; and
- public education.

NPS grants to SHPOs must be matched by nonfederal contributions—either money or in-kind services. NPS audits the SHPOs periodically, not only to ensure that their grants are being well administered, but that the programs are being run as NPS thinks they should be. Some of the things NPS thus encourages SHPOs to do are—in my opinion—pretty silly and counterproductive, and they get in the way of efficient and effective SHPO participation in project review under NEPA and section 106. Some of these problems will become apparent in later chapters.

Many SHPOs carry out functions under state laws as well as under federal law; examples include maintenance of state registers, historic preservation easement programs, participation in state environmental reviews and state versions of section 106 review, and state-funded grants programs.

The SHPO is designated by the governor. Some states constrain the governor's discretion by stipulating that the SHPO will be, say, the director of the state historical society, answerable to the society's board of directors; others do not. SHPOs tend to be political animals, and some preservation purists decry this fact. In my experience, it's mostly to the good; if an SHPO is going to be effective, she or he needs to know how to play the state's political system. SHPO *staff* must meet standards promulgated by NPS—that is, the staff must include specialists in history, archeology, architectural history, and other fields who meet NPS professional qualifications standards. There also must be a state review board with qualified members, whose primary function is to review National Register nominations.

At the national level, SHPOs are represented by the *National Conference of SHPOs* (NCSHPO), a membership organization whose president sits on the Advisory Council. Some SHPOs who haven't joined NCSHPO claim not to be represented by it. Generally speaking, this leaves them simply unrepresented, because as far as agencies like the

ACHP and NPS are concerned, when it comes to national issues, NC-SHPO speaks for the SHPOs.

SHPO staff are the government officials with whom most CRM practitioners come into contact most often—and indeed lots of CRM practitioners *are* SHPO staff. It's important to remember who the SHPO is and is not. The SHPO is the representative of the state's interests in historic preservation. The SHPO is not the representative of the ACHP or of NPS, nor is he or she necessarily an advocate for historic preservation *uber alles*. Perhaps most important of all, the SHPO is not responsible for doing a federal agency's work for it—for identifying historic properties that the agency's actions may affect, telling the agency what the effect will be, or dictating to the agency what to do about the effect. The SHPO consults with the agency, assists the agency, but is not supposed either to boss the agency around or to perform functions on the agency's behalf.

Tribal Historic Preservation Officers[70]

The 1992 amendments to NHPA contained a number of provisions designed to increase and improve participation by Indian tribes, Alaska Natives, and Native Hawaiians in the historic preservation system. One of these provisions was for the substitution of tribal preservation programs for SHPO functions on tribal lands. To substitute for the SHPO, a tribal program must be approved by NPS. The tribe can also substitute its preservation procedures for those of the section 106 regulations, provided the ACHP agrees.

NPS-approved tribal programs are headed by tribal historic preservation officers (THPOs). Just as the SHPO serves at the pleasure of the governor, so does the THPO at the pleasure of the tribal government. The THPO's responsibilities and authorities are largely exercised within the external boundaries of reservations; it is within these boundaries, for instance, that they can substitute for the SHPO in section 106 review. These boundaries may embrace a good deal more territory than simply the lands that the tribe owns in fee, or that are held by the federal government in trust for the tribe. They may include large tracts that have been lost to states, federal agencies, local governments, and nongovernmental entities during the federal government's periodic attempts to do away with tribes and parcel out their lands. The THPO may also be designated by the tribal government to represent its interests (or some of its interests) beyond reservation boundaries, including participation in section 106 review *with* the SHPO and others. Some THPOs do what they can (which may be a good deal) to assert tribal authority over ancestral sites and other culturally important places throughout their traditional territories and beyond. And like SHPOs, THPOs may carry out functions under other laws, both federal (e.g., NEPA) and tribal. Quite a few tribes have their own environmental and historic preservation statutes. Many tribes also assume federal functions on their reservations under the Indian Self-Determination and Education Act of 1975,[71] often including things like road building, timber management, and housing, which themselves may require review under NEPA, section 106, and other authorities.[72]

Indian Tribes and Native Hawaiian Groups

Indian tribes are important participants in CRM regardless of whether they have set up THPO programs, and to some extent Native Hawaiian groups have similar authorities and roles. There are a number of things that are special about tribes that a CRM practitioner needs to understand.

Government-to-Government, Fiduciary, and Treaty Relationships

A special set of relationships exists between the U.S. government and the governments of federally recognized tribes. A federally recognized tribal government, as the term suggests, is one whose official existence is recognized by the federal government. The Bureau of Indian Affairs (BIA) publishes an annual list of the several hundred recognized tribes.

Tribes, of course, were sovereign nations long before Europeans landed. For some centuries it was uncertain whether the natives or the invaders would gain the upper hand, or whether some sort of truce would emerge. By law today, federally recognized Indian tribes remain sovereign nations, to which the laws of the United States apply only as Congress explicitly determines. In many respects, the sovereign character of tribal governments gives them a superior position to those of states and local governments, which are subdivisions of the United States.[73]

Federal agencies have to respect the government-to-government relationship between tribal governments and the government of the United States. President Clinton usefully reminded agencies of this ongoing duty in Executive Order 13175 in 2000[74] and President Bush acknowledged it in Executive Order 13336 on education in 2004.[75]

What does "government-to-government" mean? Something pretty simple, but powerful. As one tribal representative summed it up to me, "Your policy people talk to our policy people before your technical people talk to our technical people." Agencies are supposed to deal with tribal governments at an official, executive level. You don't send your archeologist to chat with the tribal chairman, unless she's invited. You don't send your consultant, or your engineer, or your lawyer. The line officer, that is, the official who's in the line of authority down from the president, is the one to make official contact—the area manager, the regional administrator. Staff can set up consultation meetings and follow up on them; the "technical people" can get together, once the "policy people" have agreed it's appropriate. But staff-level consultation isn't a substitute for executive consultation, and you don't send staff to talk with the tribal executive unless you're invited to.

The federal government also has a fiduciary, or trust, relationship with tribes, which is grounded in treaties not only with the tribes[76] but with other nations—for example Great Britain, which sought to protect its Indian allies through the Treaty of Ghent at the end of the War of 1812.[77] In effect, the federal government is supposed to look out for the interests of tribes. The extent of the "trust responsibility" is often the subject of debate. One interpretation is that the federal government must protect the interests of tribes in land the government holds "in trust" for tribes—basically, reservation land—and in "trust resources" or "trust assets" like timber and mineral resources on or under such land. A broader interpretation is that the government is responsible for protecting tribal interests, period—making sure that tribes get a square deal from other parties and that their rights under law and treaty are respected. In 2006, the Ninth Circuit Court of Appeals gave credence to the broad interpretation—and constructed a linkage with NEPA and section 106—in *Pit River Tribe et al. v. U.S. Forest Service et al.*[78] The court found that the federal government failed in its fiduciary duty in not addressing the Pit River Tribe's cultural concerns as part of proper and timely EIA when considering a geothermal drilling project on federal land.

Many tribes also have specific rights under treaties with the U.S. government, and some interpretations of treaty rights have broad implications. In the typical treaty, the tribe ceded vast tracts of land to the United States in return for a reservation, food, other forms of support, and, particularly, peace. But often, specific rights were retained by the tribe—rights to fish or hunt, for example.[79] These treaty provisions continue in force today, except where Congress has explicitly extinguished them.[80] The Supreme Court established long ago as a "canon" of treaty construction that if a tribe didn't explicitly give up a right, it retained it.[81] So arguably, while a tribe may have ceded ownership of its land, and hence the right to farm it, log it, and have exclusive access to it, it did not give up the right to protect and use its spiritual places or the burial places of its ancestors. More and more, tribes are making this sort of argument as a basis for exerting power over ancestral places beyond the boundaries of their reservations.

Another of the Supreme Court's "canons of construction" is that if there's a question about how a law affecting Indians can be interpreted, it's to be interpreted in favor of the tribe.[82] So a federal agency should interpret its responsibilities under laws like NEPA in ways that favor tribal interests, unless there is an awfully good rationale for doing otherwise.

For all these reasons, an agency can't treat a federally recognized Indian tribe as just another interest group, just another part of the public. American Indians are U.S. citizens, with all the rights that status implies, but they're also citizens of their own nations, and those nations have a special relationship with the U.S. government that must be reflected in government dealings with them, in cultural resource matters as in all others.

Native Hawaiian groups are in rather a different category. Although the Kingdom of Hawai'i was very much a sovereign nation, it was never defeated by the United States—its land and sovereignty were simply stolen. So there's no treaty, no trust responsibility, no government-to-government relationship, though Native Hawaiian groups are lumped with tribes under such laws as NHPA and NAGPRA. It's a neither fish nor fowl situation, in which agencies try to treat Native Hawaiian groups more or less like tribes, but without much guidance in law. Native Hawaiians and their supporters in Congress are working on ways to achieve a more general recognition of Native Hawaiian sovereignty; at this writing all this is a work in progress.[83]

Finally, there are Indian tribes that aren't federally recognized. Some have lost recognition during one of the U.S. government's periodic infatuations with absorbing tribal people into the great American melting pot (and distributing their land to others). Other times they were so quickly overwhelmed by Anglo-American society that they never had a chance to establish a government-to-government relationship. Such tribes have the same rights as any other interest group—the Sierra Club, the National Rifle Association—under laws like NEPA and NHPA, but that's about it. Except that they're minority communities, and usually low-income communities, and should be given consideration under executive order 12898. And except that they may *become* recognized; many have applied for recognition and are in the process of getting it. And except for the fact that some agencies, sometimes, recognize a moral responsibility to address their needs. If you can work with a nonrecognized tribe in the same way you'd work with one that's recognized, it's probably a good idea, but it's not always possible.[84] When push comes to shove, a nonrecognized tribe is a group of American citizens, with all the rights of citizens but no more.

As mentioned earlier, the United Nations General Assembly in late 2007 adopted a *Declaration on the Rights of Indigenous Peoples.*[85] The declaration is quite wide ranging; among many other things it asserts the rights of indigenous peoples to maintain, protect, and develop manifestations of their culture, their traditions and ceremonies, and their histories and languages, as well as to be safe from molestation in their homelands. How this declaration will affect the rights and practices of tribes and other indigenous groups under U.S. law remains to be seen, but it is likely to have some effect on the interpretation of laws dealing with indigenous people, however little the government may want this to be so.

Applicants

Applicants for federal permits, licenses, and assistance do—
or at least pay for—a lot of the legwork involved in compliance
with the cultural resource laws. There are different kinds of applicants, depending mostly on what they're applying for and
what kinds and amounts of money they have to deploy to support their applications.

Applicants for large federal grants—state departments of transportation, for example, applying for Federal Highway Administration assistance—usually have their own full-scale environmental
compliance programs. They have state money to support what
they do and can usually apply portions of their federal grants to
compliance as well. They tend to work within well-developed systems established by their granting agencies, with which they may
have pretty complicated relationships. Generally, though, they are
pretty well organized to do their part in compliance—which
means doing all the legwork subject to approval by their granting
agency, often up to and including preparing all the necessary documentation for agency signature.

Applicants with delegated authorities are a bit different in that
they can actually act for the federal agencies whose assistance they
seek or administer. Local governments receiving grants from some
(but not all) Department of Housing and Urban Development
(HUD) programs fall into this category. They basically act as
though they were federal agencies. Depending on how big they are
(*Chicago v. Peachpit Junction*) and how big their grants are, they may
or may not have substantial environmental compliance programs,
historic preservation officers, and expertise in dealing with the
laws.

Applicants for big permits—for instance, a mining company
seeking to extract minerals from federal land, or a developer looking for a Clean Water Act permit from the Corps of Engineers for a
big marina development—probably have a good deal of money to
put into helping the responsible agency through the compliance
process, but may or may not have much expertise in how to do it.
In my experience many big applicants put lots of money into
lawyers and maybe into consulting firms to help them with environmental compliance, but the lawyers often see their job as being
to help their clients bull their way through the review process, and

the consultants may feel the same way. Both are often deeply igno-rant of what the laws require. There are exceptions, though: some of the best, most responsible and creative clients I've had have been applicants for big permits.

Applicants for little permits, like a mom and pop boat rental out-fit that wants to put in a dock and needs a permit from the Corps of Engineers, are in the terrible position of having neither money nor expertise, and thus are pretty much at the mercy of their regu-lators and other players in the environmental review process. Some of those players try to cut them slack—it's not uncommon, for example, for SHPOs to apply much more lenient standards of review to small-scale permit applicants than to large ones and to invest staff time in helping them. Others won't, and often can't. The Natural Resources Conservation Service (NRCS) and other as-sistance agencies in the Department of Agriculture try to find cre-ative ways of helping small farmers and ranchers participate in review of assistance they apply for—help building stock ponds, for example, or converting from one kind of crop to another—but the agriculture agencies are limited in what they can do by their own financial constraints and limited professional staff.

The laws and regulations don't distinguish among these differ-ent kinds of applicants. Some agency-specific regulations apply different review standards to projects over and under particular size or dollar thresholds. NEPA allows this in a programmatic kind of way, while section 106 of NHPA doesn't, and leaves it to be dealt with, if it's dealt with, on a case-by-case basis. And since many as-sistance and permit projects have to be done in compliance with several different federal laws, administered by several different agencies, the life of an applicant in the cultural resource manage-ment system can be very complicated and frustrating—for appli-cants, for the agencies to which they're applying, for review agencies, and for the interested public.

Some assistance and permitting agencies don't help matters by imposing on applicants their own peculiar interpretations of the law. For example, the Corps of Engineers has a strange, convoluted interpretation of its responsibilities toward historic properties in is-suing clean water act permits, examining some kinds of impacts on some kinds of properties but leaving other impacts and other prop-erties unconsidered. Since no review agency (and no court, for that matter) has accepted the Corps' approach to its responsibilities, this can result in all kinds of rancorous argument, which the applicant is often powerless to resolve.

It's a messy situation, and it results in applicants playing a wide range of roles—as supplicants, as whipping boys, as bullies, as Daddy Bigbucks, and occasionally as creative, willing managers of cultural resources frustrated by their inability to be all that they can be.

Everybody Else

Almost everybody has culture, so you might think that everybody would be players in the cultural resource game. You'd be both right and wrong. Most of the cultural resource laws make nods toward involving the public in decision making, but sometimes they're not easy to perceive. NEPA, for example, requires consultation with government agencies and other ostensible authorities, but lets others get involved only as reviewers of draft documents. NAGPRA focuses only on consultation between agencies or museums and tribes; nobody else has a role. NHPA provides for much broader consultation among interested parties, particularly in the section 106 regulations and NPS guidelines for section 110. This is one reason I try to apply section 106 to as broad a segment of the cultural environment as possible; it's one of the few federal laws that treats citizens as human beings worthy of attention.

Laws like NEPA are holdovers from an era when government thought that most problems could be best addressed by experts, and the best thing citizens could do was show respect for the experts' decisions. This was also the era that gave us urban renewal and the Vietnam War. In the 1980s and 1990s, in CRM and EIA as in other aspects of life, a new respect for diversity in knowledge and perception, often jargonized under the rubric "postmodernism," began to open up decision-making systems to citizen interests.[86] It seems to me that this promising development, which found expression in new legal authorities like Executive Order 12898, rather withered on the vine after the 2000 presidential election; federal agencies today give lip service to the interests of the public, but in my experience are behaving more arrogantly than ever. So there are ways for all kinds of interested parties to take part in many aspects of CRM, but it's seldom easy, and it can be intensely frustrating.

In a nutshell, those are the players in CRM. But at what do they play, and what are the rules of the game? Well, it depends, but let's begin by looking at one of the major games[87] that most of them play, the process of review under NEPA.

Notes

1. Formerly "Truk"; now one of the states of the Federated States of Micronesia.

2. For information and links regarding the African Burial Ground, see www .africanburialground.gov/ABG_Main.htm (accessed December 24, 2007).

3. See John P. McCarthy, "Who Owns These Bones? Descendant Communities and Partnerships in the Excavation and Analysis of Historic Cemetery Sites in New York and Philadelphia," *Public Archaeology Review* 4 (2): 312.

4. See, for example, *The Heritage Journal* at www.heritageaction.org/?page= theheritagejournal (accessed December 24, 2007) and *The International Journal of Heritage Studies* at www.tandf.co.uk/journals/routledge/13527258.html (accessed December 24, 2007).

5. Frank Vanclay, "International Principles for Social Impact Assessment," *Impact Assessment and Project Appraisal* 21 (1) 2003: 6. See also Interorganizational Committee on Guidelines and Principles for Social Impact Assessment, "Guidelines and Principles for Social Impact Assessment," *Environmental Impact Assessment Review* 15 (1) 1993: 11; NOAA 1994: 1.

6. NHPA section 301(8).

7. NHPA section 301(5).

8. See, for instance, David Rubenstein, Jerry Aroesty, and Charles Thompsen, *Two Shades of Green: Environmental Protection and Combat Training*. Santa Monica, CA: Rand National Defense Research Institute R-4220-A, 1992.

9. For NIMBY-oriented advice about NHPA section 106 review, see T. F. King, *Saving Places That Matter: A Citizens Guide to the National Historic Preservation Act*. Walnut Creek, CA: Left Coast Press, 2007.

10. See Helen Y. Herman, "Why is Paris Arguably the World's Most Beautiful City?" *Preservation in Print* 31 (5) 2004: 12–13.

11. 16 U.S.C. 431–33.

12. 16 U.S.C. 461–67.

13. William J. Murtagh, *Keeping Time: The History and Theory of Preservation in America*, rev. ed. (New York: John Wiley & Sons, 1997), 59.

14. 16 U.S.C. 469.

15. For example, The Hague *Convention for the Protection of Cultural Property in the Event of Armed Conflict* in 1954, the *Recommendation on International Principles*

Applicable to Archaeological Excavations in 1956, and the *Recommendation Concerning the Safeguarding of the Beauty and Character of Landscapes and Sites* in 1962. As part of the same trend, the *International Council on Monuments and Sites* (ICOMOS) was chartered in Venice in 1964.

16. 44 U.S.C. Chapter 33.

17. See Mindy Thompson Fullilove, *Root Shock: How Tearing Up City Neighborhoods Hurts America, and What We Can Do About It* (New York: Ballantine, 2004).

18. U.S. Conference of Mayors, *With Heritage So Rich* (New York: Random House, 1967). Released as a report in 1965.

19. See Antoinette J. Lee, "Discovering Old Cultures in the New World: The Role of Ethnicity," in *The American Mosaic*, ed. Robert Stipe and Antoinette J. Lee. (Washington, DC: U.S. Committee for the International Council on Monuments and Sites [US/ICOMOS], 1987); and various papers in Beth L. Savage (ed.), *African American Historic Places* (Washington, DC: National Register of Historic Places, 1996).

20. Rachel Carson, *Silent Spring* (Cambridge, MA: Houghton Mifflin, 1962).

21. See, for instance, William R. Freudenburg, "Social Impact Assessment." *Annual Review of Sociology* 12 (1986): 451–78.

22. Variously known as the Archeological and Historic Preservation Act and the Archeological Data Preservation Act, and widely ignored by federal agencies.

23. And parenthetically to ensure the author's first job in the federal government, working for NPS writing Moss-Bennett regulations that, as the political winds shifted, never were published for effect.

24. See W. D. Lipe and A. J. Lindsay Jr., *Proceedings of the 1974 Cultural Resource Management Conference*. Museum of Northern Arizona Technical Series No. 14, Flagstaff, AZ, 1974. However, Louis Wall, then a preservation planner with the National Park Service working with the National Register, also has a good claim to having invented the term.

25. See Thomas F. King, "How the Archeologists Stole Culture. A Gap in American Environmental Impact Assessment and How to Fill It," *Environmental Impact Assessment Review* 18 (2) 1998: 117–34; and King, "Doing a Job on Culture: Effective But Self-Serving Communication With One of Archeology's Publics," *Thinking About Cultural Resource Management* (Walnut Creek, CA: AltaMira Press, 2002), 4–14.

26. 25 U.S.C. 450–51n, 455–58e.

27. 42 U.S.C. 1996.

28. 20 U.S.C. 2101.

29. 16 U.S.C. 1701 et seq.

30. 16 U.S.C. 1600 et seq.

31. 449 F.2d 113 (9th Cir. 1974).

32. 16 U.S.C. 470aa–mm.

33. 460 U.S. 766, 103 S.Ct. 1556 (1983).

34. Pub. L. 93-383.

35. 16 U.S.C. 470a note.

36. NHPA Sec. 101(e)(3)(B).

37. 25 U.S.C. 3001–13.

38. 485 U.S. 439.

39. Senate Report No. 191–85.

40. Patricia L. Parker, ed., *Keepers of the Treasures* (Washington, DC: National Park Service, 1990).

41. *Guidelines for Evaluating and Documenting Traditional Cultural Properties.* NPS 1990. Bulletin 38 can be accessed at www.nps.gov/nr/publications/bulletins/ nrb38/. For history see T. F. King, *Places That Count: Traditional Cultural Properties in Cultural Resource Management* (Walnut Creek, CA: AltaMira Press, 2003), chapter 2.

42. 43 U.S.C. 2101–6.

43. UNESCO, *Convention on the Protection of the Underwater Cultural Heritage.* Adopted at Paris, November 2, 2001. See http://portal.unesco.org/en/ev .php-URL_ID=13520&URL_DO=DO_TOPIC&URL_SECTION=201.htm (accessed December 24, 2007).

44. Thus creating "THPOs."

45. CEQ, *Federal Actions to Address Environmental Justice Under NEPA.* February 11, 1994. www.epa.gov/fedrgstr/eo/eo12898.pdf (accessed December 24, 2007).

46. *Locating Federal Facilities on Historic Properties in Our Nation's Center Cities*, May 21, 1996, www.wbdg.org/pdfs/eo13006.pdf; and Indian Sacred Sites, May 24, 1996, www.cr.nps.gov/local-law/eo13007.htm (both accessed December 24, 2007).

47. See also Thomas F. King, *Federal Planning and Historic Places: The Section 106 Process* (Walnut Creek, CA: AltaMira Press, 2000); and King, *Thinking About Cultural Resource Management: Essays from the Edge* (Walnut Creek, CA: AltaMira Press, 2002), 35–100.

48. See www.achp.gov/army.html#aap for the army's description of its alternative procedures. See www.blm.gov/heritage/docum/finalPA.pdf for the Bureau of Land Management's national programmatic agreement; and www.blm .gov/heritage/why.htm#NatProg for BLM's description of its national program (all accessed December 24, 2007).

49. *Preserve America*, March 3, 2003, www.achp.gov/news-preserveamericaEO .html (accessed December 24, 2007).

50. Facilitation of Cooperative Conservation, August 26, 2004, www .whitehouse.gov/news/releases/2004/08/20040826-11.html (accessed December 24, 2007).

51. UNESCO, *Convention for the Safeguarding of the Intangible Cultural Heritage.* Adopted at Paris, October 17, 2003. See www.unesco.org/culture/ich/ (accessed December 24, 2007).

52. United Nations General Assembly, *United Nations Declaration on the Rights of Indigenous Peoples.* Adopted by the General Assembly, September 13, 2007. See www.un.org/esa/socdev/unpfii/en/declaration.html, (accessed December 24, 2007).

53. See www.achp.gov (accessed December 24, 2007).

54. CEQ Web site, www.whitehouse.gov/ceq/.

55. See www.epa.gov/, especially www.epa.gov/compliance/environmental justice/ (accessed December 25, 2007).

56. 42 USC 9601 et seq.

57. CERCLA § 113(h), 42 U.S.C. § 9613(h). It would be an odd thing for a federal agency to claim that it need not comply with a law simply because a citizen suit could not compel it to.

58. See www.ecr.gov/ (accessed January 8, 2008).

59. CEG, *A Citizen's Guide to the NEPA: Having Your Voice Heard.* December 2007, www.nepa.gov/nepa/Citizens_Guide_Dec07.pdf (accessed January 8, 2008).

60. Executive Order 13287, *Preserve America,* Sec. 3(e).

61. See www.achp.gov/pubs-stewardship.html (accessed December 25, 2007).

62. See www.achp.gov/pubs-stewardship.html (accessed December 25, 2007).

63. See www.cr.nps.gov (accessed December 25, 2007).

64. See www.nps.gov/hdp/about.htm (accessed December 28, 2007).

65. See www.nps.gov/history/hps/abpp/ (accessed December 25, 2007).

66. See crmjournal.cr.nps.gov/Journal_Index.cfm (accessed December 25, 2007).

67. AFC Web site, www.loc.gov/folklife/.

68. See www.nationaltrust.org/ (accessed December 25, 2007).

69. See www.ncshpo.org/ (accessed December 25, 2007).

70. See www.nathpo.org/ (accessed December 25, 2007).

71. 25 USC §§ 450–450n, and when enacted, Public Law 93–638; often referred to in Indian country as "638."

72. For a detailed discussion of tribal programs, see Darby C. Stapp and Michael S. Burney, *Tribal Cultural Resource Management* (Walnut Creek, CA: AltaMira Press, 2002).

73. See Charles Wilkinson, ed., *Indian Tribes as Sovereign Governments* (Oakland, CA: AIRI Press, 1997).

74. Executive Memorandum on Government-to-Government Relations with Native American Tribal Governments, April 29, 1994; Executive Order 13175, *Consultation and Coordination with Indian Tribal Governments,* November 6, 2000.

75. Executive Order 13336: *American Indian and Alaska Native Education,* April 30, 2004.

76. Example of treaty language: "In consideration of the rights and privileges acknowledged in the preceding article, the United States bind themselves to protect the aforesaid Indian nations against the commission of all depredations by the people of the said United States, after the ratification of this treaty." Treaty of Fort Sheridan with the Sioux and other tribes, September 17, 1851, Article 3.

77. "Treaty of Peace and Amity between His Britannic Majesty and the United States of America, Concluded at Ghent, December 24, 1814, Article IX: The United States of America engage to put an end, immediately after the ratification of the present treaty, to hostilities with all the tribes or nations of Indians with whom they may be at war at the time of such ratification; and forthwith to restore to such tribes or nations, respectively, all the possessions, rights, and privileges which they may have enjoyed or been entitled to in one thousand eight hundred and eleven, previous to such hostilities. Provided always that such tribes or nations shall agree to desist from all hostilities against the United States of America, their citizens and subjects, upon the ratification of the present treaty being notified to such tribes or nations, and shall so desist accordingly."

78. 04-15746, D.C.No. CV-02-01314-DFL.

79. Example of treaty language: "It is, however, understood that, in making this recognition and acknowledgement, the aforesaid Indian nations do not hereby abandon or prejudice any rights or claims they may have to other lands; and further, that they do not surrender the privilege of hunting, fishing, or passing over any of the tracts of country heretofore described." Treaty of Fort Sheridan with the Sioux and other tribes, September 17, 1851, Article 7.

80. See, for instance, the decision in *Minnesota v. Mille Lacs Band of Chippewa Indians*, 526 U.S. 172 (1999).

81. See, for instance, *United States v. Winans*, 198 U.S. 371 (1905): "In other words, the treaty was not a grant of rights to the Indians, but a grant of rights from them—a reservation of those not granted."

82. See, for instance, *Choctaw Nation v. Oklahoma*, 397 U.S. 620, 630-31 (1970).

83. See, for instance, www.hawaii-nation.org/ (accessed December 25, 2007).

84. For one reason, because the recognized tribes are sometimes offended if you give a nonrecognized tribe too much respect.

85. United Nations General Assembly, *United Nations Declaration on the Rights of Indigenous Peoples*. Adopted by the General Assembly, September 13, 2007. See www.un.org/esa/socdev/unpfii/en/declaration.html, (accessed December 24, 2007).

86. For an insightful and not too jargon-laden exposition of this perspective, see Frank Fischer, *Citizens, Experts, and the Environment: The Politics of Local Knowledge* (Durham, NC: Duke University Press, 2000).

87. Some readers have criticized my use of a sports metaphor for the practice of CRM, saying it suggests a lack of seriousness. I think there's danger in taking oneself too seriously. Others have objected that the metaphor unduly emphasizes adversarial relationships, and that, I think, is more on point. But games don't have to be adversarial; the term embraces hide-and-seek as well as NFL football.

2

Cultural Resources in the Broadest Sense: Practice Under the National Environmental Policy Act (NEPA)

What Is It?

NEPA is a cultural resource management law, a natural resource management law, a pollution prevention law, a clean water law—a law requiring federal agencies to manage the impacts of their actions on the "human environment," which is defined as "the natural and physical environment and the relationship of people with that environment."[1]

So in terms of cultural resources, NEPA's umbrella is an expansive one, covering *all* types of resources having anything to do with the way people relate to the built and natural environment—that is, all the kinds of resources we'll be discussing in subsequent chapters and maybe others.

NEPA has two parts. The first, section 101, establishes national policy, declaring that:

> It is the continuing policy of the Federal Government, in cooperation with state and local governments, and other concerned public and private organizations, to use all practicable means and measures, including financial and technical assistance, in a manner calculated to foster and promote the general welfare, to create and maintain conditions under which man and nature can exist in productive harmony, and fulfill the social, economic, and

other requirements of present and future generations of Americans.

To carry out this policy, section 101(b) goes on to articulate:

The continuing responsibility of the Federal Government to use all practicable means, consistent with other essential considerations of national policy, to improve and coordinate Federal plans, functions, programs and resources to the end that the Nation may—

- fulfill the responsibilities of each generation as trustee of the environment for succeeding generations;
- assure for all Americans safe, healthful, productive, and esthetically and culturally pleasing surroundings;
- attain the widest range of beneficial uses of the environment without degradation, risk to health or safety, or other undesirable and unintended consequences;
- preserve important historic, cultural, and natural aspects of our national heritage, and maintain, wherever possible, an environment which supports diversity, and variety of individual choice;
- achieve a balance between population and resource use which will permit high standards of living and a wide sharing of life's amenities; and
- enhance the quality of renewable resources and approach the maximum attainable recycling of depletable resources.

The part of NEPA that federal agencies deal with day-to-day is section 102. Section 102 begins by saying that to the fullest extent possible:

The policies, regulations, and public laws of the United States shall be interpreted and administered in accordance with the policies set forth in this Act.

It goes on to direct that—again to the fullest extent possible:

All agencies of the Federal Government shall . . . (u)tilize a systematic, interdisciplinary approach which will insure the integrated use of the natural and social sciences and the environmental design arts in planning and in decision making which may have an impact on man's environment.

It further tells agencies to:

Identify and develop methods and procedures, in consultation with the Council on Environmental Quality . . . which will insure that presently unquantified environmental amenities and values may be given appropriate consideration in decision making along with economic and technical considerations.

Finally, it lays out the procedural requirement to:

Include in every recommendation or report on proposals for legislation and other *major Federal actions significantly affecting the quality of the human environment, a detailed statement* by the responsible official on—(1) The environmental impact of the proposed action; (2) Any adverse environmental effects which cannot be avoided should the proposal be implemented; (3) Alternatives to the proposed action; (4) The relationship between local short-term uses of man's environment and the maintenance and enhancement of long-term productivity; and (5) Any irreversible and irretrievable commitments of resources which would be involved if the proposed action should it be implemented [emphasis added].

Regulations by the Council on Environmental Quality (CEQ) direct agencies in carrying out the procedural requirement. The regulations, which are extensive and not (in my opinion) very logically organized, are at 40 CFR 1500-1508.[2] CEQ has recently published a *Citizen's Guide to the NEPA*[3] that outlines the regulatory process in fairly plain English.

MFASAQHE

Section 102's requirement for a detailed statement is the only part of NEPA many agencies seem to know about. This is too bad, because without the underlying policy it's a throwaway, and it results in fixation on "major federal actions significantly affecting the quality of the human environment" (MFASAQHE, pronounced "Mafasakwee").

NEPA's scope actually embraces all kinds of federal actions—as it must given the policy articulated in section 101. MFASAQHE is the threshold for writing the detailed statement of environmental impacts—which is called an environmental impact statement (EIS). But an agency has to do some level of environmental analysis even to determine whether an action *is* a MFASAQHE, and that's what most NEPA work is really about.

According to the CEQ regulations, the range of actions to which NEPA applies includes:

1. Adoption of official policy, such as rules, regulations, and interpretations; treaties and international conventions or agreements; formal documents establishing an agency's policies which will result in or substantially alter agency programs;
2. Adoption of formal plans which guide or prescribe alternative uses of federal resources, upon which future agency actions will be based;
3. Adoption of programs, such as a group of concerted actions, to implement a specific policy or plan; and
4. Approval of specific projects, such as construction or management activities, located in a defined geographic area.[4]

It's in the context of the last class of action that most practice occurs under NEPA. "Projects," the regulations say, include "Actions approved by permit or other regulatory decisions as well as federal and federally assisted activities."

Categorical Exclusions

CEQ's regulations direct federal agencies to develop their own NEPA procedures. One thing these do is to list "categorical exclusions." A categorical exclusion—usually referred to as a "CX," "CATEX," or "CatEx"—is:

A category of actions which do not individually or cumulatively have a significant effect on the human environment and which have been found to have no such effect in procedures adopted by a Federal agency in implementation of these regulations.[5]

In other words, agencies decide (subject to CEQ approval of their procedures) which actions don't have the potential to be MFASAQHEs and hence don't require analysis. CATEXs are necessary to government operations; otherwise, agencies would have to analyze the environmental impacts of every paperclip purchase.

But actions can be miscategorized, so the regulations go on to say that:

Any procedures under this section shall provide for extraordinary circumstances in which a normally excluded action may have a significant environmental effect.

So, in fact, agencies have to perform some level of environmental review even of CATEX actions, to determine whether an "extraordinary circumstance" exists.

In 1996 I helped the General Services Administration (GSA) rework its NEPA procedures, and we spent a lot of time debating CATEXs. GSA builds and manages federal buildings, among other things, that can have environmental impacts—particularly on the urban sociocultural environment. But the great bulk of GSA's actions are routine administrative matters—legitimate CATEXs. Many others have some remote potential for impact on the environment, but it's so slight that it would be a waste of tax money (which, believe it or not, federal employees *do* worry about) to spend much time reviewing them.

We distinguished between two types of CATEX. One is the "automatic CATEX" (also called the "no-brainer"), which requires no environmental review at all. This is the kind of action where it's virtually unthinkable that an extraordinary circumstance could exist; examples are hiring and firing people and purchase of office supplies.

The other type is the "checklist CATEX" (or "low-brainer"), which requires a quick checklist review to ensure that extraordinary circumstances don't exist.[6] Examples include:

- Acquisition of land that is not in a floodplain or other environmentally sensitive area and does not result in condemnation;

- Acquisition of space by Federal construction or lease construction, or expansion or improvement of an existing facility, where all of the following conditions are met:
  1. The structure and proposed use are substantially in compliance with local planning and zoning and any applicable State or Federal requirements (referenced in appendix);
  2. The proposed use will not substantially increase the number of motor vehicles at the facility;
  3. The site and the scale of construction are consistent with those of existing adjacent or nearby buildings; and
  4. There is no evidence of community controversy or other environmental issues.
- Disposal of properties where the size, area, topography, and zoning are similar to existing surrounding properties and/or where current and reasonable anticipated uses are or would be similar to current surrounding uses (e.g., commercial store in a commercial strip, warehouse in an urban complex, office building in downtown area, row house or vacant lot in an urban area).

Review of a GSA checklist CATEX naturally involves a checklist, which is shown in figure 2.

Applying even automatic CATEXs requires some analysis; during preparation of the agency's NEPA procedures you have to think through whether, as a category, hiring or firing people or buying office supplies could affect the environment. As figure 2 shows, checklist CATEXs require a fair bit of case-by-case analysis.

Sociocultural issues need to be considered in checklist CATEX review. Deciding whether "community controversy" exists, for instance, requires knowledge of and discussions with the community in which such controversy may arise. And completing the checklist requires someone to find out whether the project may be "inconsistent with locally desired social . . . conditions," or "affect a significant aspect of the sociocultural environment."

An obvious question here is "What if the checklist's filled out by somebody who doesn't know anything, or who lies?" That's a

Action Name:
Action Location:
Action Description:
Category:

Part A: All Checklist CATEX Actions

	YES	NO	Need Data
A. Is the action likely to be inconsistent with any applicable Federal, State, Indian tribal, or local law, regulation, or standard designed to protect any aspect of the environment?			
B. Is the action likely to have results that are inconsistent with locally desired social, economic, or other environmental conditions?		.	
C. Is the action likely to result in the use, storage, release and/or disposal of toxic, hazardous, or radioactive materials, or in the exposure of people to such materials?			
D. Is the action likely to adversely affect a significant aspect of the natural environment?			
E. Is the action likely to adversely affect a significant aspect of the sociocultural environment?			
F. Is the action likely to generate controversy on environmental grounds?			
G. Is there a high level of uncertainty about the action's environmental effects?			
H. Is the action likely to do something especially risky to the human environment?			
I . Is the action part of an ongoing pattern of actions (whether under the control of GSA or others) that are cumulatively likely to have adverse effects on the human environment?			
J. Is the action likely to set a precedent for, or represent a decision in principle about, future GSA actions that could have significant effects on the human environment?			
K. Is the action likely to have some other adverse effect on public health and safety or on any other environmental media or resources that are not specifically identified above?"			

CONCLUSIONS:

1. The action is a CATEX and requires no further environmental review.

2. The action is a CATEX but requires further review under one or more other environmental authorities (list).

3. The action requires an EA.

4. The action requires an EIS.

_____   _____
Program Staff   Date   REQA Representative   Date

Figure 2.   General Services Administration CATEX Checklist

problem, and it can never be wholly solved. If people really want to get out of looking at an environmental impact, there's usually a way to do it. In trying to plug the holes in any environmental review system, you have to balance costs and benefits: how thoroughly can we protect ourselves from errors and omissions without creating a system that's too complex, or too expensive? In the GSA NEPA procedures, each checklist is supposed be signed by a trained environmental staffer, and there are guidelines for responding to each checklist question. For example:

> Think about whether your action is likely to cause changes in the ways members of the surrounding community, neighborhood, or rural area live, work, play, relate to one another, organize to meet their needs, or otherwise function as members of society, or in their social, cultural, or religious values and beliefs. Is your action likely to:
>
> - Cause the displacement or relocation of businesses, residences, or farm operations;
> - Affect the economy of the community in ways that result in impacts to its character, or to the physical environment;
> - Affect sensitive receptors of visual, auditory, traffic, or other impacts, such as schools, cultural institutions, churches, and residences; or
> - Affect any practice of religion (e.g., by impeding access to a place of worship)?
>
> Give special attention to whether the action is likely to have environmental impacts on a minority or low income group that are out of proportion with its impacts on other groups. Consider, for example, whether the action is likely to:
>
> - Result in the storage or discharge of pollutants in the environment of such a group;
> - Have adverse economic impacts on such a group;
> - Alter the sociocultural character of such a group's community or neighborhood, or its religious practices; or
> - Alter such a group's use of land or other resources.
>
> Also consider possible impacts on historic, cultural, and scientific resources. Think about whether the action is likely to have physical, visual, or other effects on:
>
> - Districts, sites, buildings, structures, and objects that are included in the National Register of Historic Places, or a state or local register of historic places;
> - A building or other structure that is over forty-five years old;
> - A neighborhood or commercial area that may be important in the history or culture of the community;

- A neighborhood, industrial, or rural area that might be eligible for the National Register as a district;
- A known or probable cemetery, through physical alteration or by altering its visual, social, or other characteristics;
- A rural landscape that may have cultural or esthetic value;
- A well-established rural community or rural land use;
- A place of traditional cultural value in the eyes of a Native American group or other community;
- A known archeological site or land identified by archeologists consulted by GSA as having high potential to contain archeological resources; or
- An area identified by archeologists or a Native American group consulted by GSA as having high potential to contain Native American cultural items.

Particularly in rural areas, give special consideration to possible impacts on Native American cultural places and religious practices. For example, consider whether the action is likely to alter a place regarded as having spiritual significance by an Indian tribe or Native Hawaiian group, impede access to such a place by traditional religious practitioners, or cause a change in the use of, or public access to, such a place.

Is anybody really going to do all this kind of thinking and questioning when they fill out a checklist? Well, in theory, GSA people are supposed to be trained to do so. And for most actions, there shouldn't be that much thinking and questioning to do. Checklist CATEX (i), for example, is "Disposal of . . . personal property, dismountable structures, transmission lines, utility poles, railroad ties, and track."

It shouldn't take long for someone to run through the guidelines and decide that a CATEX (i) action has no earthly potential for significant effects on the sociocultural environment. A CATEX (j) action, which involves land disposal, requires more consideration.

Each agency has its own list of CATEXs, and its own way of screening CATEX actions to make sure they don't involve extraordinary circumstances. Many use checklists. How carefully they're used varies from agency to agency and person to person. Making any CATEX decision properly, though, requires at least some thought about potential impacts on the environment, including the sociocultural environment.

Let's suppose, now, that you have an action that's not a CATEX, but it also isn't obviously a MFASAQHE. What do you do?

The Environmental Assessment (EA)

If you don't know whether something is a MFASAQHE you have to do some analysis to figure out the answer. This analysis is referred to as an environmental assessment (EA).

According to the regulations, an EA is:

A concise public document for which a Federal agency is responsible that serves to:

1. Briefly provide sufficient evidence and analysis for determining whether to prepare an environmental impact statement or a finding of no significant impact;
2. Aid an agency's compliance with the Act when no environmental impact statement is necessary; and
3. Facilitate preparation of a statement when one is necessary.[7]

Something like fifty thousand EAs are done each year across the federal establishment, as compared to about a tenth that many EISs. It can be fairly said that EAs are the bread and butter of NEPA review.

The regulations aren't very informative about what an EA should contain. They only require that the resulting document:

Include brief discussions of the need for the proposal, of alternatives . . . , of the environmental impacts of the proposed action and alternatives, and a listing of agencies and persons consulted.[8]

But what an EA *must* do is provide the basis for deciding whether an action is likely to significantly affect the quality of the human environment. The regulations provide some detail about what "significantly" means, and their language is redolent with relevance to the sociocultural environment:

"Significantly" as used in NEPA requires considerations of both context and intensity:

Context. This means that the significance of an action must be analyzed in several contexts such as society as a whole (human, national), the affected region, the affected interests, and the locality. Significance varies with the setting of the proposed action. For instance, in the case of a site-specific action, significance would usually depend upon the effects in the locale rather than in the world as a whole. Both short- and long-term effects are relevant.[9]

Intensity. This refers to the severity of impact. The following should be considered in evaluating intensity:

1. Impacts that may be both beneficial and adverse;
2. The degree to which the proposed action affects public health or safety;
3. Unique characteristics such as proximity to historic or cultural resources, park lands, prime farmlands;
4. The degree to which the effects on the quality of the human environment are likely to be highly controversial;
5. The degree to which the possible effects are highly uncertain;
6. The degree to which the action may establish a precedent;
7. Whether the action is related to other actions with individually insignificant but cumulatively significant impacts; and
8. The degree to which the action may adversely affect districts, sites, highways, structures, or objects listed in or eligible for listing in the National Register of Historic Places, or may cause loss or destruction of significant scientific, cultural, or historical resources.[10]

The EA should hold the action's potential effects up against the regulatory definition of "significantly," and ask, "Given the context of the action, and applying the measures of intensity, will the action significantly affect the quality of the human environment?"

You first need to ask, "In what context(s) may effects occur?" Suppose we're planning a timber sale on the Kindling National Forest. In terms of geography, there clearly will be effects in a local context—the context of the forest and its environs, or of the ecosystem. Perhaps there will be regional impacts—on the economy of the region, or on the regional wildlife habitat. In terms of society, there may be economic, visual, and auditory impacts, among others, on a local community—the nearby town of Matchless, say—but you'd also need to think about other contexts. Perhaps there's an Indian tribe that used to occupy the area, but that was long ago relocated to Oklahoma. This tribe might have concerns about the area, and they might even have treaty rights to resources there. The bottom line is that you've got to do some thinking, some research, to establish the context(s) in which analysis should be done. And don't make the mistake of thinking that the sequence given in the regulations—"society as a whole (human, national), the affected region, the affected interests, and the locality"—represents a hierarchical ordering. The regulations are just trying to say that you don't ignore the local negative effects, or the negative effects on affected groups, because the effects on society as a whole will be positive.

Having established our contexts—let's say they comprise the National Forest and its neighborhood, and the concerns of the Motomak Tribe—we then turn to intensity and look at each measure of intensity given in the regulations. So, for example:

1. Impacts that may be both beneficial and adverse . . .

We're going to stimulate the local economy and give people jobs (beneficial). We may muck up the ecosystem (adverse). We may disturb places of cultural significance to the Motomak (adverse).

2. The degree to which the proposed action affects public health or safety . . .

Cutting on slopes greater than 30 percent could cause erosion that would increase downstream flooding, possibly drowning people or polluting the Matchless water system.

3. Unique characteristics . . . such as proximity to historic or cultural resources park lands, prime farmlands . . .

We'll need to do studies[11] of some sort to identify historic and cultural resources—consult with the Motomak and others who may have cultural links to the area, look for archeological sites, check for historic buildings, and so forth. This is often taken as a rationale for doing archeological surveys, but it can require both less and more than that. If we're planning to do helicopter logging, or logging over snow, there may not be much need for archeological surveys because we won't mess up the ground much. Even if this is the case, though, if the sale will result in a swath of clear-cut visible from a nearby peak, we'd better talk to the Motomak and others to make sure the peak isn't a spiritual place whose use requires a natural view—or a place where everybody goes to enjoy the scenery.

4. The degree to which the effects on the quality of the human environment are likely to be highly controversial . . .

There's only one way to find out about this: we've got to talk with people—both locals and people at a distance who may be concerned, like the Motomak.

5. *The degree to which the possible effects . . . are highly uncertain . . .*

Suppose we're planning to log over snow, but we don't really know how effective that's going to be for the protection of sensitive plants and surface archeological sites; or suppose we don't know whether that peak is a place where Motomak people go to seek visions. These sorts of uncertainty need to be addressed, and if possible eliminated, in the EA.

6. *The degree to which the action may establish a precedent . . .*

Maybe if this project is "successful" in controlling environmental impacts, the Forest Service is going to make logging over snow standard practice. If this is likely, we'd better be sure we've really thought through all its impacts, and we'd probably better go back and rethink the contexts in which we're doing our analysis. Now maybe we'd better look at a nationwide context and think about different regions. If we do logging over snow where the buffalo roam, for example, is it going to create trails that bison will follow from the high country down onto the cattle range, raising the fear of spreading brucellosis? Not a problem on the Kindling, where the biggest animal is the jackalope, but if the project is a precedent for logging on the Big Blue Bison National Forest, it could be another matter.

7. *Whether the action is related to other actions with individually insignificant but cumulatively significant impacts . . .*

How much logging has already gone on in the area? Are we creeping toward a point at which we could go over some critical threshold and lose a resource? Is the speckled mugwump's habitat so mucked up by logging, road building, and mushroom gathering on the Kindling that one more timber sale will push it into extinction? Or in a cultural context, is there now just enough old growth timber on the forest, or in the Stony Owl drainage, or on the east slope of Mt. Moron, to allow the Motomak to carry out their Universe Salvation ritual, and will this timber sale reduce the old growth below critical levels? Or will the sale reduce the number of mine sites left from the 1876 quartz rush to a point where we'll never be able to answer important research questions about this fascinating part of Washafornia's history? Cumulative impact analysis is supposed to look at how severe the current project's impacts are when added to the impacts of all past, current, and reasonably foreseeable future impacts, regardless of who may be responsible for them.[12] Many analysts find cumulative effects particularly hard to figure out, so there's a tendency to ignore them. This is too bad not only because it provides a tempting target to anyone who wants to litigate—considering cumulative impacts is required by the regulations, after all—but precisely *because* they're hard to figure out. They're hard to figure out because they're subtle. You may be looking at a little bitty project, with little bitty direct effects, but maybe it's part of a pattern of development that's fundamentally changing the character of the environment. If you don't understand that big pattern, you're not really assessing the project's effects.[13]

8. The degree to which the action may adversely affect districts, sites, highways, structures, or objects listed in or eligible for listing in the National Register of Historic Places, or may cause loss or destruction of significant scientific, cultural, or historical resources . . .

This too requires a hard look—not only within the boundaries of the sale, but in areas where visual, auditory, land use, or other effects might occur. This look should be coordinated with work under section 106 of the National Historic Preservation Act (see chapter 4), but this measure of intensity isn't limited to *historic* places, or even to *places* at all. The clause about "significant scientific, cultural, or historical resources" must mean something other than historic properties, or it wouldn't be there as a separate clause. So—

- We need to think about scientific resources like paleontological sites, and pack rat middens that can provide information on past climates.
- We need to think about cultural resources like the religious practices of the Motomak, the use of Stony Owl Creek for baptismal purposes by the local Pentecostal Church, the gathering of mushrooms on the slopes of Mt. Moron for the annual Mushroom Festival, and use of the area by landscape painting classes from Southeastern Washafornia State University.
- We need to think about historical resources like the records of the Mt. Moron Mine, locked in a safe in the old mine head-

quarters, like the oral history of medicinal plant use in the area, and like the history of local logging itself.

Some of these resources may relate to historic places, but others don't. They are resources that can be affected by the action, whether they're subjects of concern under laws like the National Historic Preservation Act or not, and impacts on them ought to be considered in the EA. And, importantly, finding out about a lot of them requires talking with people, consulting with them, getting their opinions. Although the CEQ regulations don't say much about public participation in EA preparation, it's an absolute necessity with respect to cultural effects, because it's in people's collective consciousness that such resources reside and such effects take place.

So preparing the EA is an analytical activity that should be organized around the regulatory definition of the word "significantly." It must lead to a report, which answers the question: "Are significant effects likely?"

The EA has one of two results. Either you do an EIS because the action *is* likely to have significant impacts, or you don't because it *isn't*. In the latter case, your agency issues a "Finding of No Significant Impact" (FONSI or FNSI) before proceeding. Many times, the FONSI will include actions the agency has decided to do— or agreed to do—to reduce impacts below a significant level. Some litigants have questioned the appropriateness of "mitigated FONSIs," but most courts have found that they're reasonable, cost-effective ways to handle impacts without going through a lot of unnecessary review. The important point to remember, though, is that in order to have a legitimate mitigated FONSI, the agency must be able to *show that it has mitigated or will mitigate the impacts down to a level of nonsignificance.*

The "Socioeconomic Exclusion"

Section 1508.14 of the NEPA regulations says that:

Economic or social effects are not intended by themselves to require preparation of an environmental impact statement. When an environmental impact statement is prepared and economic or social and natural or physical environmental effects are interrelated, then the environmental impact statement will discuss all of these effects on the human environment.[14]

The Supreme Court, in *Metropolitan Edison Co. v. People Against Nuclear Energy*[15] (commonly called the PANE decision), similarly concluded that social and *psychological* impacts were not sufficient by themselves to require an EIS.

Agencies have been known to interpret this to mean that impacts on social, economic, and cultural resources don't have to be considered under NEPA.[16] Neither the regulations nor the Court in PANE said this. What the regulations and PANE say, taken together, is that if an action will have effects only on social, economic, or psychological factors, then the proponent agency *doesn't have to do an EIS.* That's a lot different than saying the agency doesn't have to consider these factors under NEPA. In fact, an agency *does* have to consider them in its EA, along with all other possible environmental impacts. If it turns out that there are only social, economic, or psychological effects, then the project does not rise to the level of a MFASAQHE, and environmental impact analysis ends with a FONSI. If there are social, economic, or psychological effects that are linked somehow to significant effects on the physical (natural or built) environment, then an EIS has to be done.

Suppose that Mr. Jones really, really, really likes the view from his front window out across the valley of Stony Owl Creek. Suppose that Megazap Corp. plans to build a 750 kV power line through the valley, crossing Mr. Jones' view. If Mr. Jones can't find anything wrong with Megazap's proposal except that it's going to upset him, cause his social standing to decline, or decrease his property value, he's not going to be able to force whatever federal agency is regulating Megazap to do an EIS. But his concerns *will* have to be considered in any EA that's prepared on the project, and if he can show that there are impacts that go beyond his psychological, social, or economic well-being, then perhaps he *can* force preparation of an EIS.

What might Mr. Jones find as an impact that goes beyond the social, economic, and psychological? Well, obviously he might find that construction will cause erosion, or that endangered owls will alight on the lines and be fried, but as a reflection of his own concerns, he might argue that the project will have serious cultural effects.

Note that the "exclusion" provided by the regulations and PANE extends to social, economic, and psychological effects; nothing is said about *culture*. So if Mr. Jones can argue that the Stony Owl Creek valley may be a historic property, a place of high cultural attachment for the people of Matchless, a spiritual place in the eyes of the Motomac Tribe (or the Zen Buddhists, or the Baha'i), or a popular local picnic place, then he may be able to give Megazap a run for its money. How much of a run he can give them will depend on how good a case he has, and how well he's able to make it.

Note, though, that there's very little in the CEQ regulations to force Megazap or its regulator ever to talk with Mr. Jones or anybody else, as long as all they're doing is an EA. The regulations go on at length about public participation in EIS preparation and review, but don't say much about such participation in EAs. It's possible for an agency never to reveal its EAs to the public except in response to Freedom of Information Act requests. This doesn't make much sense—one can't very well figure out the intensity of an impact on affected interests without ascertaining what those interests are and talking things over with them, but there's nothing in the regulations that comes right out and says "talk with people." That's a serious flaw in the regulations that cultural resource managers need to be careful about.

The Environmental Impact Statement (EIS)

The EIS is the "detailed statement" that is required on any action that's a MFASAQHE. In contrast with their terseness on EAs and CATEXs, the CEQ regulations go into great detail about what goes into an EIS, and how it's prepared and reviewed.

You begin by deciding what the purpose and need for the proposed action are. This may seem self-evident—you'd obviously better know why the project's needed if you're thinking of doing it. There are good reasons for thinking carefully about purpose and need, however, because the way you define them limits the range of alternatives you'll consider. If you define the purpose of your project as meeting the need to alleviate traffic congestion in East Armpit, you can consider a wide range of alternatives—rapid transit, bicycle subsidies, euthanasia—but if you say the purpose is to move traffic more efficiently from downtown East Armpit to the suburbs, you're pointed pretty clearly in the direction of highway improvements.

Having decided why you need to do the project, you publish a Notice of Intent (NOI) in the *Federal Register.* The Federal Register (not the National Register, which is another thing entirely) is a daily publication of federal agency announcements, draft and final regulations, guidelines, standards—just about everything but a "Personals" section. Few real people ever read the Federal Register, of course, so if an agency seriously wants people to know about its EIS, it will publish notice elsewhere, too.[17]

Then comes "scoping"—one of the most widely abused elements of the NEPA process. Scoping is a terribly sensible thing to do—it means figuring out what the scope of the EIS should be. You don't want to hire water quality specialists to work on your EIS if the scope of effects doesn't include doing anything to the water. According to the regulations, scoping includes:

- Inviting interested parties to participate in the EIS work;
- Identifying significant issues for analysis;
- Eliminating non-significant issues;
- Allocating assignments for the work that's to be done;
- Identifying other studies being done that relate to the subject of the EIS, so work can be coordinated;
- Identifying environmental review requirements other than NEPA that need to be addressed; and
- Establishing the relationship between preparation of the EIS and the project planning schedule.[18]

The regulations go on to say that as part of scoping, the agency may set page limits on the EIS, set time limits on preparation, combine scoping with EA preparation, and *hold a public scoping meeting.* Unfortunately, some agencies and consultants read that last clause and seem to ignore everything else, reducing scoping to the conduct of a public meeting. More on this later. Scoping is supposed to be an analytic activity—you take a look at the project and the area, and try to get an idea of what you need to do to identify impacts. Getting public input is an important part of this analysis, but it's only one part, and it doesn't have to involve a mind-numbing public hearing. It can involve interviews, workshops, focus groups, facilitated working sessions—whatever makes sense under the circumstances. And again, it shouldn't be the only thing you do; you also ought to apply your own brain, and those of your interdisciplinary colleagues, and those of others you consult, to the questions "what impacts might this action have, and what kinds of environmental factors may need to be considered?" Your conclusions are going to be provisional, of course; you may discover unexpected impacts as you go along, or find that some anticipated impacts really aren't going to occur.

Although the regulations talk about scoping only in the context of EIS preparation, it's really necessary in planning how to do an EA, too, and even in screening a CATEX. Whether you call it scoping or not, you've got to figure out what you're going to do, and you ought to do so systematically, based on analysis and consultation with knowledgeable and interested parties.

Having established the scope of the EIS, the next step is to carry it out—whatever that may entail. Naturally, this is a flexible process; you do such analysis as is needed to identify and make sense of the project's impacts. Of course, if you haven't done a good job of scoping, you may wind up analyzing the wrong things.

The regulations spell out what the format of an EIS should be; in outline, it goes like this:

- Cover sheet
- Summary
- Statement of purpose and need for the proposed action
- Description of alternatives, including the "no action" alternative (not taking the action at all). All reasonable alternatives are to be "rigorously explored," and the agency's preferred alternative is to be identified, if there is one. Mitigation measures can also be described.
- Description of the environment affected by each alternative
- Discussion of the environmental consequences of each alternative, including direct, indirect, and cumulative impacts
- List of preparers
- Appendixes as needed[19]

So, the core of the EIS answers the following questions:

- What are our options (alternatives) for meeting the purpose and need?
- What is the environment that would be affected by each option?
- What impacts will each option have on the environment?

The analysis leads to a draft EIS (DEIS), which is circulated for comment to agencies with jurisdiction or expertise, to local governments, Indian tribes, and other groups, and made available for public review. Once the comment period is up, comments are considered and—unless the project has been blown out of the water by public opposition or canned for some other reason—a final EIS (FEIS) is prepared. The FEIS must respond to all comments received and presumably adjusts the analysis to address deficiencies identified by commenters.[20]

The FEIS is then considered by whoever makes the decision about whether and how to proceed with the project. He or she makes a decision, whereupon a record of decision (ROD) must be published, telling the world what the decision is. The ROD may (and should) include a description of whatever the agency has decided or agreed to do to mitigate environmental impacts.[21]

NEPA and Cultural Resources

Now that we have a handle on the basic NEPA process, let's look at how the cultural environment can—and, I suggest, should—be addressed. Then we'll look at how it usually *is* addressed in the real world.

Remember that NEPA requires agencies to consider *all* environmental impacts, on *all* aspects of the environment. Thus it's NEPA that gives agencies their broadest authority, and direction, to address the sociocultural environment writ large, as well as its interactions with the biophysical environment. NEPA is often referred to metaphorically as an umbrella that extends over all the resource-specific laws, but it also extends beyond them, to cover aspects of the human environment that are *not* the subjects of more specific laws and executive orders.

Let's start with scoping—and by scoping I mean formal scoping for an EIS, the less formal scoping needed in planning an EA, and the even more informal scoping involved in figuring out whether extraordinary circumstances exist that prevent an action from being regarded as a CATEX.

During scoping, an agency should try to figure out what sociocultural issues may need to be addressed—what sociocultural aspects of the environment may be affected. This is not necessarily going to be apparent as the result of a public meeting or two, though interactions with the public during scoping are vital. Scoping should involve whatever consultations are necessary with authorities and stakeholders, as well as background research. Where traditional communities are concerned—for example, many Native American communities—it's often important to consult with them before any sort of public discussion of the action, because they may have cultural concerns (e.g., about spiritually important places or practices) that can't be revealed in public. Consultation with federally recognized tribes must be carried out on a government-to-government basis that respects tribal sovereignty.[22]

Scoping may reveal issues—impacts on traditional land uses, lifeways, hunting, gathering, or agricultural practices, social interactions, religious practices, historic places—that affect what kinds of people make up the study team that will perform the NEPA analysis and in designing the analysis itself.

Scoping defines the character of the analysis that's needed, but there are also some basic principles the analysis should follow. Some years ago the American Social Impact Assessment community produced a set of *Guidelines and Principles for Social Impact Assessment*.[23] The nine principles established there can usefully be applied to all kinds of sociocultural impact analysis.[24]

1. *Involve the diverse public.* Figure out who the affected "publics" are, and involve them in ways that are sensitive to cultural, economic, linguistic, educational, and other differences. The NEPA analysis must be carried out in *consultation* with the people who may be affected. Consultation should mean more than having meetings or sending letters; it ought

to involve face-to-face exchanges of information and ideas. Special efforts may have to be made to make it meaningful—for example, use of each group's own language, and paying attention to local social norms that may be foreign to the analyst.

2. *Analyze impact equity.* Try to determine who'll win and who'll lose if the proposed project or an alternative is pursued. As we'll discuss later, Executive Order 12898 provides specific direction about this aspect of the analysis.

3. *Focus the assessment.* As the *Guidelines and Principles* say, the analyst should "deal with issues and public concerns that really count, not those that are just easy to count." What's of interest to the analyst, or what the analyst finds easy to deal with, is not necessarily what's important to the people. On the other hand, of course, what people don't know *can* hurt them or the environment. One shouldn't be slavish to the concerns of the affected public; you need to look both at what specialists think is important and what the locals are concerned about.

4. *Identify methods and assumptions and define significance.* The steps you go through to reach your conclusions should be understandable to others. And the bottom line of any impact analysis is to determine how significant the impacts may be. In a NEPA context, this means analyzing impacts with reference to the definition of significance in the regulations—analyzing the intensity of the impacts in their relevant contexts.

5. *Provide feedback to project planners.* The analysis should be dynamic; a continual flow should exist back and forth between analysts and planners. Feedback to stakeholders is vital, too.

6. *Use qualified practitioners.* NEPA calls for interdisciplinary research. It's important to distinguish between *inter*disciplinary and *multi*disciplinary research. *Multi*disciplinary research simply means a bunch of specialists working on the same project; *inter*disciplinary research means interaction among the specialists—and presumably a fruitful symbiosis. The specialists needed for the sociocultural side of a NEPA analysis will probably be social scientists—anthropologists, sociologists, cultural geographers, archeologists—

practitioners of such fields in the humanities as history and architectural history, and people in hybrid disciplines like landscape history. It's important to have them work with the other scientists involved in the assessment effort. The people doing the water quality studies, for example, will have much to say to the people studying the affected community's use of fish, shellfish, aquatic plants, or water itself.

7. *Establish monitoring and mitigation programs.* This, of course, should be one of the end results of the analysis, assuming the proposed action goes forward in some manner.

8. *Identify data sources.* Adhering to this principle can present problems where sensitive sociocultural information is involved. It may not be possible for a traditional religious practitioner to reveal much about a spiritual place, and if he or she does, it may be inappropriate for you to put it in print, or say where you got the information. But to the extent you can, it's necessary to the NEPA administrative record to say where your data came from.

9. *Plan for gaps in data.* It's unlikely that you'll get all the information you'd like to have. The important thing is to recognize the missing information *as* missing, and decide explicitly how important it is. Then you can decide whether it's worth the effort to get it.

In the case of a MFASAQHE, the analysis results in a DEIS, which gets circulated for review. This shouldn't be the only time the analysts interact with the interested public, but it's one important opportunity. Review of the DEIS should be an opportunity for creative communication, for identifying gaps and flaws, for filling the former and correcting the latter, for challenging assumptions, and defending or adjusting conclusions. It should also be an opportunity to make sure the affected public knows what the hell the analysis is about, and understands what impacts the various alternatives may have on their lives and cultural values. It should involve a carefully constructed program of public review and participation.

The public review period is also a key time for consultation with regulatory/advisory agencies like the state historic preservation officer (SHPO). The analysis leading to the DEIS should have at least generally defined the affected resources and the character of the effects, so it becomes feasible at this point to consult about how to manage the former and resolve or mitigate the latter. This consultation needs to be coordinated with the public review, so that each can inform and be informed by the other.

In an EA/FONSI case, the regulations don't require public review, but the wise agency will provide for it to the extent the issues seem to demand it. The same principles apply to this sort of informal review as to review of an EIS.

The results of public review and consultation with oversight bodies should be organized, responded to, and reflected in the final EIS/ROD or EA/FONSI. Then they should be considered in making the agency's final decision about whether and how to proceed, and any needed mitigation measures should be developed and implemented—again in consultation with the affected parties.

That's the way it ought to be done. Now, in the real world . . .

It is common to hear EIS consultants talk blithely about "the scoping meeting" as though that's all scoping is. And, in fact, that's the way they often behave. Scoping is often thought of as a pro forma exercise in public relations. I've heard this referred to as "the rent-a-gym syndrome"—set up a meeting in some local public facility, explain the project in great detail to the public, stonily absorb such comments as the (by now stunned and somnolent) attendees can launch, and then say goodnight. Since such meetings often have little evident influence on the actual analysis, this is also referred to as the "Triple-I" approach: "Inform, seek Input, and Ignore."

Having thus engaged the public, the analysts go on to perform a study that matches their—the analysts'—template of a proper EIS. This may have more to do with the background and experience of the preparer's staff than with the potential impacts of the action.

Where the NEPA analysis is an EA, and there is no formal requirement for public participation, there may not be any. The entire analysis is performed in the blackest possible box, with as little public input as possible, in order to minimize costs and expenditures of time.

In preparing EAs, analysts often follow CEQ's directions for the preparation of EISs. This is understandable, since the regulations are so much more verbose about the latter than the former, but it fails to recognize a very important point. An EA is designed to answer a single question—*will there or will there not likely be a significant impact on the quality of the human environment?* The answer to this question—yes or no—has specific regulatory implications; if yes, you have to do an EIS; if no, you're through with NEPA and can issue a FONSI. An EIS serves no such crystalline purpose; it merely reveals impacts so the decision maker and the public can consider them. When an EA is done following the standards for an EIS, it may analyze all kinds of impacts but never make a case as to whether they're significant. The writers of the EA then make an essentially unsubstantiated judgment call—usually with heavy encouragement to conclude that the impact will be insignificant.

This approach can have serious, costly results for the project proponent. Example: the National Aeronautics and Space Administration (NASA) proposed to help the University of Hawaii expand the Keck Observatory, a major astronomical facility on the volcano Mauna Kea. The mountain is regarded as a spiritual place by Native Hawaiians, and many of them objected strongly to the project's impacts on their spiritual environment. Clearly the project had the potential for impacts on cultural resources, and clearly it was controversial—two of the "intensity" measures of significance set forth in the NEPA regulations.[25] Yet NASA did an EIS-like EA[26] on the project and concluded it had no significant impact. Litigation halted the project until NASA agreed to do an EIS. Continued controversy eventually forced NASA to withdraw from the project entirely, and at this writing it has been halted by still more litigation.[27]

This failure to acknowledge the significance of impacts is a problem with regard to all kinds of impacts, on all kinds of resources. In the case of the environment's sociocultural aspects, the problem is exacerbated by another definitional issue. In both EAs and EISs, the affected sociocultural environment typically is divided into two parts. There is usually a section on "cultural resources" and another on "social (or socioeconomic) impacts." In most cases neither term is defined. When they are, however—and by implication when they aren't—"cultural resources" are equated with "historic properties" (i.e., places included in or eligible for the National Register of Historic Places) or sometimes with archeological sites, or occasionally with historic properties and Native American cultural objects (see chapter 6). "Socioeconomics," meanwhile, is typically reduced to variables that, in the pungent words of the *Guidelines and Principles*, are "easy to count":[28] demographics, use of services, numbers of kids in school, purchasing power, tax base, employment. Everything else of a sociocultural nature falls through the cracks between these two narrowly defined foci of interest, and isn't discussed at all.[29]

So the DEIS, or EA, ends up addressing historic properties at one end of the spectrum, and easy-to-count socioeconomic phenomena at the other, and then if it's an EIS, and sometimes if it's an EA, it goes out for public review. Members of the public may be frustrated that things of cultural importance to them aren't addressed, and they may comment on this when they review the DEIS, but they are in a slippery position. Suppose you don't feel that a DEIS has properly considered the effect of a reservoir on the places where your community has fished for the last several generations. What do you call these places? Are they historic properties? Well, you can try to call them that, but the response is likely to be that the analyst's archeologist looked over the place and determined there was nothing there because, after all, the sandbars from which you fish move around all the time. Hence there are no intact archeological deposits and so, you're told, there's nothing eligible for the National Register of Historic Places, and hence no historic property.

Or you can complain about the EIS's failure to consider the importance of subsistence fishing to maintaining your community's traditional lifeways. This complaint will get bounced to the socioeconomist to answer, and he or she will spew out a bunch of statistics about fish yield and per-pound market value, probably showing that fish aren't nearly as important as frozen dinners in your diet—never mind how they figure in your weekly interfamily gatherings.

This sort of obscurantism doesn't necessarily mean that anybody is trying to ignore your fishing place; it merely means that nobody knows how to deal with it, because they're all looking at impacts through narrow, disciplinary lenses.

You can get past all this if you know how, but most people don't. You can argue that the sandbars comprise a National Register eligible traditional cultural property. You can point out that NEPA is about more than National Register properties. You can talk about the special sociocultural importance of fishing in your community, and about how taking away the fish may be a disproportionate adverse impact on your low-income or minority group, thus raising the red flag of environmental justice (see chapter 7). But you've got to know how to do this sort of thing, to speak this way, to say the right things at the right time to the right people. And most people don't know all those obscure words and concepts.

So the chances are excellent that the project will go forward with impacts on the most important parts of the sociocultural environment—at least those that are most important to you—virtually undisclosed, and entirely unconsidered by the agency in making its decision.

So what do you do? If you can afford to, you hire somebody like me to help you frame your argument, get yourself a lawyer, and sue the bastards. And if you're lucky, you may force them to back up and do more analysis—perhaps even an analysis that's relevant to the impacts you're concerned about. Maybe.

Return to the African Burial Ground

The African Burial Ground in New York City—discussed in chapter 1 to show how the unrecognized complexity of cultural resources can cause an agency trouble—is also an example of NEPA gone bad. The NEPA analysis was an EA, leading to a FONSI, despite the fact that it revealed the mapped location of a "Negro burial ground" on the site. It was assumed, first, that NEPA analysis was just a hoop through which the project's proponents had to jump—never mind what it revealed. And it was a foregone conclusion that the project would have no significant effects—after all, this was downtown Manhattan. The burial ground was noted, of course, but it was assumed that if anything remained of it, it would be something the contract archeologists could take care of. So, there was no EIS, and hence no formal scoping, no organized context in which the concerns of the African American community might have surfaced. The project went forward, and, of course, did have significant impacts, for which the General Services Administration (GSA) paid dearly.

The African burial ground also illustrates the need for interdisciplinary coordination in NEPA analyses. The archeologists reasonably enough assumed that most of the burial ground would have been destroyed by the basements of buildings that had been built on the site during the nineteenth century. Better coordination with geomorphologists involved in site characterization might have revealed that the burials had taken place in a swale between sand dunes and that the nineteenth-century basements had gone mostly into the fill that had been dumped into this low spot to level it—thus preserving much of the burial ground *under* the basements but right in the path of GSA's construction.

Conclusion

It's in the context of NEPA that cultural resources as a whole have the best chance of being considered early enough in planning a project that changes can be made to protect them. But there are plenty of things to keep a NEPA analysis from being successful from a cultural point of view. The project may be miscategorized as a CATEX. It may be the subject of an ill-planned EA that's done without adequate consultation with affected people or experts outside the agency, or even with internal agency experts. Scoping may be so poorly done that significant issues aren't identified, or aren't identified until too late. Or the issues may be identified, and even discussed, but ignored in decision making. All these things can happen, but they don't need to. If you're working inside the agency or as a consultant to the agency, it should be your business to keep them from happening. If you're an affected citizen, you need to know enough about the NEPA process—and I hope you've just learned it—to stand up and insist that the resources you're concerned about get properly considered and that you get a say in how they're treated.

Always remember, though, that in the final analysis there's nothing in NEPA that says an agency can't nuke the environment. The agency has to *consider the environmental impacts* of its project, but it doesn't have to refrain from having them.

But on the other hand, the agency *is* required—in theory—to explain itself if it concludes that an action will not significantly affect the quality of the human environment. If it issues a FONSI it should be able to justify that finding with reference to the measures of significance in the regulations. And if it fails to ratchet its impacts down to a level of insignificance, then it's not supposed to do a FONSI. A significant impact will occur, and it's supposed to go through the extra time and expense of doing an EIS and attending to its results. If it does an EIS and then decides to blow away important parts of the environment, it has to justify that in its ROD. And it's required to consider reasonable mitigation measures; if it doesn't adopt such measures, then it has to document in the ROD *why* it hasn't adopted them.[30]

Given these requirements, project opponents and regulators, like state historic preservation officers, do have a bargaining chip or two. Suppose an agency sits down to negotiate how to treat a cultural resource but won't really negotiate. The agency has decided that all it can do is excavate the archeological site and bulldoze it; they won't consider leaving it in place even though it's of great cultural value to the community. If you're an SHPO or a community group negotiating with the agency, you may rightly conclude that although the proposed "mitigation" measures really won't mitigate the impacts, you don't have the leverage to get the agency to do anything better. So you sigh and sign an agreement, whereupon the agency issues a FONSI and proceeds. If you're in this kind of situation, you may want to consider saying "OK, we'll agree to this mitigation measure because you're such SOBs that you won't accept anything else, but we *do not* think it reduces your impacts below significance, and we'll file a formal objection if you issue a FONSI based on adoption of this kind of mitigation." Agencies don't like to do EISs; they take time and money and are exposed to a lot of scrutiny. If you can threaten the validity of the agency's FONSI, you may find the agency becoming a lot more reasonable.

On the other hand, if you're a project proponent—in an agency or looking to an agency for a permit or assistance—you ought to anticipate this kind of situation and do everything you can to reach agreement on measures that really do reduce the impact below significance. Or suck it up and do an EIS. It may be costly in the short run, but if it avoids lengthy appeals and litigation, it will probably save money and time in the long run.

Notes

1. 40 CFR 1508.14.
2. For guidance about NEPA implementation, see (for instance) Larry Canter, *Environmental Impact Assessment*, 2nd ed. (New York: McGraw-Hill, 1996); David P. Lawrence, *Environmental Impact Assessment: Practical Solutions to Recurrent Problems* (New York: John Wiley & Sons, 2003).
3. CEQ, *A Citizen's Guide to the NEPA: Having Your Voice Heard* (Washington, DC: CEQ, 2007), www.nepa.gov/nepa/Citizens_Guide_Dec07.pdf (accessed January 8, 2008).
4. 40 CFR 1508.18.
5. 40 CFR 1508.4.
6. GAS, *NEPA Desk Guide* (Washington, DC: Public Buildings Service, 1999); see www.gsa.gov/gsa/cm_attachments/GSA_DOCUMENT/NEPA_Desk_Guide _R2E-c-q-v_0Z5RDZ-i34K-pR.pdf (accessed December 25, 2007).
7. 40 CFR 1508.9.
8. 40 CFR 1508.9.
9. 40 CFR 1508.27(a).
10. 40 CFR 1508.27(b).
11. Including, but not limited to, the studies and consultation necessary to comply with section 106 of the National Historic Preservation Act (see chapter 5).
12. See Council on Environmental Quality, *Considering Cumulative Effects Under the National Environmental Policy Act* (Washington, DC: CEQ, 1997), www.nepa .gov/nepa/ccenepa/exec.pdf (accessed December 25, 2007).
13. Regarding litigation risks in poor cumulative effect analysis, see Michael D. Smith, "Cumulative Impact Assessment Under the National Environmental Policy Act: An Analysis of Recent Case Law," *Environmental Practice* 8 (4) (2006): 228–40, http://journals.cambridge.org/action/displayAbstract;jsessionid=43FDD9C76B97 BA080BA52F776FAE1A78.tomcat1?fromPage=online&aid=690264 (accessed December 25, 2007).
14. 40 CFR 1508.14.
15. 460 U.S. 766, 103 S.Ct. 1556 (1983).
16. J. G. Thompson and Gary Williams, "Social Assessment: Roles for Practitioners and the Need for Stronger Mandates," *Impact Assessment Bulletin* 10 (3) (1992): 43–56.
17. And, of course, if it doesn't, it won't, or it may publish only in the *Federal Register* because its people lack the initiative and imagination to do anything more.
18. 40 CFR 1501.7.
19. 40 CFR 1502.10-18.
20. 40 CFR 1502.9.
21. 40 CFR 1505.2.
22. This means, in effect, consultation between a line officer of the agency and the tribal government, though on the basis of such consultation, day-to-day coordination may be delegated by each to technical staff.

23. Interorganizational Committee on Guidelines and Principles for Social Impact Assessment, "Guidelines and Principles for Social Impact Assessment," *Environmental Impact Assessment Review* 15 (1) (1993): 11–43; NOAA, *Guidelines and Principles for Social Impact Assessment*, 1994.

24. As can many of the broader principles set forth in the more recent International Principles for Social Impact Assessment (Frank Vanclay, International Principles . . . ," *Impact Assessment and Project Appraisal* 21 (1): 5–11), but because these *are* broader, and designed to relate to wide range of international conditions, some of them are less directly relevant to U.S. practice than are their progenitors, the Interorganizational Guidelines and Principles.

25. 40 CFR 1508.27(b)(3), (4), and (8).

26. NASA, *Environmental Assessment for the Outrigger Telescopes Project, Mauna Kea Science Reserve, Island of Hawai'i* (Washington, DC: Office of Space Science NASA, 2002).

27. See timeline summary at www.mauna-a-wakea.info/news/index.html (accessed December 25, 2007).

28. NOAA, *Guidelines and Principles*, 20.

29. Thomas F. King, "How the Archeologists Stole Culture. A Gap in American Environmental Impact Assessment and How to Fill It," *Environmental Impact Assessment Review* 18 (2) (1998): 117–34; King and Ethan Rafuse, *NEPA and the Cultural Environment: An Assessment of Effectiveness* (Washington, DC: CEHP for Council on Environmental Quality, 1994).

30. 40 CFR 1505.2(c).

3

Historic Properties as Cultural Resources: The National Register of Historic Places

What Is It?

In chapters 4 and 5, we'll focus on laws and practices involving a type of cultural resource called "historic properties." In the interests of simplifying the discussion, I think it would be wise to be clear about what "historic properties" are. There's a succinct statutory definition of the term: a historic property is a "district, site, building, structure, or object included in or eligible for the National Register."[1]

That's the *National Register of Historic Places*, the U.S. version of the national list conceived by the French back in the early nineteenth century. The U.S. Register was created by the National Park Service (NPS) in response to the 1966 enactment of the National Historic Preservation Act (NHPA). Initially, the Register was cobbled together from several preexisting lists of historic places that NPS had compiled, notably the list of National Historic Landmarks (NHLs) designated under the Historic Sites Act of 1935. The list has grown exponentially over the years and now contains well over eighty thousand entries. The Register—as outlined in the last chapter—is also a group of people in NPS who maintain the list, headed by the "keeper."

International Models

Over the last two centuries the notion of a definitive, official list of significant historic places (and sometimes other types of cultural resources) has become deeply embedded in the world's collective psyche. Every developed nation has one, or more, and developing a list is almost always the first thing a developing nation decides to do when it sets up a historic preservation apparatus within its government. Virtually every UNESCO convention and recommendation on cultural heritage establishes, dictates, or promotes listing the things that ought to be preserved. Listing seems to be a sort of reflex.

The uber-list is the *World Heritage List*, created by UNESCO in 1972 via the Convention Concerning the Protection of the World Cultural and Natural Heritage (World Heritage Convention). At this writing 181 nations are "states parties" to the Convention, officially binding themselves to its terms. States parties nominate places that they believe have "outstanding universal value" as parts of the "World Cultural and Natural Heritage." They also theoretically obligate themselves to care for the places they nominate. A World Heritage Center in Paris oversees the program, and a World Heritage Fund helps states parties manage properties inscribed in the list.[2] As of late 2007, 851 properties are listed in 141 countries, categorized as "cultural," "natural," and "mixed." A *Recommendation Concerning the Protection, at National Level, of the Cultural and Natural Heritage*, adopted at the same time as the convention and not binding on states parties, encourages nations to set up similar programs within their own governmental structures.[3] The United States was somewhat ahead of the curve, setting up its National Register six years before UNESCO adopted the World Heritage Convention, but of course other nations did so much earlier. Some nations maintain truly national lists; others have lists at state, provincial, or district levels, others at both. Some lists are narrowly focused on historic landmarks, usually of an architectural sort, while others include archeological sites, landscapes, natural areas, and, in some cases, animals, plants, people, documents, artifacts, and social institutions. The U.S. National Register is a middling sort of list in terms of its inclusiveness, focusing only on "historic properties" but defining that term fairly broadly.

In some nations, as with the World Heritage List, and many landmarks lists maintained by local governments, listing a property requires that it be protected to some degree. This tends to produce a relatively short, elite list, and to make listing a political act with real economic consequences. The United States (wisely, I think) chose not to link listing to protection, except to the extent that federal agencies, as we'll see in chapter 4, must consider the effects of their actions on places included in (or eligible for) the National Register. Some states and local governments (unwisely, in my opinion) give higher levels of protection to listed properties. Listing is often a prerequisite to qualifying for grants and tax benefits encouraging preservation.

How the Register is Expanded

NHPA directs NPS to "maintain and expand" a National Register. The Register is maintained by the NPS National Register division, in partnership with the state historic preservation officers (SHPOs) and, to the extent NPS can prevail on them to do so, the tribal historic preservation officers (THPOs). It's expanded through nominations by agencies, states, tribes, local governments, organizations, and citizens. If you want to nominate a place, there's a ponderous, counterintuitive nomination form that must be filled out, accompanied by precisely prepared maps and photographs. The form then has to be reviewed at the state level and, assuming it passes muster, by the keeper's staff. If all goes well, the nominated place is entered in the Register and that's that. It's on the list.

Eligibility and Its Determination

As we'll see in the next chapter, federal agencies, thankfully, are not required only to pay attention to historic places listed in the Register. If that were the only requirement, as it was when NHPA was first enacted, an agency could ignore historic places with impunity if it could just keep anyone from nominating them to the Register. To keep the onus on the agencies to figure out what impacts their actions will have, rather than leaving it to others, NHPA section 106 was amended as discussed in chapter 1, requiring attention not only to registered properties but to those *eligible for* the Register.

Cultural resource practitioners in the United States spend a great deal of time—volunteer and professional, some of the latter quite well compensated—figuring out whether things are eligible for the National Register. Let's discuss how that's done.

In simplest terms, we apply the Criteria of Eligibility, which are found in NPS's National Register regulations at 36 CFR 60.4 (see textbox below). But doing this is nothing like as simple as it may seem.

The National Register Criteria

There are four National Register Criteria, labeled *A* through *D*. Lee Wyma, a preservation architect and attorney,[4] long ago developed a way to keep track of them. *A* is for "association," *B* for "big

---

The National Register Criteria (36 CFR 60.4)

The quality of significance in American history, architecture, archeology, engineering, and culture is present in districts, sites, buildings, structures, and objects that possess integrity of location, design, setting, materials, workmanship, feeling, and association and

a. that are associated with events that have made a significant contribution to the broad patterns of our history; or
b. that are associated with the lives of persons significant in our past; or
c. that embody the distinctive characteristics of a type, period, or method of construction, or that represent the work of a master, or that possess high artistic values, or that represent a significant and distinguishable entity whose components may lack individual distinction; or
d. that have yielded, or may be likely to yield, information important in prehistory or history.

people," C for "cute buildings," and D, of course, boringly, for "data." Or perhaps "dig."

A is for "Association"

Is the property associated with some important event, set of events, or pattern of events, that's important in our past? The word "our" can refer to us local folks, us members of a community, us members of an Indian tribe, us residents of a state or region, us Americans, or us residents of the world. Historic properties are judged in whatever spatial and social contexts are relevant.

A property can be eligible under Criterion A if it's associated with a specific event, such as a battle, an invention, the first occurrence of this or the last occurrence of that. Or it can be associated with a pattern of events—westward movement, the development of a complex political organization in the prehistoric Midwest, the growth of the poultry industry in Sonoma County. The events can be traditional events in, say, the oral history of a Native American group—Universe Maker's battles with the monsters; the emergence of the ancestors from the lower world.

B is for "Big People"

Again, the people here can be "big" in a variety of contexts. George Washington is a Big Person, but so is Marin de Likatuit, the early nineteenth century Coast Miwok chief who launched a revolt against the Spanish in northern California. So is Montgomery Blair, whose plantation became Silver Spring, Maryland. The "person" also doesn't have to be a demonstrable member of the human race. Tahquitz Canyon in southern California is included in the Register in part for its association with the spirit Tahquitz, who in the traditions of the Cahuilla tribe comes down the canyon in the form of a blue comet to devour people's souls.

C is for "Cute Buildings"

Criterion C could also be called "catch-all," though, to be nice, let's call it the "characteristics" criterion. A property that displays the characteristics of a class, a style, a school of architecture, a period of construction—all these can be eligible under criterion C. Generally speaking, this is the architectural historian's favorite criterion—a dog-trot house, a Classical Revival courthouse, a parkway designed by the Olmsted Brothers—can be eligible simply for being what it is. So can an example of engineering like, say, a rocket launch tower or a nuclear reactor, a sewer system or an automobile assembly plant—or a piece of artwork like a WPA mural or a prehistoric rock art panel.

A place can display characteristics if it's *typical* of its class—a good example of a shotgun house. On the other hand, it can be eligible if it's the *best or only* example—the last tobacco barn in Emphysema County—or if it's an *atypical* example, like the biggest or smallest tobacco barn.

Finally, there's that marvelous last clause: a property can be eligible if it represents a "distinctive entity, the individual components of which may lack distinction." Say what? This is what "districts" are all about—the whole can be greater than the sum of the parts. A historic mining area may have shafts, adits, chunks of rail line, spoil heaps, collapsed buildings, garbage piles—any one of which, by itself, might be of little or no historical value, but when you put them all together, the whole complex is pretty neat. Such a "distinctive entity" can be eligible as a district, even though its individual components "lack distinction."

D is for "Data"

The archeologist's fave, criterion D, says a place is eligible if it contains—or may contain—information significant in history or prehistory. Some archeologists think D is the *only* National Register criterion—that a place can't be eligible unless it contains significant data. This, of course, is not true; there are three other, quite independent, criteria, and a property need meet only one of them to be eligible.

Arguably, though, to be eligible under criterion D a place must also be eligible under criterion A. How can a place have important information about the past if it's not associated with some important pattern of events? A rhetorical question; it really doesn't matter.

It's not necessary to know *for sure* that a place contains significant data; it's enough to think it probable. This is helpful because it means you don't have to dig the bejeebers out of an archeological site to determine whether it's important, and hence eligible. You can give it the benefit of the doubt, based on informed judgment.

Archeological sites of all ages and types can be eligible under criterion D, and so can any other kinds of property. A building that can be studied to learn about eighteenth-century carpentry, a landscape that can be studied to learn about Shaker agricultural practices, a highway that can tell us about early twentieth-century engineering—all these can be eligible under criterion D, as well as, probably, other criteria.

Integrity

There's another thing a place must exhibit in order to be eligible for the National Register: "integrity." The regulations refer to "integrity of location, design, setting, materials, workmanship, feeling, and association." One can go into great detail about what this means,[5] but the bottom line is that the place can't be so screwed up that it no longer contains or exhibits whatever made it significant in the first place. The National Register's first keeper, Dr. William Murtagh, used to use the example of the place in St. Louis, Missouri, where the immigrant trails to the West began. Clearly a tremendously important historic site, but now it's downtown St. Louis, and there's simply nothing left there to convey its association, or the feeling of the place's history.

Of course, things like feelings can be pretty tricky to define. Who does one have to impress in order to demonstrate integrity? Right—it depends.

Rationally, it ought to depend on two major factors:

1. *What's it significant for?* If you think the place is important for its possible contribution to historical or archeological research, then it has integrity if the information in it is intact enough to be studied; it doesn't matter a bit what sort of "feeling" it has, or what it looks like.[6] If you think it's important because of the feelings of inspiration, enlarged vision, or historical perspective it can engender, then integrity of feeling—generally requiring a visually intact property

and environment—is necessary. Of course, this answer begs another question: what do we mean by visually intact? The Gettysburg Battlefield can inspire, enlarge one's vision, give one historical perspective, and it's not "intact" in the sense of gun smoke in the air and gore underfoot. Yet if it were covered with tract housing, surely it would not inspire. But it's OK, apparently, that it's covered with monuments. Where do we draw the line? There's no obvious answer, but a partial answer may be found in the other factor on which integrity ought to depend.

2. *Who thinks it's significant?* If the people of Bayonne, New Jersey, regard a place in Bayonne as significant to them, then surely it should be up to them to decide how much and what kind of integrity it needs to have. National Register Bulletin 38 is most explicit about this with regard to "traditional cultural properties," (TCPs) when it says that:

> The integrity of a traditional cultural property must be considered with reference to the views of traditional practitioners; if its integrity has not been lost in their eyes, it probably has sufficient integrity to justify further evaluation.[7]

But the same principle surely applies to all kinds of historic properties. Archeologists think that sites with interesting data in them are significant, and they are the best judges of how messed up those data can be before a site loses integrity. Architectural historians like buildings that are good examples of particular styles or that represent deviations from standard forms; they're the best judges of how much change a building can handle and still retain its significant elements. The people of Bayonne value the places that represent—to them—the character of their community and are the best judges of whether they retain their integrity.

We sometimes lose track of this basic principle, particularly when "we" are employees of the National Register, or SHPO/THPO staff who deal routinely with registration. We begin to think that *we* ought to be the arbiters of integrity, treating the National Register as though it were designed for us rather than for the American people.

Consider, for example, the case of Mount Shasta, an extinct volcano in northern California, and a place of great spiritual significance to several Indian tribes (among other people). To make a long and complex story short, the Forest Service, which administers most of the mountain, determined that its upper slopes were eligible for the Register in connection with section 106 review of a proposed ski facility. The tribes said the whole mountain was significant, and hence eligible for the Register. The matter was referred to the keeper of the National Register, who, after much deliberation, agreed with the tribes. Local property owners were furious, because California law provides special protections for Register-eligible properties, which they felt would impinge upon their property rights. They and their representative in Congress put political pressure on the keeper, who felt it and became inclined to undo his decision. But how to do it? Integrity showed the way. The keeper toured the mountain (without talking with the tribes) and observed, to his consternation, that the lower slopes had long ago been transformed from forest primeval to timber plantations. Obviously, the keeper then opined, the lower slopes had lost integrity and the Forest Service had been right all along. The keeper revised the eligible property's boundary accordingly.

The problem here, of course, is that it wasn't the keeper to whom the mountain was significant; it was the tribes. Hence it should have been for the tribes to decide what did and did not compromise its integrity. Had the keeper done his job honestly, he would have talked to the tribes, asked them whether the long-ago conversion of the woodland from natural to managed forest made it lose integrity in their eyes, documented the results and opined accordingly. By substituting his own taste in forests for theirs, the keeper acted as though the Register were his own plaything, rather than a tool to be used in the service of people who value their heritage.[8]

So integrity is very much in the eye of the beholder, and it is possible to get into some pretty esoteric arguments about whether a place has it or doesn't. The best advice I can offer is, go with the opinions of those who value the place. If their opinions seem strange to you, it's perfectly appropriate to get them to explain them, but I do not believe that it is your business or mine to impose our judgment on places valued by other people.

One last word about integrity. In discussions of the subject, much is often made of whether the property retains the ability to "convey" its significance. This notion that the property must somehow speak to the viewer results from the National Register origins in the traditions of architectural history—where the appearance of a building is key—and in the National Park Service, where interpretation for the public is a central concern. Surely the property must convey something to someone, but we ought to be careful not to slide into thinking of integrity entirely in terms of what the property might convey to a visitor seeking enlightenment about the property's life and times. An archeological site may convey its significance only to an archeologist armed with appropriate tools; a Native American spiritual place may convey its significance only to someone initiated in the traditions of the tribe. Again, we need to consider integrity through the eyes of those who value the property. If those people are interested in public interpretation, fine, but it's not only the public in general to whom historic properties may convey something.

This brings us to a simple rule of thumb that the National Register sometimes uses in considering integrity; it asks "would a person from the property's period of significance recognize it?" If the answer is "yes," it has integrity; if "no," it doesn't.

Like most simple rules, this one has to allow for a lot of exceptions. A resurrected Clovis mastodon hunter probably wouldn't today recognize central Cleveland, where he or she sat down twelve thousand years ago to flake a spear point, but his flaking station may well retain its integrity as an archeological site. Even where feeling and association are key variables, recognition by a person associated with the place may not be the major thing to consider. A place that has been radically transformed may—even as a result of its transformation—convey something important about the past to a viewer. A resurrected geisha incinerated at Ground Zero in Hiroshima or Nagasaki would be unlikely to recognize the place today, but the very transformation of the cities, both by atomic bombs at the end of World War II and by postwar recovery, conveys history-based feelings to any visitor with an iota of sensitivity.

The "recognizability to those associated" rule of thumb is ONE rule to apply, but we ought to remember that history and culture are dynamic, so the significance of a property may lie less in how well it represents the character of its times than in the role it plays in today's culture.

The Criteria Considerations

It's not enough for a place to meet one of the National Register criteria and have integrity. It also must *not* reflect one of a series of "criteria considerations" shown in The Criteria Considerations and Exceptions textbox on page 98—except that often a property can exhibit such a "consideration" and still be eligible.

Say what? It's probably clearest to explain the considerations one at a time, and discuss why a place that reflects each one normally isn't eligible but sometimes is.[9]

Cemeteries

The criteria considerations say that cemeteries are not ordinarily eligible, but one can be if it derives its "primary significance" from graves of people who were of "transcendent importance," or from age, distinctive design features, or association with historic events.[10]

With all those exceptions, it's not too hard to find that a cemetery is eligible. Ancient or just old cemeteries are determined eligible all the time because of their age and association with historic events like, say, the development of mortuary ritual in an ancient society. Somebody who looks pretty commonplace from one person's perspective may be of transcendent importance from another's. And so on. If you want a cemetery to be regarded as eligible, you can usually make it happen.

Birthplaces and Graves

Birthplaces are a little more clear-cut. If all that ever happened someplace is that someone important got born there, the property is not therefore eligible for the Register. Yes, Christians, it's a good thing the National Register isn't how significance is judged in Bethlehem.

Similarly, if the only thing a person of importance ever did on a particular plot of ground was to get buried, that plot is not eligible for

The Criteria Considerations and Exceptions (36 CFR 60.4)

Criteria considerations. Ordinarily cemeteries, birthplaces, or graves of historical figures, properties owned by religious institutions or used for religious purposes, structures that have been moved from their original locations, reconstructed historic buildings, properties primarily commemorative in nature, and properties that have achieved significance within the past 50 years shall not be considered eligible for the National Register. However, such properties will qualify if they are integral parts of districts that do meet the criteria of if they fall within the following categories:

a. A religious property deriving primary significance from architectural or artistic distinction or historical importance; or
b. A building or structure removed from its original location but which is significant primarily for architectural value, or which is the surviving structure most importantly associated with a historic person or event; or
c. A birthplace or grave of a historical figure of outstanding importance if there is no appropriate site or building directly associated with his productive life.
d. A cemetery which derives its primary significance from graves of persons of transcendent importance, from age, from distinctive design features, or from association with historic events; or
e. A reconstructed building when accurately executed in a suitable environment and presented in a dignified manner as part of a restoration master plan, and when no other building or structure with the same association has survived; or
f. A property primarily commemorative in intent if design, age, tradition, or symbolic value has invested it with its own exceptional significance; or
g. A property achieving significance within the past 50 years if it is of exceptional importance.

its association with the stiff. If this seems slightly at odds with the fact that a cemetery can be eligible if it contains transcendently important dead bodies—well, let's not be slaves to consistency.

A birthplace or grave can be eligible if it's associated with the productive life of the person who was born or buried there. Martin Luther King's home in Atlanta, Georgia, is on the Register not because he was born there but because he lived there as he was beginning his ministry. And if there's no place remaining that reflects the person's productive life, then that person's birthplace or grave can be eligible. Of course, this means that in order to determine a birthplace or grave eligible you have to demonstrate that there's no place else that reflects the person's productive life—a daunting task.

Religious Properties

"Properties owned by religious institutions or used for religious purposes" are not supposed to be eligible, but may be eligible if they derive "primary significance from architectural or artistic distinction or historical importance." The bugaboo word here is "primary." "Primary" to whom? In what social or historical or artistic context? At what point in time?

The "religious consideration" was included among the criteria considerations in order to avoid running afoul of the Establishment Clause of the First Amendment to the U.S. Constitution, which says "Congress shall make no law . . . respecting the establishment of religion." The fear was that recognizing a religious property as eligible for the Register because of its significance in religion would be taken as governmental endorsement of the religion and, hence, establishment. The "primary significance" exception-to-the-consideration was then tacked on to accommodate the fact that religious places may have lots of nondoctrinal, supradoctrinal, or extradoctrinal kinds of significance.

It's easy to see that a church can be eligible if it's a fine example of, say, Romanesque architecture. It's also easy enough to see that a synagogue could be eligible if it was the site where proto-fascists tarred and feathered a leader of the local Jewish community before World War II (I'm sorry to say this happened in my hometown). It's not hard to understand that a mosque might be eligible as the community center for Moslem immigrants to a community.

Things get a little trickier when we get to Native American spiritual places, which are given considerable attention in National Register Bulletin 38 as traditional cultural properties. The problem is that those who value such properties, through whose eyes we are supposed to consider their significance, often express their significance in spiritual—that is, religious—terms. So if we recognize a place as eligible for the National Register because those who value it regard it as spiritually significant, are we not placing the government's imprimatur on those people's religious doctrine? Are we not establishing religion?

Hold that question for a moment and look at the First Amendment's other religious clause—the "Free Exercise" clause. Congress, the First Amendment says, not only will make no law respecting the establishment of religion, it will also make no law "prohibiting the free exercise thereof." Just as an agency cannot constitutionally interpret the law in such a way as to "establish" religion, it cannot administer the law in a way that it prohibits someone from the free exercise of her or his religion.

Both the Establishment and Free Exercise clauses have been bases for voluminous litigation, and case law provides extensive if sometimes confusing guidance about how both are to be interpreted. Suffice to say that agencies must operate in a sort of "window" between the clauses, carrying out their affairs in such a way as to avoid prohibiting anyone from carrying out their religions while not going so far as to support—that is, "establish" the beliefs or practices of a particular religion.[11]

It's pretty obvious that destroying someone's place of worship may prohibit that person from practicing his or her religion— though of course this depends on how integral the place is to the practice. In Native American traditional religions there tends to be close association between place and practice, so it's a fair general statement that an agency should try not to destroy Native American spiritual places lest it run afoul of the Free Exercise clause. On the other hand, it's equally obvious that if the government sets a place aside for use only by Native Americans in carrying out religious rituals, and prohibits others from using the place, it may be supporting traditional religion in a way that is probably at variance with the Establishment clause. Between these extremes there's a host of situations and possibilities to be sorted out, some of which have been addressed by the courts, some of which have not.

What does all this have to do with the National Register and the religious properties criteria consideration? First, we have to ask does recognizing a property as eligible for the National Register "establish" religion? The answer, as usual, is "it depends."

Consider the example of the "Sacred Wood" in upstate New York. According to the traditions of the various churches of Jesus Christ of Latter Day Saints (LDS—including but not limited to the "Mormon" Church), it was here that the founder, Joseph Smith, received a vision from God telling him to found the new religion. If we were nominating the Sacred Wood to the National Register and said "The Sacred Wood is significant because it was here that God told Joseph Smith to start his own religion," the Register would do well to look at our nomination askance, because we'd be asking the U.S. government to validate the doctrine of the LDS churches. If instead we said that "The Sacred Wood is significant because in the traditions of the LDS churches it was here that God told Joseph Smith to start his own religion, which led to the creation of the LDS churches, which are of great cultural importance to those who subscribe to their beliefs," the Register could be much more comfortable about accepting our nomination. We would not be asking the government to support anybody's religion; we would simply be asking it to recognize the importance of a set of beliefs in the cultural life of a community, and the association of that set of beliefs with a place.

Consider, then, the other side of the coin. If we built a highway through the Sacred Wood, would we prohibit the free exercise of LDS religion? Once again, of course, it depends—in this case on how tight the association is between the Sacred Wood and the integrity of LDS religious practice. We don't know whether bulldozing the woods will destroy LDS religion, and we certainly won't find out if we don't consider the significance of the Sacred Wood to LDS practitioners. Viewing the Sacred Wood as eligible for the National Register, and hence giving it the attention required by section 106, is one way of ensuring that its significance will be considered.

And if we don't consider the Sacred Wood eligible for the Register, may we not run afoul of another amendment to the Constitution—the Fourteenth? Are we not discriminating against LDS practitioners on the basis of their religion, saying that because they happen to ascribe religious importance to the Wood, it cannot be considered in agency decision making, while the old building down the road can and will be considered? This particularly becomes an issue where Native American spiritual places are concerned, because Indian tribes and other indigenous groups tend not to make bright-line separations between the secular and the sacred. If we decline to consider impacts on properties simply because an Indian tribe talks about them in terms of spirits and supernatural power, we may be discriminating against the tribe's cultural values, on the basis of the tribe's ethnicity and religion.[12]

The bottom line is that religious places can be, and routinely are, determined eligible for the National Register, but in determining them so, one has to be careful not to appear in any way to be giving the government's blessing to the values ascribed to a property in the doctrine of the group that values it. We regard a spiritual place as eligible because of the important roles that beliefs about it have in the cultural life of a community, not because the government endorses those beliefs.[13]

Moved Properties

If a property has been moved from its original significant location, it is generally taken not to be eligible for the Register. The Register does not want to encourage the creation of architectural petting zoos, in which historic buildings are relocated into theme park settings. Historic properties are supposed to remain in their cultural and environmental contexts.

Of course, a property that is inherently mobile—an airplane, or a ship—can be moved with impunity and retain its eligibility. You have to be careful about where it's moved, though. A railroad car that's moved along a rail line is one thing; one that's moved to the middle of a shopping mall is something else again. Even this, though, depends on, say, the character of the mall; if it's the Railyard Mall, built around and incorporating an old roundhouse, moving the car there might be just fine.

A moved property can also become significant on its new site. Fort John Wayne is dismantled and reconstructed fifty miles away as Fort Clint Eastwood, where it gains significance in the Madison County Bridge wars.

Districts that contain some moved buildings, or buildings that include a moved-in wing or two, don't automatically become ineligible, nor does a building that's moved up or down on its foundation—but as always, it depends. It's a matter of degree; if your proposed district contains one old building in place and sixteen that are moved in, it's not going to be eligible as a district (the single *in situ* building may be eligible), but if it's sixteen buildings in place and one moved in, it probably *will* be eligible. If you raise the building six inches on its foundation it's probably no problem; if you raise it twenty feet it's probably another matter.

Reconstructed Properties

If you reconstruct a vanished building or structure, it will probably not be eligible for the Register, because it lacks integrity—it's not the real McCoy. This doesn't mean you can't remodel a real historic building and have it retain its eligibility, though, of course, if you remodel it too much, or with too little sensitivity to its original character, it will lose integrity and become ineligible. How much remodeling is too much? Check the *Secretary of the Interior's Standards and Guidelines for the Treatment of Historic Properties*[14] and related NPS publications for guidance.

The reconstruction criteria consideration is meant to keep what amounts to speculative reconstructions off the Register. If you've got the foundations of Fort Clint Eastwood, and you make up what the walls and innards of the place looked like based on your impressions from old movies; the fort is not likely to be eligible.

As always, though, there are exceptions. If you do a really good job of reconstruction, accurately reconstructing the place based on good historical, archeological, and other information, and if it's in an appropriate environment (usually its original environment), then it may be eligible. Any reconstruction is going to be viewed by the Register with something of a jaundiced eye, though, so if you want to have such a property considered eligible, be prepared for some tough questions.

Commemorative Properties

A statue or other marker of some historical (or other) event is not itself eligible for the National Register, though, of course, the site of the event it commemorates may be eligible. Gettysburg Battlefield is eligible; the monuments that litter it are not themselves eligible—though by now, they have become such parts of the scene that they may in a way contribute to the battlefield's integrity.

A commemorative property can be eligible for its design—as an indicator of the designs associated with a particular period, or because it's the work of a master. Or if it's really something special—the Statue of Liberty—it may be eligible. Actual direct association with (as opposed to commemoration of) an important event may also make a commemorative property eligible. There's a statue on the island of Guam representing the indigenous leader who misguidedly welcomed Spanish colonists to the island; it's not eligible for the Register for its association with indigenous culture or Spanish colonists. A few years ago, however, an important local political figure chained himself to the statue and committed suicide; it may be that history will show this to be an important event, association with which will make the statue eligible.

Properties Whose Significance Extends Less Than Fifty Years into the Past

Finally, there's what's widely referred to as "the Fifty Year Rule." This criteria consideration is often misstated as "a property isn't eligible if it's less than fifty years old." Actually a property can be *more* than fifty years old and still not be eligible if it didn't become significant until less than fifty years ago. The reclaimed surface mine near Shanksville, Pennsylvania, was doubtless over fifty years old on September 11, 2001, when United Flight 92 crashed there, but nobody had (as far as I know) considered it Register eligible. Had Flight 92's passengers succeeded in taking the plane back from the hijackers, the Shanksville landscape probably wouldn't today be regarded as eligible for the National Register. But clearly it *is* eligible, which illustrates the exception to the rule. A property whose significance lies less than fifty years in the past may be eligible if it is of "exceptional significance." The September

11 events are obviously regarded as exceptionally significant, so the Flight 92 crash site is eligible.

The notion of "exceptional significance" begs one to ask: "exceptionally significant to whom?" The answer to this question is not always as clear as it is in the case of Shanksville. For instance, consider properties associated with the Cold War. In 1991 Congress directed the Department of Defense (DoD) to:

> inventory, protect and conserve the physical and literary property and relics of the Department of Defense, in the United States and overseas, connected with the origins and development of the Cold War.[15]

With more enthusiasm than good sense, some DoD officials decided that this meant that Cold War properties were by definition exceptionally significant and therefore eligible for the National Register, even though such properties were almost universally less than fifty years old. Upon realizing that it had backed itself into viewing virtually all its domestic real estate holdings as historic properties, DoD tried to recover by holding that really, a Cold War property was eligible only if it was "nationally significant"—that is, a National Historic Landmark. The Alaska SHPO, among others, rightly objected to this contention, pointing out that the Register includes properties of national, state, and local significance. Surely, she argued, a Cold War property can be "exceptionally significant" in a state context—for example, the context of Alaska's socioeconomic development. Although the Register appears to agree with this position, and although it is manifestly logical, DoD does not as yet seem to have bought into it.

In any event, properties that have been regarded as significant for less than fifty years usually aren't eligible for the Register. The reason for this rule is obvious; we need some historical perspective in order to judge something's historical significance. Fifty years is the rule of thumb the Register uses, though it is careful to point out that it's a sliding rule that shouldn't be applied rigidly. When the significance of a property—or for that matter, the property itself—has hung around for forty years or so, one ought to start thinking about whether it might be eligible; on the other hand, the mere fact that a property has turned fifty doesn't automatically make it eligible. If you want to assert the eligibility of something whose significance lies less than fifty years in the past, be prepared for some argument.

Conclusion: Living With the National Register

One could go on and on about the National Register, the intellectual contortions involved in its interpretation, and the politics of its administration. NPS never talks about the politics, but has put out hundreds of pages of guidance[16] about the Register's meaning and interpretation—and particularly about its importance. NPS sees the National Register as the centerpiece of the whole U.S. historic preservation program, and—regrettably, I think—there's some truth in this. Much of the time of many American cultural resource managers is devoted to National Register matters—preparing nominations, reports on eligibility, arguing about what is and isn't eligible under which criteria, about what has integrity and what doesn't. This has become such a specialized enterprise that many of our reports and much of our jargon is impenetrable to the public we're presumably supposed to serve. The Register has become something that only professionals can understand, only specialists can influence. I think that's a serious problem that in time is likely to bring down the whole fragile structure of historic preservation in the United States.

But for the moment, we're stuck with the National Register. For better or worse, it's one of the major tools we use in carrying out the requirements of NHPA. But "tool" is a poor word to apply to the Register. It's not really a tool; you can't actually do anything with it. It's simply a list and a set of criteria and caveats-on-criteria that has, I think, an inordinate influence on the truly functional aspects of NHPA. In the next chapter we'll turn to one of NHPA's most useful, most significant, and most despised provisions—section 106.

Notes

1. NHPA Sec. 201(5): 16 USC 470w–Definitions.
2. See http://whc.unesco.org/en/convention/ for information on the World Heritage Convention, List, and Centre (accessed December 29, 2007).

3. See www.unesco.org/culture/laws/national/html_eng/page1.shtml (accessed December 28, 2007).

4. And, as Lee Keatinge, for many years a senior staff member at the ACHP.

5. See National Register, *How to Apply the National Register Criteria for Evaluation*, www.nps.gov/nr/publications/bulletins/nrb15/ (accessed December 25, 2007). This bulletin was formerly known as National Register Bulletin 15, but with a fine attention to the needs of librarians and scholars the Register has deleted numbers from its bulletins; thankfully after a hiatus of some years they have restored dates.

6. See Thomas F. King, "Integrity Among Archeologists: The Dirty Truth," *Thinking About Cultural Resource Management: Essays From the Edge* (Walnut Creek, CA: AltaMira 2002), 154–63.

7. National Register of Historic Places, *Guidelines for Evaluating and Documenting Traditional Cultural Properties*, National Register Bulletin 38 (but see note 2); see www.nps.gov/nr/publications/bulletins/nrb38/ (accessed December 25, 2007).

8. And pay the keeper's keep.

9. The order of criteria considerations given here is the order in which they are initially listed in 36 CFR 60.4. In National Register guidance (e.g., National Register Bulletin 15), the considerations are reordered by the way they appear in the *exceptions* to the considerations, also given in 36 CFR 60.4; thus the "religious property" consideration becomes Consideration *A*, the "moved property" consideration becomes *B*, and so on.

10. See 36 CFR 60.4 for this and the other "considerations," and National Register Bulletin 15 [*sic*], 26–43 for discussion.

11. For discussion, see King, *Places That Count*, 259–63; and Lydia T. Grimm, "Sacred Lands and the Establishment Clause: Indian Religious Practices on Federal Lands," *Natural Resources and Environment* 12 (1) (1997): 19–24.

12. As well as indulging in environmental injustice or environmental racism; see Executive Order 12898 and chapter 6.

13. The *Access Fund v. United States Department of Agriculture et al.*, D.C. No. CV–03–00687–HDM, www.ca9.uscourts.gov/ca9/newopinions.nsf/9ADD9 D7E47C1097B88257344005879D0/$file/0515585.pdf?openelement (accessed December 25, 2007).

14. National Park Service, *Secretary of the Interior's Standards and Guidelines for the Treatment of Historic Properties*, 36 CFR 68, see www.access.gpo.gov/nara/cfr/ waisidx_02/36cfr68_02.html (accessed December 25, 2007).

15. Department of Defense Appropriations Act of 1991, section 8120.

16. For National Register publications see www.nps.gov/history/nr/ publications/ (accessed January 10, 2008).

4

Managing Impacts on Historic Properties: Section 106 of the National Historic Preservation Act

What It Is and How It Works

If NEPA is the broadest of the cultural resource authorities, section 106 of the National Historic Preservation Act[1] (NHPA) is one of the narrowest. It requires federal agencies to do two deceptively simple-seeming things (see the Section 106 of NHPA textbox on page 110):

- "Take into account" the effects of their actions on "districts, sites, buildings, structures and objects included in or eligible for inclusion in the National Register [of Historic Places]— that is, on "historic properties," and
- "Afford the Advisory Council [on Historic Preservation] . . . a reasonable opportunity to comment" on such actions.

An intricate project review process has grown from these two requirements over the last forty years.

Section 106 in Historical Perspective

When NHPA was enacted in 1966, one of its authors, the late Robert R. Garvey Jr., became the first executive secretary (later executive director) of the fledgling Advisory Council on Historic Preservation (ACHP) and had to decide what section 106 meant.

Section 106 of NHPA

The head of any Federal agency having direct or indirect jurisdiction over a proposed Federal or federally assisted undertaking in any State and the head of any Federal department of
independent agency having authority to license any undertaking shall, prior to the approval of the expenditure of any Federal
funds on the undertaking or prior to the issuance of any license,
as the case may be, take into account the effect of the undertaking on any district, site, building, structure or object that is
included in or eligible for inclusion in the National Register.
The head of any such Federal agency shall afford the Advisory
Council on Historic Preservation . . . a reasonable opportunity
to comment with regard to such undertaking.

How were agencies to "take effects into account?" What did it
mean to give the ACHP a "reasonable" opportunity to comment?

At the time, another question was easily answered. The only
thing agencies had to give the ACHP an opportunity to comment
on, or to take into account, were effects on places *already on* the National Register—section 106 at the time referred only to "districts,
sites, buildings, structures, and objects *included in* the National
Register." Nothing about unregistered but eligible properties.

Since the Register was as new as the ACHP, there weren't many
places on it, so section 106 business was slow for awhile. However,
a National Register was assembled by NPS using its existing list of
National Historic Landmarks (NHLs) and its inventory of buildings documented by the Historic American Buildings Survey
(HABS). Agencies began finding that they *did* have section 106 to
deal with from time to time. But what did this mean?

Based on what seemed to work in the first few cases in which
the ACHP took part, Garvey and his colleagues, then embedded in
NPS, decided that "taking into account" meant figuring out what
effects one's action was likely to have and considering ways to reduce or mitigate any effects that were adverse. Since most agencies
didn't know beans about historic preservation, this should be done
in consultation with people who *did* know something about it—the

ACHP's small NPS-based staff and the newly created state liaison officers (later state historic preservation officers or SHPOs). Finally, because the rationale for even *having* a section 106 was that preservation was in the public interest, consultation should be done in public.

In the late 1960s, the ACHP put out nonbinding procedures for section 106 review. President Nixon's Executive Order 11593 added clarity to the ACHP's role, and brought eligible but unlisted historic places under the section 106 umbrella. President Carter gave the ACHP rulemaking authority, through the backdoor mechanism of a presidential memorandum on water resource management. Congress eventually made this authority, and the inclusion of eligible properties, official. It also separated the ACHP from NPS, giving it independent status. Section 106 procedures were issued as regulations in 1979 and revised in 1986 and 2000 with further adjustments in 2004. They're codified at 36 CFR 800—that is, Title 36, Part 800 of the Code of Federal Regulations.

36 CFR 800 Today

36 CFR 800 was the subject of regulatory reform during the Reagan administration. This was when I was employed at the ACHP, and I hope someday to write about it—it was Reagan and the environment in microcosm, and it taught me a lot about how Washington works. The revised regulations that emerged reflected a lot of compromise. We were able to preserve the public, consultation-based process that Garvey and his colleagues had invented, but controls were inevitably placed on it to protect project proponents against the rapacious preservationists. The Reagan-era regulations worked all right for a dozen years, but in 1992, after NHPA was significantly amended, the ACHP began revising them again.

The ACHP had a great opportunity, in the environmentally oriented Clinton administration, to prescribe a simple, balanced, effective process for reaching public interest decisions about conflicts between historic preservation and development. But the ACHP insistently ducked this opportunity; instead it just tinkered with the 1986 regulations, guided by no evident philosophy or vision. Adjustments were made here and there to make things work better from the standpoint of whoever was pushing the particular adjustments. If such adjustments raised howls from people who felt they went too far, the ACHP made more adjustments to satisfy the aggrieved parties, and then more to satisfy those unhappy with the adjusted adjustments. The result is something of a camel.

But in 1999 the revised regulations were issued, promptly challenged in court, revised some more, and reissued with minor changes in 2000. More litigation followed, leading to more tweaks in 2004.

Some Conventions

Before we begin to look at the regulations, let's be clear about some conventions.

Terminology

Wherever I refer to "the regulations" or "the section 106 regulations" I mean 36 CFR 800 as revised and published by the ACHP in 2004. Where it's necessary to contrast them with earlier versions, I'll refer to them as "the 2004 regulations."

By "Advisory Council," "Council," or "ACHP" I mean the Advisory Council on Historic Preservation. By "SHPO" I mean state historic preservation officer; by "THPO" I mean the SHPO's equivalent in an Indian tribe. The regulations routinely refer to the "SHPO/THPO," recognizing that these officials fulfill the same roles within their respective jurisdictions. I'll follow the same convention. The regulations also provide that where an action has effects on tribal lands—that is, lands within the exterior boundaries of a reservation—and there's no THPO, the tribe has the same rights as the THPO2.[2] They don't thereafter refer to such tribes; it's understood (in theory) that they're included in the term "THPO." I'll follow that convention, too, so please understand that whenever I refer to the THPO I mean "THPO or tribe-without-THPO-with-respect-to-impacts-on-tribal-lands." Clear as mud?

The regulations use the term "agency official" for the person in the agency that's doing section 106 review who's responsible for making sure the review happens. I don't follow this convention, instead just referring to the "agency," because compliance is a corporate endeavor. On the assumption that many readers are employed by agencies, or are thinking about being thus employed, or at least can imagine being thus employed, I also just call the agency official "you," or sometimes "we" or "us."

Case Study

I'll illustrate each step in the process with a real-world (if elderly) case—the "GO Road" in Northern California, and with other cases where they help clarify the process and its pitfalls. Each time I use the GO Road case (except at the very end), I'll pose questions for the reader's consideration, to help make sense of what's just been discussed. Some of the questions will have pretty obvious answers, others won't; answers will be discussed in the prelude to the next use of the example.

What's It All About?

As we begin to look at the process, and as we work our way through it, it's important to keep some things in mind.

Purpose

First, what's the section 106 process *for*? Despite what some whose projects are reviewed think, its purpose is not to complicate their lives or deplete their bank accounts. Despite what some consultants think, its purpose is not to keep them employed. Despite what some archeologists think, its purpose is not to require archeological surveys, and despite what some architectural preservationists think, its purpose is not to keep old buildings standing.

The regulations articulate the purpose of the process rather succinctly:

> The section 106 process seeks to accommodate historic preservation concerns with the needs of Federal undertakings through consultation among the agency official and other parties with an interest in the effects of the undertaking on historic properties, commencing at the early stages of project planning.[3]

Some key words here: "seeks," "accommodate," "consulta-tion," "other parties with an interest," "early stages of project plan-ning." The section 106 process is not about preserving historic properties at all costs; it's about accommodation, compromise, seeking win-win solutions to conflicts between historic preserva-tion and other public interests.

But it only *seeks* such solutions; it does not guarantee they'll be found. It seeks them through *consultation* between the agency and other interested parties, and it has to start *early* if it's going to be ef-fective.

Many, maybe most, of the problems that arise in section 106 re-view result from forgetting one of these elements of the process's purpose. We forget that we're trying to accommodate and just try to win. We consult too narrowly, or not at all. We start too late. And unfortunately, there are aspects to the process, and the way it's usually practiced, that encourage some of these mistakes—particularly the last one.

Consultation

Almost uniquely among federal regulatory processes, the sec-tion 106 process is based on *consultation* among concerned parties. Other review systems—under NEPA, for example—provide for notifying people of what's proposed, getting their views, consider-ing their views, and advising them of decisions, or for consultation with official bodies like local governments or agencies with ex-pertise, but it's rare for a regulation to require consultation with all concerned parties, aimed at reaching binding agreements. This em-phasis on consultation, I think, is the central genius of the section 106 process.

Why Consult?

In the ACHP's introductory section 106 class, we used to use a wonderful John Cleese video called "Decisions, Decisions,"[4] in which one of the protagonist's business colleagues, impersonating Queen Elizabeth I, observes that "consultation is a process factual and a process psychological." She then drops out of character to explain that "there are two dead good reasons to consult with people, baby." The reasons are (1) to get information that might influence your decision, and (2) that when people feel like their concerns have been addressed, they're more likely to accept the decision when it's made.

If everyone attended to Her Majesty's sturdy advice, there'd be fewer silly arguments about who has the "right" to be a consulting party under section 106. But even in these enlightened times, with a zillion self-help and management books around advising folks to talk with one another, there are still people who think they can best advance their interests by not listening to anybody else and by keeping others from knowing what they're up to. Such people—and their lawyers—get terribly exercised about who they have to consult under section 106, what has to be discussed, how long consultation must take, and whether one need only suffer through it or actually do something in response.

Consulting Parties

Although agencies ought to consult broadly under section 106, the regulations give special attention to the state historic preservation officer (SHPO) and the tribal historic preservation officer (THPO).[5] Other consulting parties called out in the regulations are:

- Indian tribes whose lands may be affected by the action (that is, lands within the external boundaries of their reservations);[6]
- Indian tribes and Native Hawaiian organizations who may attach religious and cultural significance to affected properties, regardless of where they occur;[7]
- Local governments with jurisdiction over affected areas;[8]
- Applicants for federal assistance (e.g., state highway departments applying for funds from FHWA, or a low-income housing provider seeking HUD assistance); and
- Applicants for federal permits, licenses, or other approvals (e.g., the applicant for a FERC certificate or a right-of-way from BLM).[9]

Agencies are also supposed to consult with other "individuals and organizations with a demonstrated interest in the undertaking

. . . due to the nature of their legal or economic relation to the undertaking or affected properties, or their concern with the undertaking's effects on historic properties."[10] That embraces pretty much everybody, but the agency can, if it wishes, decline to consult with those not explicitly named as having consulting party rights.[11]

My strong recommendation is consult with everybody; get everybody to the table. It's the best way to get a bulletproof solution. And even if the section 106 regulations don't require you to consult with a particular party, that party may be able to invoke other authorities, such as the Administrative Procedures Act,[12] the Federal Advisory Committees Act,[13] or status as an environmental justice population under Executive Order 12898,[14] to force consultation.

Finally, the agency has to provide for public participation in the process, in a manner appropriate to the project and its effects.[15] It's out of the public that consulting parties bubble up to join the process.

Consultation Methods

The regulations are unspecific about how to consult. This is, I think, as it should be. You consult for as long as it takes, using whatever methods are necessary to address people's concerns.

Don't mix up consultation with notification, holding public hearings, or public relations. Consultation means talking with people, trying to resolve whatever issues need to be resolved, negotiation. Nicholas Dorochoff's *Negotiation Basics for Cultural Resource Managers*[16] provides solid advice about how to do it, as does a host of other books.[17]

A Word About Flexibility

The section 106 regulations—or the core of the regulations, at least—comprise a series of steps (figure 3), and the ACHP often talks about the process as one that proceeds "step by step." This stepwise process is not supposed to be rigid; on the other hand it's not supposed to be spineless. As interpreted by its various participants, however, it can be either—or even both at the same time.

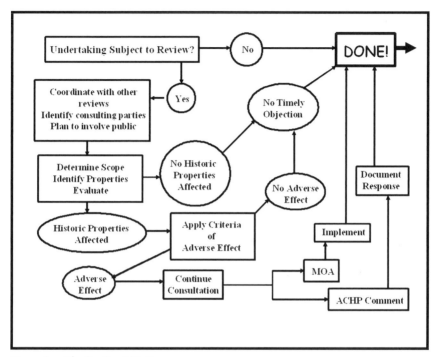

Figure 3.   The Section 106 Process

I think flexibility is vital, as long as it advances, rather than de-feats, the purpose of the process. As we go along, I'll try to point out places where the process can usefully be flexed, but there is logic to a stepwise approach, so we'll use a step-by-step explana-tion to structure this chapter.

Getting Started: Does the Action Require Review?

You'll recall that the NEPA process filters out projects with little po-tential for significant effect by "categorically excluding" them from review. The Section 106 regulations do something similar. They ask first whether the proposed action is an "undertaking" under the law, and second whether it's the kind of undertaking that has the potential to affect historic properties.

First Question: Is It an "Undertaking"?

Section 106 deals with the effects of agency "undertakings." Section 301(7) of NHPA defines an "undertaking" as any:

> project, activity, or program funded in whole or in part under the direct or indirect jurisdiction of a Federal agency, including—
>
> 1. those carried out by or on behalf of the agency;
> 2. those carried out with Federal financial assistance;
> 3. those requiring a Federal permit, license, or approval; and
> 4. those subject to State or local regulations administered pursuant to a delegation or approval by a Federal agency.[18]

In a nutshell, an "undertaking" is anything a federal agency undertakes to do itself, have done for it, assist someone else in doing, permit someone else to do, delegate to a state or local regulatory body, or oversee such a body in doing.[19] So the first question to ask about a proposed action, in terms of the statute, is: "is there some kind of federal involvement in the action?" Or, as it's often put, "is there a federal handle?"

This is a point that people sometimes miss. Section 106 (like NEPA) applies only to actions with federal involvement. If the Mount Vernon Ladies' Association, which owns George Washington's old home, wants to cover its facades with vinyl siding and add a twenty-story tower complete with battlements, it is perfectly free to do so under federal law, provided it doesn't use federal funds or need a federal permit. And no, the fact that Mount Vernon is a real important historic place does not mean that the Ladies' Association needs a permit to muck about with it. Why not? Because Congress hasn't made it so, and one reason they haven't made it so is that there's no evident constitutional basis for doing it.

However, Congress *has* dictated that you need a permit to discharge fill into certain wetlands—section 404 of the Clean Water Act requires that, and it's constitutionally justified under the Commerce Clause.[20] So if the Ladies' Association wanted to bulldoze Mt. Vernon into the Potomac River, they'd need a section 404 permit, and *that* would trigger section 106 review. The statutory definition of "undertaking" embraces actions carried out by, for, with the assistance of, or under the regulatory authority of a federal agency, and the federal arm can be pretty long.

But just as with NEPA, if section 106 review had to be done on every action the federal government is involved in, either the wheels of government would grind mighty slow, or we would have to develop a very attenuated section 106 process. So just as CEQ invented categorical exclusions (CATEX) to avoid reviewing things that couldn't plausibly have significant effects on the environment, in the section 106 regulations the ACHP included a way to filter out actions that don't have the potential for effect. It's important to note, however, that many CATEX actions under NEPA require review under section 106. The opposite is not necessarily true; in some agency NEPA regulations, if an action requires review under section 106 it *can't* be a CATEX.

Second Question: Is It the "Type of Activity That Has the Potential to Cause Effects"?

To avoid applying section 106 to things like the hiring and firing of agency office staff or driving a government-owned car, an undertaking gets reviewed only if it's the "type of activity that has the potential to cause effects on historic properties."[21] So if an agency wants to fire its mail room attendant, that doesn't require section 106 review, nor does the agency's purchase of office supplies. But if the agency wants to build a new mail room, or convert the old one, or build a road to carry the office supplies from one place to another, that *does* have to be reviewed, because it's the type of action that has the potential to change buildings or land, hence affecting any historic properties that may be standing or lying in the vicinity.

Note that you don't need to know that there'll *be* an effect, or that historic properties are lurking in the neighborhood. Knowing that something is the *kind* of action that has the *potential* to affect is different from knowing there's something to be affected. Checking to see if something *is* indeed there and *will* be affected is what you do after, and because you recognize the *potential* for effect.

If I want to pull the pin out of a live grenade and toss it out the window, I know this may injure someone walking by. I don't need to know that somebody's out there to recognize this *potential*. Knowing that the possibility of hurting someone exists—and assuming I don't want to hurt them—I need to take a look before I throw, or I should leave the pin in the grenade. In the same way, I know that knocking down a building, or digging up the ground, or painting a facade, or changing traffic patterns through a neighborhood, may affect historic properties. Recognizing this, I need to find out if anything is out there to be affected, and that's the next step in the section 106 process.

Who Decides?

The regulations leave it up to the responsible federal agency to decide whether an action requires review—that is, to determine whether it's (1) an undertaking and (2) the kind of thing that has the potential for effects. This leaves agencies a lot of discretion, which some agencies abuse—intentionally or otherwise. Most often, I think, the abuses are unintentional; common examples include figuring that an action doesn't require review if it's categorically excluded under NEPA, and assuming that there's no need for review if you don't know of any historic properties in the neighborhood. The only way I know of to deal with these problems is by education inside the agencies and vigilance outside.

The Question of Delegation and Oversight

In 2003 the Court of Appeals for the District of Columbia, in *National Mining Association v. Fowler*,[22] held that section 106 does not apply to state and local permit actions under programs delegated or overseen by federal agencies. The court reasoned that despite the general NHPA definition of the word "undertaking," section 106 by its own language applies only to actions carried out by agencies, with agency assistance, or with a federal agency license. So actions like a state's issuance of coastal zone management permits, state clean water permits, and surface mining permits under authorities delegated by federal agencies are not subject to review under section 106, even though they are clearly defined as "undertakings" by NHPA.

This decision has not had much evident impact, probably for two reasons. First, no state or local agency I know of carried out section 106 review on its permit actions *before* the court decision, so not being required to do it hasn't made much difference. Second, the court allowed, rather in passing, that the decision of an agency to delegate or oversee a permit program might *be* subject to review, and when the ACHP tweaked the regulations in response, it said that such decisions *are* subject to review. So agencies that delegate or oversee ought to be doing section 106 review on each decision to delegate and on the conduct of their oversight.[23] In doing such review, which would have to be done programmatically rather than on a case-specific basis, there might be interesting opportunities to craft creative approaches to project-level impact assessment and resolution. But in the political climate of the last few years, the ACHP hasn't pushed the point.

Was the GO Road Subject to Review?

In the mid-1970s, the Forest Service proposed to construct a logging haul road across the Six Rivers National Forest in northern California, from the town of Gasquet to the town of Orleans (hence, called the G-O or just GO Road). The purpose was to open up virgin timber reserves on the interior, eastern side of the north coast ranges and make them accessible to financially strapped sawmills on the coast. No historic properties were known to exist in the vicinity of the proposed road.

Discussion Question: Was construction of the GO Road an undertaking subject to section 106 review?

Initiating Review

So, suppose we're a federal agency proposing to do something, or assist something, or permit something, and we decide that yes indeed, it does require review under section 106. What then?

One very useful thing the ACHP did in the 2004 regulations—it had been a soft spot in the 1986 regulations—was to detail how to initiate review. Unfortunately, lots of agencies, SHPOs, consultants, and others haven't yet tumbled to the "new" requirements.[24] This is too bad, because some of the most common ways agencies fail to comply with section 106 are by forgetting to start, or putting it off until it's too late, or starting wrong.

The regulations list four things to do in initiating review:

- Coordinate with other reviews—like NEPA (chapter 2) and the other cultural resource laws discussed in chapters 5 through 7;
- Identify which SHPO(s) and/or THPO(s) to consult;
- Plan to involve the public; and
- Identify other consulting parties.

I can't overemphasize how important these are, and how it messes things up when agencies fail to do any one of them. Too often agencies do only the second item in the list—they figure out what SHPO or THPO to consult and send them a letter—often asking just for their comments, or even their "clearance." Or they'll task a cultural resource contractor with doing an archeological survey of the project site and submitting the resulting report to the SHPO/THPO for approval; they think this is what section 106 review is about. Let me be even clearer than the regulations (which are, unusually, pretty clear on this point): *that's not section 106 review.* Even if the SHPO/THPO tells you it is.

Failure to coordinate with other requirements means that things get out of synch—so, for example, the agency is deciding under NEPA that it can issue a FONSI when it hasn't even started section 106 review. Commonly in such a case, the agency shrugs and says, "No problem; we won't have any significant impact on 'cultural resources' [*sic*] because section 106 review will reduce any such impact to insignificance." But even if this were consistent with NEPA (which after all requires *considering* effects, not brushing them under the rug), it wouldn't be reasonable. Section 106 review may or may not render impacts insignificant in NEPA terms; there is absolutely no guarantee. To say nothing of the fact that Section 106 doesn't deal with "cultural resources"; it deals only with historic properties.

Failure to figure out how to involve the public results in a "black box" review carried out only by the agency and SHPO/THPO. Many agencies and many SHPO/THPOs still think this is what they're *supposed* to do. Figure it all out without talking to the people who may be affected. That's not the way the regulations say to do it; the regulations demand transparency. The interested public has to know what's going on and have the opportunity to participate.

And if they really want to participate, they can become "consulting parties"—who, the regulations say, the agency is supposed to try to identify at the outset. Being consulting parties means that they participate in discussions about how to identify properties, consider effects, and resolve effects that are adverse. If people who are concerned enough to be consulting parties aren't identified at the outset, the agency may not know about their concerns until the bulldozers are ready to roll and the agency is served with a subpoena or blasted on the front page of the newspaper.[25]

Identifying Historic Properties

Once initiated, the process moves into the next phase: identification of historic properties. Actually that's a bit simplistic in two ways. First, the transition from initiation to identification is usually a seamless one; getting the process started blends naturally into the beginning of identification—scoping. Second, what identification is about is not simply identifying *historic properties*, though that's the way the regulations present it. You're really trying to determine effects; identification of properties is just one step toward doing so.

Unfortunately (I find myself using that word a lot), we often act like identification stands on its own, is done for its own sake, and must be completed in accordance with specific standards (usually established by the SHPO/THPO) before anybody even thinks about effects. Lots of time and trouble and angst are generated by identification work that doesn't bear any relationship to the likely effects of the project.

Identification needs to be done *only to the extent necessary to address effects*; addressing effects is what section 106 is all about.

Scoping

The 2004 regulations introduced section 106 practitioners to the useful NEPA notion of "scoping"[26]—that is, in this case, figuring out the scope of one's identification effort. Unfortunately (there's that word again), not everyone has welcomed the introduction.

Scoping doesn't seem necessary if one employs a one-size-fits-all approach to identification. If you think you always must do a Class IB5 survey according to the SHPO's standards, what's the point in thinking further about the scope of your efforts? Unfortunately(!), lots of 106 practitioners and SHPOs prefer simple, universally applicable standards. It's understandable; they're overworked, they don't have much time to think, and universal standards make life predictable. But just doing a standard thing leads to work that's not necessary to address a project's impacts and to failing to do what *is* necessary.

Scoping involves looking at the likely effects of your project and thinking about what you need to do to identify historic properties that may be subject to such effects. Thinking about it and *talking* about it with concerned parties—those "consulting parties" you've identified. Why talk? Because those parties may have important ideas about how best to do identification; they may know something about the area, and in any event, it's wiser to involve them than to leave them carping on the sidelines.

The regulations call for doing three things as parts of scoping: establish the area of potential effects, review existing information on that area, and seek information from others, paying particular attention to Indian tribes and Native Hawaiian groups (in Hawaii) who may have concerns about places of cultural importance to them.[27] That first requirement is often messed up.

The Hairy APE

If I'm going to identify historic properties (or anything else), I need to decide where I'm going to look. This is called defining the "area of potential effects," or APE.

Going back to our grenade analogy, in order to be sure I won't blow anyone up, one thing I need to know is the grenade's blast radius. It's within that radius that I want to be sure no one's strolling around. To determine the radius, I'll have to consider several variables. How powerful is the grenade? Will the wall through whose window I'll toss it deflect the blast away from itself? Are there other walls, rocks, cliffs, groves of trees that will shape the blast's effects? Are there secondary sources of explosive power—cars with gas in their tanks, an ammunition dump, a fireworks stand? What kind of grenade is it? Will it spew shrapnel? Is it incendiary? Will it discharge tear gas or mustard gas or botulism? Will it blind people?

In the same way, I need to figure out the size and shape of the area within which my proposed undertaking may affect historic properties. This is the APE, which the regulations define as:

> The geographic area or areas within which an undertaking may directly or indirectly cause alterations in the character or use of historic properties, if any such properties exist.[28]

One common mistake agencies make is to equate the APE with the undertaking's "footprint"—for example, the construction site. This is like considering the APE of a grenade to be only where it may bonk somebody on the head.

As with my grenade's blast radius, a lot of things can affect the size and shape of the APE. Obviously the place where the undertaking will have direct physical effects (if there is such a place) is part of the APE, but it's only part—analogous to the precise location where the grenade lands. Just as the grenade's effects may be felt in different locations and different ways depending on the character of the area, the grenade itself, the wind direction, atmospheric conditions, and so forth, so the effects of an undertaking are shaped by the character of the undertaking, the local environment, and other factors. Typically, in defining the APE you'll need to consider not only direct physical effects but at least the potential for:

- Secondary physical effects (things like erosion downstream from a dam or commercial development around an improved highway interchange);
- Visual effects (the areas within which the undertaking's effects will be visible);
- Auditory effects (the areas within which the undertaking's noise, if any, will be audible);
- Sociocultural effects (the areas within which the undertaking may cause changes in economic activity, land use, tax rates, traffic, quality of life); and
- Effects on culturally significant natural resources such as plants or animals used in subsistence or for religious purposes.[29]

All these kinds of effects need to be considered regardless of whether they're the direct, obvious outcomes of the action or less direct—foreseeable but likely to happen later than the action itself, or at a greater distance.

Cumulative effects also have to be considered—that is, the effects of the action under review added to the effects of everything else that may be messing up historic properties in the area, including things that have messed them up in the past, or are likely to do so in the future, regardless of who's responsible for the messing.[30] Section 106 practitioners often have even more trouble understanding cumulative effects than NEPA analysts do, but these effects are just as important with respect to historic properties as they are in a general environmental context.

I hear the question: "How do I figure all this out?" As usual, talk to people, but in this case not only people concerned about the project and its effects, but also people involved in other parts of the agency's overall impact analysis. Very likely, as part of the NEPA impact analysis, somebody is working on visual effects, auditory effects, and so on. They may be able to tell you where such effects are anticipated. Remember that under NEPA you're supposed to be working as an interdisciplinary team. *Use* the expertise of those other disciplines. And, of course, use your own brains, too, both to translate what others tell you into terms that are meaningful for cultural resources and to make your own projections. Your hypotheses about what kinds of effects may occur, and where, are just as good as anyone else's.

Defining the APE based on multiple variables often results in several differently bounded areas—an APE for physical effects, an APE for visual effects, and so on. This is all right. In fact, a troop of APEs is perfectly expectable. The cumulative effects APE is likely to be a big one, with soft, fuzzy edges, and that's OK too; it's the nature of the beast.

It may not be possible even to define APE boundaries. This is all right, too, as long as you're honest about it. In the case of Crandon Mine, a copper-zinc mine in Wisconsin urgently opposed by the Mole Lake Band of Great Lakes Ojibwa on cultural grounds (among others), the Corps of Engineers (which had section 106 responsibilities because it has regulatory authority under section 404 of the Clean Water Act) decided that the APE for archeology was the mine site and its access roads, power lines, and the like, but the APE for "traditional cultural properties"— in this case, places of cultural importance to the Ojibwa—had no boundaries at all. As a Corps representative quipped, if someone wanted to complain about impacts on a traditional cultural property in Los Angeles, this would be perfectly OK, because the Corps wouldn't have to waste much time on considering such an implausible impact.

The Bureau of Indian Affairs (BIA) and Rural Electrification Administration (REA)[31] got themselves in trouble in New Mexico by defining the footprint of a proposed power substation as its APE. The substation, designed to supply power to San Ildefonso Pueblo, was adjacent to a graded parking lot used by the Hispanic community of El Rancho. BIA and REA had the project site surveyed for archeological sites (without talking with the El Ranchitos) and, having found nothing, proceeded with construction. The El Ranchitos took BIA and REA to court for violating section 106. The parking lot, it developed, was where the community carried out its Matachines Dance, a culturally important tradition that made the place eligible for the National Register of Historic Places. The power station, the El Rancho people argued, would intrude on their performance of the dance, adversely affecting the integrity of the site. The project was halted for close to a decade because of the agencies' failure to comply properly with section 106.[32] Had BIA and REA considered visual and auditory impacts in defining the project's APE and talked to the community about such effects, they probably would have sited the station elsewhere and avoided the whole problem.

Some agencies try to limit the APEs of their projects to the areas over which they have jurisdiction—the land they control or, in the case of the Corps of Engineers, which frequently tries this ploy, the land or water over which it has regulatory authority. The area of jurisdiction is an apple to the APE's orange; it's like saying that I don't need to consider who'll get blown up by my grenade unless I own the street into which I'm tossing it. The law requires agencies to consider effects, not just effects on stuff that's under their jurisdiction. The APE is the area (or areas) where effects will occur, regardless of who may control the land.

The GO Road's APE

The Forest Service recognized that the GO Road was an undertaking, since it was under the jurisdiction of a federal agency. It recognized that it represented a kind of action with the potential to affect historic properties. So the Forest Service initiated section 106 review and needed to define the APE.

Discussion Question: What factors should the Forest Service have considered in establishing the GO Road's APE?

The Rest of Scoping

The remainder of scoping involves doing background research and consulting with people. Of course, you should consult about establishing the APE, too; consultation is the main thing to do throughout the 106 process. Exactly what kind of consultation, and what kind of background research, you need to do depends on the circumstances—the nature of the project, the area, and so on.

You need to find out what's already known about the APE. What studies have been done, what historic properties have been identified? What areas have been studied and found not to contain anything, or not to contain particular kinds of historic property?

At a higher level of abstraction, what can we find out that may *suggest* what kinds of historic properties are there, or where they might be? What do the area's history, traditions, sociology, geography, geomorphology tell us about what people in the past may have been left there? Or about what people do there now, or think is important about the area?

And what do people think might be there, and why? What can be said by extrapolation from other areas, or based on sociological, anthropological, or other theory?

I know, this is beginning to look like a lot of research, but as usual, it depends. For a small area, where it's relatively easy to see what's standing or lying around on the ground, you're probably not going to have to do as much research as you are for a bigger, more complex area, or for a project with extensive, complicated effects.

One caution about background research: don't reduce it to a records check. This happens a lot—California is a particularly bad example, where people seem to think that if they've just gone to the local records center and checked previous archeological surveys, they've done their job. Records checks will tell you, not surprisingly, what's already been recorded, but they won't give you a basis for imagining what's *not* been recorded, and that's what you need to do. Imagine—based on the geography and environment of the area, its history, its ethnography, its prehistory—what kinds of historic properties might be out there in the APE, what they might look like, and what you may have to do to find them. Generate predictions, think about how to test them. Then design the actual scope of work to test the predictions.

Finding Historic Places: Some Myths

Before we move on to actually finding historic places, let's dispense with some widely held but erroneous beliefs about the identification process.

There's a widespread belief that section 106, or the regulations, require agencies to do a *survey*. They don't.

A related myth is that agencies have to identify *all* historic properties in the APE, usually by doing some kind of "complete" survey. This too is myth, all myth.

The regulations don't require any particular kind of identification. They require a "reasonable and good faith effort" to "identify historic properties."[33] And that's "historic properties," not "*all* historic properties." The regulations don't require identification of everything for two reasons. First, it's impossible; you can't know what you haven't found. Second, it's unnecessary. The rule of thumb is that you should do enough to understand what effects are likely and what can be done about them.[34] How much and what kind of identification that means depends on the nature of the likely effects, the nature of the area, and the nature of the likely historic properties, among other things.

Then there's the myth that you have to do some standard kind of survey, perhaps called a "Class One" or "Phase One." This isn't true either, and it's a terrible idea because it encourages rote thinking. Standards for Class One surveys—and Phase Two, Type IIB, and so on—are variously set forth in state, regional, and agency guidelines. They vary from place to place, but one thing is pretty universal: they emphasize archeological field survey. They go into loving detail about how closely spaced [*sic*] archeologists should be over the landscape, and at what intervals they should dig holes, in order to find "all the sites." But some historic properties aren't "sites," and some aren't best found or evaluated by looking at or digging in the ground. Historic buildings, districts, landscapes, and traditional cultural properties require different strategies, ranging from aerial remote sensing to talking with local residents to background historical research to geomorphology. Whenever we assume that a particular "class" of survey will automatically be sufficient—and that it is automatically required—we fail to think through what kinds of study are really needed. This can lead us to miss important stuff, however closely we pack our archeologists and space our holes.

Bottom line: There's no specific kind of survey you've got to do to satisfy section 106; what you have to do depends on the character of the project and its likely effects, and on the character of the properties likely to be present—which can only be determined through background research and consultation. You don't necessarily have to identify every historic property subject to effect, but you do need to consider all kinds of historic properties, not just those you happen to be trained to identify and appreciate. The basic rule is make a reasonable and good faith effort.

In almost no case, though, is it enough just to send an archeologist (or anybody else) out to look around, whether they're just looking aimlessly or looking in a highly organized manner on five-meter transects digging holes every four meters. There was a case in Indiana in which the archeologists surveying a highway borrow source missed the big Hopewell mound into which it would be dug, because it was so big it dwarfed the survey area. That's a pretty unusual situation in archeology, but it's easy to have a historic landscape or an urban historic district that stretches far, far beyond the project site, or even beyond the boundaries of the APE. You've got to back up and look at the big picture in order to see it. Some kinds of properties don't look like anything at all—or rather, they just look like hills or streams or rock outcrops or groves of trees or meadows or commercial streets. To understand their importance you've got to talk to the people who value them, find out what they think is important. To figure out who to talk with, you need to think about and read about and talk with people about what's known and believed about the area. That's what background research is all about. Incidentally, this sort of background assessment—or overview, as it's sometimes called—is another piece of work that's sometimes referred to as a Class One or Phase One survey, to the endless confusion of those who use the same term to mean a basic field inspection.

The "Reasonable and Good Faith Effort" Standard

So, you've scoped your identification effort and discovered, let's say, that:

- The APE includes the Hoitytoit Historic District, made up of mansions along Hoitytoit Road, a locally designated historic district that's included in the National Register.
- The Motomak Indian Tribe, now resident on a reservation fifty miles away, used to occupy the area.
- Part of the APE is a floodplain covered with sediments deposited in the last five thousand years.
- Much of the floodplain is farmed by Amish families.
- The Town of Crossroads, near the east end of the APE, has been occupied by African American families since the end of the Civil War.
- The Crooked Bend Unpleasantness, in which local militiamen massacred fleeing Motomaks, occurred somewhere along a bend in Messy Creek, which flows through the APE.
- The overworked, understaffed SHPO's office has given you a form letter recommending a "Class II.A cultural resource survey."
- Professor R. T. Toulle of Giant State University's Geographic Research Center advises that the area may produce information important in the study of climatic change over the last ten thousand years; this information may be present both in archeological sites and in natural floodplain deposits.

The regulations require that—based on your scoping—you make a "reasonable and good faith effort" to identify historic properties. In this case, given the above data, what does this mean?

One of the commonest and least useful responses is to do what the SHPO tells you to do. This is not meant to insult SHPOs; it's just that in this case, as often happens, the SHPO's staff person has been busy with other things and has given you an off-the-cuff recommendation that isn't useful.

What does the SHPO mean by a "Class II.A cultural resource survey?" Like a Class One or Phase One survey (which naturally leads to a Class Two or Phase Two), it's probably a standard kind of fieldwork promoted up by the state's archeological community. It probably means particular personnel qualifications, spacing of archeologists on the ground, and test pit intervals. Or it may be product-oriented: "a sufficiently detailed study to permit determining eligibility for the National Register." When you ask what this means, you're usually told something about test excavations.

The problem, of course, is that a survey that assumes the need for test excavations to determine eligibility may not identify anything but archeological sites. And a standard-form archeological survey that doesn't consider local conditions may not even identify archeological sites if they're deeply buried in those floodplain sediments. You may spend a lot of time and money traipsing archeologists over the floodplain, digging holes every few meters, and never getting down to the level where there are actually archeological sites. And, of course, while you're spending your time and money on all this, you're probably not identifying any of the non-archeological historic properties that *are* there.

So what should you do? Use your background data and your head.

- The Hoitytoit Historic District is already listed in the Register, but don't trust the Register data to be comprehensive. It may be that Hortense Hoitytoit nominated the district back in 1972 based on a very narrow range of significance criteria. Perhaps she considered only the district's association with Harry Hoitytoit, her grandfather, who brought the railroad to the area. So the documentation doesn't tell you that the district's elegant homes look eastward over the adjacent valley and are subject to visual impacts by, say, a highway passing up the valley as much as five miles away. It may not tell you about the mature oak trees in the district that are subject to damage by air pollution. Hortense may have drawn the boundaries of the district more or less arbitrarily and left properties out that are significant in their own right. There may be buildings outside the district that are identical with those inside, or maybe a little bit younger or less high-style but still significant. There may be a group of commercial buildings a block away, important in the history of the community's economic development. Hortense probably ignored the two-thousand-year-old archeological site that lies under 725 Hoitytoit Road. None of this indicates that Hortense was ill intentioned or stupid; she just nominated what was important to her, and the Register accepted it. The point is, the fact that something is included in the Register doesn't mean it's the only eligible thing around or that its eligibility has been comprehensively considered. You need to take another look at the District with specific reference to the potential impacts of your project, and you're going to need to reconsider its boundaries and character, too. All this is probably a job for a historian and/or an architectural historian. In addition, you're going to need to look for other kinds of historic properties.

- The fact that the Motomak Tribe occupied the area tips you off that it may contain places that are culturally important to the tribe. These may be archeological sites, and/or traditional cultural properties,[35] which may comprise whole landscapes. To find them, you may need to do some kind of archeological survey, which may or may not fall into the Class II.A category. But most important, you need to get out and talk with the Motomak. This may be a job for someone who knows the Motomak well—perhaps for a member of the tribe—and for an agency line officer if the Motomak are federally recognized.

- Speaking of archeological sites, the fact that the APE includes a floodplain covered with five-thousand-year-old sediments suggests a couple of things. First, there may be buried archeological sites in those sediments that could be quite old and, perhaps quite significant for research and public interpretation. Second, as mentioned, surveying the surface of the floodplain may be a pretty fruitless endeavor—though this, of course, depends on how fast the floodplain has built up and how young the sediments are on the surface.

- With deeply buried archeological sites, you also need to think about whether your project can actually affect them. If the project will disturb only the top meter of the floodplain, and the sites are likely to be twelve meters down, there's probably not much point in disturbing the sediments to find them; you may do more damage than construction will.

- Since the floodplain is farmed by Amish families, you need to consider whether as a working landscape it's got historical value for its association with the Amish and their traditional lifeways. And you'll need to talk with the Amish, too—again, work for a knowledgeable person who appreciates Amish ways.

- Similarly, you need to talk with the people of Crossroads and look into the community's history, to see whether it constitutes a historically or culturally significant resource or whether there are places that its residents value—the pool in the creek where baptisms are carried out, perhaps, or the fishing bridge. More work for the specialist in living cultures.

- Archival research into the Crooked Bend Unpleasantness, perhaps coupled with aerial photography or other forms of remote sensing, may help you identify the massacre site, which may be eligible for the National Register. Interviewing willing Motomaks is likely to be important, too; there may be traditions about the place and the event that can help pinpoint its location and elucidate its significance.

- Finally, in considering the possible significance of archeological sites in the floodplain, you'll need to respect Professor Toulle's concerns about climatic change. These research interests aren't the only basis for regarding archeological sites (or other sites) as eligible for the National Register, but they certainly are *one* basis, and an important one.

So, it looks like you need to deploy an army of historians, architectural historians, archeologists, landscape historians, and cultural anthropologists to figure out what's in your project's APE. In some cases this is true, particularly if your project is a big one with lots of far-reaching, complex, potential effects. But in most cases it doesn't have to be true; you need to look at what kinds of impacts your project is actually likely to have, and adjust your identification accordingly. If you're planning a 500 kV power line on giant towers marching through the countryside, you're going to have to worry a lot about visual effects on things like historic buildings, districts, and landscapes, and a lot less about impacts on archeological sites. If you're planning a fiber-optic cable in the ground through the same landscape, archeology's going to be a problem but visual effects probably won't. The nature of the likely effect determines the kinds of properties likely to be affected, and how they're likely to be affected, and hence the kind of work you need to do to identify them and the kinds of specialists you need to do the identifying.

In some cases—particularly where the project is a relatively small one, with a limited range of probable impacts—all the requisite expertise may reside in a single head. Because they've mostly been the ones who've wound up running "section 106 shops" in the agencies, SHPO/THPO offices, and consulting firms, there are quite a few archeologists who have become more or less able to identify and evaluate things other than archeological sites—buildings, structures, landscapes, traditional cultural places. Some historians, too, have become jacks and jills of all historic preservation trades, and sometimes you'll find an architectural historian who's developed multidisciplinary, multiresource expertise. People who've come through "historic preservation" or "cultural resource management" (CRM) graduate programs or graduate certificate programs may have developed this kind of expertise, too, but don't count on it; lots of "historic preservation" programs basically train people in applied architectural history and historical architecture, while many CRM programs teach little more than applied archeology.

Hint for students: If you want to be really employable in CRM, get training in more than one preservation-related discipline. It will make you a hot commodity.

One last point. It's during identification—notably during the first step, assessing information needs—that you can most effectively identify not only historic properties but also people who may be concerned about the project's effects. The regulations encourage consulting people who may have knowledge of or concerns about historic properties in the area.[36] Treat this as an opportunity, not an onerous requirement. Better to identify concerned people, ascertain their concerns, and consult them at this early stage than to have them pop up in court when you're ready to go into construction.

The Las Huertas Canyon Standard

We have guidance from one court of law about what constitutes a "reasonable and good faith" identification effort under section 106. In 1995 the Tenth Circuit Court of Appeals ruled in *Pueblo of Sandia v. United States*,[37] a case involving a proposed management plan for Las Huertas Canyon on the Cibola National Forest, near Albuquerque, New Mexico.

The Forest Service's preferred alternative involved changes to the road up the canyon and to visitor-use facilities. During review under NEPA and section 106, the Forest Service determined that there were no traditional cultural properties (TCPs)[38] in the canyon and that the undertaking would have no effect on historic properties. The SHPO concurred.

The tribal government of Sandia Pueblo filed suit charging violation of section 106, alleging that there were important spiritual sites in the canyon and, in effect, that the canyon as a whole was a TCP. The District Court granted summary judgment for the Forest Service, largely on the basis of the SHPO's concurrence. The Pueblo appealed.

Meanwhile the SHPO received information from the Pueblo backing up its contention about the canyon's cultural importance: an affidavit by the Pueblo's own cultural anthropologist and a resolution by the Pueblo's council. It turned out that the Forest Service had this information at the time it made its no TCPs determination and had withheld it from the SHPO. The SHPO withdrew his concurrence.

The Court of Appeals reversed the District Court's decision and remanded the case for further proceedings. The ruling largely speaks for itself: "The Forest Service mailed letters to local Indian tribes. . . . The letters requested detailed information."

Rather astonishingly, the Forest Service wrote tribes in the area and asked them for written descriptions of any TCPs in the canyon, together with a description of their significance and a 7.5 minute U.S. Geological Survey quadrangle showing the sites and their boundaries. "None of the tribes or individuals provided . . . the type of information requested."

Hardly a surprise. The Forest Service was asking the tribes to do its work for it and to reveal sensitive cultural information.

> We conclude, however, that the information the tribes did communicate to the agency was sufficient to require the Forest Service to engage in further investigations, especially in light of regulations warning that tribes might be hesitant to divulge the type of information sought.

By "regulations" the Court seems actually to mean National Register Bulletin 38.[39] The Court cited Bulletin 38 repeatedly as a methodological guide and as an explanation as to why the tribes might not have been willing to provide the requested details:

> National Register Bulletin 38 warns that knowledge of traditional cultural values may not be shared readily with outsiders, "as such information is regarded as powerful, even dangerous, in some societies."

The Court said that the Forest Service had the obligation to make its own reasoned decision about what kind of identification effort was needed; it could not do nothing just because the tribes hadn't provided precisely the kind of information it requested.

Going on to discuss what the Forest Service should have done to make a "reasonable" effort to identify TCPs, the Court said:

> Determining what constitutes a reasonable effort . . . "depends in part on the likelihood that such properties may be present," National Register Bulletin 38. . . . The information communicated

to the Forest Service as well as the reasons articulated for the lack of more specific information clearly suggest that there is a sufficient likelihood that the canyon contains traditional cultural *properties to warrant further investigation.*

So the Forest Service should have used the data from the tribes—together with other information as available, one might add—to determine what kinds of identification were needed. The tribe's statement that there were important cultural qualities to the canyon should have been enough to tip off the Forest Service to the need for detailed study.

Turning to what constitutes a good-faith effort, the Court focused on the Forest Service's misleading interaction with the SHPO:

Affording the SHPO an opportunity to offer input on potential historic properties would be meaningless unless the SHPO has access to available, relevant information. Thus, consultation with the SHPO mandates an informed consultation.

By withholding relevant information from the SHPO during the consultation process . . . the Forest Service further undermined any argument that it had engaged in a good faith effort.

I think we can extrapolate from *Pueblo of Sandia* to establish some standards for what constitutes a "reasonable and good faith effort" to identify not only TCPs but historic properties of all kinds:

- Writing letters is all right as part of background research, but it's not enough. The agency has to analyze all its relevant information and reach a defensible decision about what kind of identification to do.
- Factors that may affect someone's willingness to communicate about historic properties have to be thoughtfully considered.
- National Register bulletins provide guidance on identification that should be thoughtfully considered; and
- Consultation must be *informed* consultation; an agency isn't acting in good faith if it withholds important data.

Identification on the GO Road

The Forest Service never explicitly defined an APE for the GO Road, but implicitly, it acted as though the construction corridor—the right-of-way itself and a rather ambiguously defined buffer on each side of it—was the APE.

Discussion Question: Having defined the APE, what should the Forest Service have done to identify historic properties?

Evaluation

OK, suppose you've done identification—whatever this may have entailed—and you've found something that *might* be eligible for the National Register, but you don't know whether it *is*. How do you decide?

First let's think about the phrase, "something that might be eligible for the National Register." In deciding that this thing might be eligible, and this other thing surely is not, we're making value judgments that we ought to be careful about. It's generally good practice to assume something might be eligible unless it clearly, demonstrably isn't. Why? Maybe because you really, really don't want to mess up something important. If you're not that altruistic, there's this: finding that something you thought was insignificant really *is* significant, late in the game, can be embarrassing and costly. Suddenly your agency's or client's project is stopped, the bulldozers are idling and eating up money, the contractor is charging quintuple fees for sitting around twiddling his thumbs, your boss or your sponsor or your congressperson is screaming about obstructionists, and the local citizenry, or the archeological community, the Indian tribe, the SHPO, or somebody is screaming about violating the nation's cultural patrimony.

But, of course, there has to be a rule of reason. The scatter of beer cans along the roadside is not something that qualifies as a "might be eligible." Unless, of course, the road is pretty old, and the people who drank out of the cans were pretty important, and—

Well, where do you draw the line?

As usual, it depends. Age is part of the answer. Last night's beer cans don't plausibly make up a site that might be eligible for the Register, but a scatter of cans from seventy-five years ago just might. Association is another factor. Your cans or mine don't make an eligible site, but cans left by the first Vulcan expedition to Earth would be another matter. But how do you know whether the cans—or the old foundation or the nondescript building—are associated with someone or something important?

You don't. You have to guess. When push comes right to shove, we have to exercise more or less unsubstantiated judgment, or we'd never get anything done. We look at the scatter of cans, or the corrugated tin garage, or the fence line with adjacent cow trail, or the concrete foundation slab, or the local gas station, and say, "No, it's not worth even thinking about." And having made that statement, feeling comfortable that nobody will argue with us about it, we then ignore the place and don't think about it any more.

Of course, an educated guess is a lot better than an uneducated one. This is one reason local expertise and background research are important. Knowing the area and its history because I've studied it, I know that this isolated concrete slab may be all that remains of the abortive real estate development that serendipitously led to the discovery of gold in the area, so I know we'd better pay some attention to it. You haven't studied the area, so you don't know that the old slab may be important, and this may get you or your client in trouble.

In an attempt to level the playing field and objectify the threshold of "might be significant," people sometimes establish more or less arbitrary criteria for historic property-ness. Archeologists are prone to this—if there are fifteen flakes of chert per square meter, it may be a significant site; if there are only fourteen, it's not. Applying such measures is fraught with problems, of course—variation among observers, with season, with vegetation cover, with the number of cows that have walked over the site, and so on, and the uncertain relationship between what's on the surface and what's present at depth—to say nothing of the fact that it is, at base, an arbitrary measure whose relationship to the actual significance of a place is tenuous at best.

I belabor all this because some people get preoccupied with it, and it can be a source of great, and sometimes expensive, frustration. One SHPO of my acquaintance used to be terribly worried about making people spend money on insignificant archeological sites. To avoid this odious result, he insisted that the significance of any site be proved through intensive subsurface testing. Testing, of course, costs money and takes time, so project proponents sometimes found themselves spending far more of both than they probably would have if they'd just accepted sites as significant and gotten on with managing them.

And you have to remember that a place can be significant for multiple reasons. The site may actually contain only those 5.3 flakes you see on the surface, but be the place where, in the eyes of the Motomac Tribe, the ancestor Universe Maker fought the star monster. To the Motomac it may not matter whether there are any flakes there. In fact, the only flakes the Motomac may notice are the archeologists asking dumb questions.

Bottom line: there aren't any simple answers. We make judgment calls about what might and what might not be significant, and sometimes we're wrong—just as we're sometimes wrong about the decisions we make about marriage, child rearing, and which way to turn on an unfamiliar road. That's life.

So we come out of an effort to identify historic properties with a list of places that we think might be eligible for the National Register. How do we decide whether something *is* eligible?

Naturally, we apply the "Criteria of Eligibility," 36 CFR 60.4, discussed in chapter 3. The agency—usually meaning the agency's or regulated project proponent's consultants, overseen by the agency—applies the criteria in consultation with the SHPO and other consulting parties and tries to decide whether the property under consideration meets the criteria and hence is eligible, whether it falls under one of the "Criteria Considerations" and therefore is *not* eligible, and whether it falls under a criteria consideration but also meets one of the exceptions, in which case it's eligible after all. Got that?

Evaluation is often the most time-consuming part of the section 106 process and one of the most contentious. Specialists can get into incredibly tedious arguments about whether a given criterion, criteria consideration, or exception is met and about whether a given place has sufficient integrity to even be considered for eligibility. We'll return to this issue later.

Significance, Eligibility, and What You Want to Do With the Place

Remember that when you're evaluating a property to determine its historical significance, that's *all* you're doing. You're not determining what will be or should be done with the property. To put it another way, you're not letting management affect your evaluation. Evaluation is supposed to be done solely on the basis of historical, cultural, and other aspects of significance. You're not supposed to consider what you, or your client, or anybody else wants to do with or to the place. You may be working for somebody who really wants to knock the old building down, and you may entirely support this intent—maybe it's a matter of national defense or maybe the building is full of toxic wastes that are poisoning the community—but that's no reason to say the building isn't historically or architecturally significant if it really is. It's perfectly all right to say, "It's historically significant and we want to knock it down"; what's *not* all right to say is, "We want to knock it down, and therefore it's not historically significant."

By way of analogy, imagine that you're examining a wetland. You're up to your knees in muck, alligators nibbling at your tush. Your client wants to fill the wetland to build a hospital for abandoned urchins. You don't say that the wetland is dry just because you want to see the project go forward, or even because you're tired of the 'gators. You acknowledge that it's a wetland and go on to ask the Corps of Engineers for a permit to fill it. It's the same thing with a historic property. It may well be that nobody wants to preserve the thing—that doesn't matter. If it's historically significant, you determine it to be, and *then* think about whether to preserve it and, if not, what else you can do with it—for example, document it and let it go.

This is a big difference between federal law and the historic preservation ordinances of most local governments. When something is declared a local historical landmark, that usually means it's going to be preserved, period—so there are lots of practical reasons for people to argue about whether its significant enough to be designated. Under section 106, recognizing the significance of a place doesn't mean it's got to be protected—it merely means it has to be considered in planning.

That's an important but poorly understood distinction, with important ramifications. If you believe that everything that's historically significant must be preserved, then you're either going to make it impossible to meet the changing needs of society, or you're going to have to be very selective (as local governments tend to be) about what you call historic. The latter course of action is the only reasonable one, of course, but if it's adopted, what happens to all the historically significant places that can't practically be preserved if we're going to get on with life? The world is full of stuff that's got historic value but can't realistically be physically preserved—maybe shouldn't be preserved even in the most perfect of worlds—but should be documented before it's destroyed, or commemorated in some way, or compensated for. If you let physical preservation and significance get equated, you're inevitably going to wind up recognizing only a very narrow range of properties as significant.

As an example, consider a steel launch tower at Vandenberg Air Force Base in California, used during the Cold War to launch intercontinental ballistic missiles on test firings into the Pacific. Steel, rusting on an active military base, no potential for public interpretation. Should we invest scarce tax money in preserving such a tower? Probably not. Should we document it before we demolish it? Probably so. But if we say that historical significance means a place must be preserved, we cannot recognize the historical significance of the launch tower without committing ourselves to preserving it. Frugal responsibility for the taxpayer's dollar will accordingly drive us to consider the tower to be nonhistoric and therefore not even record it.

The bottom line is that you don't consider management factors when evaluating whether a place meets the Register criteria. That's not to say that you don't consider such factors when you decide how much analysis you need to do to determine eligibility or how far you have to go to "prove it." Agencies regularly agree that something's eligible and get on with figuring out how to manage it, rather than going through the trouble of exhaustively analyzing its significance. On the other hand, project sponsors who feel they're being pressured to preserve submarginal properties may want to invest the time and treasure needed to nail down or disprove eligibility. Yep; it depends.

"Potential Eligibility" and Still Another Definition of "Cultural Resource"

So, let's say you've found something you think might be eligible, and it hasn't been formally evaluated. Perhaps you're a consultant, and you've applied the National Register Criteria and decided the thing is eligible, but the sponsor agency and SHPO/THPO haven't done so officially. Or perhaps even *you* haven't applied the criteria yet; maybe you don't think you have enough data. What do you call this thing?

Sometimes people call such places "potentially eligible." This seems sensible enough on the surface, but it's a mistake. Remember that section 106 requires agencies to consider impacts on places that are *included in or eligible for* the National Register, not *potentially* eligible. In theory—and, in fact, this has happened in practice, particularly in the regulatory program of the Corps of Engineers—an agency can say "well, we need to consider properties that have been *determined* eligible, but we don't have to consider properties that are only *potentially* eligible until somebody—other than us—determines them eligible." This effectively puts us right back where we were before Executive Order 11593, when section 106 applied only to properties *included* in the Register. The agency can ignore its impacts on a property until the SHPO/THPO or the keeper or maybe God determines it eligible.[40]

The eligibility determination process and the notion of agency responsibility for formally unevaluated properties turn on the notion of "inherent eligibility." Under this doctrine, a property either inherently does or inherently doesn't meet the Register criteria. A property that nobody's ever even seen can be lying out there in the woods, throbbing with eligibility, while another is weeping softly for its failure to possess this happy quality.

Of course, this notion is epistemologically absurd. Eligibility is a human mental construct, not a fundamental characteristic of a place like "yellowness," or "acidity," or "Pony Trussness," or "Dogtrotness." And what's not eligible today may be eligible tomorrow, or vice versa. But if you carry this thinking very far, the whole National Register concept becomes pretty silly. A point worth considering,[41] but for the moment let's just note that unless we assume that eligibility is inherent, we have no logical basis for saying that agencies have the responsibility to concern themselves with—and hence even *identify*—places that may be eligible; they are responsible only for those that are *known* to be eligible.

Going back to our wetland analogy: when we go out to see if there's a wetland on a development site, and we sink into the muck up to our knees, we don't say, "This is a potential wetland." We say, "This looks and feels and smells a helluva lot like a wetland; let's check it against the definition in the Corps of Engineers' section 404 regulations." Wetness is an inherent quality of the property; our task is to recognize it and hold it up against established criteria to see if it's wet enough to merit attention in the regulatory process. Just so with historic properties.

But if we don't call our unevaluated place "potentially eligible," what do we call it?

Some people, unfortunately, call it a "cultural resource." There's some logic in this; since "cultural resource" embraces a wider range of phenomena than "historic property," it's reasonable to say that something is a cultural resource but may or may not be a historic property. However, this doesn't really solve the problem of ensuring agency responsibility for considering the place—or at best, it complicates it. You're really saying that the agency has to consider the place as a cultural resource under NEPA and other authorities, but it has responsibilities under section 106 only once somebody determines it to be eligible for the National Register by applying the Register criteria. Worse, it leads to the impression that "cultural resource" means "ineligible property" or "property whose eligibility is undetermined," as opposed to all the other, broader things that the term logically embraces.

So, what to call a place until its eligibility has been determined, either formally by the keeper or informally by agency-SHPO/THPO consensus? I'd call it a "property that may be eligible," or a "property whose eligibility has to be determined," or "property that appears to be eligible" (or ineligible)—or something like that. Something that makes your uncertainty clear without implying that the place falls into some category other than eligible or ineligible. This may seem like a pretty inelegant way to express uncertainty, and hardly preferable to some simpler term like "potentially eligible," but you've got to remember that your reports may wind up being interpreted in a court of law, by people who don't know what you're talking about, and who may have reasons to give your words their own particular twists. You need to be careful not to give the court a basis for concluding that a property is not eligible (by virtue of being only "potentially" so) until somebody officially pronounces on its status.

Determining Eligibility

All right, then. You've found something that may be eligible, but you don't know whether it is eligible. What now?

Section 106 regulations are flexible about this. The SHPO/ THPO and responsible agency can agree to "regard" a property as eligible for the Register. When they do, they treat the property as eligible for purposes of section 106.[42] Technically, this is not a formal "determination" of eligibility; only the keeper makes formal determinations. But it's often referred to as a "consensus determination of eligibility."

The regulations don't spell out documentation requirements for a consensus determination; it can be based on whatever the agency and SHPO/THPO agree on. The National Register wants everyone to use National Register forms, and pushes SHPO/ THPOs to do the same. SHPO/THPOs often accept this or demand that their own forms or standards be used. There's nothing in the law or regulations requiring agencies to accede to such demands, but they usually do, because it would take more trouble to argue with the SHPO/THPO than just to do what he or she says. As a result, this step in the process is where a good deal of delay and unnecessary costs are generated by "requirements" not only for completing particular forms but for collecting the information needed to do so—for example, through intensive archeological testing.

The SHPO/THPO and agency can also agree to "regard" a property as not eligible, in which case (with the exception discussed below) as far as section 106 is concerned, it can be blown away without further consideration. This is not to say that it doesn't need to be considered under NEPA and other authorities, but in practice it generally means that it's not going to get very much consideration under any statute, unless somebody really makes a fuss about it.

If the SHPO/THPO and agency don't agree, then the agency has to seek a formal determination of eligibility from the keeper. Before we look at how that's done, let's consider another circumstance in which a formal determination must be sought. It may be clearest to give some historical background.

In the early 1980s, the Forest Service was considering issuing a permit for expansion of ski facilities at the Arizona Snow Bowl, a resort on the San Francisco Peaks in Arizona. The San Francisco Peaks comprise a very important sacred place for both the Navajo and Hopi, as well as for other tribes. In Navajo cosmology they make up one corner of the world; to the Hopi they're home to the Kachina, very important spirit beings. The Navajo and Hopi both alerted the Forest Service to the cultural importance of the Peaks and said they were eligible for the Register.

The Forest Service had an archeological survey done, which revealed nothing. Accordingly, the Forest Service determined that the project would affect no eligible properties. The SHPO, allegedly under pressure from the governor, concurred. The tribes disagreed, pointing out that the very significance of the Peaks discouraged people from going there and creating archeological sites and that Kachinas leave no artifacts. The Forest Service and SHPO didn't listen.

Under the regulations then governing eligibility determinations,[43] an agency had to seek a determination from the keeper under either of two circumstances:

1. *When the agency and SHPO agreed that a property was eligible.* Their agreement was meaningless unless the keeper also agreed.
2. *When a "question" existed about eligibility.* Under the regulations, a question existed when the responsible agency determined it did.

You can doubtless see the problem; all an agency had to do was decide the property was not eligible, get the SHPO to concur, and determine that there was no "question" about ineligibility, in order to avoid considering impacts on the place.

Parenthetically, I reviewed the Register's draft regulations in the early 1970s and questioned letting the agency decide whether a question existed. I was rather grandly advised by the solicitor calling the legal shots that no agency would ever be so crass as to decide a question did not exist when one actually did. The solicitor and I are both a good deal older and, I hope, wiser now.

Because, of course, the Forest Service displayed precisely such crassness in the Snowbowl case. The tribes had gone to court insisting that the Peaks were eligible. The keeper and the advisory council had both written the Forest Service recommending that it seek a formal determination of eligibility. In the face of this, the Forest Service determined that since the SHPO concurred in its opinion about eligibility, no question existed. Taking the regulatory language at face value, the court agreed, and the project proceeded without further section 106 review.[44]

This case obviously illuminated a large loophole in the section 106 process, which we sought to seal up in the 1985 version of 36 CFR 800. At the same time, we tried to do away with the manifestly ridiculous requirement to have the agency seek the keeper's blessing when the agency and SHPO agreed that a property *was* eligible. Our revisions remain in the 2004 regulations.

So, under the section 106 regulations, an agency must seek a determination from the keeper if:

- the agency and SHPO/THPO don't agree; *or*
- the ACHP or keeper so request.

The second provision is designed for situations like the Snowbowl, without going so far as to require keeper review every time anybody objects to an agency-SHPO/THPO determination for however frivolous a reason. The keeper and ACHP serve as a screen, but if either so requests, the agency must seek the keeper's determination.

So if the agency and SHPO/THPO don't agree, or the keeper or ACHP requests that the agency seek a determination from the keeper, the agency needs to bundle up all the pertinent documentation and send it to the keeper. It's in the agency's interests to organize the documentation so it's clear and complete and gives the keeper a rational and easy-to-use basis for making a decision. Other parties can, of course, supply the keeper with their own documentation and make their own arguments.

The keeper reviews the documentation, talks with people as necessary, and makes a decision. The keeper's determination is theoretically final, though as we saw in chapter 3 in the case of Mount Shasta, political pressure can force the keeper to rethink a decision.

Eligibility and Nomination

The fact that the agency, the SHPO/THPO, or the keeper decide that something is eligible does not mean that anybody has to, or even should, nominate it for inclusion in the Register. Eligibility determination and nomination are completely different things.

Since you determine eligibility as part of the section 106 process, it often would make no sense for the property to become a permanent part of the National Register, because the action under review may very well destroy it. In other cases, there's just no practical reason to nominate the property; preparing a nomination may not be where you want to put your limited financial and personnel resources.

This kind of thinking upsets people at the National Register and people who make a living doing nominations. Here are some of the arguments they make for nomination, with some responses:

1. Nomination is required by law. Nope, it's not. It used to be, to the extent that section 110(a)(2) of NHPA required agencies to nominate "all" historic properties under their control. This provision was removed in the 1992 amendments; what's required now is simply a program that *includes* nomination. Congress (that is, the drafters of the amendments) recognized that agencies can take perfectly good care of historic properties without nominating them. So why require them to go to the trouble and expense of nomination?

Executive Order 11593 does require agencies to nominate all properties under their jurisdiction, but they were supposed to get this done by July 1973. Needless to say, nobody succeeded. So is the requirement still effective? Some people who make money off nomination work would like to think so, but I think they're on shaky ground. Congress has had repeated opportunities to incorporate the executive order's provision into law and hasn't done so. Or rather, they at first did include it, at section 110(a)(2), and then explicitly removed it.

2. It protects the property. Well, sometimes. It depends. Actually, the condition under which nomination is encouraged by the statute—when a property's in federal ownership—is precisely the one where nomination is least useful as a preservation device. Federal agencies, remember, are required to manage historic properties under their jurisdiction or control, and historic properties are defined as properties included in or *eligible* for the National Register. So if the property's eligible, the agency's responsible for managing it, whether it's on the Register or not.

Of course, some people are impressed by registration. It's sometimes helpful to have a property on the Register if, say, we're going to seek funding to rebuild its roof, and our budget people are more likely to approve a new roof for a Register property than for one that's simply eligible. But do we want to encourage this kind of thin understanding of what NHPA's all about, if we can help it?

3. It's a good thing to do. Says who? Nomination is paperwork; it doesn't change the property in any way. More often than not it does nothing for preservation. I think it's fair to say that nomination has no moral content whatever.

4. It helps keep track of the property. Well, yes, as does any registration, but the same argument cuts against the Register. If there's another way to keep track of the property, that's no more expensive and no less effective, what's the benefit of the Register? If a land management agency keeps records of its resources in a geographic information system (GIS), for example, integrating historic property data into that system is probably going to be much cheaper, more flexible, and more likely to influence agency planning than putting things on the Register, so why not invest scarce dollars in the GIS rather than in nomination?

5. It's an aid to research. This is one of the Register staff's fallback positions; they honestly think that the Register can be a great research tool. This strikes me as utter bunk. Considering that the Register now represents—and surely always will represent—a nonrandom selection of properties that have been nominated and accepted based on quite uncontrolled and uncontrollable variables, what kind of legitimate research is anyone going to use it for? Besides, most research in most of the preservation disciplines is done on a regional basis, where regional records would be at least as useful as a national database. Finally, is the possibility of future research by preservation specialists a legitimate justification for investing tax dollars?

6. *It's an educational tool.* The Register staff really likes this one, too, and it's true, to an extent. Educators do use the Register. But educators would, could, and do use alternatives to the Register, too—like local inventories, state inventories, the databases of land management agencies, Indian tribal data—and these might well have greater pedagogical value than the Register.

7. *It honors the property.* Yep; sure does. That's what the Register is really good for, and if you feel the need to honor a property, you ought to nominate it. If you simply want to manage it, you'll find other tools more useful. And we ought to be careful about bestowing the Register's honors too far and wide; the owner of the fine antebellum plantation house may feel that his property's Register status is somewhat cheapened when he finds that it's shared with a tin can scatter in southeast Wyoming.

In a rational world, the Register would be an honorific tool and we'd use other, simpler, cheaper, more flexible tools for planning purposes. We don't live in such a world, so we try to use the Register and its eligibility criteria for both honorific and planning purposes. But that doesn't make it sensible, or necessary, to mix up the planning functions of eligibility determination and the honorific function of registration.

A Word About Documentation

Section 106 regulations don't require any particular documentation as the basis for deciding to treat a property as eligible. It does say that agencies are supposed to be guided by the *Secretary of the Interior's Standards for Identification,*[45] but these are pretty flexible. In point of fact you can agree to treat something as eligible based on a one-page description, a Polaroid photo, or no documentation at all. This kind of flexibility can be very useful.

For example, suppose an Indian tribe wants a spiritual place to be considered in planning but doesn't want to reveal much about it—because to do so, in the tribe's belief, would dissipate its power or cause that power to turn to evil, do harm to people. It may be very helpful, efficient, cost-effective, and productive of harmony to be able to say, "OK, we'll treat this mountaintop as eligible without pursuing why it is. Now, what can we do to manage impacts on it?"

Or imagine you have seven hundred old houses scattered through an area that may be affected by a redevelopment program. It may save a lot of time and money to say, "We'll treat every building over forty-five years old as eligible, and apply the *Secretary of the Interior's Standards for Rehabilitation* (see chapter 5) to each one." Hundreds of local governments have agreements with their SHPOs and the ACHP under which they do this, in lieu of project-by-project section 106 review.

Or consider a project with five alternative sites, some of which can't be physically inspected in full at the time analysis is performed under NEPA. If you can make judgments about the relative likelihood of eligible properties in each alternative's APE, you can consider and resolve at least some adverse effects early in planning. If you have to wait until you can get on the land, dig holes in it, measure its buildings, or whatever, by the time you get around to addressing historic preservation issues, most of the decisions about the project will have been made. It's this kind of thing that causes section 106 review to cause last-minute conflicts.

The National Register staff doesn't worry about such practicalities, however. It's an article of faith at the Register that an eligibility decision should be based on the same kind of information as a nomination. If you go to the keeper for a formal determination of eligibility, you're going to be asked for something equivalent to a nomination package—a detailed description of the property, with maps, plans, photos, and the like, together with a detailed analysis of its significance.

For the same reason, in auditing SHPO performance, NPS leans on SHPOs to insist on nomination-level documentation when evaluating Register eligibility. Since NPS holds the SHPOs' federal purse strings, SHPOs tend to respond to NPS expectations.

Of course, some SHPO/THPOs may want substantial documentation for their own reasons—which may be good ones (e.g., not wanting to give undue protection to insignificant resources) or not so good ones (e.g., consistency with some standard operating procedure).

The thing to remember is that the section 106 regulations *themselves* don't require any particular documentation, so what is required should be negotiable and should—if you'll excuse it—depend on the circumstances.

Boundaries

The keeper of the National Register frets greatly about boundaries—where they should be drawn, how they should be justified, and so forth. This is necessary where a property is nominated for inclusion in the Register, because it's going to be plotted on maps, perhaps referenced in property ownership and local planning documents, so one really does need to know where the thing starts and stops. Boundaries are far, far less important in the world of eligibility determinations. In an eligibility determination we are not listing a property in perpetuity—we may, in fact, destroy it—so there's no long-term recordkeeping rationale for detailed boundary definition. And boundaries are often irrelevant to planning needs. The effects we need to plan for—visual, auditory, and atmospheric effects, for example—may result from actions that take place far outside the property's boundaries. In fact, defining boundaries may mislead people into thinking that if they can just physically stay outside the boundaries, they've avoided adverse effect; this is seldom true. On the other hand, sometimes it *is* true. If we can physically avoid an archeological site that's valuable only for research, we probably have avoided affecting it. So once again, it depends. In consulting about whether to regard something as eligible, you should think about the extent to which there's a practical need for boundaries. Don't get wrapped up in trying to do so if it's not useful. But if you have to refer the matter to the keeper, expect to go into excruciating detail about boundaries, and to draw them someplace even if doing so is entirely irrelevant to your project and its effects.

Eligibility and the GO Road

The Forest Service conducted an archeological survey along the GO Road right-of-way and identified a few prehistoric and historic sites, including some rock cairns at the crest of the coast range. It didn't undertake any special consultation with interested parties, but local tribes voiced concerns. They said there was a very important spiritual place in the high country, probably close to the road right-of-way. Here, they said, there was a hole in the sky through which knowledgeable religious practitioners could gain access to other worlds of knowledge. It was also an important place for medicine gathering, and those rock cairns were prayer seats, constructed by people seeking visions.

After some hemming and hawing, the Forest Service contracted with a cultural anthropologist for an ethnographic study of possible Indian spiritual places along the right-of-way. Based on extensive interviews and work in the field with tribal consultants, the ethnographer confirmed that people used the high country for spiritual purposes and that a particular area, smack dab on the GO Road right-of-way at the crest of the coast range, was viewed as a particularly important place for medicine making and communication with the spirit world.[46]

Discussion Question: Don't worry about the archeological sites; they were taken care of. Aside from these sites, do you think there's an eligible property here? Apply the National Register Criteria and the criteria considerations. If you think there is an eligible property, what do you think it is? How should it be documented? How should its boundaries be established?

Determining Effect

I've belabored identification and eligibility determination because they're where a lot of myths accumulate, and many project reviews get hung up—and because they're the reasons for a lot of professional practice. They're only steps in the process, however. It's important to remember, and to remind others who may not understand the process as well as you do, that eligibility does not mean you can't blow a property away or muck it up. It just means that you have to consider and consult about ways of managing it and mitigating effects.

To figure out how to mitigate effects, you need to have some idea what those effects are. So the regulations prescribe that once you've identified something as eligible, you determine what effect your project may have on it.

"No Historic Properties Affected"

You may, of course, come out of the identification process having found nothing that's eligible for the National Register. In this case, you determine that no historic properties will be affected, give the SHPO/THPO and other consulting parties thirty days to comment, and if the SHPO/THPO doesn't object within that time, you're through with section 106 review.[47] You may have to deal with noneligible properties under NEPA or other laws, but section 106 review is done.

The regulations also say that you can find "no historic properties subject to effect" if there are eligible properties in the APE but the project won't affect them in any way—positively or negatively.[48] This might be the case if, say, there was an archeological site, useful only for research, within the visual impacts APE.

But in most cases, if you have historic properties in your APE, you're going to have to assume that the project will have some kind of effect on them, so you move on to the next section of the regulations: "assessment of adverse effects."

The "Criteria" of Adverse Effects

Deciding whether an action's effects will be adverse involves applying the "criteria of adverse effects." There is actually only one criterion:

> An adverse effect is found when an undertaking may alter, directly or indirectly, any of the characteristics of a historic property that qualify the property for inclusion in the National Register in a manner that would diminish the integrity of the property's location, design, setting, materials, workmanship, feeling, or association.[49]

Applying this criterion may not be easy. You have to decide what aspects of the property make it eligible for the Register, which may not be obvious. Suppose we have a building that's been on the Register since 1976, and we want to gut it to create office space. We need to know whether the interior helps make it eligible for the Register, because if it doesn't, then gutting it may not adversely affect it. But whoever nominated the building back in 1976 probably wasn't explicit about what did and did not contribute to its eligibility; National Register forms don't really elicit that information very well. So we may not know whether the interior contributes or not. This is why the regulations go on to say:

> Consideration shall be given to all qualifying characteristics of a historic property, including those that may have been identified subsequent to the original evaluation of the property's eligibility for the National Register.[50]

Even if we're not dealing with some antique nomination or eligibility determination—even if we're looking at the historicity of a property for the first time—reasonable people can disagree, and there's a world of potential for disagreement about what does and doesn't contribute to a property's eligibility.

Assuming we can reach consensus on what contributes, then we have to decide whether what we're planning to do will diminish its integrity. OK, so gutting the interior is pretty obvious, but what if we're planning only to paint it? Or remove asbestos? Or bring it up to code? Again, lots of room for argument.

And what if we can do things to reduce the effect? What if everybody thinks painting it puce would be an adverse effect, but painting it teal would be OK?

The Examples

The regulations provide a set of examples that most people use, most of the time, to avoid dealing with the abstractions inherent in the core criterion of adverse effect. These examples are what most people mean when they refer to the "*criteria* of adverse effect."

The examples are:

Physical destruction of or damage to all or part of the property. If you're going to knock the building down or bulldoze the archeological site, or tear down a wing of the former or drive a trench through the latter, that's an adverse effect. No-brainer, though honorable people can disagree about what constitutes "damage."

Alteration that's not consistent with the *Secretary of the Interior's Standards for the Treatment of Historic Properties*.[51] A bit trickier. The *Secretary's Standards* prescribe how alterations should be done when you're "preserving" (i.e., maintaining), restoring, re-constructing, or rehabilitating a building or structure. If you're consistent with the *Standards*, your project is taken to have no ad-verse effect; if you're not, the effect is adverse. The problem, of course, is demonstrating that your project will be consistent—if, that is, you don't want to acknowledge adverse effect. We'll go over the *Standards* in chapter 5, because they're useful in several contexts.

Removal. If you're going to move a property away from its his-toric location, that's an adverse effect, even if you're moving it for protective reasons. If a property doesn't have a historic location—as is arguably the case with a historic ship or aircraft— then pre-sumably removing it isn't an adverse effect. But consider the case of the USS *Missouri*, the battleship on which the Japanese surren-dered to end World War II. When it was up for recommissioning to go lob shells at Lebanon during the Reagan administration, it had sat in port at Bremerton, Washington, for years and had become a popular tourist attraction. Was moving it from Bremerton an ad-verse effect? The Bremertonians certainly thought so—as they have more recently when the Mighty Mo, once again off duty, was relo-cated to Hawaii to serve as a museum ship.

Changing use. Even if you don't touch the property, if you change the way it's used this may have an adverse effect. If you drive up tax rates to the point where low-income families may not be able to remain in their old houses, or family farmers are unable to hold onto their land, or if you close off the trail that the Indian tribe uses for access to its sacred site, you're having an adverse effect.

Altering the setting. Changing the setting of a property can have adverse effects—again without touching the property itself. If you build something visually incompatible with a building whose vi-sual qualities are important, that's an adverse effect. A classic ex-ample of setting alteration—and use alteration—is the case of the Matachines Dance site in El Rancho, New Mexico. As you'll recall from chapter 3, in this case the proposed action was building a power substation next to the parking lot where the dance was held. The people of El Rancho said that this alteration of setting would so compromise the character of the site that they would no longer be able to dance there; this was clearly an adverse effect on the site.

Obviously, though, sometimes an alteration of setting may be irrelevant to the significance of the property. For example, archeological sites are notoriously insensitive to visual impacts.

The regulations try to deal with this disparity by saying that a change in the setting is an adverse effect only if it changes physical features within the setting that contribute to the property's significance. This opens the door for some truly wonderful arguments about what does and what doesn't contribute. Some of these doors are closed by the next criterion.

Introduction of intrusive elements. If you erect a cell-phone antenna on the margins of a historic district whose visual integrity is important, this is obviously an adverse effect. The regulations at this point speak to visual, atmospheric, and audible elements, so they cover things like air pollution and introduction of noise as well as things you can see. The introduction, like a change in setting, must somehow diminish the integrity of the property's significant elements in order to be an adverse effect.

There's a cell-phone antenna on the edge of the "woodhenge" at Cahokia, the ancient urban center east of St. Louis, Missouri. Does this diminish the woodhenge's, or Cahokia's, significant elements? I'd certainly say so and probably most people would agree. But does it really? Aren't the significant elements of the woodhenge the holes into which the poles were stuck to create the structure? What's really affected is the visitor experience at Cahokia, which is probably never discussed in the documentation covering the woodhenge's historical importance, but is surely one of the major reasons the place is preserved and interpreted. Here again it's possible to get into hair-splitting arguments about abstract matters of definition—which will distract people from getting on to the real issues of resolving adverse effects.[52]

Neglect. If you control a historic property and neglect it so it falls apart, falls down, gets vandalized, or is otherwise negatively affected, the neglect itself is an adverse effect—except, say the regulations, where deterioration is something the property is *supposed* to do according to an Indian tribe or Native Hawaiian organization. This caveat is intended to handle situations like Indian cemeteries, where the tribe may want the remains of its ancestors to return to the earth, or even wash into the river, rather than be dug up.

Neglect is a hard effect to deal with because agency decision makers seldom wake up in the morning and say, "I'm going to neglect the Joe Smith Plantation House today." But agencies *do* make decisions all the time that are neglectful of historic properties— budget decisions, decisions about the priority of projects, and so on. In *National Trust for Historic Preservation v. Blanck*[53] the U.S. District Court for the District of Columbia found that in neglecting historic buildings at the Walter Reed Army Medical Center Annex in Maryland the army had failed to comply with NHPA, though it also determined (using rather contorted logic) that NHPA did not require agencies to spend substantial amounts of money to maintain historic properties. This decision left all concerned scratching their heads about just what agencies are supposed to do about neglect.[54]

Transfer out of federal ownership. Federally controlled properties are subject to the protections not only of section 106 but of other sections of NHPA and other federal laws. If you transfer a property out of federal ownership—sell it, give it away, exchange it—it's deprived of these protections, and that's obviously an adverse effect.

Again the regulations contain a caveat. Transfer is all right if you impose adequate and enforceable restrictions to protect the property. What constitutes adequacy or enforceability? That's left for negotiation, as it must be; what works in one state or with one kind of property won't work in another. In the state where I live, for example, there's an active, well-enforced historic easement program, and that's the system the SHPO wants used to protect transferred property. The recipient of the property grants the SHPO an easement under which the recipient agrees to preserve specified characteristics of the property.

Questions have arisen as to whether this criterion applies to properties transferred from one federal agency to another. Some argue that such transfers aren't even subject to review, because the legal status of the property doesn't change; it's still protected by section 106 and other legal requirements. The trouble with this argument is that it ignores the regulatory definition of what requires review. The regulations require review of all federally involved actions that fall within types that have the potential to affect historic properties; they don't carve out an exception for agency-to-agency transfers. It seems to me that an agency must look at its proposed transfer and consider whether it has the potential to affect historic properties. When the Bureau of Land Management (BLM) transfers land to the army for use in training exercises, this has the potential to affect historic properties. Sure, BLM and the army are both bound by section 106, but the army drives tanks and explodes ordnance; BLM doesn't. Their uses of the land are fundamentally different, whatever legal requirements apply. As far as I can see, federal agency-to-agency transfers may or may not have adverse effects, depending on what the recipient agency may do with the property. One has to apply all the *other* criteria to determine this: Will the transfer lead to destruction? Alteration? Change in use? Introduction of incompatible elements?

Other Kinds of Adverse Effects

So, those are the examples of adverse effect that illustrate the core criterion. They're so widely used and so thoroughly embedded that they're referred to as the "criteria of adverse effect," though they're really only examples. There can be other kinds of adverse effect, as long as they meet the core criterion.

Like what? Well, how about if somebody is living on public land, under a permit of some kind, and takes it upon himself or herself to keep watch over a cave full of ancient pictographs? The resident keeps track of visitors to the cave, talks to them, encourages them to respect the paintings, and not contribute their own spray-can additions. The permit expires and the federal agency proposes not to extend it; the resident will have to move. Is the agency destroying the cave? No. Is it altering the cave? No. Is it changing the "character of its use?" Well, one might make an argument for this, but it would be a pretty long bow to draw. Is it altering the setting? No. Is it introducing elements that diminish its integrity? Probably not. The regulations talk about "visual, atmospheric, or audible elements," and while spray-can vandals presumably could be seen, might smell, and can probably be heard, it would still be hard to squeeze them into this example. Is the agency neglecting the cave? Well, yes, but no more than it's already been neglecting it, and it will probably say that it will, of course, protect it just fine. Is it transferring the cave? No. But is it doing something that, indirectly at least, can alter characteristics that qualify the cave for the National Register? Sure it is.

What to Do With a Determination

Having applied the criteria of adverse effect, the agency has to decide: either the project will have an adverse effect or it won't. If you determine that it *will*, you move on to the next step. If you determine that it *won't*, you notify whoever you've been consulting with—at minimum the SHPO or THPO and any Indian tribe that "has made it known . . . that it attaches religious or cultural significance to a historic property subject to the finding"[55]—and send them supporting documentation.[56] Section 800.5(c) of the regulations gives the SHPO or THPO thirty days to review the finding, and section 800.5(c)(2)(i) gives any consulting party the opportunity to object within the same period.

If any consulting party objects in writing within the thirty-day window, the agency either has to persuade them to withdraw the objection or ask the ACHP to review the determination. The ACHP may also ask to review the determination on its own initiative—though that probably won't happen unless they've been asked to do so by some unhappy consulting (or nonconsulting) party. If the ACHP asks to review the determination, the agency has to give it the information it needs to do so.[57] The ACHP then has fifteen days to decide whether it thinks the agency has correctly applied the criteria of adverse effect.[58] The ACHP's finding—that the agency has applied the criteria correctly or that it's screwed up—is advisory to the agency and the other consulting parties. A court would afford the ACHP's advice a good deal of respect, however. And the ACHP has the option of submitting its finding to the very head of the agency, and whoever it's submitted to must respond in a public document. This makes it hard for an agency to ignore a council finding.

"Conditional" No Adverse Effect Determinations

Often an agency, SHPO or THPO, and others will agree on conditions they think will keep adverse effect from occurring. The resulting determination is commonly referred to as a "conditional no adverse effect" (CNAE) determination. The regulations don't use this terminology, but they provide for CNAEs by saying that the agency can find no adverse effect when "the undertaking is modified or conditions are imposed . . . to avoid adverse effects."[59] The regulations offer as an example of such conditions an agreement on later review of a building's rehabilitation plans to make sure they comport with the *Secretary of the Interior's Standards for Rehabilitation*. This is a very common kind of CNAE. As another example, imagine that an agency says that constructing a new building will have no adverse effect on a nearby historic cemetery because a vegetative buffer will be created between the building site and the cemetery. We might agree in principle that this measure is adequate, but how does the agency translate the principle into on-the-ground reality? What kind of buffer will it be? What kinds of plants will be used? Evergreen or deciduous? Big or small? How big? How close together? A CNAE can nail all this down.

The regulations don't prescribe what kind of document is needed; often the agreement is documented by an exchange of letters. But the documentation should be thorough, complete, and understandable to the "cold reader"—the person who walks in off the street and picks it up. The project will probably be implemented by people who didn't prepare the documentation; they need to be able to understand what any condition requires them to do. The condition may be interpreted in court, so you need to write with judges and lawyers in mind. This does not mean you've got to lace the document with obscure Latinisms and allusions to parties of the first part; it means that you've got to make it clear and complete.[60]

Another thing to remember is that any condition that's agreed on must actually—at least, in the eyes of a reasonable person—keep adverse effect from happening. For example, if you're building a road close to an archeological site that's useful only for research[61] and you agree to put up a fence and install mine fields and watch towers to make sure the bulldozers don't wander into the site, you can probably find that there'll be no adverse effect. But you can't agree to send archeologists in to dig the site up before you put the road through it and call *that* not an adverse effect.[62]

Finally, the project has actually to be carried out in accordance with any conditions adopted, or the agency has to start over.[63] In other words, you can't agree to rehabilitate following the *Secretary's Standards*, or put up the visual screen, or avoid disturbing the archeological site, and then do something different. Or rather, you *can*, but you won't have complied with section 106.

Some Advice

Like the eligibility determination process, the process of determining effect can generate a lot of argument over abstractions, fine points, and procedural issues. My recommendation to clients about such arguments almost invariably is, don't get into them. If someone thinks there's an adverse effect, there's almost always a way to show that there is, given how vague the criterion and its examples are. If you don't think there's an adverse effect, but somebody else does, it's probably not worth arguing about it. And if you can find some lawyerly way to split a procedural hair, somebody else can probably find a lawyerly way to splice it back together or find a hair that's less ratty under some other law. Don't play games; accept the argument that you'll have adverse effects (even if you don't agree) and get on with the process.

The Effects of the GO Road

The Forest Service felt that the spiritual place identified at the crest of the coast range was not eligible for the National Register because of the religious property criteria consideration. The SHPO, following the lead of the tribes, disagreed. The matter was referred to the keeper of the Register.

The keeper determined that the spiritual place was eligible as a district, called the "Helkau Historic District." The keeper dismissed the religious property criteria consideration argument by noting the intense cultural significance of the property, the role it played in maintaining traditional culture, and its clear association with important local Indian traditions.

The keeper, as is the keeper's wont, worried greatly about the boundaries of the property and eventually established them along the contour line that enclosed all the locations where the ethnographic study indicated that people sought visions and medicine; this enclosed all the prayer seats, but it was a pretty small area.

By the time the determination was made—because the Forest Service had not refrained from construction while the process went on—the road was built to the east and west boundaries of the district.

Discussion Question: Assuming the Forest Service wanted to complete the road, what sort of effect determination should it have made?

Resolving Adverse Effect

If there will be an adverse effect, naturally the next step is to see if there's a way to keep it from happening or reduce its severity. Mitigate it or, as the regulations put it, "resolve" the adverse effect. You figure out how to resolve the adverse effect through more consultation. But the regulations don't provide much guidance about how to consult and even less about what the agency itself might do to seek resolution—think about the matter, do studies, and most critically, consider alternatives.

What the regulations at this point *do* talk a lot about is whether the ACHP participates in consultation. Before this point the ACHP has not been formally involved; now it is, but its involvement is kept on a pretty tight leash.

Advisory Council Involvement

In a nutshell, the agency has to notify the ACHP that it's found adverse effect and is continuing consultation, providing supporting documentation. And it must invite the ACHP to participate in the consultation if:

- It wants to (this does happen sometimes),
- The adverse effect will be to a National Historic Landmark (NHL)—that is, a place designated by the secretary of the interior under the Historic Sites Act of 1935 as "nationally significant" (elitism raises its ugly head) in the "commemoration and illustration of the nation's history,"[64] or
- The agency wants to negotiate a Programmatic Agreement (more on this later).

The ACHP then decides whether it wants to participate. It can also decide to participate without being asked.[65]

If the ACHP comes into the consultation, everybody consults; if it doesn't, everybody but the ACHP consults and the resulting Memorandum of Agreement (see below) is filed with the ACHP.

The regulations require the agency to provide the consulting parties with the documentation they need in order to participate in the process.[66] And the agency must inform the public of what's going on, provide the public with documentation, and consider the public's views.[67]

Consultation

The agency then consults with those already at the table (those consulted during identification, evaluation, effect determination) and is supposed to welcome new parties to the process.[68] But the agency calls the shots as to whom it *will* consult, other than the ubiquitous SHPO/THPO and affected tribes.

In a way it's unfortunate that this section of the regulations focuses so heavily on consultation. I say this because people get so wrapped up in who to consult, who has what rights, who gets to be at the table instead of around the edges of the room, and so on, that they lose track of the consultation's *purpose*. However devoted we are to good consultation, we can't make it accomplish anything if we don't attend to its substance. The agency responsible for the action has primary control over substance; it's the one that can either consider an alternative or decline to do so, get more data about something or not, apply expertise to a problem or not, pay attention to someone else's expertise or not. Under NEPA and its regulations, the agency is required to do substantive analysis—of its impacts and what to do about them. Although pragmatically an agency must do the same kinds of analysis to take into account effects on historic properties, section 106 regulations are vague about it, while going into excruciating detail about who has consultation rights. Moreover, the agency's consultation responsibility is overwhelmingly focused on the SHPO/THPO, which encourages agencies to transfer their substantive responsibilities to the SHPO/THPO as well. Alternatives? What does the SHPO/THPO say we should do? Can we avoid an adverse effect? What does the SHPO/THPO think?

Bottom line: consultation needs to have substance; it needs to be informed. And it's not a substitute for the agency's own, independent, analysis of impacts and what to do about them.

The regulations say that we consult about ways to avoid, minimize, or mitigate adverse effects.[69] These three terms are not defined in the regulations, and in the NEPA regulations the first two are subsumed under the third.[70] Some 106 practitioners think of the three terms in hierarchical order. We first seek ways to avoid the impact altogether; if this doesn't work we look for ways to minimize it, and if we can't find these we seek agreement on mitigation measures. "Mitigation" in this formulation gets equated with things like archeological data recovery and architectural recordation. We let the property go, but we make a record of it.

Such a simple hierarchy doesn't relate well to the real world's complexity. Suppose we have a highway that's going through an archeological site. Suppose we move the right-of-way a mile from the site's boundaries. Have we avoided adverse effect? Sure—except that the new highway may stimulate development that will destroy the site. And suppose the property isn't an archeological site but a historic building, and the highway, while physically distant, is still in its view shed? Now have we avoided adverse effect or only minimized it? Suppose we plant trees along the highway; does this minimize the effect further? Or suppose we move the highway not a mile from the archeological site, but three feet, and provide construction monitoring in case the site has oozed out beyond what we think its boundaries are. Have we avoided effect, minimized it, or mitigated it? What if we're not talking about a highway but a footpath? A power line? What if there's a three-foot horizontal separation but a three-hundred-foot vertical drop? What if the site is a Native Hawaiian spiritual site where silence is important, particularly in the trade wind season, and that's when we have to build? Or not build?

"Avoidance," "minimization," "mitigation" often grade into and among each other, depending on the nature of the action, the nature of the property, the measures proposed, and a range of other factors. We get into a lot of silly arguments when we let ourselves believe that they have absolute definitions. Some Indian tribes, for example, insist that "you can't mitigate adverse effects on a spiritual place." Why? Because they've dealt mostly with archeologists in section 106 review and have come to think that "mitigation" means archeological excavations. What they're really saying is "you can't dig up spirituality and put it in a museum." This is doubtless true, but that doesn't mean you can't mitigate impacts on a spiritual place. It depends on the nature of the place, the nature of the impacts, and the nature of the mitigation.

What we should have in our consultation is an open, free-wheeling, informed discussion of the proposed project, its effects, and what to do about them. We should consider alternatives, weighing and balancing costs and benefits of all kinds.

Here's another myth: that we can consult only about "historic preservation matters," which usually means archeology, architectural recordation, rehabilitation, and the like. Agencies and other project proponents promote this myth because they don't want preservation people questioning, say, their traffic volume calculations or their assessment of economic benefits. Preservationists accept it because they don't want to think outside their technical specializations. In fact, of course, if we limit ourselves to "avoidance, minimization, and mitigation measures" that are within the ambit of the historic preservation disciplines, we're going to have a mighty narrow range of measures to consider.

Remember that one purpose of consultation is to reveal and consider new information. It's a "process factual," in the words of the Virgin Queen. The relevant information may or may not have much to do with historic preservation per se. Building the new shopping mall will create five hundred new jobs, but will they be jobs that local residents will be able to get, or will they require skills that must come from outside? If the latter, do the proponent's assertions about local economic development, upon which the local government has relied to justify tearing down a bunch of historic buildings, really make sense? If we swing the proposed airport runway fifteen degrees to avoid flying over the historic district, what does this do to fuel consumption and safety? These kinds of questions have to be addressed and answered with real data, or consultation has little chance of accomplishing anything.

On the other hand, considering such issues not only requires that proponents be willing to gather and share pertinent information, but that preservationists take the information seriously. If the jobs at the mall really will go mostly to local people, or if altering the runway alignment will cause aircraft to crash into mountains, scare endangered ducks away from a wetland, or cause a five dollar per ticket increase in airline fares, these facts can't be ignored as irrelevant to historic preservation.

How Is Consultation Done? Some Process Suggestions

In stressing the need for substance, I don't mean to denigrate process. A colleague in the Department of the Interior commented to me once that the older he got, and the longer he spent in the bureaucracy, the more he came to equate "success" with "good process" as opposed to "good outcome." I think this is an entirely reasonable position—especially in a public servant. As we grow older and more experienced, unless we shut down our thought processes altogether, we come to recognize a wider and wider range of outcomes that we can regard as "good." Particularly if we work for the public, which almost by definition has multiple, conflicting desires, most of them justified one way or another, we come to be suspicious of simple "good-bad" distinctions. If we believe in serving the public, then we pretty soon come to be satisfied—even happy—with a process that gives everybody a fair crack at making his or her preferences prevail.

Consultation under section 106—and for that matter under NEPA, AIRFA, and the other statutes—is by definition a process, and what constitutes a "good" outcome, as usual, depends. In this case it depends on your point of view; did the process arrive at what you think is desirable?

But the process itself can be good or bad, depending on how level it makes the playing field, how fairly it allows different opinions to be heard and debated, how open it makes decision making to varying ideas and alternatives.

There are ways to make consultation work and ways to make it a sham. Unfortunately, a lot of people know only how to do the latter. Not necessarily because they want sham consultation, but because they can't imagine anything else. This is particularly sad since there is substantial literature on how to make consultations of various kinds work.[71] There's widely available training, and there's a national organization—the Association for Conflict Resolution (ACR)[72] that's composed of people for whom consultation is a way of life and a way of making a living.

Consultation-to-agreement under section 106 is a classic example of what's widely referred to as "alternative dispute resolution" (ADR). It's called "alternative" because it's mostly lawyers who've named it, defining it as an alternative to suing your opponent's eyes out.

There are several kinds of ADR—arbitration, mediation, the mini trial. Section 106 consultation slips and wiggles around three types: negotiation, conciliation, and mediation.

Negotiation is where disputants get together without anyone helping them out, to butt heads and work through to a solution. Of course, the extent to which there's head butting depends on how far apart the negotiators are and how serious their beefs are with one another. The great majority of section 106 cases—perhaps all of them to some extent—involve negotiation.

In *conciliation*, there's a third party who helps the disputants communicate with one another. This is a form of what's popularly called "facilitation," but facilitators don't work just in ADR; they help in a variety of decision-reaching and team-building contexts. The conciliator is neutral and helps the disputants exchange views. Sometimes this can be as basic as persuading them to sit in the same room and talk; often it requires trying to get them not to drive one another out in a huff. Sometimes it includes helping them interpret data or use language in something like comparable ways.

Mediation is much like conciliation, but a bit more structured and the mediator is a bit more a person with a mission. But it's an entirely processual mission; the mediator doesn't care what the resolution is, as long as there is a resolution that the disputants are reasonably happy with. The mediator is rather more in control of the process than the conciliator is; he or she sets the rules and does his or her best to enforce them. The rules are designed to keep people talking, break down communication barriers, achieve understanding, and, where possible, agreement. If agreement is reached, the mediator is equipped to help the parties put the agreement in writing.

In section 106 review, it is not uncommon for the SHPO/THPO or ACHP staff to serve—informally and almost always without professional training—in a conciliator or mediator role between a project proponent and project opponents. When I've served in this role, both as an ACHP staff member and as an outside consultant, I've often found it to be tremendously rewarding both intellectually and emotionally.[73] Often I find that the parties are simply talking past each other, or that one side or the other is locked into some kind of absolutist position that's unnecessary or even counterproductive to resolving the issue that one or both sides are concerned about. Often there's a hang-up on abstractions—is this really subject to review, is this place really eligible—that can be dissolved if you can get people beyond it to talk about what really concerns them. There's a principal in mediation that says you ought to get the disputants away from staking out positions and into discussing their interests. When you can do that, the results can be almost magical.

So how do we consult? Naturally, it depends—on who you represent and what you're trying to do. If you want to clog up the process and bring things to a grinding halt, there are ways to do that. If you want to advance your point of view over everybody else's, there are ways to do that, too—to an extent, but as we'll see, it's always possible for someone to pull the plug and terminate consultation. That's the safety valve in the section 106 process that keeps consultation from turning into gridlock. But let's assume that your job is to try to resolve the dispute over adverse effect that's brought the parties to the table. Let's suppose that you're the honest broker—which you can be even if you're working for one of the parties, as long as your role is clearly understood.

Everybody is human. Whoever you're working for, try not to perceive the person on the other side of the table as the devil incarnate. And if you're in any kind of broker position, try to encourage everyone to think of one another as people with legitimate, if conflicting, needs.

Keep it small. If possible, limit the number of people at the table. This can't always be done, and the process has to be an open one, in which all points of view are represented, but if you can keep the cacophony of voices down, it will help. Sometimes this can be done gradually—you have a great big chaotic meeting at first, and by the second or third meeting everybody's beginning to think they should designate spokespeople or form coalitions.

But not too small. Be wary of people who want to exclude others because they're "disruptive" or "just want to make their points." It's astounding how thin-skinned some people are, even people who routinely deal in conflict. An attorney once told me he didn't want a citizen activist at a meeting because she was "just preparing for litigation," and would "use the meeting as a forum for expressing her views." Better, presumably, to exclude her and thus help build her court case.

First, we kill. . . . Speaking of courts, be careful about participation by lawyers. You can't keep the devils out of the room, but don't take any guff from them. Despite their self-perceptions, they are not the sole receptacles of all wisdom, and their training and personalities are often at odds with the interests of dispute resolution. That said, I should acknowledge that quite a few attorneys are getting trained in ADR, which helps a lot, and there are plenty of lawyers who manage to be human. But don't count on it, and don't be afraid to ask them to explain their obscure legalisms in English.

Seek equity. Try to make the playing field as level as possible. Some of your consulting parties may not understand section 106 or NEPA very well—may not know a FONSI from a fuzzy bear or that it's legal to knock down a National Register building. Some may not have English as their first language or may have cultural barriers to communication. You may have people with disabilities to be accommodated. Make sure you accommodate them not only physically but by trying to keep the discussion sensible to them. Stop and summarize from time to time, try to rephrase things in plain language. Watch their eyes; are they glazing over? Narrowing to suspicious slits? Time to stop and regroup.

Interests, not positions. Try to get people to explain the interests that lie behind their positions. For example, when somebody says:

"This project will wipe out our community's whole connection with its past . . ."

Before you let somebody else say:

"It will not, as we've explained a hundred times . . ."

Ask:

"Can you explain how it's going to do that?"

Try to get past sweeping generalizations and down to specifics. How will it wipe out the community's connections with its past? By eliminating the only place where people can park to shop at local stores in rehabilitated historic buildings, thereby driving the stores out of business and thereby causing our downtown to dry up. Well, there's a germ of a solution here, isn't there?

But be careful about suggesting the solution, if you're the honest broker; it's much better to let the parties find it themselves. And often they will.

"You mean that's your problem? What about if we add a parking garage?"

That sounds overly simple, of course, but you'd be surprised how often seemingly intractable conflicts are conflicts between positions, rather than between interests. In other cases, addressing the interests that people are willing to talk about may ultimately reveal things that they aren't so willing to discuss but that are really bases for solutions.

Trial solutions. Try to get people to put trial solutions on the table. What would you like to see done? Of course, when you're starting out with one side just wanting the other to go away, and the other wanting its opponent to shut up, this may not be feasible. But you can try to explore hypothetical options, anyhow.

Lots of options. Explore as wide a range of options as possible. Particularly if there are lots of people involved, a technique like brainstorming can be useful—where everybody tosses up ideas and nobody shoots them down until they've all been articulated.

Look for mutual gain. There may be something that party A wants badly enough to put up with a contentious impact if it gets it. Even if party A is in favor of preservation and against the project, that something may not be strictly a preservation kind of something. I've known of cases in which Indian tribes accepted impacts to traditional cultural places in return for financial assistance to cultural revitalization programs. Or the possibility may not relate directly to the property affected. There have been cases in which demolition of buildings has been accepted in return for developing community revitalization plans, purchase of facade easements, or creation of rehabilitation revolving funds to encourage preservation of other buildings or neighborhoods.

Restate it. Try restating things, in the simplest terms possible. Get beyond the abstractions, find the concrete meaning:

"We insist that the *Secretary of the Interior's Standards for Rehabilitation* be met."

"So you don't object to changing the building, but you want everything that's architecturally significant about the building preserved?"

Explore implications. On the other hand, explore the implications of expansive statements:

"We'll guarantee that this project will do no damage whatever to any significant historic property."

"You mean you're not going to do anything that could have any physical, visual, auditory, social, any kind of impact at all to any of these properties?"

Try deconstruction. Break the problem down into its constituent parts:

"It seems like we have three problems here: visual impacts on the Old North Church, bulldozing the Magnificent Midden, and access to Spirit Peak. Can we look at each of these individually?"

Or

"It seems like there are different problems surrounding construction and surrounding operations and maintenance. Can we look at each in turn?"

Or

"Each group has outlined its interests. Now can we look at each one by itself, pretending for the moment that none of the others exist? Then we can see what conflicts exist between addressing one set of interests and another."

Document and move on. If points of agreement develop, record them and move on. If there are points that seem intractable, try setting *them* aside and working on issues where agreement may be possible. The intractable issues may evaporate as other things get resolved.

Be flexible. Don't get hung up on rules of procedure—even rules of proper ADR procedure. Adapt the consultation to the situation.

Recognize cultural variation. It may be inappropriate in a given cultural group for a young person to speak in the presence of his elders, or for meetings to begin without prayers, or for some things to be discussed by women in front of men. The person negotiating for the Indian tribe may not be able to commit the tribe to anything without consulting the elders. Some things may not be discussible in public at all, and some negotiation methods that Euroamericans are comfortable with—including some of those I've just recommended—may be utterly unacceptable to a non-Euroamerican community.[74] Try to make sure you understand these factors going into the consultation, and design it to accommodate them.

174 / Chapter 4

Understanding such factors may require prior research—informal discussions with the group involved, perhaps advice or study by a cultural anthropologist or sociologist. One group of practitioners in dispute resolution routinely conducts a social assessment on a community before trying to consult, to ascertain what groups should be brought to the table and what constraints there may be on their participation.[75]

Recognize political and legal realities. If consultation involves a federally recognized Indian tribe, it's important to make sure that it constitutes—or is preceded by—government-to-government consultation between the tribal government and the agency. Don't expect the agency's consultant to be able to waltz in and start negotiating with tribal elders before an appropriate line officer in the agency has consulted with the tribal government.

In the government context, recognize that negotiators may be constrained by the positions of their superiors. On the other hand, don't take these kinds of constraints at face value. When the Corps of Engineers cultural resource manager says, "My colonel has instructed me not to consider that idea," it is perfectly within reason to suggest that this is a damned counterproductive position for the corps to take, and if it wants to have a reasonable consultation, the colonel ought to rethink his position—and then to go on and discuss the idea while the corps representative sits on his hands.

And recognize that there are legal limits on the authority an agency can grant to a group of consulting parties and rules of the game that the group must follow. Under the Federal Advisory Committee Act of 1972[76] (FACA), an agency decision maker cannot give over his or her decision-making authority to an outside advisory group—the group must be advisory only. Under the same statute there are definite limits to how closed the meetings of such a group may be. However sensitive the issues to be discussed, however much the group may need to reason together in private, its meetings may have to be open to the public. Under FACA, in fact, the very formation of an advisory group is fraught with complexity, all to keep special interests from having backdoor influence on federal decisions. Here is a place where, if you're representing a federal agency, you're going to need to talk with your lawyers. But tell them what you want to do, and don't take "no" for an answer without an explanation of why it has to be "no."

What's the Result of Consultation?

Consultation under section 106 results in one of three things: agreement, termination, or project abandonment. The last option isn't mentioned in the regulations, but it's always a possibility and probably happens more often than people think. Some projects just aren't very good ideas, and when confronted with problems, their proponents abandon them. But assuming the project's not abandoned, adverse effects end up being "resolved" either using a memorandum of agreement (MOA) or through an agency decision after issuance of ACHP comment.

Memorandum of Agreement

In most cases, consultation about adverse effects results in an MOA. Appendix 4 is a model MOA for a hypothetical project. There's no particular magic to the format, but there is a logic to it.

- *The Title.* The title should be designed to give the cold reader an immediate fix on what the agreement's about. It needs to contain the name of the action and the key players.
- *The "Whereas" Clauses.* These clauses spell out the rationale for the agreement and outline relevant actions that have led up to it, data supporting it, and so forth.
- *The Stipulations.* These detail what will be done to resolve the adverse effect, who will do each thing, when, and what standards will be employed.
- *The Signature Blocks.* Signatures in these blocks represent agreement by the signatories and concurring parties.
- *Appendixes.* Appendixes are often attached, providing things like detailed plans, reference documents, exceptions to standard practices, and systems for monitoring performance.

Writing an MOA

Writing MOAs is something of an art.[77] The basic rules are to make it clear to the cold reader—the manager or lawyer or judge who has to interpret it—and to make it complete. Don't leave things out; cover all the bases. Describe what the consulting parties have agreed will be done, and include provisions to ensure—insofar as is possible—that the things agreed to *will* be done.

Signing an MOA

The MOA is signed by the consulting parties, but some parties *must* sign it to make it official, while others don't.

The regulations are a bit confusing on this point. First, they identify the federal agency, the SHPO/THPO, and the ACHP (where it's taken part in consultation) as the signatories.[78] Then it (magnanimously, if a bit gratuitously) gives the agency the authority to "invite additional parties" to sign, specifically highlighting Indian tribes and Native Hawaiian organizations that ascribe cultural or religious importance to affected historic properties and parties assuming responsibility under the MOA. These are referred to as "invited signatories,"[79] but later are lumped with the agency, SHPO/THPO, and ACHP as signatories.[80] The failure of an invited signatory doesn't keep the core signatories from putting the MOA into place; the failure of a core signatory more or less does (but see below).

Got it so far? OK, now, anybody else in the world can be a "concurring party," provided the signatories (it's not clear at this point whether this includes the invited signatories) agree. The failure of a concurring party to concur—like the failure of an invited signatory but not a core signatory to sign—doesn't invalidate the MOA.[81]

If this seems a tad precious, I agree, but there it is. In simplest terms, generally speaking the SHPO/THPO and agency must sign the MOA for it to go into effect. In some cases the ACHP also must sign.[82] Anybody else may be invited to sign, but if they don't sign, the MOA can go into effect anyway.

So in the vast majority of cases, it's the agency and SHPO/THPO who really have the muscle in executing an MOA and in the consultation process generally. The ACHP has equal power—in some ways more than equal power vis-à-vis the SHPO—in certain circumstances. Everybody else is a second-class citizen.

Is this right? Just? Democratic? User-friendly? I don't think so, but it's what the regulations say, so there you are.

Termination and Comment

If an MOA isn't achieved—that is, if the agency, SHPO/THPO, or ACHP terminates consultation in accordance with the regulations —then the ACHP renders a comment to the agency. The regulations go into some detail about the termination process, but we don't need to here; it doesn't happen often, and in principle the same thing happens however it's done. Most practitioners go through life without ever dealing with a termination and comment; if you have to, you can read the regulations.[83]

What the regulations don't say much about is how ACHP comment is rendered. It's important to understand that rendering ACHP comment is not a staff function. Or more accurately, if it is carried out by staff, it's done with a lot of oversight by the council itself—that is, by the twenty-member panel of presidential appointees, agency heads, and others that comprises the actual Advisory Council on Historic Preservation. The comment may take the form of a letter signed by the chair, or it may be developed by a panel of council members or by the full council sitting in review. Depending on the case (usually depending on its political visibility), the council may hold public meetings, on-site inspections, and other information gathering or deliberative activities. The agency must assist the council in carrying these out. However it's done, the comment has to be rendered within forty-five days after it's requested, unless the agency agrees to a different timetable.[84]

Under section 110(l) of NHPA,[85] the comment goes to the agency head. In other words, if the project is a highway, the comment goes to the secretary of transportation or the administrator of FHWA—not just to the regional FHWA staff or the state DOT that's directly responsible for the project. If it's an NPS project it goes to the secretary of the interior or the director of NPS. If it's a HUD project it goes to the secretary of HUD, unless HUD has legally delegated its responsibilities to the local government, in which case it goes to the head of the local government. Also under section 110(l),[86] the agency head must document whatever decision is made (if any) once he or she has considered the comments, and can't delegate this responsibility. Presumably this doesn't mean that the secretary of defense has to sit down at his or her own laptop and bang out a response to ACHP comments on an army project, but it does mean that the responsibility can't just pass down the chain of command to the base commander. The secretary has to be personally involved, and this involvement may have career implications for those responsible for attracting the ACHP's attention.

What does the agency have to do in response to the comment? Nothing, other than document its decision, indicating why it's decided what it's decided and how it considered what the ACHP said it ought to do, providing a copy of this documentation to the consulting parties, and making it available to the public.[87]

People are sometimes surprised that, in the final analysis, the advisory council really is advisory; that its only ultimate authority under section 106 is to render those comments that the agency has to give it the opportunity to render. Citing this limited authority, some preservationists—and some project proponents who are used to the more dictatorial powers of, say, the Environmental Protection Agency under the Clean Air Act—dismiss the ACHP, and the section 106 process, as paper tigers. This is neither reasonable nor accurate. It's not reasonable because in creating section 106, Congress didn't mean to make historic preservation superior to all other public interests; it merely meant to ensure that preservation concerns were weighed and balanced with other interests. It's not accurate because, in fact, few projects wind up going to the ACHP for comment; the great majority gets a memorandum of agreement. Particularly since section 110(l) was added in 1992, ensuring high level consideration of ACHP comment, with a predictable trickle-down effect, agencies are reluctant to terminate consultation, so they really try to reach agreement. Whether the agreements reached are good agreements is, of course, another matter.

Resolving the GO Road's Effects

The Forest Service acknowledged that building through the Helkau Historic District would have an adverse effect on it. It proposed to mitigate this effect in three ways. First, it would place the road in such a way that it didn't take out any prayer seats or other specific locations where people carried out spiritual activities. Second, it would keep the shoulders of the road narrow, so people wouldn't be able to park to watch the funny Indians doing their rituals. Third, it would color the pavement brown to blend in with its surroundings.

The tribes pointed out that the Forest Service was proposing to drive a road down the aisle of their cathedral and allow 18-wheelers to rumble along it loaded with logs. Avoiding the pews on either side, coloring the road to match the floor, and keeping people from stopping as they trundled through didn't exactly mitigate the project's effects. The SHPO and ACHP agreed with the tribes and argued for rerouting the road.

The Forest Service terminated consultation and referred the matter to the ACHP. The ACHP's comment proposed that the Forest Service abandon several miles of the road and build along another set of ridges, removing it not only from the Historic District but from its view shed.

The Forest Service thanked the ACHP and decided to proceed as originally planned, with the mitigation measures it had proposed. The tribes took the Forest Service to court, charging violation of section 106, NEPA, and other laws.

Discussion Question: What do you suppose the ACHP's position was on the Forest Service's compliance with section 106? What do you suppose the court decided?

What's Usually Done to Resolve Adverse Effects?

What can the consulting parties agree to as ways to resolve adverse effects? Anything they want to, as long as it's legal.

What's Legal?

Is it legal to destroy a historic property? Absolutely, as far as federal law is concerned. It's not legal to destroy it without taking its effects into account—that's what section 106 requires, and, of course, the way you do that is by following the regulations. But once you've done that, you can destroy the property, subject to whatever agreement you've reached under section 106—and subject to any other legal authorities that apply.

Such legal authorities *do* exist and constrain the flexibility of the consulting parties a bit. As a result, and also as reflections of long-standing practice, there are certain types of things that are commonly agreed upon to resolve adverse effect.

Section 110(b) of NHPA says that an agency must document any historic property that it damages or destroys, or assists anyone in damaging or destroying. So at a bare minimum, an MOA on destruction or damage has to provide for documentation. What kind of documentation, the level of documentation, and where the documentation gets filed are decided by the section 106 consulting parties. The legislative history of section 110(b) indicates that the documentation is to be whatever's appropriate to the type of property—it can be architectural or engineering drawings, historical research, oral historical research, archeological data recovery— whatever fits. The level of documentation can range from superdetailed architectural drawings on acid-free paper and multivolume archeological reports, to—in theory—crayon sketches. Consulting parties have agreed to documentation in the form of videos, popular publications, Web sites, and databases. The only more or less absolute standard is that if the property is a National Historic Landmark, then the NPS guidelines for section 110 implementation as issued in 1988[88] specify that the standards of the Historic American Buildings Survey/Historic American Engineering Record (HABS/HAER) must be met, and that the results must be filed with the Library of Congress (see chapter 5). However, the revised section 110 guidelines issued by NPS in 1998 don't deal with section 110(b),[89] so even this rule is rather up in the air.

If the MOA deals with archeological resources on federal or Indian lands, then standards that flow from the Archeological Resources Protection Act (ARPA; see chapter 6) must be met. Excavations must be professionally supervised, must follow approved research designs, and the resulting information and material must be curated in accordance with regulations (36 CFR 79; see chapter 6). So you can't have an archeological site on federal or Indian land dug up by the Amalgamated Graverobbers of America, with artifacts sold to fund the work (some of us find this a bit restrictive, but there you are).

If the effects will occur on federal or Indian lands, then Native American ancestral remains and cultural items have to be dealt with following the Native American Graves Protection and Repatriation Act (NAGPRA; see chapter 6) and its implementing regulations.[90] These require plans of action (POA) whose terms should be consistent with any 106 MOA—and the MOA must be consistent with the POA. You don't want your POA to say that everything will go to Tribe X, while your MOA says everything will go to the state museum.

What's Possible?

Besides what's legally required or prohibited, anything goes, provided you don't stipulate murder, treason, environmental degradation, or some other illegal or manifestly offensive act. Some things that have been agreed to in MOAs include:

- Restoration or rehabilitation and adaptive use of buildings and structures
- Demolition and removal of properties that don't contribute to the historic or architectural significance of an area (or, of course, those that do, if it's justified)
- Transfers of development rights
- Redesign of projects to preserve specific properties, vistas, access points, landscapes, neighborhoods
- Relocation of buildings and structures
- Implementation of maintenance plans
- Design of projects like power lines to merge with the landscape and reduce visual effects
- Transfer of historic lands to Indian tribes, local governments, nonprofit organizations
- Donation of easements on landscapes, facades, buildings, structures, and sites
- Development and implementation of community, neighborhood, and regional plans
- Creation of historic preservation revolving funds or funds to support specific preservation-related purposes
- Establishment of design review procedures and groups to implement them
- Construction of museums, cultural centers, and curatorial facilities
- Installation and maintenance of interpretive facilities
- Public participation and education programs

- Intentional neglect and monitored deterioration
- Burial of archeological sites
- Creation of managed open space
- Visitor information facilities

Really, what the consulting parties can agree to is limited only by their collective imagination. One MOA I wrote regarding impacts of a U.S. courthouse expansion on adjacent historic residential districts dealt with the control of lawyers—to the extent of providing denizens of the courthouse with a brochure describing the historic and architectural qualities of the districts and encouraging use of appropriate standards when converting residential buildings to law offices. Another provided for moving dozens of houses in a National Historic Landmark district to make way for an expressway expansion and donating them to the local public housing authority, which agreed to rehabilitate them to stabilize the deteriorating district. There's no end to the possibilities.

What's Reasonable? Anzalone's Adages

Of course, it's possible for one or more of the consulting parties to go crazy and demand things that are completely off the wall. You need to remember that you're trying to mitigate impacts in the public interest, not to make points, punish your opponents, or throw your weight around. Ronald Anzalone of the ACHP long ago outlined some hardy rules of thumb for judging whether what you're proposing is reasonable in terms of public benefit.[91]

Standard 1: Apply a combination of common sense, professional judgment, and civic responsibility.

Guideline: Sell the idea to yourself as if you were an intelligent, concerned, informed citizen (which hopefully you are!).

Standard 2: Reject silly mitigation; subject all proposals to the "laugh test."

Guideline: "The American people are a very generous people and will forgive almost any weakness, with the possible exception of stupidity."—Will Rogers

Standard 3: Reject useless mitigation.

Guideline: Understand what is required as well as the flexible application of such requirements, but do not propose or accept mitigating measures just to have some if there is no particular purpose served.

Standard 4: Understand, explain, and justify mitigation.

Guideline: Be prepared to try to explain your position and justify the expenditure of time, money, and other resources to:

1. A spouse or close friend who's not "in the business";
2. Your parents; and/or
3. Mike Wallace.

What's Required?

Anzalone mentioned "what's required," and one of the most frequent questions by people who are being asked to pay the bill is precisely that: "What is required?" The answer is pretty simple: not much. An MOA has to provide for documentation, because that's required by section 110(b), but the kind of documentation it provides for is up to the consulting parties. It has to accommodate the terms of a NAGPRA POA if there may be Native American graves or cultural items involved on federal or Indian lands. Beyond these, there aren't any explicit requirements.

However, there are some general guidelines. Section 110(d) of NHPA says that agencies are to conduct their affairs, to the extent compatible with their missions, in ways consistent with the purposes of the statute, and consider ways to advance those purposes. The purposes of NHPA are set forth largely in section 2,[92] in a widely ignored statement of national policy. Some of the policies that are particularly germane to the content of MOAs are:

> to foster conditions under which our modern society and our prehistoric and historic resources can exist in productive harmony and fulfill the social, economic, and other requirements of present and future generations.
>
> [to] provide leadership in the preservation of . . . prehistoric and historic resources . . .
>
> [to] administer federally owned, administered, or controlled prehistoric and historic resources in a spirit of stewardship . . .
>
> [to] contribute to the preservation of nonfederally owned prehistoric and historic resources and give maximum encouragement

to organizations and individuals undertaking preservation by private means . . .

[to] encourage the public and private preservation and utilization
of all usable elements of the Nation's historic built environment.

OK, all motherhood and apple pie, but if federal agencies are
supposed to carry out their activities in a manner consistent with
these policies, then the policies surely ought to be reflected in the
MOAs they negotiate. So it's required that MOAs be aimed at fos-
tering productive harmony between historic resources and the modern world, providing for stewardship of federally owned resources,
and so on. NEPA and other authorities point us in the same direction. In a nutshell, "taking effects into account" as section 106 requires doesn't mean just saying "lookee there, we're knocking down
that old building," it means considering and, if feasible, adopting
means of treating historic properties in positive ways or mitigating
adverse effects on them. That's the overall requirement. How the
consulting parties meet this requirement—depends.

Coordination with NEPA

The regulations try to encourage good NEPA coordination. They
establish as a principle that NEPA and 106 should be coordinated
as early as possible in the planning process. They call on SHPOs
and THPOs to work with agencies to initiate section 106 at early
stages in planning. They tell agencies to include historic preservation concerns in environmental assessments (EAs) and findings of
no significant impact (FONSIs), and in environmental impact statements (EISs) and records of decision (RODs), and to review categorical exclusions (CATEXs) to see whether they need to do section
106 review.[93] There's also a way to substitute a NEPA analysis for
the standard section 106 process; we'll get to that in chapter 8.

Figure 4 shows how section 106 review ought to be coordinated
with EA and EIS development. Scoping, identification, evaluation,
and initial effect determination are coordinated with EA or DEIS
preparation, and consultation to resolve adverse effects takes place
as needed before the EA or EIS is finalized and the FONSI or ROD

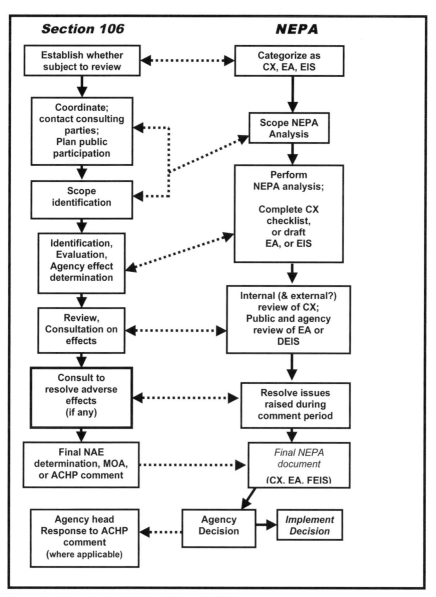

Figure 4.   Coordinating Section 106 and NEPA

is issued. This way the public can be fully informed about the results of section 106 review through its review of draft NEPA material, and the consulting parties under section 106 can be fully informed of public views obtained by the agency through the NEPA process. Everything moves along smoothly, there's no redundancy, nothing falling through the cracks.

Of course, it doesn't always—or perhaps even often—work this way. At least as often as not, the agency or the SHPO or the ACHP or all concerned understand section 106 to require such detailed information on properties and effects that it can't possibly be gathered when NEPA review is being done on a project's multiple alternatives. So section 106 gets put off until after a preferred alternative has been selected, even after the ROD's been issued or, even more dangerous, after the FONSI's been signed, specifying that there will be no significant impact when impacts on historic properties haven't even been determined. Obviously that's not what should be done, but as long as people think that the identification, eligibility determination, and effect determination steps in section 106 review require highly detailed information, it's probably the way it's going to continue.

Discoveries

So, you've completed your section 106 review, you've done, or are doing, whatever your MOA calls for (or maybe you've found that there are no historic properties subject to effect, or no adverse effect), and all of a sudden you run into something you hadn't bargained for. What do you do?

Anticipation

Let's begin by saying that you *shouldn't* encounter something you hadn't bargained for. During your section 106 consultation and your NEPA analysis you ought to think about what might pop up, and bargain for it—develop procedures for dealing with it, and put these procedures in your MOA or no adverse effect documents. Actually this is more than just something you *should* do; the 2004 regulations *require* it.[94]

NAGPRA

If you're operating on federal or Indian land, and what you encounter is something that may be human remains or a Native American cultural item as defined by NAGPRA, then you have separate and distinct responsibilities under that statute and its regulations. If you've really done your job right, you have a plan of action for dealing with such discoveries, and you can follow it. If you don't, you're going to need to stop what you're doing and consult relevant tribes, per the NAGPRA regulations (see chapter 6).[95] This doesn't relieve you of your section 106 responsibilities, but it needs to be coordinated with whatever you do to comply with section 106.

No Plan

Let's suppose you don't have a predeveloped plan embodied in an MOA, and just to keep it simple let's assume that NAGPRA doesn't apply—your project isn't on federal or tribal land, or the discovery has no chance of being related to an Indian tribe or Native Hawaiian group.

If your discovery happens before the undertaking has been approved—during geological testing as part of EIS preparation, let's say, you go back and consult in the standard manner, to arrive at an MOA or obtain ACHP comment.[96]

Alternatively, if the agency, SHPO/THPO, and any involved tribe or Native Hawaiian group agree that the discovery is of value only for its "scientific, prehistoric, historic or archeological data"— the subjects of the Archeological and Historic Preservation Act of 1974 (AHPA, see chapter 6)[97] then you can comply with that act in lieu of redoing section 106 review. This means that you can conduct data recovery or pay NPS to do so.[98]

If the project *has* been approved and you find something—during construction, for example—then the agency simply decides what it can do to resolve adverse effects. It then notifies the SHPO/ THPO, tribe or Native Hawaiian group, and ACHP within forty-eight hours after the discovery, gives them forty-eight hours to respond, takes the responses into account, and implements whatever it decides to do.[99]

So—you rip the aluminum siding off the undistinguished-seeming oldish building that you're about to demolish to expand the expressway and find that it's Daniel Boone's log cabin. You've completed section 106 review and have an MOA that doesn't deal with the building because nobody thought it was historic. What do you do?

You probably won't be able to get agreement that the cabin should be treated under ADPA, so you'll probably come up with your own proposal. You propose, let's say, to document the cabin and move it to the local city park where it can be restored and interpreted. You whip this plan out within forty-eight hours (during which time the regulations require you to "make reasonable efforts to avoid, minimize or mitigate adverse effects"[100]) and notify the SHPO and ACHP. If you're smart you'll notify other concerned parties, too, but the regulations don't require this except in the case of concerned Indian tribes and Native Hawaiian groups (we can imagine reasons why a tribe might be interested in Boone's cabin, but let's assume they aren't).

The SHPO comes back within forty-eight hours and says, "We think you ought to relocate the highway." The ACHP doesn't respond. At this point your agency can say, "Thank you very much, Ms. SHPO, but we're going to do what we planned to do in the first place." Or it can accede to the SHPO's direction, or it can negotiate. It's up to the agency.

Of course, at this point you might have a lawyer for the Greater Appalachia Daughters of Dan'l' or the Tribes United to Destroy Evidence of Oppression knocking at your door pointing out that since you were only preparing the right-of-way and construction had not really commenced, the regulations don't allow you to use the forty-eight-hour provision, and you've got to go back into standard section 106 consultation and address their concerns. Or they might insist that you really should have anticipated the presence of the cabin when you did your MOA and, hence, have violated the regulatory requirement to include provision for discoveries in agreement documents. But absent such challenges, you can do pretty much what you want.

Which seems to provide rather thin encouragement to agencies to do the kinds of up-front planning the regulations call for.

Incidentally, under the discovery provisions the agency can assume that a newly discovered property is eligible for the National Register without consulting anyone, though for obscure reasons it has to specify (to whom is not indicated) the National Register criteria under which the property is assumed to be eligible.[101]

NAGPRA Again

If you have the kind of situation we've just discussed, but NAGPRA *does* apply, then you have to do what's outlined above, but you need to coordinate it with NAGPRA compliance. And if your discovery takes place on tribal lands, you follow tribal procedures and do whatever the tribe tells you to do.[102]

If 106 Has Not Been Completed . . .

The discovery provisions are not a substitute for regular section 106 review. They can be invoked only for discoveries that occur after review has been finished. If you haven't done section 106 and you discover something, you are way up a creek, and the only way you can legally paddle back down is by going through the full, regular 106 process.

Emergencies

If you're an agency that's likely to deal with emergencies, the regulations (and good sense—but see below) encourage you to develop procedures for dealing with historic properties affected by your emergency work. You're to do this in consultation with all the usual parties, and the procedures have to be approved by the ACHP.[103] Once approved, you can follow the procedures in lieu of regular section 106 review. Alternatively, you can cover emergency situations in a programmatic agreement,[104] and then follow *that.*

If you don't have procedures in place and don't have a programmatic agreement and you're confronted with a disaster or emergency, then you're supposed to contact all the usual parties and give them seven days to comment, *if* you determine that that this is feasible; if not, comment is to be invited during whatever time is available.[105]

Interestingly, the regulations don't provide for the agency to do anything substantive at all. There's probably the assumption that the agency is going to do what it can to take care of historic properties, but there's no explicit requirement to this effect. So the "emergency" section seems to create a pretty big loophole in the process. Declare an emergency, give folks fifteen minutes to comment, and go ahead. The saving grace in this section, however, is that its provisions apply only to actions taken within thirty days after the disaster or emergency has been declared.[106] So you can't say, "Well, we had this earthquake last year and now we have to demolish these damaged houses, so we'll call up the SHPO and give him half an hour to provide his advice. . . ." At least, you're not supposed to.

Alternatives to the Standard Process

The regulations identify several kinds of program alternatives to the standard section 106 process—agencywide alternative procedures, exemptions, standard treatments to be described by the ACHP, council comment on whole programs.[107] A number of agencies have developed such alternative systems in the last few years, and others are doing so all the time.

Program alternatives can be useful when a particular program is so structured that it just can't relate effectively to the standard section 106 process. But they can also be very confusing, especially to people outside an agency. You ask an agency how it's complying with 36 CFR 800, and they say, "Oh, we don't have to; we comply with our alternative procedures." Then you have to find and look at the alternative procedures—or exemptions, or program comment, or whatever they're using—and see if they're using them right.

The regulations provide extensively for public participation and consultation during development of program alternatives, but this isn't really happening. Some pretty weird alternatives have been developed or are under development, in some pretty black boxes. Those put in place thus far—one developed by the army, for example, and another by the Bureau of Land Management[108]— don't give me much cause for cheer.

Programmatic Agreements

The program alternative that's been most extensively tested is the programmatic agreement (PA).[109] PAs, long ago called PMOAs,[110] have been around since the 1970s; there are lots of them in place—some good, some bad, some very, very indifferent. PAs are by far the most common kind of program alternative, and they can exemplify both the reasons for pursuing alternatives and the pitfalls in doing so.

- You're an official of the U.S. Bureau of Good Works, and Congress directs you to provide grants to orphanages for building renovation. The grants are to be awarded through State Good Works agencies, which will decide which orphanages will get fixed up. By the time it's known which buildings will be affected, you, the federal agency, will no longer be involved in the grants process (having turned the money over to the state). Most of the repairs will be pretty small-scale operations. How do you comply with section 106?
- You're a federal official responsible for the newly established kudzu eradication program, which is going to hire unemployed and homeless people throughout the South to dig up and burn the noxious plant that has been consuming the area since it was introduced some decades ago to control erosion. Your program may cause superficial damage to archeological sites, but doesn't have much other potential impact. You have to maintain a high level of flexibility in deploying your forces, based on the level of unemployment and homelessness in different regions on a month-to-month basis. How do you comply with section 106?
- You're the federal alternative power authority (FAPA), and you're reviewing a request by Sunshine Superco to license a solar power plant in Maine. The venture capital to support the project—including things like detailed historic property identification—won't be advanced by Sunshine's backers until it has all its federal licenses in hand. How can you comply with section 106 without requiring the company to do studies before it has the money in hand to do them?

- You're the economic development officer for the City of East Westerly, and you've got Community Development Block Grant (CDBG) funds to support low-income housing rehabilitation throughout the city. HUD has delegated its section 106 responsibilities to you. The program will involve dozens of small-scale rehab projects each year, each of which will be reviewed by the city historical architect to make sure that good preservation standards are followed. Standard section 106 review seems unduly costly and pointless. But you've got to comply, so how do you do it?

These are the kinds of situations in which a programmatic agreement (PA) is useful. They're situations in which the standard section 106 process just can't realistically be done.

Under such a circumstance, the responsible agency (or local government, in the case of a CDBG program), the ACHP, if it elects to play, some representative of SHPO-ness, and (in theory) other interested parties, including but not limited to Indian tribes and Native Hawaiian organizations, sit down and negotiate an alternative way of meeting the requirements of section 106 and other pertinent authorities. This alternative is embodied in a PA, which is signed by all the parties and then governs how the program is carried out.

I said that some representative of SHPO-ness has to be involved. That representative will be the SHPO if the action takes place in a particular state, a group of SHPOs if several states are involved, or the National Conference of SHPOs if the PA will have national effect. Some SHPOs claim not to be represented by the National Conference and therefore argue that a PA executed by the conference is not applicable in their states. This is a myth. SHPO participation in PA development, execution, and implementation is an artifact of the regulations, not a matter of right. The regulations say that the National Conference is the SHPO representative in nationwide PA matters, and that's simply the way it is, however much an individual SHPO may not like it.

PAs are negotiated and executed very much like MOAs— except that the ACHP must always be invited to participate in consultation[111]—and are subject to the same kinds of drafting principles.

Let's consider what kinds of alternatives we might set out under PAs for the four actions described above.

For the orphanage grants program, we might provide for the federal agency to delegate its section 106 responsibilities to the state, which would then follow 36 CFR 800. We might exempt certain actions from review, if we thought them unlikely to do damage. We might provide for expedited review of others, perhaps involving local preservation agencies. We might provide for those doing the projects to be trained in applying the *Secretary of the Interior's Standards for Rehabilitation*.

For the kudzu eradication program, we might provide for the eradicators to be trained in the identification of archeological sites, and for quick recordation and data recovery whenever one was found.

For the power project, we might have FAPA use background data and predictions about historic property distributions, developed as part of its NEPA review, in making its license decision, and consult extensively to identify and resolve any big conflicts that appear to exist, but defer detailed survey, evaluation, and treatment planning until after the license is issued.

For the CDBG program, we'd almost certainly execute a very standard kind of PA, versions of which are working successfully in hundreds of cities, under which projects would require no review beyond that performed by the city historical architect as long as the *Secretary of the Interior's Standards for Rehabilitation* were met.

Of course, there are pros and cons to all these kinds of options, and they would be the subjects of lively debate in PA consultation. What would finally be adopted would—what a surprise—depend on what the parties were willing to agree to.

If you don't reach agreement on a PA, then what you do depends on the nature of the action to which the PA would have applied. If the action involves multiple individual subactions—multiple orphanage rehabs, for example—then if there's no PA the agency has to follow the standard section 106 process for each subaction.[112] The same goes for a whole agency program that doesn't get a PA—the kudzu cleanup program, for instance.[113] Where a single complex project is at issue—FAPA's Sunshine license, say—then a failure to agree on a PA *may* (the regulations are less than clear on this point) lead to a council comment.[114]

Some Dumb Ideas About PAs

PAs—and other program alternatives—are the subjects of several groundless, silly, and counterproductive beliefs and practices. For instance:

Polly Parrot PAs

It seems to be assumed in some quarters—I've never had anybody explicitly state it, but have seen scores of PAs that reflect it—that a PA or other alternative must more or less parrot or paraphrase the standard section 106 process. This is nonsense. If the standard process works for you, why prepare an alternative? And paraphrasing not only is wasteful, it's dangerous, because when you start changing words without intending to change meaning, you risk changing meaning inadvertently—or at least you tempt people to think that you meant to change the meaning. If you're drafting a PA and find it sounding a lot like the standard process, stop and think: do I really need this?

Undeserving Agencies

Some SHPOs and ACHP staff have suggested that an agency doesn't deserve a PA until it has shown that it can handle the standard section 106 process. A moment's thought might reveal that if the agency can handle the standard process, it probably doesn't need a PA. Conversely, if an agency *doesn't* handle the standard process well, this may not mean that its officials are evil or stupid, but just that the standard process doesn't work very well for their programs—the precise reason for *doing* a PA.

PAs Are Sexy

Some agencies seem to have concluded that a PA is simply a good thing; in some quarters PAs have become faddish. Be careful about this. There's nothing in law saying you have to have a PA, and you ought to go to the trouble of doing one only if there's some value in it.

Recommendations

Be very careful about taking on development of a PA—or any other kind of program alternative. Remember that it substitutes for the regulations; once it's in place, the regulations no longer apply, except to the extent the PA includes portions of them by reference. So you're very likely inventing a whole new section 106 process for your program. Be sure you're up to the challenge, and that you really need it.

The prime directive ought to be go back to the law; *don't* be bound by what's in the regulations. Your alternative has to satisfy the statutory requirements, but it ought not do so in the same way the regulations do. If it does, you're wasting everybody's time.

Don't make the alternative more complicated than it needs to be, and certainly don't make it more complicated than the standard process. Perhaps the most common fault I've seen in reviewing PAs is getting carried away. What's needed may be some small surgical adjustment to the standard process—simplifying review of a class of actions that follows particular standards, assuming the eligibility of a given class of properties and getting on with determining how to deal with them—and people tie themselves into knots trying to redesign the universe around these minor adjustments. In most cases you're trying to simplify your compliance; don't make it more complicated.

Always, always, always provide for periodic reporting, monitoring, and opportunities for course corrections. Your PA is going to be in place for awhile—maybe indefinitely—and you need to make sure that it works and is responsive to changing conditions.

Guard against misinterpretation. Make the document as clear and understandable as possible, and provide ways for people to be reminded of (1) its existence and (2) how to interpret it. A training component is often appropriate, and so may be some sort of provision for briefing new personnel—for example, new commanding officers on a military installation where a PA guides planning.

Don't just follow an example. The fact that a PA was signed on somebody else's program doesn't mean that it's a good model for yours. We learn more about what works and what doesn't all the time, so an older PA is almost certainly inadequate by today's standards. And the circumstances that motivate agencies to develop PAs are unique; you can't easily apply a system that's appropriate in one case to another. Finally, PAs may be accepted when they're not especially good, and then they become enshrined in folklore as "successful," whereupon people start using them as models.

A classic example of misguided adherence to a model began with a very complicated PA developed by the Forest Service to cover salvage logging after forest fires in California in the mid-1980s. The ACHP signed onto it with major misgivings, based on the Forest Service's assurance that it was something that would really work. It didn't. It was so complicated, so convoluted, that only one forest ended up being able to follow it; the others stuck with the standard process. But the PA, having been signed, was assumed to have been successful, so when Hurricane Hugo downed a lot of timber in South Carolina awhile later, the Forest Service there adopted it as a model. For reasons not entirely clear, the ACHP again signed off, but as far as I know the arrangement didn't work any better in South Carolina than it had in California. But now having been "successful" on both sides of the continent, it was naturally adopted when timber borers attacked the Southwest. This time the ACHP rejected the draft, to the Forest Service's dismay, judging it impossible to implement. When I reviewed the Southwestern iteration of the PA, I was astounded at its incomprehensibility and asked what a number of its provisions meant. It soon became apparent that nobody had any idea, but everyone assumed the PA was the thing to do, since similar documents had been "successful" elsewhere.

Before you even start on the PA, establish clearly what you're trying to accomplish. The more explicit you can be about your goals, the easier it will be to stay focused and get a good product.

At the same time, think about what you're *not* trying to do that you nevertheless need to take into account—the things that may facilitate or frustrate your PA's implementation. Step back and look at the real-world operational context in which your PA is going to have to work, and think about related issues that you may need to address.

And generally, think ahead; try to anticipate issues and make sure they're resolved, that you're not shooting yourself or someone else in the foot.

For example—and this illustrates not only the need to think beyond your immediate need but also something of how broad and flexible a PA can be—consider the "World War II Temporaries PA," also known as "the World's Largest Demo Memo."

In the late 1980s Congress directed the Department of Defense to do away with all its World War II temporary buildings. The military services, of course, have a fair number of these buildings—thousands, in fact—and there was much head scratching about how to do section 106 on their wholesale demolition. Eligibility was a particular problem, since the buildings were built to standard designs and it was pretty hard to figure out why one might be more significant than another. This was clearly a job for PA-Man.

I got to draft the PA, and was (and am, for that matter) rather proud of it. It was simple. It assumed that all the buildings might be eligible and that was it for evaluation. It accepted the fact that they were coming down, sooner or later—being in theory "temporary" and in view of Congress' direction. It provided for DoD to sponsor a study of the contribution of World War II temporary architecture to the architectural history of the United States and to document buildings that represented different types and designs. DoD was also to advertise with veterans' groups and others to see if anybody had really strong feelings about preserving a particular building or building group and to consider these desires in deciding which ones to demolish when. With those things done, the services could demolish World War II temporaries at will.

Whether you like this result or not (as it turned out, the Gulf War mobilization and subsequent events greatly slowed the demolition, but eventually, no doubt, all the buildings will be gone), I think you'll have to grant that it was an elegant solution.

A few years went by, and then the air force asked Pat Parker, by now an executive in NPS, to judge a competition for an air force preservation award. One of the strong candidates was an installation that had taken a World War II temporary building, moved it to an appropriate location, and rehabbed it to serve as a museum on women in the air force. Not wanting to vote for a project that might be out of compliance with section 106, Pat asked me what I thought. "Not a problem," I said, "there's this PA . . ." and then I went and looked, and I realized that the only thing the PA permitted without regular section 106 review was *demolition*. A *re-hab* project had to go through the standard process. So I'd neatly made it easier for a military service to knock down a historic building than to keep it up. Stupid, and the direct result of not thinking through all the ramifications of the issues I was trying to address in the PA. Try to be smarter than I was.[115]

Preemptive Destruction

"Well," says Farmer Brown, irritated by all this fuss over some old building or bunch of artifacts that stands in the way of her feder-ally assisted stock pond, "I think I'll just crank up my bulldozer and solve my problem." Can she?

Anybody who can drive a bulldozer can bulldoze, of course, but Farmer Brown may be jeopardizing her federal grant if she knocks over the old house or roots up the site. Section 110(k) of NHPA says that:

> Each Federal agency shall ensure that the agency will not grant a loan, loan guarantee, permit, license, or other assistance to an ap-plicant who, with intent to avoid the requirements of section 106, has intentionally significantly adversely affected a historic prop-erty to which the grant would relate.[116]

Section 110(k) goes on to allow such a grant to be provided only if the agency, after consulting the ACHP, determines that some sort of justifying circumstances exist. So it's not an absolute prohibition on giving Farmer Brown her grant, but there's likely to be a considerable delay, a lot of questions asked, and, unless Farmer Brown can offer some awfully good explanations or pull some well-connected strings, she's unlikely to get money from Un-cle Sugar.[117]

Of course, the trick is to show that Farmer Brown *intentionally* knocked over the building, with *intent* to avoid the requirements of section 106. Doing so or failing to do so usually turns on whether one can demonstrate that she knew what those requirements were. If she did and wasn't bulldozing in her sleep, one has to assume that she knew what she was doing and did it to avoid the require-ments that she knew would otherwise apply.

Section 110(k) can be useful in preventing people from doing damage to historic places. An Indian tribe I know was concerned about the proposed (nonfederal) logging of a spiritual place on private land by a company that was also seeking a federal permit for a mine in the same area. The tribe wrote the company with copies to the world, alleging that the place was eligible for the National Register, that therefore section 106 would require consideration of impacts on it during the federal permit process, and that therefore if the place was logged, arguably destroying its significance, the permitting agency would be prohibited by section 110(k) from granting the permit. The warning seems to have worked; such logging as has taken place there seems to have been very selective and discretely done—no clear-cutting.

Some Conclusions About Section 106

We've spent many pages on the section 106 process. It may seem to you that it's pretty complicated, perhaps confusing, likely to be unduly time-consuming. I think you're right.

A lot of other people do, too, but most agencies and practitioners seem to accept it as given that it's the way it's got to be. This has results that I think are unfortunate.

One problem is that because the section 106 review is too complicated to be easily done early in planning, agencies tend to disconnect section 106 and NEPA. They put off the former until the latter is well advanced or even completed. In a study I supervised in 1994, which looked at a large sample of EISs, we found that about 42 percent deferred section 106 review until later—presumably until after the decision was made about how to proceed and the ROD was issued.[118] They'd say things like "cultural resource studies are not yet complete, but impacts on cultural resources will be mitigated pursuant to section 106"—and then essentially ignore cultural resources thereafter. Only 16 percent of the EISs clearly documented completion of section 106 review prior to issuance of the FEIS and ROD.

The effect of deferral is to increase greatly the chances of conflict between development and preservation and greatly decrease the chances of successful resolution, because by the time section

106 is done, many alternatives have been eliminated and the agency is pretty well set on its preferred course of action. Of course, it also frustrates the purposes of NEPA, which after all is designed to inform decision makers and the public about impacts *before* decisions are made.

Deferral results, I'm certain, from the complexity and property-specific character of section 106 review as it's commonly understood. An agency often simply can't do the kinds of detailed studies and consultations the regulations appear to demand when it's looking at a large number of alternatives under NEPA, so it puts things off until it can focus only on a single preferred alternative.

The complexity of the process also generates high costs in money and time. These are often associated with activities that are of marginal relevance to the real issues of impact identification and resolution. Massive amounts of time can be spent arguing over the details of eligibility or over precisely which examples of the Criterion of Adverse Effect apply.

The heavy focus of the regulations on the role of the SHPO has at least two unfortunate results. One is that agencies—assuming the process is all about satisfying the SHPO—often feel no need to develop or use expertise of their own. Why pay for pricey experts of our own if we're going to do whatever the SHPO's experts tell us to do? Thus the responsible agency, which has the best chance of doing something intelligent about historic preservation early in and throughout the planning process, doesn't. Instead, section 106 review becomes a rote matter for the agency—jumping through the hoop of "SHPO clearance."

The other result is that the SHPO is given great opportunity, and great temptation, to act in arbitrary and dictatorial ways, and to sweat the small procedural stuff rather than dealing with the large policy and substantive issues. Even if the SHPO doesn't do this sort of thing intentionally, it's easy for an agency or project proponent—particularly if they lack expertise of their own—to conclude that they're being jerked around by the SHPO and respond accordingly. The SHPO then develops quite pragmatic reasons for thinking that the agency or proponent is antagonistic and not to be trusted and so ratchets up the pressure, and the vicious cycle continues.

Meanwhile, a nonfederal applicant for assistance or a license is likely to get the impression—even be told by the agency responsible for issuing the permit or license—that the process is taking so long because the SHPO is being a butthead and just won't issue clearance. The applicant, if he or she has the wherewithal to do so, may then feel justified in calling up the governor to suggest that something be done to bring this uncooperative state employee to heel.

And while the agency and SHPO and applicant dance their intricate dances, everyone else who may be interested in the project and its effects can get shut out—because what's forgotten in the process of all this is that it's not just the SHPO who has to be consulted; other interested parties have roles to play, too.

I hasten to say that these problems have understandable historical roots. The strong emphasis on SHPO review made sense thirty years ago, when agencies and project proponents didn't have access to much expertise, the method and theory of environmental review in general weren't very well developed, and there weren't a lot of groups who knew enough about the process to be "interested" in a knowledgeable way. But it's a different world today, and the ACHP doesn't seem able to understand this. I'll also hasten to say that during my tenure at the ACHP, I subscribed to its approaches and contributed to the problem. There were historical reasons for this, too, but I still regret it.

So what's needed? A thorough rethinking of the process, I believe, at least going back to the basic requirements of the law and seeing how they could best be met given contemporary conditions. But this didn't happen during the late 1990s revision of the regulations, and there's no sign that it's going to happen anytime soon. So we're all stuck with the complexities I've outlined in such mind-boggling detail in this chapter. Good luck to us all.

Notes

1. For details and further discussion, see Thomas F. King, *Federal Planning and Historic Places: The Section 106 Process* (Walnut Creek, CA: AltaMira Press, 2001); and King, "What Is Section 106 Review Anyway? Two Views," in *Thinking About Cultural Resource Management: Essays From the Edge* (Walnut Creek, CA: AltaMira Press, 2002), 38–47.

2. 36 CFR 800.2(c)(2)(B).
3. 36 CFR 800.1(a).
4. See www.johncleesetraining.com/Decisions_Decisions_John_Cleese.htm (accessed December 26, 2007).
5. 36 CFR 800.2(c)(1).
6. 36 CFR 800.2(c)2)(i).
7. 36 CFR 800.2(c)(2)(ii).
8. 36 CFR 800.2(c)(3).
9. 36 CFR 800.2(c)(4).
10. 36 CFR 800.2(c)(5).
11. 36 CFR 800.3(f).
12. 5 USC 551 et seq. www.archives.gov/federal-register/laws/administrative-procedure/ (accessed December 26, 2007).
13. PL 94–463, http://epic.org/open_gov/faca.html (accessed December 26, 2007).
14. See chapters 1, 2, 7, and www.epa.gov/region2/ej/exec_order_12898.pdf (accessed December 26, 2007).
15. 36 CFR 800.2(d).
16. Left Coast Press 2007, Walnut Creek, CA, see www.lcoastpress.com/book.php?id=101 (accessed December 26, 2007).
17. I particularly like the "principled negotiation" espoused by Roger Fisher and William Ury, *Getting to Yes: Negotiating Agreement Without Giving In*, ed. Bruce Patton (New York: Penguin, 1991); and by William Ury, *Getting Past No: Negotiating Your Way from Confrontation to Cooperation* (New York: Bantam, 1993); for cross-cultural consultation see Raymond Cohen, *Negotiating Across Cultures* (Washington, DC: U.S. Institute of Peace Press, 2002).
18. 16 USC 470w(7).
19. However, see *National Mining Association v. Fowler*, 324 F.3d 752 (D.C. Cir. 2003).
20. For discussion, see, for example, Robert Meltz, *The Commerce Clause as a Limit on Congressional Power to Protect the Environment*, http://digital.library.unt.edu/govdocs/crs/permalink/meta-crs-969:1 (accessed January 10, 2008).
21. 36 CFR 800.3(a).
22. 324 F.3d 752 (D.C. Cir. 2003.
23. Since such activities are clearly under their "direct or indirect jurisdiction" (section 106) and are "carried out on behalf of the agency" (section 301(7)(A) and usually "with federal financial assistance" (section 301(7)(B).
24. See, for instance, King, "What Is Section 106 Review Anyway?" in *Thinking about Cultural Resource Management*.
25. See King, *Federal Planning and Historic Places*, 38–40.
26. 36 CFR 800.4(a); the word actually was first included in the 1999 draft regulations; see also 40 CFR 1501.7, 1508.25.
27. 36 CFR 800.4(a)
28. 36 CFR 800.16(b).
29. In some recent cases involving Native American concerns—for example at Mauna Kea in Hawai'i, Fence Lake Mine in New Mexico, and Crandon Mine in

Wisconsin—the quality of water within or underlying historically significant landscapes has been an issue.

30. 36 CFR 800.16(b): "in which the undertaking may directly or indirectly cause changes"; 36 CFR 800.5(a)(1): "Adverse effects may include reasonably foreseeable effects caused by the undertaking that may be later in time, be farther removed in distance, or be cumulative." CEQ (at 40 CFR 1508.7) defines cumulative effect or impact as "the impact on the environment which results from the incremental impact of the action (being reviewed) when added to other past, present, and reasonably foreseeable future actions regardless of what agency (Federal or non-Federal) or person undertakes such other actions."

31. Now mostly part of the Rural Utilities Service (RUS).

32. *El Rancho La Communidad v. United States*, No. 90–113 (D.N.M. May 21, 1991); see also Thomas F. King, *Places That Count: Traditional Cultural Properties in Cultural Resource Management* (Walnut Creek, CA: AltaMira Pres, 2003), 3–5, 136–37, 175, 281.

33. 36 CFR 800.4(b)(1); 800.4(b).

34. See National Park Service 1983; Standard 1: "Identification is done to the extent necessary to make a management decision."

35. King, *Places That Count.*

36. 36 CFR 800.4(a)(3) and references to oral history and interviews in 36 CFR 800.4(b)(1).

37. 50 F.3d 856 (10th Cir. 1995).

38. See King, *Places That Count*, for details about TCPs.

39. Thomas F, King and Patricia Parker, *Guidelines for Evaluating and Documenting Traditional Cultural Properties* (Washington, DC: National Park Service, 1990, rev. 1992 and 1998).

40. See King, "What's In a Name? The Case of 'Potentially Eligible' Historic Properties," *Thinking About Cultural Resource Management*, 65–69.

41. For consideration, see King, "An Uninspired Centerpiece: The National Register of Historic Places," *Thinking About Cultural Resource Management*, 19–25.

42. 36 CFR 800.4(c)(2).

43. 36 CFR 63, which astonishingly are still on the books, even though they are entirely inconsistent with 36 CFR 800.5(c). When the Advisory Council changed section 106 regulations in 1985–1986, NPS assured us that it would do away with 36 CFR 63 and replace it with regulatory language paralleling what we said in 36 CFR 800. NPS then got cold feet about opening regulations up for review during the Reagan administration and shelved the project. By the time a more sympathetic administration took over, there was a higher degree of tolerance for confusion at both NPS and the Advisory Council, and nothing has been done about the inconsistency between the regulations. 36 CFR 63 is generally honored in the breach today, but it does still exist. You can use it if you'd like to make some mischief and clog up the system by insisting that agencies comply with contradictory requirements.

44. The same facility has been the subject of further recent (as of 2007) litigation, with interesting results under the Religious Freedom Restoration Act; see *Navajo Nation et al. v. U.S. Forest Service et al.*, cited in chapter 7 notes.

45. Part of the National Park Service, "Secretary of the Interior's Standards and Guidelines for Archaeology and Historic Preservation," 48 *Federal Register* 44716–78: 1983.

46. The 450-page report has never been published, but a short summary is at http://sorrel.humboldt.edu/~jae1/emenLyngTR.html (accessed December 27, 2007).

47. 36 CFR 800.4(d)(1). The regulations also provide for the ACHP to object "if it has entered the section 106 process," but afford no way for it to have entered the process, which makes the provision a bit vacuous. At the same time, they require notifying all the other consulting parties but don't say that their objection triggers further review, so the point of the notification provision is unclear. I think these provisions are supposed to allow an aggrieved consulting party to object to the ACHP and get the ACHP to object on his or her behalf, but if that's the intent, the regulations are pretty obtuse about expressing it.

48. 36 CFR 800.4(d)(1); see also 800.16(i).

49. 36 CFR 800.5(a)(1).

50. 36 CFR 800.5(a)(1).

51. 36 CFR 68.

52. See Thomas F. King, "In the Eye of the Beholder: Visual Impacts and Section 106 Review," *Thinking About Cultural Resource Management*, 70–74.

53. 938 F. Supp. 908 (D.D.C. 1996).

54. But the army has transferred the property to NPS, which has entered into an arrangement with private interests to rehabilitate it and put it to productive use. See www.nationalparkseminary.com/ (accessed December 27, 2007).

55. This seems to imply that the tribe must go knocking at the agency's door to let their concerns be known, but remember that the agency was supposed to contact interested tribes when it initiated the process, and it should have been consulting with them throughout the identification and effect determination process.

56. 36 CFR 800.5(b), (c).

57. 36 CFR 800.5(c)(2).

58. 36 CFR 800.5(c)(3).

59. 36 CFR 800.5(b).

60. See chapter 15 in King, *Federal Planning and Historic Places*; the National Preservation Institute (www.npi.org) provides training and online assistance in writing CNAEs and other section 106 documents.

61. And hence not subject to visual, auditory, and other nonphysical effects.

62. Under the 1986 regulations this was permissible; the so-called research exception, thankfully, was struck from the 2004 version.

63. "Implementation of the undertaking *in accordance with the (NAE) finding as documented* fulfills the agency official's responsibilities under section 106 and this part. If the agency official will not conduct the undertaking as proposed in the finding, the agency official shall *reopen consultation*," 36 CFR 800.5d(1), emphasis added.

64. Regulations for the designation of NHLs are at 36 CFR 65; see www.access.gpo.gov/nara/cfr/waisidx_01/36cfr65_01.html (accessed December 27, 2007).

65. 36 CFR 800.6(a)(1).

66. 36 CFR 800.6(a)(3).

67. 36 CFR 800.6(a)(4).

68. 36 CFR 800.6(a)(2).

69. 36 CFR 800.6(a).

70. 40 CFR 1508.20.

71. For example Nicholas Dorochoff's *Negotiation Basics for Cultural Resource Managers* (Walnut Creek, CA: Left Coast Press, 2007). See also Raymond Cohen, *Negotiating Across Cultures* (Washington, DC: U.S. Institute for Peace Press, 2002); Cathy A. Constantino and Christina Sickles Merchant, *Designing Conflict Management Systems* (San Francisco: Jossey-Bass Publishers, 1995); Roger Fisher and Scott Brown, *Getting Together: Building Relationships as We Negotiate* (New York: Penguin Books, 1988); Roger Fisher and William Ury, *Getting to Yes* (New York: Penguin Books, 1981); Phyllis B. Kritek, *Negotiating at an Uneven Table* (San Francisco: Jossey-Bass Publishers, 1994); William Ury, *Getting Past No* (New York: Bantam Books, 1991). Training is offered at a number of institutions and through government and private-sector organizations. Sadly, it's unusual to find an SHPO or ACHP staff person with any training in the subject.

72. See www.acrnet.org/ (accessed December 27, 2007).

73. Particularly since I got training in how to do it—which I strongly recommend.

74. See Cohen, *Negotiating Across Cultures*.

75. Matthew S. Carroll et al., "Social Assessment for the Wenatchee National Forest Wildfires of 1994: Targeted Analysis for the Leavenworth, Entiat, and Chelan Ranger Districts," Gen. Tech. Rep. PNW-GTR-479. Portland, OR: U.S. Department of Agriculture, Forest Service, Pacific Northwest Research Station. See www.treesearch.fs.fed.us/pubs/2961 (accessed December 27, 2007).

76. Federal Advisory Committees Act (FACA), 5 U.S.C. App. 1.

77. I've discussed this art form in chapters 14 and 15 of *Federal Planning and Historic Places: The Section 106 Process* (Walnut Creek, CA: AltaMira Press, 2001).

78. 36 CFR 800.6(c)(1).

79. 36 CFR 800.6(c)(2).

80. 36 CFR 800.6(c)(8), as interpreted in the preamble to the *Federal Register* publication of the regulations in 2000.

81. 36 CFR 800.6(c)(3).

82. That is, where it has been a consulting party, unless it decides to drop out of the consultation. There's also a provision for the agency and council to sign an MOA over the SHPO's head (but not the THPO's) in the event of a disagreement (36 CFR 800.7(a)(2).

83. Specifically, 36 CFR 800.7.

84. 36 CFR 800.7(c).

85. And 36 CFR 800.7(c)(3).

86. And 36 CFR 800.7(c)(4).

87. 36 CFR 800.7(c)(4).

88. NPS 1988 110 guidelines.

89. NPS 1998 revised 110 guidelines.

90. 43 CFR 10.

91. Ronald Anzalone, "Remarks for 'Public Benefit of Mitigation'" (Annual Meeting of the National Conference of State Historic Preservation Officers, Washington DC, March 27, 1995).

92. 16 U.S.C. 470-1.

93. 36 CFR 800.8(a) and (b).

94. 36 CFR 800.13(a).

95. 43 CFR 10.

96. 36 CFR 800.13(b)(1).

97. ADPA, aka Archeological and Historic Preservation Act of 1974; see chapter 6.

98. 36 CFR 800.13(b)(2).

99. 36 CFR 800.13(b)(3).

100. 36 CFR 800.13(b).

101. 36 CFR 800.13(c).

102. 36 CFR 800.13(d).

103. 36 CFR 800.12(a).

104. 36 CFR 800.12(b)(1).

105. 36 CFR 800.12(b)(2).

106. 36 CFR 800.12(d).

107. 36 CFR 800.14(a), (c), (d)(e).

108. Army: see www.achp.gov/army.html#aap (accessed December 24, 2007); BLM: www.blm.gov/heritage/docum/finalPA.pdf (accessed December 24, 2007).

109. 36 CFR 800.14(b).

110. For "Programmatic Memorandum of Agreement"—prior to 1986.

111. It doesn't have to participate, however, in which case the PA is negotiated and executed by everyone else and filed with the council just like most MOAs are.

112. 36 CFR 800.14(b)(3)(d), second sentence.

113. Implicit in 36 CFR 800.14(b)(2)(v).

114. 36 CFR 800.14(b)(3), first sentence.

115. For assistance in drafting PAs and other section 106 documents, see chapters 14 and 15 of King, *Federal Planning and Historic Places*; also available at www.npi.org under "tools for cultural resource managers."

116. 16 U.S.C. 470h-2(k).

117. The regulations, at 36 CFR 800.9(c), provide for a remarkably limited sort of "consultation" with the council—the only place in the regulations where "consultation" is defined as just giving someone a period of time in which to comment. This seems to me to significantly undercut the utility of section 110(k).

118. Thomas F. King and Ethan Rafuse, *NEPA and the Cultural Environment: An Assessment of Effectiveness* (Washington, DC: CEHP for Council on Environmental Quality, 1994).

5

More About Historic Places

Section 106 isn't the only section of the National Historic Preservation Act (NHPA) with which cultural resource managers deal. Nor is NHPA the only historic preservation law. In this chapter we'll examine some other historic preservation authorities under which CRM practitioners practice, organized roughly by the types of properties and special situations to which they relate.

The International Context

In looking at the U.S. historic preservation authorities, it's useful to remind ourselves that they did not exactly spring, Athena-like, from the heads of their legislative and executive sponsors. Other nations have evolved similar approaches to historic preservation and developed a general consensus about what historic preservation should entail. For instance, in 1968—two years after the United States enacted NHPA—UNESCO issued *Recommendation Concerning the Preservation of Cultural Property Endangered by Public or Private Works*[1] essentially addressing the subject of NHPA section 106, though with somewhat broader scope. The recommendation calls for nations to conduct inventories of "cultural property," defined as both what in the United States we would call "historic properties" and movable items found within such properties. While predictably calling for listing ("scheduling") such places, it notes that "unscheduled" properties are embraced by its definition. It encourages nations to establish and impose preventive and corrective measures aimed at the impacts of urban expansion and renewal, "injudicious modification and repair," highways, dams, pipelines, transmission lines, farming, industry, and other development. Priority should be given to preserving cultural property in place, but where this isn't possible, data recovery or documentation is appropriate, as is relocating properties into new, accessible ensembles—something very much discouraged under NHPA. Surveys should be done well in advance of construction, as should preservation and recovery work. Construction should be delayed if needed to accommodate such work, which should be adequately funded either by government or as "part of the budget of construction costs"—an early articulation of the principle of "let the destroyer pay." Governments should establish administrative bodies to oversee surveys and preservation work, provide inducements to private parties through grants, loans, and tax relief, and should penalize violators. Especially important places should be acquired by government, and public education should be provided.

In 1976 UNESCO adopted its *Recommendation Concerning the Safeguarding and Contemporary Role of Historic Areas.*[2] "Historic areas" were defined to include "historic and architectural (including vernacular) areas," such as "groups of buildings, structures and open spaces including archaeological and paleontological sites, constituting human settlements in an urban or rural environment, the cohesion and value of which, from the archaeological, architectural, prehistoric, historic, aesthetic or sociocultural point of view are recognized"—presumably by some cognizant authority. The overall thrust of this recommendation is to encourage a sort of holistic planning and preservation; it urges that historic areas be considered in their totality, as coherent entities, and protected from fragmentation. Nations should recognize that such places are endangered by urbanization and by the standardization of building forms. The recommendation seems to look beyond project-by-project review à la section 106 of NHPA, to encourage principled national policies affecting planning. When it comes to specifics, however, it falls back on the usual mechanisms of scheduling, establishment of administrative authorities, and the application of technical expertise. Historic areas should be identified, studied, listed, and made the subjects of "safeguarding plans," which should be implemented as parts of urban and land-use planning.

With these international expectations in mind, let's look at how U.S. law deals with several particular kinds of historic properties and situations affecting them—starting with the most obvious such property type.

Taking Care of Historic Buildings and Structures

A *building*, in National Register parlance, is a construction designed to hold people or activities, a house, a barn, a courthouse, a grocery store, a church. A *structure* is designed for some other purpose—a tunnel, a mine shaft, a power plant, a fortification, a road, a bridge. Ships and aircraft are also classified as structures. These categories have permeable boundaries, of course; fortifications and power plants house activities. And the function of a construction can change through time; a power plant can be converted into offices, a silo can become a hotel. Specialists argue over whether something is a building or a structure, but only if they don't have much else to do.

What sets buildings and structures apart from other kinds of historic properties is that they are entirely (or mostly, as in the case of a structure built into a cave) human constructions. They exhibit design features that reflect their times and functions and the thought processes of those who designed and built them. Unlike many sites and districts, they are also clearly bounded; they have walls, floors, roofs. In many cases they are occupied, and can continue to be occupied or reoccupied, to meet contemporary needs. The things we do with and to buildings and structures reflect these characteristics. We document their design elements, and we try to preserve these elements while facilitating their continuing use or reuse.

One of the major tools used in facilitating continuing use and reuse is a set of standards issued by NPS on behalf of the secretary of the interior, often referred to simply as "the Secretary's Standards."

The Secretary of the Interior's Standards for the Treatment of Historic Properties

The secretary of the interior, through NPS, has long promoted standards for doing good things with historic buildings and structures. In 1992 these were gathered together into *The Secretary of the Interior's Standards for the Treatment of Historic Properties.*[3] The title is inaccurate; the standards are really for buildings and structures. The inaccuracy results from their authorship by NPS's architectural gurus, who have never really internalized the fact that a place can be a historic property without being a building or structure.

But the Standards, and the extensive guidelines that back them up, are helpful and generally commonsensical, if you just substitute "buildings and structures" for "properties" throughout.

The Standards address four kinds of treatment: preservation, rehabilitation, restoration, and reconstruction. An obvious fifth—demolition—is not entertained.

Preservation

"Preservation" means something different in the Standards than it does under NHPA. Section 301(8) of NHPA defines "preservation" to include everything from identification to documentation. It includes "rehabilitation" and "restoration," which the Standards *contrast* with "preservation." But let's not quibble. The Standards define preservation as "the act or process of applying measures necessary to sustain the existing form, integrity, and materials of an historic property."

Under the Standards, then, preservation means keeping the building or structure in its existing form, preserving its integrity, respecting its materials. It "focuses upon the ongoing maintenance and repair of historic materials and features."

There are eight Preservation Standards:

Standard 1: A property shall be used as it was historically, or given a new use that maximizes the retention of distinctive materials, features, spaces and spatial relationships.

We use a barn as a barn, or we can probably get away with using it as a farm museum, but if we want to convert it into office space, we probably can't call it preservation under the Standards. You *can* call it preservation under NHPA section 301(8). Practitioners seem able to live with this ambiguity.

Standard 2: The historic character of a property shall be retained and preserved. The replacement of intact or repairable historic materials or alteration of features, spaces, and spatial relationships that characterize a property shall be avoided.

Leave the place pretty much alone, although . . .

The limited and sensitive upgrading of mechanical, electrical, and plumbing systems and other code required work to make properties functional is appropriate within a preservation project.

So we can bring the place up to code and keep it there, as long as the work done is "limited" and "sensitive" to its historic fabric.

Standard 3: Each property shall be recognized as a physical record of its time, place, and use. Work needed . . . shall be physically and visually compatible, identifiable upon close inspection, and properly documented for future research.

This standard is tricky; it seems to say two contradictory things. Anything we do should be "physically and visually compatible" with existing fabric, but it should be "identifiable upon close inspection." So if we have to replace some deteriorated woodwork, it ought to look and feel just like the old woodwork, but close inspection by somebody who knows his or her stuff should reveal that it's not of the same vintage as the original. And the work should be documented so a future scholar doesn't have to rely entirely on her or his own senses.

Standard 4: Changes to a property that have acquired historic significance in their own right shall be retained and preserved.

The Jose V. Toledo Federal Building and U.S. Courthouse in Old San Juan, Puerto Rico, is—in part—a beautiful four-story Beaux Arts/Spanish revival-style building built in 1914 with a grand entrance facing the sea. In 1941 a rather ugly addition was built, wiping out the entrance and extending several more stories into the unclouded Caribbean sky. When the courthouse needed major rehabilitation in the 1990s, a proposal was floated to demolish the addition. There was violent and successful opposition to this proposal, because the addition—a visual landmark in Old San Juan, if a less than distinguished one—had acquired its own historical significance.

Standard 5: Distinctive materials, features, finishes, and construction techniques or examples of craftsmanship that characterize a property shall be preserved.

This standard is pretty obvious, but often takes a good deal of research to apply. We have to determine what the distinctive features, finishes, and construction techniques *are*, and they may not be obvious, particularly if the building has undergone a lot of changes over the years—changes which, themselves, may have achieved historic significance and therefore be things we shouldn't strip away willy-nilly.

Standard 6: The existing condition of historic features shall be evaluated to determine the appropriate level of intervention needed. Where the severity of deterioration requires repair or limited replacement of a distinctive feature, the new material shall match the old in composition, design, color, and texture.

In following this standard, of course, we have to make sure that people in the future don't mistake today's replacement for yesterday's original. If half our wall light sconces are deteriorated beyond repair, we're going to want to replace them, and we ought to copy the existing sconces—make them look essentially identical with the originals. But somehow we need to make sure that careful examination will distinguish the old from the new. Why? Architects will tell you that it's a matter of honesty.

Standard 7: Chemical or physical treatments . . . shall be undertaken using the gentlest means possible. Treatments that cause damage to historic materials shall not be used.

The second sentence of this standard may be a tall order. Arguably any treatment that alters a piece of architectural fabric causes some damage. But applied sensibly, this is a very important standard. No doubt you've seen those brick walls in your local brew pub, nice and clean and rough-surfaced. They've been sandblasted, which has removed the hard surface of the brick. They look fine now, but in a few years, or decades, or perhaps centuries, depending on what they're exposed to, they'll deteriorate and eventually the wall will fall down. Sandblasting—or blasting with pretty much anything—will also destroy surface details, such as sculptural elements. So you shouldn't do it, ever. Water and a soft-bristle brush are the recommended cleaning agents for most kinds of historic architecture; sometimes mild detergent is OK, and there are some acceptable chemical treatments, but (of course) it depends—on the material, the gunk we're trying to remove, the environmental conditions, and so on. One thing *doesn't* depend, however; there is—as far as I know—no circumstance under which sandblasting is OK.

Standard 8: Archeological resources shall be protected and preserved in place. If such resources must be disturbed, mitigation measures shall be undertaken.

This sop to archeology is found in each set of standards. Like a lot of the standards, it contains a mild internal contradiction. Are we to preserve and protect in place, or are we to mitigate? In real-world terms, what it means is that as we bring our preserved building or structure up to code and have to upgrade utilities or clean up landscaping, we ought to be careful about whatever's in the ground and plan for data recovery if we're likely to disturb something. That something may be associated with the building or structure itself—the remains of a demolished wing or bay, an old cistern, a privy pit—or something unrelated but important, like a prehistoric site or the buried ships that lie under waterfront commercial rows in New York and San Francisco.

It's worth noting—though unfortunately people usually don't—that the "archeological standard" should be applied to buildings themselves, not just to the ground underneath them. There's stuff in the walls of old buildings—newspapers, shoes, guns, body parts—that have historical value. Paintings, signs, and graffiti *on* the walls may be interesting, too, and there are closed-up rooms, cellars, and crawl spaces that may contain all kinds of treasures. These are just as much archeological resources as are those found in the ground.[4]

Rehabilitation

The *Standards for Rehabilitation* may be the most important of the lot. Rehab is:

> the act or process of making possible a compatible use for a property through repair, alterations, and additions while preserving those portions or features which convey its historical, cultural, or architectural values.

The idea behind NHPA and other historic preservation authorities is not to fossilize historic buildings and structures in their original conditions but to keep them alive, as parts of modern life. Living things have to change, and rehab is our means of making necessary changes while retaining the characteristics that make the place important.

The rehab standards are particularly important because developers have to meet them in order to qualify for certain investment credits on their federal income tax. "Tax Act" work generates a lot of rehabilitation, and each project must be reviewed by the SHPO, under NPS oversight, to make sure the rehab standards are met.

Rehab is not perfect preservation; something's always lost. But that's life. What rehab can do is keep a good old building standing and functional, serving a purpose. It can extend the life of the investment the building represents. Rehab permits "adaptive use"—that is, use for something other than the one for which it was originally intended—without completely sacrificing the characteristics that make it important.

There are ten rehab standards:

Standard 1: A property shall be used as it was historically or be given a new use that requires minimal change to its distinctive materials, features, spaces, and spatial relationships.

Similar to Preservation Standard 1, but more permissive of change. But what constitutes minimal change? How much change is too much? It depends, of course, and it often and perhaps inevitably depends on some highly subjective factors. Perhaps including the side of bed on which a reviewer arises in the morning, or how much he had to drink the night before. There are horror stories about SHPO and NPS reviewers of rehab projects getting terribly sticky about some things and being loose as a goose about others, with no apparent rationale for the difference. Some people seem to feel that, since architecture is an art, the reviewer of architectural issues should have a whole lot of artistic license in accepting or not accepting things based on gut feelings. Perhaps, but the reviewer or planner in a CRM context should remember that she or he is dealing directly or indirectly with the taxpayers' money, and it's to those taxpayers that we have to be responsible.

Standard 2: The historic character of a property shall be retained and preserved. The removal of distinctive materials or alteration of features, spaces, and spatial relationships that characterize a property shall be avoided.

This reads a lot like Preservation Standard 2, but it's subtly different. Where the preservation standard talks about avoiding replacement of *historic* materials, the rehab standard talks about avoiding removal of *distinctive* materials. This may seem like hairsplitting, but the difference between *all* historic materials and those that are distinctive can be considerable. Say we've got an old office building with a lot of woodwork, including some really nice woodwork in the public spaces and some pretty boring woodwork in the offices. All of it is historic, and if we're following the Preservation Standard we're going to need to respect it all. But if we're rehabilitating, we may decide that the woodwork in the public space is what's distinctive, and the garden variety woodwork elsewhere can go, or be substantially altered.

Standard 3: Each property shall be recognized as a physical record of its time, place, and use. Changes that create a false sense of historical development, such as adding conjectural features or elements from other historic properties, shall not be undertaken.

Here the contrast with the equivalent preservation standard is a bit starker. We're still recognizing the building or structure as a record of its time, place, and use, but rather than insisting on compatibility with, but distinctiveness from, existing fabric, we're simply saying "don't lie." Don't slap a false front on the old store to turn it into the Deadwood Saloon. Don't stick phony muntins between the panes of the double-glazed aluminum frame windows to make them look like they have old-timey multiple panes.

Standard 4: Changes to a property that have acquired historic significance in their own right shall be retained and preserved.

This one is precisely the same as its preservation equivalent and has to be interpreted in the same way.

Standard 5: Distinctive materials, features, finishes, and construction techniques or examples of craftsmanship that characterize a property shall be preserved.

This one, too, is identical with its preservation counterpart. In practice, though, it's often interpreted with more flexibility.

Standard 6: Deteriorated historic features shall be repaired rather than replaced. Where the severity of deterioration requires repair or limited replacement of a distinctive feature, the new material shall match the

old in composition, design, color, texture, and, where possible, materials.
Replacement of missing features shall be substantiated by documentary
and physical evidence.

Oddly, this standard actually seems more absolute than its preservation equivalent, which does not flatly prescribe repair rather than replacement. It's not meant to be, though. The important distinction is that the preservation standard demands rigorous evaluation to "determine the appropriate level of intervention needed," while the rehab standard simply says we ought to repair rather than replace. The research requirement is less strenuous. The fact that the Standards routinely say "thou shalt" or "thou shall not" when they mean "thou oughta" or "thou shouldn't" was pointed out to NPS when the Standards were rewritten in the late 1980s, and NPS acknowledged that they didn't mean precisely what they say. NPS wanted to speak firmly, and did, but in practice, a rule of reason applies. In the case of Standard 6, the need for reasonableness is indicated by the obvious contradiction between the first and second sentences. If we were always to repair rather than replace, there would be no need for matching new material with old. The actual rule is that we should repair rather than replace unless it's unreasonable to do so, whereupon we should make sure the replacement matches the original.

Note that Preservation Standard 6 says nothing about using matching material in replacement, but Rehabilitation Standard 6 does. This is probably because the NPS standard setters couldn't imagine the designer of a preservation project replacing, say, wood-frame windows with vinyl-clad, but they could well imagine it of a rehab project designer. Note, too, that the rehab standard says we match materials "where possible." While it's arguably almost always "possible" to replace something with the same material as the original—to replace "in kind"—this language is usually taken to mean "where feasible," considering factors like availability, cost, and effectiveness.

But such considerations need to be justified. It's too easy for a building manager who wants to improve energy efficiency to tumble for triple-glazed windows in aluminum frames, without exploring the costs and benefits of alternatives like interior storm windows. Often when these costs and benefits are accurately calculated, it turns out to be more cost-effective, and just as energy-effective, to repair and upgrade the existing windows.

Standard 7: Chemical or physical treatments . . . shall be undertaken using the gentlest means possible. Treatments that cause damage to historic materials shall not be used.

Same as the preservation standard, with the same rationale. It's not desirable to let the wall of a historic building get sandblasted and fall down, whether we intend to preserve the building or rehabilitate it.

Standard 8: Archeological resources shall be protected and preserved in place. If such resources must be disturbed, mitigation measures shall be undertaken.

Same as the preservation standard, same rationale, same implications.

Standard 9: New additions, exterior alterations, or related new construction shall not destroy historic materials, features, and spatial relationships that characterize the property. The new work shall be differentiated from the old and shall be compatible with the historic materials, features, size, scale and proportion, and massing to protect the integrity of the property and its environment.

This one is unique to the Rehab Standards, for obvious reasons. One does not do new construction as part of a preservation project as defined in the Standards (though, of course, one could do so on a preservation project as defined in NHPA).

This standard prescribes a narrow path to walk in designing a new-construction component of a rehab project—a new wing on a building, or a new building in a complex of old ones. On the one hand the architect is to "differentiate" the new work from the old; on the other he or she is to make sure the two are "compatible" in terms of "materials, features, size, scale and proportion, and massing." It's a path with very subjective boundaries; architects can argue endlessly about whether a given project has achieved a good result.

Suppose we're dealing with a Victorian ironfront commercial building, and we need to provide access for the disabled. Suppose the only economically feasible way to do this without really mucking up the building is by adding an outside elevator shaft. What do we make this shaft look like?

The Standard indicates that we don't make it look like a little skinny Victorian ironfront standing next to the original; I think most people would agree that this would look pretty stupid. But suppose we can kind of tuck it in against a wall of the building and extend a facade a little to disguise it? The Standard discourages this, too, because we're not "differentiating" the new from the old. But reasonable people might ask who cares, if the relationship between the old and the new is a visually pleasing one. The answer an architect may give—if someone has the temerity to ask—is that disguising the new to look like part of the old is not honest and that it may confuse people in the future. Take that for what it's worth.

Some architects lean so strongly toward differentiating between the old and the new that they'd build a plain concrete box to house the elevator, or maybe something in anodized aluminum. The Standard discourages this, too, because this solution isn't "compatible with the historic materials, features, size, scale and proportion, and massing to protect the integrity of the property and its environment."

What the Standard encourages is something that tends to be pretty pleasing when you see it—a new building or wing that doesn't pretend to be old, but echoes the existing building in interesting, subtle ways. The color's similar, though probably not identical. If the original is made of brick, so is the new, or perhaps it's not but it doesn't contrast shriekingly with the brick. Windows are in line with those in the original and of about the same scale. It's not grossly out of proportion with the original. One of the things that makes such a solution pleasing to the eye, I think, is that it obviously takes intelligence to design, and it requires a certain amount of intelligence to interpret and appreciate. It adds something more than just an elevator shaft to the built environment. Anybody can copy something, and anybody can build something that doesn't respect its surroundings. Designing something that isn't a copy but does respect what's around it requires some thinking, and it's pleasant to experience the result of such thinking. So in some ways, the best thing about this Standard is not what it says, per se, but that it encourages thoughtful design that enriches the visual environment. And it also encourages some wonderful arguments among architects.

Standard 10: New additions and adjacent or related new construction shall be undertaken in such a manner that, if removed in the future, the essential form and integrity of the historic property and its environment would be unimpaired.

This standard, also unique to the Rehab Standards, is straight-forward. We ought to build our addition so that if and when it's taken down, the original building or structure is still there, without big holes in it.

There's an example of this at the Old Post Office in Washington, D.C., where the ACHP has its offices. A glass passage has been added connecting commercial spaces on the lower floors with an adjacent commercial area. The passage links to the old building through a window and just sort of snuggles up against the wall around the opening. If it's ever taken down, the sashes can be re-hung in the window opening, and no one will be able to tell that the glass connector was ever there. Of course, if this doesn't happen until the connector has achieved historical significance in its own right there will be other problems to confront.

Restoration

Restoration is:

the act or process of accurately depicting the form, features, and character of a property as it appeared at a particular period of time by means of the removal of features from other periods in its history and reconstruction of missing features from the restoration period.

Had GSA taken down that 1941 addition to the Old San Juan Courthouse and rebuilt the grand entrance, this would have been restoration.

Restoration Standards 1, 2, 3, 5, and 6 are virtually the same as their equivalent Preservation Standards, except that they focus on the period to which the property is restored rather than to all pertinent historic periods. Restoration Standard 8 is the same as Preservation Standard 7 (Use gentle methods.), and Restoration Standard 9 is the same as Preservation Standard 8 (Be nice to archeology.). Restoration Standard 4, rather than requiring preservation of changes to the property that have acquired historic significance, says to document them.

Restoration Standards 7 and 10 are peculiar to restoration. Standard 7 requires documentary or physical evidence to support replacement of missing features from the restoration period and prohibits the creation of:

> a false sense of history . . . by adding conjectural features, features from other properties, or by combining features that never existed together historically.

Standard 10 points in the same direction, elegantly stating that "Designs that were never executed historically shall not be constructed."

Both standards discourage speculation and frivolity, and promote honesty. If we don't know and can't prove that the McDuck Bank Building had twelve-over-twelve windows in its heyday, we don't make it so when we restore it—or if we do, because we've got to put something in the window openings, we don't represent them as what used to be there. If the bank never had a money bin, we don't build one to match Walt Disney's vision.

Reconstruction

Reconstruction, according to the Standards, is:

> the act or process of depicting, by means of new construction, the form, features, and detailing of a non-surviving site, landscape, building, structure, or object for the purpose of replicating its appearance at a specific period of time and in its historic location.

Most of the Reconstruction Standards have no counterparts among the Preservation, Rehabilitation, and Restoration Standards. Reconstruction is rarely enough done that we won't devote much space to discussing its standards, but in brief:

Standard 1: Reconstruction shall be used . . . when documentary and physical evidence is available to permit accurate reconstruction with min-

imal conjecture, and such reconstruction is essential to the public under-standing of the property.

We don't reconstruct unless we need to and can do it accurately.

Standard 2: Reconstruction . . . shall be preceded by a thorough archeological investigation.

Archeology should be used to get physical evidence of what the property was like, and archeological sites—including those related to the thing being reconstructed, and other sites (e.g., a prehistoric site underlying Fort Benedict Arnold)—shouldn't be unnecessarily mucked up. One thing that is sometimes forgotten is that for archeology to be helpful in planning reconstruction it has to be done well in advance of design. Too often designs are developed based on conjecture, and then archeology is done only to "salvage" data that implementing the design will destroy.

Standard 3: Reconstruction shall include measures to preserve any remaining historic materials, features, and spatial relationships.

This really isn't much different from Standard 2. If there is anything original there—in the ground or elsewhere—it should be preserved.

Standard 4: Reconstruction shall be based on . . . accurate duplication . . . rather than on conjectural design or the availability of different features from other historic properties.

If we can't prove that Fort Benedict Arnold's walls were seventeen feet high and made of redwood logs, we don't build them to that height, of that material, or if we do (because we have to build them to some height, out of something), we explain that we really don't know quite how high they were or what they were made of. And we don't haul in old buildings from Fort Aaron Burr to add to Arnold's ambience.

Standard 5: A reconstruction shall be clearly identified as a contemporary re-creation.

Put up a sign. Don't fool the public.

Standard 6: Designs that were never executed historically shall not be constructed.

If Fort Benedict Arnold didn't have a tower from which the troops could watch for attacking Indians, we don't add one because we saw a fort on TV that had one and it really looked neat.

The Standards and the Laws

Some architects follow the Standards simply because they're good advice for historic buildings and, for that matter, in general. But for the most part, the Standards are employed in order to comply with one of several legal authorities.

The Tax Code[5]

If you own the McDuck Bank Building and preserve it as an operating bank, rehab it as a bed and breakfast, or restore it as a museum of banking, you can take a preservation credit on your federal income tax, *if* you can show the Internal Revenue Service that your work meets the relevant Secretary's Standards. You show this by getting your project reviewed and approved by the SHPO, with the blessing of NPS. Many historical architects make their living designing or consulting on the design of tax code–supported rehab projects, and others spend their lives reviewing such designs on behalf of SHPOs or NPS.[6]

Section 106

If we want to use a federal grant to rehab the McDuck Bank Building, and if we want a determination of "no adverse effect" on that grant under section 106 we're going to have to meet the Secretary's Standards.

You may be told that architectural work done under a section 106 memorandum of agreement (MOA) must meet the Secretary's Standards, but this is a myth. It's nice to meet the Standards, but it's not necessary. An MOA prescribes measures to mitigate a project's adverse effects. There's no requirement that the measures we choose be consistent with any particular standards, as long as they're not illegal.

Example: A low-income housing provider who was part of a development project at a closed military base believed he had been burned on an earlier by-cost overrun resulting from Tax Act review. He refused to participate in the new project if its MOA required that the Standards be followed. Rather than lose his participation, we executed an MOA stipulating use of the Standards as *guidance*, without being strictly bound by them. Whether you like this solution or not, it was legal.

Technical note: If you refer to the Secretary's Standards in a section 106 document—or any document that you expect people to follow—don't refer to them simply as "the Secretary's Standards." There are a lot of Secretary's Standards—for archeology and historic preservation, for the documentation of historic watercraft, and, who knows, probably for the classification of infirm raptors. Give a complete citation, such as *The Secretary of the Interior's Standards for Restoration, National Park Service 1992*. Remember the "cold reader," and don't assume that he or she will know which Standards you're referring to.

Federal Agencies in Urban Historic Districts

NHPA was enacted in substantial part because of rampant demolition in the nation's urban centers, occasioned by the generally misguided assumptions of urban renewal. Discouraging federal agencies from knocking down the center cities didn't stop people and capital from fleeing to the suburbs, however, and it soon became apparent that the government ought to do something to stabilize and stimulate the nation's central business areas (CBAs). Since many CBAs contain lots of historic buildings, often comprising historic districts, and since clearly, the best way to preserve such properties is to keep them in active use, interests in CBA stabilization and historic preservation have often coincided.

The Public Buildings Cooperative Use Act and Executive Order 12072

Back in 1976, the Public Buildings Cooperative Use Act (PBCUA)[7] was enacted, including a requirement that the General Services Administration (GSA) give preference to using historic buildings to fill federal space needs. The idea was to fight agency flight to the suburbs, filling federal space requirements via the rehabilitation of historic buildings, as a way to leverage downtown economic development. In 1978, with similar motivations, President Jimmy Carter issued Executive Order 12072,[8] directing GSA to give preference to sitting federal offices in CBAs. Although historic preservation wasn't central to this order, its intent was much the same as the PBCUA—use the federal workforce to stimulate downtown economic development.

Under the PBCUA, GSA gave a 10 percent preference to historic buildings when it leased space to fill agency needs. In other words, if I offer a nonhistoric building for $100 and you offer one for $109, all else being equal, you win.

Section 110(a)(1) of NHPA

Historic preservationists were dissatisfied with GSA's vigor in pursuing its PBCUA responsibilities, so the 1980 amendments to the NHPA included section 110(a)(1),[9] which as amended in 1992 says that:

> Prior to acquiring, constructing, or leasing buildings for purposes of carrying out agency responsibilities, each Federal agency shall use, to the maximum extent feasible, historic properties available to the agency.

Section 110(a)(1) was pretty directive. If it was "feasible"—that is, practical, economically sensible, and consistent with the agency's mission and mandates—any federal agency was *required* to give preference to historic properties. But agencies ignored Section 110(a)(1).

Executive Order 13006[10]

One might think that preservationists would have lobbied and litigated to get agencies to change their ways, but instead, the National Trust and others pushed for another executive order. Executive Order 13006, issued in 1996, directed all agencies to give preferential consideration to the use of historic buildings in historic districts in central business areas. If such buildings couldn't be found that suited the government, then they were to build compatible new buildings in historic districts. If that didn't work, they were to use historic buildings outside historic districts.

Section 110(a)(1) Again

Agencies didn't exactly fall over themselves to find historic space in response to executive order 13006; it just may be that its complicated hierarchy of preferences discouraged compliance. So the National Trust and its allies went back to Congress and got section 110(a)(1) of NHPA amended to read:

> Prior to acquiring, constructing, or leasing buildings for purposes of carrying out agency responsibilities, each Federal agency shall use, to the maximum extent feasible, historic properties available to the agency in accordance with Executive Order No. 13006, issued May 21, 1996 (61 Fed. Reg. 26071).[11]

So we have two statutes and two executive orders (one of the former incorporating one of the latter by reference) that collectively drive the federal government toward using historic buildings in historic districts in central business areas to fill their needs for offices and other spaces. Although the primary impact of all these requirements is on GSA, they affect other agencies as well, either directly when an agency does its own real estate transactions, or through GSA when GSA serves as an agency's real estate agent.

Altogether, these laws and executive orders give historic preservationists a powerful set of tools to use in promoting the reuse of urban historic buildings and historic districts. Enthusiasm should be tempered with an appreciation for a couple of realities, however.

First, the government isn't required to use historic buildings if they don't serve an agency's program needs. If the agency's employees won't fit in the building or if its use would greatly inconvenience the public or if the agency does things (e.g., some kinds of laboratory work) that are incompatible with the historic building or the neighborhood, the government doesn't have to play.

Second, it's generally up to the agency to define what its program needs are, and some agencies and their employees don't want to be in old buildings, or downtown. Some people prefer nice new buildings in the suburbs, with lots of parking space. So some agencies represent their program needs in ways that make it hard to be satisfied with historic facilities in central business areas. Where GSA is the government's agent and has the will (by no means a universal condition), it can try to jawbone its client into flexing its requirements, but if the client then wants to jettison GSA and go to a commercial agent, it can do so. The agency itself is then subject to most of the same legal requirements that constrain GSA, but it may be willing to take its chances.

Third, there are other legal requirements that more or less directly conflict with the historic or downtown requirements. The Rural Development Act of 1972[12] directs agencies to give preference to *rural* areas. Executive Order 11988—another Carter-era executive order—directs that agencies not contribute to development of floodplains. There are extensive guidelines, issued originally by the now-defunct Water Resources Council and now implemented under the oversight of the Federal Emergency Management Agency (FEMA), that prescribe a rather complicated eight-step review process for any federal project that might contribute directly or indirectly to floodplain development.[13] Although not technically regulations,[14] the guidelines are cast in directive language, and agencies follow them with some rigor. Historic center cities, of course, are often in floodplains, and FEMA—understandably, given the serious environmental, social, health, safety, and economic implications of floodplain development—can be something of a junkyard dog hounding agencies about compliance. As a result, Executive Order 11988 constrains how responsive agencies can be to Executive Order 13006 and its cohort of related authorities.

What most cultural resource managers need to know about the PBCUA, section 110(a)(1), and Executive Orders 12074 and 13006 is that they exist, that they generally promote the use of downtown historic buildings in historic districts by federal agencies, and that some agencies avoid vigorous compliance with them, for good reasons and bad. If you find yourself involved in a real estate transaction by a federal agency, you need to know about these provisions.

Parenthetically, these four laws and executive orders, together with the Rural Development Act and Executive Order 11988, also exemplify a federal government tendency that makes it increasingly difficult to do anything about anything. With the best of intent, Congress enacts laws, and presidents issue executive orders, that are inconsistent with one another and even work at cross purposes. Laws are seldom repealed, executive orders are seldom withdrawn. Instead, new laws are passed and orders issued, with neither Congress nor presidents bothering to define their relationships with those that went before. Federal agencies can spend a lot of time and effort trying to resolve the contradictions that result, instead of actually getting anything done. It's easy to "blame the bureaucrats" for this, but it's not the bureaucrats' fault; it's the nature of the beast with which bureaucrats struggle every day.

Adaptive Use

Adaptive use is simply using a building designed for one purpose to serve another. Converting the warehouse to office space, the grain silo to a hotel, the old house to a restaurant, the church to an arts center, the lighthouse to a bed-and-breakfast, the fire lookout to a campsite, the mill to a mall.[15] Adaptive use is usually what's in store for a rehabilitated building, whether the rehab is done without any federal involvement at all, or supported by federal tax credits, or the work of a federal agency. In the case of federally controlled buildings and structures, if an agency can't use a historic property for its original purpose, then section 111 of NHPA[16] requires that it pursue "alternative uses," including adaptive use.

Adaptive use by federal agencies often requires partnerships with others and mechanisms like outleasing, cooperative agreements, and comanagement. Section 111 adaptive use arrangements have to be worked out in consultation with the ACHP and are subject to section 106 review. The *Secretary of the Interior's Standards for Rehabilitation* are usually applied to maintain the architectural integrity of the buildings and structures that are usually involved, though section 111 itself doesn't explicitly require that such integrity be preserved.

Historic Building Preservation Plans

Agencies that manage historic buildings and structures, like the General Services Administration (GSA), NPS, and the military services, often develop plans for such management. NPS pioneered the former kind of plan with what it calls a "historic structures report" (HSR); the HSR model was picked up by GSA and other agencies and adapted to their needs.

"Historic structures report" doesn't exactly make one think instantly of a plan, and that's not surprising because HSRs didn't start out to be plans. An HSR was a description and evaluation of a building or structure, used as the basis for figuring out how to manage it. But this involved defining the building's significant characteristics, and it was a natural step to link those characteristics with prescribed treatments.

Because HSRs started out being largely descriptive and evaluative, they involve a lot of upfront research and, hence, a lot of investment before you get a product that can actually be used. Dissatisfaction with the high up-front costs of the HSR led GSA, with the Georgia Institute of Technology, to develop the Historic Building Preservation Plan (HBPP). Doing an HBPP involves a relatively quick and dirty descriptive and evaluative study that leads to breaking the building up into zones designated for various kinds of treatment. A "preservation zone" should be maintained intact, a "rehabilitation zone" can be rehabilitated. In a "free zone" one can have one's way with the space. Within each zone, elements like wall lights, elevator doors, and woodwork are identified and assigned treatment ratings based on significance and condition. The zones and elements are linked to standards, grounded in the Secretary's Standards. Certain zones and elements are to be preserved, others restored, others rehabbed, while others can be blown away.[17]

Other agencies have similar kinds of plans. The Corps of Engineers, for example has guidelines for "proactive maintenance plans" (PMP) for historic buildings and structures,[18] and all military bases are supposed to have "integrated cultural resource management plans" (ICRMPs) that include (among many other things) ways of managing historic buildings and structures.[19]

A plan for a historic building or structure can rationalize the use of standards like those of the Secretary, to avoid giving things more attention than they deserve while highlighting those parts of the structure that really need care. A good plan can be used to simplify compliance with section 106 if it's made the basis for a programmatic agreement (PA) or other program alternative that substitutes its implementation for standard section 106 review. There have been problems with linkages between plans and section 106 compliance, however. Ideally, if a manager is following his or her plan, he or she ought to be in compliance with section 106, but this can be the case only if the plan has been reviewed in accordance with section 106 regulations. Agencies and others sometimes develop plans but never bother to take them through section 106 review; this leaves the hapless building manager with both his plan and standard section 106 review to deal with, independent of one another. This isn't the kind of thing that's easy for a building manager to deal with, along with the zillion other day-to-day problems he or she has to juggle.[20]

Recordation

When a building or structure can't realistically be kept in continuing use, or adapted for a new use, there's nothing in federal law to keep an agency from demolishing it or letting it fall down, *provided* it complies with two sets of requirements. The agency obviously has to consider effects under NEPA, as well as section 106, and other sections of NHPA that may apply (e.g., sections 110(a)(1) and 111). This, of course, may lead to a decision that keeps the building standing. If the decision is to demolish, though, then the second legal requirement kicks in: recordation under section 110(b) of NHPA.[21] Section 110(b) requires each agency to:

> assure that where, as a result of Federal action or assistance carried out by such agency, an historic property is to be substantially altered or demolished, timely steps are taken to make or have made appropriate records.

There's a myth that recordation is the only requirement there is—that, for instance, it's all we have to consider doing under section 106. This is resoundingly not so. Alternatives to keep a building standing and in active use have to be considered if an agency is to be consistent with the purposes of NHPA as required by its section 110(d). Recordation is what we do as a fallback, when other alternatives have failed or as a supplement to more active preservation measures. When we do it under section 106, the consulting parties decide what kind of recordation it will be and where the results will be filed.

The granddaddy of recordation programs in the United States is the Historic American Buildings Survey (HABS). HABS is one of the only—perhaps the only—remaining holdover in government from the "make work" programs of Franklin Roosevelt's administration, that helped pull the United States out of the Great Depression. HABS put out-of-work architects to work documenting historic buildings, preparing detailed drawings and filing them in a special collection at the Library of Congress.[22] When the Historic Sites Act was passed in 1935, it gave NPS the authority to continue HABS indefinitely, and it did.

In the late 1960s and early 1970s, HABS got involved in recording engineering features, facilities, structures, and even processes. This required specialized skills and techniques, so eventually it became the focus of its own program—the Historic American Engineering Record (HAER).

HABS/HAER has definite recordation standards,[23] though these are not monolithic. There are very rigorous standards and not so rigorous standards, which can be applied depending on the perceived significance of the building, structure, or other facility. The HABS/HAER staff at NPS advises agencies about which standards to use and how to interpret them. HABS/HAER also does its own recordation work, in cooperation with various academic institutions.

Recordation to HABS/HAER standards and filing the results with the Library of Congress is one way to document a building or structure, but it's not the only way. SHPOs, Indian tribes, local governments, statewide organizations, and other groups have their own standards and procedures. Many section 106 MOAs spell out alternative recordation standards, though many others provide for the responsible agency to contact HABS/HAER and do as they're told.

In 2000 (luckily not 2001), HABS/HAER spawned a third acronymous recordation program, HALS for Historic American Landscapes Survey.[24] HALS, as its name suggests, has landscapes as its focus. HALS is mostly concerned with designed landscapes—parks, gardens, campuses, parkways, and the like that are formally planned and designed, usually by landscape architects. It also attends to what are usually called "cultural" landscapes or "rural historic" landscapes—landscapes that reflect human activities like farming in some more or less unplanned way.[25] Still more recently, HABS, HAER, and HALS have been joined by the less sonorous CRGIS—Cultural Resources Geographic Information System—which promotes GIS in the national parks and SHPO offices. The members of the whole HABS/HAER/HALS/CRGIS quartet are referred to by NPS, with a grand unconcern for other aspects of cultural heritage, as the "Heritage Documentation Programs."[26]

General Historic Preservation Planning

If you're responsible for managing a largish chunk of land—a military base, a national park, a wildlife refuge—and you have to comply with NHPA or just want to do right by historic properties, it's wise to develop some kind of general plan. You're probably doing, or other people are doing, a number of recurrent things on the land—training troops, handling visitors, managing wildlife habitat—that have fairly predictable effects on fairly predictable types of cultural resources. If you can formalize your predictions and prescribe more or less standard ways to manage those effects and resources, this is usually an efficient thing to do. That's what a plan is for—or should be for.

Historic preservation plans (HPPs) became popular with federal agencies, SHPOs, and some local governments in the 1980s. Such plans go under a variety of names—besides HPPs, they may be called cultural resource management plans (CRMPs), historic resource management plans (HRMPs), and, in the Department of Defense, integrated cultural resource management plans (ICRMP).[27] Whatever they're called, they almost invariably deal only with the management of impacts on historic properties as defined in NHPA—districts, sites, buildings, structures, and objects included in or eligible for the National Register. Sometimes they focus even more narrowly on archeological sites. Sometimes they include sections on things like tribal consultation and NAGPRA implementation, but for the most part they're overwhelmingly about taking care of historic places. Large-area plans like those for military training areas and wildlife refuges tend to be rather heavily archeological in orientation. Plans of this type often are embedded in, or include, geographic information systems (GIS).

Land management agencies often have statutory direction to develop and implement plans for management of their lands and resources. The Bureau of Land Management has the Federal Land Policy and Management Act (FLPMA),[28] for example, and the Forest Service has the National Forest Management Act (NFMA).[29] These laws sometimes contain more or less specific direction about aspects of CRM, and the management plans they foster can provide good contexts for historic preservation planning.

NHPA also has provisions that apply most readily to property managing agencies, notably in several subsections of its section 110. NPS has provided some rather widely ignored guidance about how to carry these provisions out, in *the Section 110 Standards and Guidelines*—or to be more precise, the *Secretary of the Interior's Standards and Guidelines for Federal Agency Historic Preservation Programs Pursuant to the National Historic Preservation Act*.[30] Further direction is provided in Executive Order 13287,[31] one of George W. Bush's contributions to the corpus of cultural resource legal authorities.

NHPA Section 110(a)(2)

Under section 110(a)(2) of NHPA, each agency is responsible for having a program that ensures, among other things:

- that historic properties under the jurisdiction or control of the agency are identified, evaluated, and nominated to the National Register; [and]
- that such properties under the jurisdiction or control of the agency . . . are managed and maintained in a way that considers the preservation of their . . . values in compliance with section 106.[32]

Although technically these provisions apply to all agencies, only agencies with historic properties under their jurisdiction or control (i.e., agencies that administer land and structures) can carry them out. So land management agencies have ongoing responsibilities to identify and manage historic properties. A few things need to be noted about these responsibilities.

Identification and Evaluation

Identification and evaluation under section 110(a)(2) can be more leisurely, long-term, and multiphased than they can under section 106. Without an impending project driving the schedule, an agency doesn't need to complete historic property identification on a particular timetable. As a result, identification work under section 110(a)(2) tends to be given low priority for funding, and cultural resource managers just have to get used to that. It's a good idea to work up plans for identification projects and have them on hand in case your agency needs to use up leftover money at the end of the fiscal year.

If you're a contractor, you may be puzzled by why a client offers you a scope of work for a section 110(a)(2) survey that's different from the one you'd have for a section 106 survey. You may be charged only with identifying historic buildings, or only landscapes, only archeology, or only traditional cultural properties. Or you may be assigned to do only background research or sample fieldwork. The reason for this is that the agency isn't trying to be comprehensive; it's moving along, identifying the kinds of places it thinks have the highest priority, with years and years ahead of it to identify the rest, and little enough money to do it with. Although the *Section 110 Standards and Guidelines* say that all kinds of properties should be identified, they also note that:

> The level of identification needed can vary depending on the nature of the property or property type, the nature of the agency's management authority, and the nature of the agency's possible effects on the property.[33]

National Register Nominations

Every agency's program has to provide for nomination to the National Register, but there's no requirement that everything be nominated, or that nomination proceed on a particular timetable. In the 1992 amendments to NHPA, Congress removed a requirement that agencies nominate everything under their jurisdiction or control— recognizing that agencies have other ways to keep track of historic properties without going to the expense and trouble of nominating them. A wise agency nominates things when it serves some purpose, and otherwise, it doesn't bother. Reflecting NPS's pro-nomination bias, the *Section 110 Standards and Guidelines* go into detail about the circumstances under which nomination may be a good idea.[34]

Management and Maintenance

How an agency manages and maintains historic properties depends on the properties and what's happening to them. It may be routine maintenance of old buildings, stabilization of archeological sites, giving assistance to an Indian tribe to manage the plant and animal resources of a gathering area—a wide range of possibilities. The allusion in section 110(a)(2) to section 106 reminds us that neglecting management and maintenance is an adverse effect under section 106 regulations, that management and maintenance activities can mitigate impacts, and that even such activities, benign as they may seem, require review under section 106. The *Section 110 Standards and Guidelines* provide a lot of advice about approaches to management and maintenance.[35] One of the more interesting recommendations relates to "demolition by neglect"—failing to maintain historic properties so that they fall down, erode away, or otherwise deteriorate:

> Where it is not feasible to maintain a historic property, or to rehabilitate it for contemporary use, the agency may elect to modify it in ways that are inconsistent with the Secretary's "Standards for Rehabilitation," allow it to deteriorate, or demolish it. However, the decision to act or not act to preserve and maintain historic properties should be an explicit one, reached following appropriate consultation within the section 106 review process and in relation to other management needs.[36]

In other words—and I think this is an important thing for agency managers to understand—it's OK to let a historic property go, or to take it down, provided there's good justification and alternatives have been duly considered, in consultation with all the appropriate parties under section 106.

Consultation

Section 110(a)(2) emphasizes consultation with others in designing and conducting agency preservation programs. Section

110(a)(2)(D) requires that each agency's "preservation-related activities"

> are carried out in consultation with other Federal, state, and local agencies, Indian tribes, Native Hawaiian organizations carrying out historic preservation planning activities, and with the private sector.

And section 110(a)(2)(E) requires each agency to have procedures for complying with section 106 that feature

> consultation with State Historic Preservation Officers, local governments, Indian tribes, Native Hawaiian organizations, and the interested public, as appropriate.

That "as appropriate" can be used mischievously, but still, the intent is clear. Agencies are to carry out their preservation work—including their identification, evaluation, management activities, and section 106 review—in consultation with everyone who's interested.

The *Section 110 Standards and Guidelines*, elaborating on section 110 consultation requirements, echo the definition of consultation found in the section 106 regulations and go on to say (among much else) that:

> Whether consulting on a specific project or on broader agency programs, the agency should:
>
> 1. make its interests and constraints clear at the beginning;
> 2. make clear any rules, processes, or schedules applicable to the consultation;
> 3. acknowledge others' interests and seek to understand them;
> 4. develop and consider a full range of options; and
> 5. try to identify solutions that will leave all parties satisfied.[37]

Executive Order 13287

The major problem with section 110(a)(2)—and other parts of section 110, but it's most obvious with 110(a)(2)—is that it contains no action-forcing mechanism. It doesn't have to be complied with "prior to" anything, as section 106 does, and there's no one with rulemaking authority over its implementation. Executive Order 13287, issued in 2003 with the title "Preserve America," reads as though it might do something about that.

The executive order begins with a statement of policy favoring preservation and, usefully, "contemporary use" of historic properties. It stresses the importance of "partnerships with State and local governments, Indian tribes, and the private sector." It goes on to direct that:

> Each agency shall examine its policies, procedures, public-private initiatives and investment in the use, reuse, and rehabilitation of historic properties.[38]

It also directs each agency to

> prepare an assessment of the current status of its inventory of historic properties required by section 110(a)(2) of the NHPA . . . , the general condition and management needs of such properties, and the steps underway or planned to meet those management needs . . . [including] . . . an evaluation of the suitability of the agency's types of historic properties to contribute to community economic development initiatives, including heritage tourism.[39]

Never mind that section 110(a)(2) doesn't require an inventory, the important thing is that this executive order appears to require agencies to do something specific about their section 110 responsibilities. The executive order further requires that each agency report the results of its assessment to the ACHP and NPS by September 30, 2004.[40] In preparing its 2004 report, each agency with real property management responsibilities was to

> review its regulations, management policies, and operating procedures for compliance with sections 110 and 111 of the NHPA . . . and make the results of its review available to the Council and the Secretary.[41]

And each such agency, by September 30, 2005, is to "prepare a report on its progress in identifying, protecting, and using historic properties in its ownership."[42]

Reports were to be submitted to the ACHP and the secretary of the interior (i.e., NPS), who were given coordinative and further reporting responsibilities. Each agency was also required to designate a senior policy level official to oversee the agency's preservation program.[43]

There is much more to the executive order, but the important parts, I think, are its direction to agencies to think about their section 110 responsibilities and the way it puts the ACHP and NPS in a position to nag at them if they don't. Thirty-five agencies submitted their initial reports, and the ACHP and NPS duly examined them and prepared a mildly critical summary and analysis.[44] Whether this will really make any difference, and whether over the long run the ACHP and NPS will carry out their authorities with vision and responsibility, remains to be seen.

Executive Order 11593[45]

Speaking of executive orders, EO 11593 is something of an anachronism today, but it was very important when President Nixon issued it in 1972.

As you may recall from chapter 1, when NHPA was enacted in 1966, section 106 required agencies to consider the effects of their actions only on properties *included in* the National Register. Naturally, the response by agencies was to keep places from being nominated to the Register, project opponents nominated properties right and left. Executive Order 11593 addressed this conflict by directing agencies to survey their lands to find and nominate historic places to the National Register. More important, until everything was nominated, the executive order directed NPS to issue guidelines for determining the eligibility of properties for the Register. Agencies were then to determine the eligibility of unevaluated properties as part of their section 106 work. If a property was eligible, it was to be treated as though it were on the Register. These provisions were eventually incorporated into NHPA itself, and into section 106 regulations, so the executive order itself is no longer very relevant today. It occasionally crops up as a rationale for insisting that agencies nominate everything they own to the National Register, or as a basis for insisting on surveys to identify all eligible properties, but the argument for such continued applicability is rather thin, I think.

The executive order directed agencies to complete their surveys and nominate everything to the Register by 1974. Nobody made it (it was rumored that the Tea Tasting Commission did, which may or may not be true). Does this leave agencies with a continuing responsibility to identify all historic properties and nominate them to the Register? If so, why did Congress in 1980 incorporate the "nominate all properties" requirement into section 110(a)(2) of NHPA and then remove it in the 1992 amendments? I don't think the executive order means much today, but it still exists, people sometimes cite it, and for historical reasons if for no other, it's good to know that it exists.

State and Local Plans

SHPOs also do plans, called State Historic Preservation Plans and specifically required by NHPA.[46] In my experience these tend to be neither fish nor fowl kinds of things, trying simultaneously to establish a general strategy for historic preservation in the state and to plan the management of the SHPO office itself. Thus the plan tries at the same time to be responsive to large statewide development pressures and social changes and to address the structure of the historic property inventory system. This doesn't often work well.

Planning is a fundamental part of local government, of course, and historic preservation at least has a long and honorable history in local planning. Cities like Charleston and New Orleans integrated their designated historic districts into city planning as early as the 1930s, and historic district planning became part of the reaction to Urban Renewal in the 1960s and 1970s.[47] The small city of Manteo, South Carolina, established a plan in the late 1980s for preserving its "sacred structure"—literally that complex of places and things that in the eyes of the town's residents gave it its special qualities. Interestingly, most of the structure's elements were not regarded as eligible for the National Register.[48]

Multijurisdictional regional plans have been tried a few times; this was something I promoted from an archeological perspective way back in the 1970s, though I then lost my way and thought that State Historic Preservation Plans would suffice. The one regional plan I've helped put together was interesting to do but sank like a stone.[49] It wasn't until the turn of the century, with the creation of a regional plan for the area around Tucson, Arizona, that I saw evidence of a regional plan that might actually work. To plan effectively and to make a plan effective, I think you've got to have a fairly delimited piece of space to work with and a somewhat limited number of entities operating on it, with some kind of common organizational, decision-making framework. In the Arizona case, although there are several jurisdictions involved, they're brought to work together by the need for an integrated habitat conservation plan (HCP) to meet the requirements of the Endangered Species Act. Historic properties have been integrated into that plan.[50]

In the late 1970s, NPS came up with what it called the "resource protection planning process" (RP3) as its preservation planning mantra. RP3 was focused on State Historic Preservation Plans, though it was supposed to be good for everything. Not surprisingly, given NPS's predilections, it focused on evaluating properties for National Register eligibility. It addressed the problems inherent in property-by-property eligibility determinations by promoting use of historic contexts—big-picture overviews of an area's historic resources that in theory would make it possible to make rational, comparative judgments about the significance of given historic properties. You'd develop a historic context on, say, "prehistoric agriculture," or "German immigrant beer brewers," and develop enough knowledge of this context to permit defensible judgments about whether this old field or that tumbled-down hop dryer was a good example of the context's constituent properties.

There was (and is, to the extent they're still being produced, and regrettably they are) a lot wrong with historic contexts. In the first place, contexts make sense if you're thinking of historic properties as sources of data (National Register criterion D,) or as places to do public interpretation (à la the intent of the Historic Sites Act of 1935). But applying a context-based evaluation to a property can blind the analyst to other—often nonresearch, noninterpretive—reasons that a place can be historically or culturally important and eligible for the Register. The bridge that's a not-particularly-good example of through-truss bridges in Minnesota might be the bridge where the mayor committed suicide in 1923 or where everybody's gone to propose marriage since 1917.

Another problem is that contexts tempt one to rank—to identify the "best" ten through-truss bridges in Minnesota and put them on the Register, then let everything else go. But even if we're not concerned with where the mayor ended it all, or where every starry-eyed swain in town has popped the question to his sweetheart, there may be good reason to be concerned about bridges that don't make the top ten. Maybe we want to try to preserve the top ten in place, but record the rest of them to provide a basis for studying variability in bridge engineering across the state. Of course, the top-ten problem really reflects the black-and-white character of the National Register: you're either eligible or you're not, and if you're not, it's good-bye, bridge. But planning ought to be more flexible than this.

And perhaps the biggest problem with contexts is that people get so enamored of producing them that they don't do any planning. Doing a context is great academic fun for a historian or archeologist, but it doesn't necessarily lead to anything but a volume on the shelf.

A plan for historic preservation in land management can usefully integrate historic preservation into an agency's larger plans for ecosystem management, land use, soil and water management, and so on. Unfortunately, not all plans *are* good; in fact, it's a safe bet that most aren't. Even plans that aren't explicitly misguided by "historic contexts" can evolve into little more than exercises in academic research, with the justification that such research is necessary to understand the property types to be managed. This rationale may be legitimate (though often it isn't), but still, a "plan" that is nothing but an inventory of properties and a lot of background information doesn't deserve to be called a plan; it provides no direction, serves no real-world purpose. Many such plans, regrettably, languish ignored on agency bookshelves.

Transportation Projects and Section 4(f)

Where a federally assisted transportation project is planned—that is, one assisted by an agency of the U.S. Department of Transportation (DOT), then the agency has to comply with section 4(f) of the DOT Act (49 U.S.C. 303)—the act that created the department. Section 4(f) says that:

> The Secretary of Transportation may approve a transportation program or project requiring the use of publicly owned land of a public park, recreation area, or wildlife and waterfowl refuge . . . , or land of a historic site . . . only if:
>
> 1. there is no prudent or feasible alternative to using that land; and
> 2. the program or project includes all possible planning to minimize harm to the park, recreation area, refuge, or historic site resulting from the use.[51]

The courts have found that any National Register property, and any property determined eligible for the National Register (at least by the keeper or an SHPO), is a "historic site" for purposes of section 4(f). They've also crafted the concept of "constructive use," which holds, in essence, that if you affect a property in such a way as to potentially alter its use, you've used it. As a result, many adverse effects under section 106 of NHPA are section 4(f) uses even if they don't physically impact historic properties. Note, too, that while 4(f) applies only to use of publicly owned land in a park, recreation area, or refuge, it applies to anybody's land in a historic site.

So section 4(f) imposes a pretty draconian requirement on transportation agencies: within some limits, they can't have an adverse effect on a historic property unless there's no prudent or feasible alternative.

There's a large body of practice involved in conducting section 4(f) analyses—not only of impacts on historic properties, of course, but on parks, recreation areas, and refuges. Such analyses are carried out in coordination with NEPA studies.

Under a long-evolving FHWA policy that became enshrined in law in 2005 as the "*de minimis* standard,"[52] section 4(f) does not apply where the section 106 process results in a finding that no historic properties are subject to effect or that there will be no adverse effect. Conversely, section 4(f) *does* apply to adverse effect situations, so transportation agencies move heaven and earth to avoid such findings under section 106. FHWA also takes the position that if an archeological site is "important chiefly because of what can be learned by data recovery and has minimal value for preservation in place," section 4(f) doesn't apply to destroying the site even though it *is* an adverse effect under section 106.[53] These arrangements reflect an understandable reaction to section 4(f)'s rather extreme protective qualities—they are attempts to avoid letting minor or technical effects on a historic property, or in-place preservation of a place that really doesn't need to be preserved in place, cause important public interests to be sacrificed. For example, it would be ridiculous to insist that hundreds of thousands of dollars be spent and, say, a whole neighborhood wiped out, in order to route a highway around an archeological site that no one thinks is worth preserving in place. But *de minimis* and FHWA's archeological site approach inevitably distort the section 106 process, causing highway agencies to categorize really damaging projects as having no adverse effect, and they close their eyes to the extra-research value of many archeological sites. It also doesn't fully take care of the problem. If a highway planner has the choice of knocking down a decrepit old building that no one cares about but that's eligible for the National Register, and taking out a retirement home whose residents really, really don't want to be moved, the retirees are going to be on the street[54] because taking down the old building will be an adverse effect.

It's important to coordinate sections 106 and 4(f) review so as to avoid complicating the latter's rigid hierarchy. 4(f) demands that we first determine whether there's a prudent and feasible alternative. If there is, we use it. If there's not, we explain this in our 4(f) documentation and go on to develop and implement "all possible planning to mitigate harm." This means that in section 106 review we need to be careful not to get deeply into negotiation about mitigation measures until we've thoroughly explored alternatives to avoid adverse effect—that is, "use"—altogether; otherwise we can seriously muddy the 4(f) process. Ideally, 106 consultation ought to be carried to the point of reaching a conclusion about avoiding adverse effect and then, if there appears to be no way to do so, section 106 review should be put on hold while the agency makes preliminary 4(f) findings and gets public response. Then section 106 review can continue, taking the public response into account, either to explore alternatives the public has raised or to identify and agree on mitigation measures. This sort of coordination is outlined in figure 5.

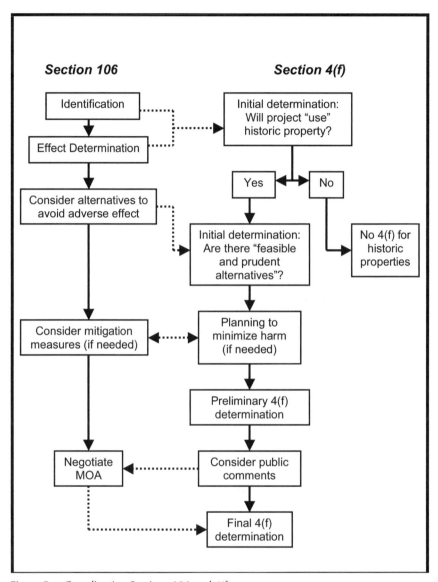

Figure 5.   Coordinating Sections 106 and 4(f)

One other point about section 4(f). It applies to "transportation programs and projects," but that doesn't mean "all actions involving transportation." Nor does it mean only "construction of transportation facilities." A road built by the Forest Service to haul logs is not subject to section 4(f) because it's not done by a DOT agency, but the Federal Aviation Administration's approval of a plan to control air traffic *is* subject to section 4(f) because the FAA is part of DOT.[55]

National Historic Landmarks

National Historic Landmarks (NHLs) are rather anachronistic today, confusingly redundant with the National Register. Created by the 1935 Historic Sites Act, the NHL program in NPS designates places determined (by NPS) to have significance in the "commemoration and illustration of the Nation's History." The program gives Congress something to do, however; every now and then some member or committee will decide that NPS should do a theme study and designate NHLs that commemorate or illustrate it.[56]

Section 110(f) of NHPA calls on agencies to give special attention to the adverse effects of their actions on NHLs. In practice under section 106 regulations, this means that the ACHP must be involved in consultation about any such impacts. If architectural, engineering, or landscape documentation has to be done on an NHL, NPS generally wants the relevant standards of HABS, HAER, or HALS to be applied.

U.S. Historic Preservation in Other Countries

Most of the U.S. cultural resource laws by design apply only in domestic contexts. NEPA's application outside the United States has been the subject of debate and litigation; it has generally been taken to apply in certain unusual circumstances (e.g., in Antarctica) but not generally. Section 106 explicitly applies only in the fifty-nine entities that are "states" for purposes of the act. Section 110(f), theoretically applies to a very few National Historic Landmark

U.S. embassies in other countries, but this is a very minor exception to the rule.

Section 402 of NHPA, a little-known provision requiring attention to impacts on places included in another nation's equivalent of the National Register, is given sporadic lip service by U.S. agencies but little more. This may change; in a recent wonderfully named court case—*Dugong v. Rumsfeld*,[57] the U.S. Department of Defense was found to have violated section 402 when it failed to consider the effects of a proposed new Marine base in Okinawa on a population of marine mammals included in Japan's equivalent of the National Register.

The Department of Defense has something it calls the "Overseas Environmental Baseline Guidance Document" (OEBGD—some wags pronounce it "Oh by God!"),[58] which directs military services to follow either the host country's environmental laws or the pertinent U.S. laws, whichever are more stringent. During the 1990s the military services paid some serious attention to this direction[59]; this interest seems to have lapsed during the first eight years of the new century.

Historic preservationists have lobbied for many years to get the United States to sign The Hague *Convention for the Protection of Cultural Property in the Event of Armed Conflict*.[60] This optimistic agreement, approved by UNESCO back in 1954, obligates signatory nations to preconflict planning for safeguarding historic places and other types of cultural property and implementing a fairly comprehensive set of protective protocols during war fighting and occupation. The United States has resolutely declined to sign onto the Hague Convention, but has assured the world that it follows it. The military services seem to have done a creditable job of compliance at least with the spirit of the convention in the Vietnam, Balkan, and Persian Gulf conflicts, but similar efforts were undercut by DOD policymakers in the early days of the Iraq war, with infamous results.[61] At this writing I'm reliably informed that real efforts are being made to bring the United States into conformance with international norms of good behavior, but high-level support appears still to be thin.

Finally, many contemporary bilateral and multilateral treaties include environmental sections or protocols;[62] those I have looked at have been rather heavily weighted toward hard-science toxic and hazardous waste control, but they may have effects on practices in historic preservation and CRM. *Glamis Gold, Ltd. v. United States of America*, as far as I know the first-ever historic preservation case considered under the North American Free Trade Agreement (NAFTA), is in process at this writing.[63]

Notes

1. See http://portal.unesco.org/en/ev.php-URL_ID=13085&URL_DO=DO_TOPIC&URL_SECTION=201.html (accessed December 30, 2007).

2. See www.unesco.org/culture/laws/historic/html_eng/page1.shtml (accessed December 30, 2007).

3. On the web at www2.cr.nps.gov/tps/secstan1.htm. See also *The Secretary of the Interior's Standards for the Treatment of Historic Properties with Guidelines for Preserving, Rehabilitating, Restoring, and Reconstructing Historic Buildings* (Washington, DC: Government Publishing Office, 1992). The Standards for Rehabilitation are integrated into regulations for federal tax act certifications at 36 CFR 67.7.

4. See discussion of the Clara Barton case, chapter 7.

5. See www.irs.gov/businesses/small/industries/article/0,,id=97599,00.html and www.nps.gov/history/hps/tps/tax/ (both accessed December 28, 2007).

6. See 36 CFR 67.

7. 40 U.S.C. 601a and 611.

8. Federal Space Management. See gsa.gov/Portal/gsa/ep/contentView.do?P=PLAE&contentId=16907&contentType=GSA_BASIC (accessed December 28, 2007).

9. 16 U.S.C. 470h-2(a).

10. 61 Federal Register 26071, "Locating Federal Facilities on Historic Properties in Our Nation's Central Cities." www.gsa.gov/Portal/gsa/ep/contentView.do?P=PLAE&contentId=10723&contentType=GSA_BASIC (accessed December 28, 2007).

11. 16 U.S.C. 470h-2(a).

12. 42 U.S.C. 3122.

13. WRC/FEMA (Water Resource Council [defunct] and Federal Emergency Management Agency [successor]), "Floodplain Management: Guidelines for Implementing Executive Order 11988," 43 *Federal Register* 6030-55, February 10, 1978. See also 44 CFR 9. Further advice on EO 11988 available from FEMA at www.fema.gov/plan/ehp/ehplaws/eo11988.shtm (accessed December 28, 2007).

14. FEMA regulations at 44 CFR 9 are consistent with and effectively incorporate the WRC guidelines.

15. For example, see NPS Technical Preservation Services memo, "Rehabilitation and Adaptive Use of Schools," www.nps.gov/history/hps/tps/tax/ITS/its_12.pdf (accessed December 28, 2007).

16. 16 U.S.C. 470h-3.

17. See GSA ADM 1020.1, Procedures for Historic Properties (August 20, 1982) and Georgia Tech, "HBPP Building Manager's Training Course," Syllabus, Geor-

gia Tech Continuing Education and General Services Administration, Atlanta, 1993.

18. Frederick J. Rushlow and Don Kermath, *Proactive Maintenance Planning for Historic Buildings*, USACERL Technical Report CRC-94/01 (Champaign, IL: Construction Engineering Research Laboratories, 1994).

19. See Department of Defense Instruction 4715.3, www.denix.osd.mil/denix/ Public/ES-Programs/Conservation/Policy/note1.html and http:// crm.cr.nps.gov/archive/24-03/24-03-3.pdf (both accessed December 28, 2007).

20. In the army, the problem is exacerbated by Army Regulation 200-4 and its accompanying instructional pamphlet (PAM 200-4), which flatly prohibit using an integrated cultural resource management plan as the basis for a section 106 programmatic agreement (see AR 200-4 Sec. 2-3(b)(4), www.gordon.army.mil/dpw/ enrmo/ar200-4.html#4-1 (accessed December 27, 2007). One has to wonder about a military service that directs its people to shoot themselves in the feet.

21. 16 U.S.C. 470h-2(b).

22. See http://memory.loc.gov/ammem/collections/habs_haer/ (accessed December 28, 2007).

23. Summarized in the "Secretary of the Interior's Standards for Architectural and Engineering Documentation," 46 *Federal Register* 44730-34, 1983. For detailed guidance see HABS/HAER, *Secretary of the Interior's Standards and Guidelines for Architectural and Engineering Documentation*, compiled by Caroline H. Russell, HABS/HAER, and National Park Service (Washington, DC: HABS/HAER, 1990); www.nps.gov/hdp/standards/index.htm (accessed December 28, 2007).

24. For information on HALS, see www.nps.gov/hdp/hals/index.htm (accessed December 28, 2007).

25. A completely natural landscape may be eligible for the National Register as a traditional cultural property for its association with the cultural values of a historically rooted living community; see National Register Bulletin 38 and Thomas F. King, *Places That Count: Traditional Cultural Properties in Cultural Resource Management* (Walnut Creek, CA: AltaMira Press, 2004) for discussion.

26. See www.nps.gov/hdp/about.htm (accessed December 28, 2007).

27. Whose department-wide adoption sadly superseded the Navy's Historic and Archeological Resource Plan, or HARP, strummed by the Navy's former federal preservation officer, Dr. J. Bernard Murphy.

28. 43 USC 35, see www.blm.gov/flpma/FLPMA.pdf (accessed December 28, 2007).

29. 16 USC 36, see www.blm.gov/flpma/FLPMA.pdf (accessed December 28, 2007).

30. National Park Service, "Secretary of the Interior's Standards and Guidelines for Federal Agency Historic Preservation Programs Pursuant to the National Historic Preservation Act," 63 *Federal Register* 20495-20508, April 24, 1998; see www.nps.gov/history/hps/fapa_110.htm (accessed December 28, 2007).

31. Executive Order no. 13287, *Preserve America*, March 3, 2003; see www.achp .gov/preserveamericaEO.pdf (accessed December 28, 2007).

32. 16 U.S.C. 470h-2(a)(2)(A) & (B).

33. Section 110 Standards and Guidelines, Standard 2, guideline (a).

34. Section 110 Standards and Guidelines, Standard 3, guidelines.

35. Section 110 Standards and Guidelines, Standard 6, guidelines.

36. Section 110 Standards and Guidelines, guideline (g).

37. Section 110 Standards and Guidelines, Standard 5, guideline (a).

38. Executive Order 13287, sec. 2.

39. Executive Order 13287, sec. 3(a).

40. Executive Order 13287, sec. 3(a).

41. Executive Order 13287, sec. 3(b).

42. Executive Order 13287, sec. 3(c).

43. Executive Order 13287, sec. 3(e).

44. ACHP, *In a Spirit of Stewardship: A Report on Federal Historic Property Management*, Washington, DC, February 15, 2006; see www.achp.gov/docs/EO.FINAL.highres.pdf (accessed December 28, 2007).

45. Protection and Enhancement of the Cultural Environment. See www.gsa.gov/Portal/gsa/ep/contentView.do?contentType=GSA_BASIC&contentId=12094 (accessed December 28, 2007).

46. Section 101(b)(3)(C); 16 U.S.C. 470a.

47. See for instance City of New Orleans, *Vieux Carre Historic District Demonstration Study* (New Orleans: Bureau of Government Research for the City of New Orleans, 1968); San Francisco (City and County), *Urban Design Plan* (San Francisco: Department of City Planning, 1972).

48. Randolph T. Hester, "Subconscious Landscapes of the Heart," Place 2 (3) (1987): 10–22.

49. Thomas F. King and Patricia P. Hickman, *The Southern Santa Clara Valley: A General Plan for Archaeology*. San Felipe Archaeology I, San Francisco State University, A. E. Treganza Anthropology Museum (San Francisco, 1973); King, "San Felipe: Designing a General Plan for Archaeology," in *Conservation Archaeology: A Guide for Cultural Resource Management Studies*, eds. Michael B. Schiffer and George Gumerman (New York: Academic Press, 1977).

50. Sonoran Desert Conservation Plan (SDCP) developed by Pima County, Arizona, with archeologist Linda Mayro guiding the cultural resource element. See www.pima.gov/CMO/SDCP/ (accessed December 28, 2007).

51. 49 U.S.C. 303.

52. See www.fhwa.dot.gov/HEP/guidedeminimis.htm (accessed December 28, 2007).

53. 23 CFR 771.135(g)(2).

54. Unless, of course, it can be shown that it's not feasible or prudent to put them there, which may or may not take a good deal of study and argument.

55. Coast Guard permits for bridges, which used to be subject to section 4(f), no longer are, because the Coast Guard is now part of the Department of Homeland Security.

56. See www.nps.gov/history/nhl/ (accessed December 30, 2007) for the official NPS word on NHLs.

57. N.D. Cal., C-03-4350, in which I was privileged to help represent the dugongs; See Thomas F. King, "Creatures and Culture: Some Implications of Dugong v. Rumsfeld," *International Journal of Cultural Property* 13 (2): 235–40; journals.cambridge.org/action/displayAbstract?fromPage=online&aid=545356 (accessed December 30, 2007).

58. See www.afpmb.org/pubs/dir_inst/OEBGD_DoD_4715.5-G_15Mar00.pdf (accessed December 30, 2007).

59. Discussed in CEHP, *Cultural Resource Law and Department of Defense International Activities*, Interim Paper, January 12, 1994, Washington, DC; CEHP, *Cultural Resource Law and Department of Defense International Activities*, Background Paper, March 1, 1994, Washington, DC.

60. See http://portal.unesco.org/culture/en/ev.php-URL_ID=8450&URL_DO=DO_TOPIC&URL_SECTION=201.html or www.icomos.org/hague/ (accessed December 30, 2007).

61. For example, see Matthew Bogdanos and William Patrick, *Thieves of Baghdad* (New York: Bloomsbury, 2005).

62. For example, see www.cec.org/ and www.fpif.org/briefs/vol4/v4n26nafta.html (both accessed December 30, 2007).

63. See www.state.gov/s/l/c10986.htm and 64.233.169.104/search?q=cache:GD2GCiC8flYJ:www.sacredland.org/endangered_sites_pages/indian_pass.html+%22NAFTA%22+%22Glamis%22+%22Quechan%22&hl=en&ct=clnk&cd=1&gl=us&ie=UTF-8 (both accessed December 30, 2007).

6

Cultural Resources in, of, and from the Land

In this chapter we'll look at laws and practice dealing with cultural land resources—things intimately associated with the land. Of course, with rare exceptions like historic aircraft in flight and historic watercraft afloat, the historic properties to which the last three chapters have been devoted stand on, lie within, or constitute parts of the land. But some kinds of historic properties are more closely related to the land than others. Some of these aren't dealt with very routinely by historic preservation specialists, so they need to be highlighted, and some land-related cultural resources, whether historic properties or not, have laws of their own that a practitioner needs to know about.

Landscapes

The broadest-scale cultural land resource is the landscape—embracing a whole big chunk of natural or not-so-natural land and all that's in it. The management of cultural landscapes, and impacts on landscapes, are matters of growing concern in CRM, despite the thin array of laws and programs specifically designed with landscapes in mind. The National Park Service (NPS) has a "cultural landscape initiative" that focuses attention on landscape management issues, primarily those involving designed and vernacular landscapes,[1] and its American Battlefield Protection Program gives special attention to battlefield landscapes.[2]

NPS guidance on landscapes is confused and confusing, referring variously to "designed landscapes," "historic vernacular landscapes," "rural historic landscapes," "historic sites," and "ethnographic landscapes."[3] The terms overlap, and at least most of them are understood not to be mutually exclusive. A historic site, of course, is a place where some more or less specific event or pattern of events took place. A designed landscape is usually the work of a landscape architect—something intentionally planned and constructed like a park, parkway, or the grounds of a great estate. A historic vernacular landscape or rural historic landscape is a landscape that reflects human activity but is not professionally designed; many farming and ranching landscapes fall into this category. The name "ethnographic landscape" was assigned to landscapes to which living communities assign cultural significance; it's rather an insulting term, I think, suggesting that these communities and their heritage places are significant as objects of anthropological research rather than in their own right. In essence, such a landscape is a large, more or less rural, traditional cultural property. There is much room for niggling argument here, but a practitioner will have a more productive life if he or she can avoid being troubled by the fine distinctions. The *Secretary of the Interior's Guidelines for the Treatment of Cultural Landscapes*, usefully defines the whole über-category "cultural landscape" as:

> a geographic area (including both cultural and natural resources and the wildlife or domestic animals therein) associated with a historic event, activity, or person or exhibiting other cultural or aesthetic values.[4]

If they are eligible for the National Register—by virtue of being battlefields, for example, or reflecting significant agricultural activities or traditional cultural values—then landscapes and their components enjoy the same consideration as do all other kinds of historic properties under section 106 and other parts of NHPA. Whether they are eligible for the Register or not, they have to be addressed in NEPA analyses, and other cultural resource legal authorities apply to those having, for example, religious significance.

Recognizing and evaluating culturally significant landscapes can present special problems. They don't fit very readily into the well-understood taxonomy of "building, site, district, structure, and object" used by the National Register—though most wind up being called "sites" or "districts." Federal agencies and state historic preservation officers (SHPOs) tend to bifurcate the world into domains of architecture and archeology; landscapes easily fall through the cracks between these categories. It may be difficult for people who are used to thinking in terms of individual sites and structures to grasp the big picture represented by landscapes. Landscapes and their components—particularly plants, animals, and human populations—are also dynamic; they change, and this may be challenging to people accustomed to thinking of historic places as static phenomena.

Landscapes also present special management issues. They are often owned by multiple parties, who may or may not have interests in common. They are subject to a host of very diffuse impacts by a wide range of change agents—indirect cumulative effects, with which CRM practitioners tend to be unfamiliar. Conversely, because they are large and somewhat diffuse themselves, they may not be as obviously affected as buildings and archeological sites are location-specific actions like highway construction or military training. Most SHPO offices, agency preservation offices, and CRM firms, dominated as they are by architectural historians and archeologists, are seldom well equipped to understand, appreciate, or even recognize landscapes.

Some large cultural landscapes have been preserved to various degrees by being recognized as "heritage areas"—areas designated by Congress, upon petition by local governments, as eligible for tax breaks and special assistance in order to encourage their preservation.[5] Local governments are usually interested in such arrangements only if they are likely to stimulate cultural tourism and the revenue it can produce. Cultural landscapes are sometimes preserved by being made into national, state, and local parks. Like designation as a heritage area, this can be something of a transforming event for a landscape, itself altering its cultural character.

In its 1962 *Recommendation Concerning the Safeguarding of the Beauty and Character of Landscapes and Sites*,[6] UNESCO proposed that nations should preserve and where possible restore "natural, rural, and urban landscapes and sites, whether natural or man-made, which have a cultural or aesthetic interest or form typical natural surroundings." Among the threats to such places noted in the recommendation are inappropriate buildings, roads, power lines and plants, gas stations, billboards, deforestation, pollution, mines, quarries, pipelines, camping, refuse dumping, and, in some cases, inappropriate noise. As is usually the case, UNESCO recommended development and maintenance of a list or schedule of significant sites and landscapes and permitting actions that would mar a scheduled place "only if the public or social welfare imperatively requires it." Nations should issue laws and regulations imposing protective management requirements and integrate protection into urban and land use planning. They should create administrative bodies to oversee protection, and they should provide public education.

Linear Resources

"Linear resources," "linear features," and similar terms are what many CRM practitioners use to refer to things like roads, trails, fence lines, ditches, and pipelines—long skinny things that snake across the countryside. Like landscapes, their evaluation and management present some particular problems.

No one could deny that many linear resources are historically and culturally important. The Santa Fe and Oregon Trails are obvious examples; innumerable named and unnamed roads and trails are significant in local contexts. Acequia systems in the Southwest are important not only for their roles in agricultural development but for the way local society was often organized around their maintenance. And so on. When the interstate highway system went over the fifty-year mark, some officials got so fretful over its obvious eligibility for the National Register that the ACHP approved a truly silly exemption from section 106 review saying in effect that it wasn't.[7] Anyone who's read a cowboy novel or watched a western movie knows how significant fences were in the settling of the West. And so on. But does this mean that every fence, every road, every ditch, is eligible for the National Register? And what about those that have remained in such continuous use over the decades or centuries that no shred of their original fabric remains? Is a jeep road eligible because it runs along the route of a wagon road or a hunting trail? You can imagine the glee with which underemployed specialists can debate these issues.

And then there's the fact that linear resources are—well, long. So suppose the Long Muddy Ditch, all three hundred miles of it, is eligible for the National Register, what kind of effect do we have if we run a road through a 100-foot segment of it? Or string a power line over it? Again, lots of room for quibbles.

There's often a relatively simple way to deal with these kinds of issues—as usual, by accepting eligibility but also accepting adverse effects unless someone feels really strongly about the matter, in which case we can address those strong feelings. But this doesn't always work, not only because some people just like to argue about things like the eligibility of an old wire fence, but because the section 106 criterion of adverse effect doesn't allow for gradations of adversity—an effect is either adverse or it's not—and because the effects we're dealing with are so often occasioned by transportation projects. As you'll recall, section 4(f) of the Department of Transportation act for the most part doesn't allow such a project to adversely affect a historic place unless there's no prudent and feasible alternative. The advisory council could probably fix this problem with a carefully crafted program comment, but it hasn't done so.

Animals, Vegetables, Minerals

Plants can be important cultural resources—consider the use of tobacco, sage, and piñon in tribal religious observances, sweetgrass and willow in basket making, wild rice and acorns in traditional tribal subsistence practices. Likewise with animals—coyote, bear, grizzly, whale, salmon, eagle, spider all play important roles in traditions, religious beliefs, and subsistence practices. And the stuff of the earth itself—its minerals—can hold cultural significance. Water, for example, is commonly regarded in tribal tradition as having sentience and spiritual qualities, as is salt in some contexts. Lava to Native Hawaiian traditionalists is the sacred stuff of the volcano goddess Pele.

Although tribes, Native Hawaiians, and other indigenous people most commonly ascribe cultural significance to plants, animals, and minerals, such significance isn't unknown to other cultures. Wild horses and burros, for instance, are regarded as cultural icons by many people—equestrians and nonriders alike. In the Wild Free Ranging Horse and Burro Act of 1971,[8] Congress found and declared that "wild free-roaming horses and burros are living symbols of the historic and pioneer spirit of the West."

The Wild Horse and Burro Act is unusual, however; for the most part, the cultural significance of animals, vegetables, and minerals are given short shrift by cultural resource laws. This sort of significance should be considered in NEPA analyses, however, and sometimes it is. Animals and plants can contribute to the eligibility of a landscape or site for the National Register; a few trees have been recognized as Register-eligible.

Dugong v. Rumsfeld, a 2006 case alleging violation of NHPA section 402, highlighted the cultural significance of animals. Section 402 obligates federal agencies to consider the effects of overseas activities on a host nation's equivalent of the National Register. Japan's official list of protected cultural resources includes the Okinawa dugong, a fleshy marine mammal thought to be the actuality behind the mermaid myth; the dugong figures prominently in many Okinawan traditions. The U.S. Department of Defense planned a new marine base whose construction would threaten dugong habitat. The dugong's defenders alleged violation of section 402; the United States argued that the Japanese list was not "equivalent" to the National Register because the Register does not include animals. The plaintiffs responded that "equivalence" did not mean word-for-word identity and that although it was true that animals are not listed in the National Register, animal habitats can be and are, with the animals serving as contributing elements. The court found for the dugongs, but actually went a bit farther. Noting that the National Register can include objects, which are defined rather loosely, and pointing to a Georgia case in which a tree had been determined eligible for the Register, the court raised the hypothetical possibility that an animal, by itself, could be eligible. The National Register has not commented on this finding.[9]

Members of the Hopi Tribe and their allies have made the cultural significance of water a major issue in the fight over mining on Black Mesa, a case that's been under review for some years under NEPA and section 106 of NHPA.[10] The nearby Zuni Pueblo used similar arguments in the course of NEPA and section 106 review of the proposed Fence Lake Mine in New Mexico, which would have endangered the aquifer feeding Zuni Salt Lake, a deeply significant traditional cultural property. As usual, neither law by itself killed the project, but the complex and contentious review processes helped persuade the responsible mining company to drop the project.[11] In the Crandon Mine case in Wisconsin, briefly mentioned in chapter 4, the cultural significance of water in a potentially affected aquifer was something on which the Mole Lake Band of Great Lakes focused in showing that the landscape overlying the ore body was eligible for the National Register as a traditional cultural property. As one of the tribe's consultants, I was impressed at the difficulty even the tribe's own water resource experts had in understanding the tribe's insistence that this water had to be kept absolutely pure. I recall one tribal official summing it up: "Only zero parts per million of pollutants is acceptable."[12]

I don't recommend pushing the notion of animals, plants, or minerals *by themselves* being eligible for the National Register; I do not think that any SHPO or the National Register staff would respond well to the idea. But certainly the cultural significance of such resources must be considered under NEPA, certainly if they have religious connotations this may trigger the protections of the Religious Freedom Restoration Act and/or the American Indian Religious Freedom Act, and certainly they may contribute to the National Register eligibility of their habitats or other places associated with them, giving those places the benefit of consideration under section 106.

"Indian Sacred Sites" and Executive Order 13007

Issued by President Bill Clinton in 1996, Executive Order 13007[13] required five things of federal agencies:

1. Accommodate access to and ceremonial use of "Indian sacred sites" by American Indian religious practitioners,

unless accommodation is clearly inconsistent with law or essential elements of the agency's mission.

2. Avoid adverse effect to the physical integrity of "sacred sites," subject to the same caveats.
3. Where appropriate, maintain the confidentiality of information on such sites.
4. Implement procedures to carry out the order, including procedures for notifying tribes of actions that might affect "sacred sites," access to such sites, or their ceremonial use. Such notification must respect the government-to-government relations between the U.S. government and Indian tribal governments.
5. Provide a report to the president[14] addressing, among other things, changes the agency thinks are needed in law, regulation, or procedure to accommodate the purposes of the executive order, to facilitate consultation with tribes and religious leaders, and to provide for dispute resolution.

The executive order contains a definition of "sacred site" that's a classic example of what you get when you let lawyers write policy documents with little advice from people in the real world:

> "Sacred site" means any specific, discrete, narrowly delineated location on Federal land that is identified by an Indian tribe or Indian individual determined to be an appropriately authoritative representative of an Indian religion, as sacred by virtue of its established religious significance to, or ceremonial use by, an Indian religion; provided that the tribe or appropriately authoritative representative of an Indian religion has informed the agency of the existence of such a site.

Well, now . . .

- What does "specific" mean? A responsible definition, I think, would be "a particular piece of real estate," not a whole class of properties. "Rocky Point," not "all sacred places in Washafornia." But how do you suppose the folks whose actions triggered *Pueblo of Sandia v. United States* would define it? You'll recall that in that case, the Forest Service wanted tribes to provide maps with the boundaries of all spiritual places marked.

- What about "discrete"? Again, the word might mean simply that the site has to have some kind of boundaries to discriminate it from the rest of the world, but it's easy to imagine a definition requiring a little red fence around the place, or a size no bigger than a breadbox.

- Then there's "narrowly delineated." Right—the more you pile these terms on top of one another, the more it adds up to "marked on a U.S.G.S. quadrangle with boundaries defined and explained." But it gets worse.

- What does "identified by an Indian tribe, or Indian individual" mean? Does the tribe or individual have to go to the agency and volunteer the site's identification? "Here's our list, Kemo sabe"? That's what the Forest Service thought it could get away with at Las Huertas Canyon, and one is tempted to think that, having failed, they or others like them got to some dim bulbs at the White House or Department of Justice and had their way with them. It's completely inconsistent with the assignment of responsibility to agencies themselves by NEPA, NHPA, and other statutes, but hey, what's a little inconsistency? Of course, "identified by a tribe or individual" could mean "identified by a tribe or individual in response to an agency request, during consultation and planning," but is there any motivation for agencies to define it that way? Perhaps, but not in the wording of the executive order.

- And then, what does "appropriately authoritative" mean? Who's to decide? Are federal agencies going to start vetting tribal representatives? To their credit, few if any agencies seem to have taken egregious advantage of the executive order. But almost all have started sending routine form letters to tribes, often written in the most incomprehensible of bureaucratese, notifying them of projects and asking them if they have any sacred sites (or National Register–eligible properties, or other cultural resources) that may be affected. Tribes are buried in such correspondence and most can't respond in a timely way. Agencies take this to mean "no problem," and proceed with their plans.

Note that a place can be a sacred site under the executive order without being a historic property under NHPA. And while it has to be a piece of real property, the site itself is not the only subject for agencies to attend to; they're supposed to protect tribal access to sites and their use for ceremonial purposes. Not all agencies attend to these fine points.

Other Religious Places

Although non-Native Americans don't have an executive order requiring attention to their "sacred sites," such sites aren't completely without protection. The Religious Freedom Restoration Act[15] discourages agencies from running roughshod over people's religious beliefs and practices, and destroying a group's sacred site is pretty rough. And any group's spiritual place may be a traditional cultural property that's eligible for the National Register and hence must be considered under section 106. Some religious places also get a degree of protection simply because everyone recognizes them as meaningful. Informal roadside memorials marking the sites of traffic fatalities are rather commonly respected by transportation departments and their CRM contractors, for example. It's not universal practice, but it's not uncommon to consult the living people associated with such places when highway improvements are being planned, seeking ways to minimize damage.[16]

Native American Graves and Cultural Items

The Native American Graves Protection and Repatriation Act—with the sonorous acronym NAGPRA, is like many other laws in being well intentioned, justified, and virtually impossible to make work well.[17] Its regulations too are grounded on excellent principles and struggle mightily to make sense of the statute, but wind up being so complicated that they are, I think, honored mostly in the breach. Many CRM practitioners claim expertise in NAGPRA, but usually when asked something specific about the regulations they get very strange looks on their faces.[18]

NAGPRA was enacted in 1989 to correct a long-standing injustice. Since the eighteenth century at least, and particularly in the late nineteenth and twentieth, the bones, grave goods, and religious objects of American Indians and other native Americans have been treated as objects of curiosity and as scientific specimens. They have been dug up, stored, handled, analyzed, displayed, and discarded with little or no consideration for their sanctity in the eyes of those whose ancestors created them, valued them, or, in the case of human remains, *were* them. They have been treated, in a word, with disrespect—for themselves and for those who ascribe cultural and spiritual value to them.

Coming out of the Indian civil rights movement of the 1960s, and as part of a worldwide resurgence of aboriginal power and dignity, Indian tribes and other native American groups (Alaska Natives, Native Hawaiians) in the 1970s became increasingly vocal about the wrongs they had suffered at the hands of white society, notably the U.S. government and archeologists. Government offenses included the quaint nineteenth-century practice of collecting parts of slain Indians' for study and storage at the Army Medical Museum and the support of archeological work that exhumed thousands of ancestral bodies. The tribes and such intertribal organizations as the National Congress of American Indians made their outrage known to Congress and state legislatures. Results were varied at the state level;[19] at the federal level, the result was NAGPRA.

I don't think a lawyer should ever be allowed to write law, and NAGPRA illustrates why this is so. It's painfully intricate, subject to many interpretations, loaded with balancing tests and shifts of the burden of proof back and forth between tribes on the one hand, and museums, agencies, and archeologists on the other. It's a wonder it works at all, and I suspect that, to the extent it does, it works in spite of itself. As long as there's good will among the parties involved, NAGPRA provides a vehicle for cooperation. Let that good will break down, and it's a different ballgame.[20]

Mostly, NAGPRA deals with repatriation of human remains and what the statute refers to as "Native American cultural items." Repatriation means giving back. NAGPRA directs federal agencies and museums that have gotten federal funds to undertake specific actions to give back human remains and native American cultural items to the Indian tribes, Alaska Native Groups, and Native Hawaiian organizations whence they came. These actions are complicated and subject to a good deal of interpretation.

The repatriation provisions of NAGPRA establish long-term, continuing responsibilities, and there is neither the space in this book nor the will in this author to discuss them all in detail. NPS and others offer training in NAGPRA, and anyone who may be involved in the repatriation of remains and cultural items should sign up. Most cultural resource managers dealing with projects and programs on the ground will encounter NAGPRA in a narrower context, which is what we'll address briefly here.

Three NAGPRA Myths

First let's dispose of a few myths.

Myth 1: NAGPRA Applies Only to Human Remains

Given its name, one might think that NAGPRA is only about graves. Not so. NAGPRA deals with graves and dead bodies, but it also deals with "Native American cultural items." Such items include a wide range of things that may be found in an ethnographic or archeological collection:

- Associated funerary objects—that is, objects associated with a body;
- Unassociated funerary objects—objects that used to be associated with a body but no longer are;
- Sacred objects—objects needed for the practice of traditional religion; and
- "Objects of cultural patrimony"—defined as objects that have historical, traditional, or cultural importance central to the Indian tribe itself, as a corporate body, rather than property owned by—and therefore subject to "alienation" (i.e., disposal, as through sale or gift) by individual tribal members.

This last term is especially open to interpretation. Clearly a totem pole is an object of cultural patrimony. It was important to a group rather than owned by an individual (though there's room for argument here). But what about an unmodified rock that was regarded by a tribe as one of the First People, turned to stone for some sort of wrongdoing? What about a complex of grinding slabs used by a village? What about a tribe's whole arsenal of arrow points? Although the NAGPRA regulations (43 CFR 10) try to keep the definition of "object of cultural patrimony" tightly bounded, questions like this are bound to come up. How, after all, are we to know what could and could not be alienated by an individual five thousand years dead?

So you're not out of the NAGPRA woods if you're unlikely to encounter graves in the course of your project or land management activity. The application of NAGPRA depends on whether you may run into a wide range of cultural items, as well as on the interests of Native American groups and how aggressively they pursue them.

Myth 2: NAGPRA Requires Reburial

It doesn't. NAGPRA requires *repatriation* to tribes and Native Hawaiian groups, who are taken to be the rightful owners of ancestral remains and cultural items. What they do with their property is up to them; they can put them in their own museums, rebury them, distribute them among households, put them out to return to nature, or for that matter sell them or grind them up for chicken feed. Of course, lots of groups want the remains of their ancestors, and sometimes their artifacts, returned to the ground, and there's nothing in NAGPRA to prohibit a federal agency (or anyone else) from helping put them there, but it's the tribe's call and the tribe's responsibility; it's not up to the agency to do.

We'll take a look at another myth later. First let's look at what NAGPRA requires of cultural resource managers.

NAGPRA in the Museums and Laboratories

If you're a museum that's received federal funds—even indirectly—or if you're a federal agency, and you manage Native American ancestral remains and/or cultural items, you're required to inventory them, consult with tribes about them, and repatriate them to tribes with which they're affiliated or to which they belong. But which items in your collection are Native American cultural items, and with whom are they affiliated? To whom should they be repatriated? With whom should you consult? The NAGPRA regulations are designed to guide you in asking and answering such questions.[21] The regulations, issued by NPS, do their best to make sense of NAGPRA's complexities, but the questions remain, sticky and with multiple possible answers. There may be half a dozen tribes with whom things may be affiliated. Each will have its own ideas about what should be done and its own special needs, interests, and obstacles to consultation—for example, the economic difficulty of sending people to a museum to inspect things, or consult about what to do with them. They may—surprise!—disagree with one another. There may be questions about whether the museum really has ownership over some items; if it can prove that it does, it can keep them, but often the records of things like old donations are ambiguous. And there may be nontribal people with significant interests in the collections—archeologists, cultural and physical anthropologists, museum administrators, university officials—who have their own ideas about what should be done with them. Some of these people may have serious power over the practicing cultural resource manager.[22]

Another complication is that museum collections have often been treated over the years with preservatives, including pesticides. Institutions have sometimes (to put it gently) not kept good records of this treatment. So if you repatriate the dance regalia to the tribe, people who use it may get sick. They may die. What's to be done about this? Studies and consultations are underway; there's no clear answer.[23]

NAGPRA on the Ground

Cultural resource managers outside the museum or laboratory setting are most likely to run into NAGPRA's two sections that deal with excavations and "inadvertent discovery." Both apply to work on federal and tribal land only, but that doesn't mean only lands owned fee simple by the government or a tribe, or held in trust for a tribe. As under the section 106 regulations, "tribal land" is defined as land within the external boundaries of a reservation—

which can include state, local, federal, and private land.[24] And "federal land" is defined as lands "controlled or owned by the United States." The definition goes on to say that "control" means the government has "a legal interest sufficient to permit it to apply these regulations without abrogating the otherwise existing rights of a person."[25] So does that mean that if an agency has an easement across my land, it's "federal" for purposes of NAGPRA? What if I'm an artifact collector; would applying the regulations and repatriating artifacts from my land abrogate my otherwise existing rights? We'll doubtless see issues like this addressed in court.

Regulating Excavation

However federal and Indian lands are understood, section 3(c) of NAGPRA says that you can't exhume, remove, or otherwise muck around with Native American bones or cultural items on such lands without a permit issued under the Archeological Resources Protection Act (ARPA), which has to be coordinated with the tribe(s) or group(s) culturally affiliated with the remains, and which has to include provision for their disposition consistent with NAGPRA.

This is pretty straightforward. Archeologists have been working under ARPA permits for decades; the only difference under NAGPRA—and it was long overdue—is that there has to be consultation[26] with tribes and repatriation.

Inadvertent Discovery

Section 3(d) is a bit trickier. Under section 3(d), if a Native American cultural item is encountered inadvertently on federal[27] land—during construction, for example—the party responsible for the project has to:

- Cease the activity in the area of the discovery, make a reasonable effort to protect the items discovered;
- Notify, in writing, the . . . head of . . . (the) agency . . . having primary management authority . . .;
- Following the notification . . . and upon certification by the . . . head of (the) . . . agency . . . that notification has been

received, the activity may resume after 30 days of such certification.[28]

In other words, the project manager must stop project work in the vicinity, protect the items discovered, provide written notification to the agency head, receive certification from the agency head that notification has been received, and wait thirty days before restarting work.

The POA

The NAGPRA regulations provide a way to avoid the danger of enduring repeated thirty-day (plus) work stoppages. They require[29] the federal agency responsible for a project on federal or tribal lands to develop and follow a plan of action (POA) for managing Native American cultural items that may be encountered. Specifically, this section of the regulations requires federal agencies to:

- Notify tribes (or Native Hawaiian organizations) likely to be culturally affiliated with the items likely to be discovered, as well as any identifiable lineal descendants of those who produced or valued such items, of the likelihood that such items will be excavated, and of the agency's intent to develop a POA;
- Consult with such tribes and descendants; and
- After such consultation, prepare a written POA meeting standards set forth in 43 CFR 10.5, and then implement it.

The advantage of having a POA, of course, is that you can follow it every time you find something, rather than stopping and going through the complicated and often pointless business of notifying people up the chain of command and twiddling your thumbs for thirty days before getting on with your project. The disadvantage, as we'll see, is that there are strict standards for what a POA must contain and how it must be developed. But whether it's useful or not, a POA is required whenever an agency thinks it's likely to have Native American ancestors or cultural items to deal with on federal or tribal land.

Developing a POA

The regulations go into considerable detail about how a POA is to be developed:

> The Federal agency official must take reasonable steps to determine whether a planned activity may result in the excavation of human remains, funerary objects, sacred objects, or objects of cultural patrimony from Federal lands.[30]

The regulations don't spell out what these steps are, but they require that the agency must:

> notify in writing the Indian tribes or Native Hawaiian organizations that are likely to be culturally affiliated with any human remains, funerary objects, sacred objects, or objects of cultural patrimony that may be excavated. The Federal agency official must also notify any present-day Indian tribe which aboriginally occupied the area of the planned activity and any other Indian tribes or Native Hawaiian organizations that the Federal agency official reasonably believes are likely to have a cultural relationship.[31]

So the agency needs to find tribes and others that may be culturally affiliated with any items that it expects it may find and notify them of its plans. Efficiency suggests that this be coordinated with the early stages of section 106 review—APE determination and identification—and with the early stages of NEPA review (scoping, defining alternatives, describing the affected environment) as well.

Note that:

> The notice must be in writing and describe the planned activity, its general location, the basis upon which it was determined that (Native American cultural items) may be excavated, and the basis for determining likely custody.
>
> The notice must also propose a time and place for meetings or consultations.[32]

So you don't just send the tribe a letter saying "we plan to train pilots by bombing Blue Mountain," you've got to describe the proposed bombing, say how you decided who to involve, and perhaps most important, propose to initiate consultation. What if the tribe doesn't respond to your written notice? "Written notification should be followed up by telephone contact if there is no response in 15 days."[33]

Who should be consulted?

> The consultation must seek to identify traditional religious leaders who should be consulted and to identify, where appropriate, lineal descendants and (tribes and organizations) affiliated with the (Native American cultural items).[34]

Various kinds of information are to be exchanged.

> During the consultation process . . . the Federal agency official must provide: (1) a list of all lineal descendants and (tribes or groups being consulted), and (2) an indication that additional information used to identify affiliation will be supplied upon request.[35]

And

> agency officials may request . . . Names and addresses of representatives, . . . Names and methods of contacting lineal descendants, . . . Recommendations on how . . . consultation . . . should be conducted (and) kinds of cultural items (to consider).[36]

Having consulted, the agency writes its POA. The regulations go into detail about what it must contain:

> At a minimum, the plan of action must . . . document the following:
>
> 1. The kinds of objects to be considered as cultural items;
> 2. The . . . information used to determine custody;
> 3. The planned treatment, care, and handling of (cultural items);
> 4. The planned archeological recording of the (cultural items);
> 5. The kinds of analysis planned for each kind of object;
> 6. Any steps to be followed to contact Indian tribal officials;

7. The kind of traditional treatment, if any, to be afforded the [cultural items] by members of the Indian tribe or Native Hawaiian organization;
8. The nature of reports to be prepared; and
9. The disposition of (cultural items).[37]

Whew! I don't know anybody who has actually prepared a POA that covers all those bases. A lot of agencies have agreements with tribes, but as far as I know none of them meet the full standards set forth in the regulations, even where they're called POAs. But obviously, agencies should have such POAs. Appendix 5 is a mockup of a POA; as you can see, it's not a simple document. Is anybody going to hold an agency to meeting the regulatory standards? Maybe not, but the closer you are to doing so, the better.

Myth 3: The Tribe Must Concur in the POA

Although the tribe (or Native Hawaiian group and lineal descendants) must be consulted during preparation of the POA, the agency is not required to obtain its concurrence where the POA applies to federal land.

> Following consultation, the Federal agency official must prepare, approve, and sign a written plan of action. A copy of this plan of action must be provided to the lineal descendants, Indian tribes, and Native Hawaiian organizations involved. Lineal descendants and Indian tribal official(s) may sign the written plan of action as appropriate.[38]

However, both NAGPRA itself and the regulations[39] require that cultural items be excavated on tribal lands only with the consent of the relevant tribe, so tribal concurrence *is* required in POAs for projects within the external boundaries of reservations and in dependent Indian communities.

POAs and Section 106

In most cases, a project that requires a POA under NAGPRA also requires review under section 106, usually resulting in an MOA. An exception would be a research excavation carried out under the Archeological Resources Protection Act (ARPA). Such excavations are exempt from section 106 requirements as long as all the agency does is issue the permit. If the agency provides people, money, vehicles, equipment, then it's a different story.

A section 106 MOA and a NAGPRA POA should be coordinated to make sure they don't contradict one another, but they shouldn't be one and the same document. The primary reason for this is that the two statutes give authority to different parties. Tribes are often involved in section 106 review, but SHPOs are the ones an agency *must* consult. Under NAGPRA, it's tribes that the agency must consult, and SHPOs don't have any role at all. Nor, of course, does the ACHP. Trying to put your MOA and POA together is almost sure to ignite arguments over who can tell whom what to do.

But *consistency* between your section 106 outcome and your POA is essential. You don't want to say in your MOA that you'll put all the artifacts in the local museum, while saying in your POA that you'll repatriate the Native American cultural items to the tribe.

Archeology

One of UNESCO's relatively early forays into cultural resource matters was its 1956 adoption of *Recommendation on International Principles Applicable to Archaeological Excavations*.[40] UNESCO advised nations to protect "archaeological heritage" in a variety of ways—for instance, by classifying archeological sites as historical monuments, creating an archaeological service to identify and care for sites, and by providing funds for research, publication, site maintenance, and dealing with accidental discoveries. Finders of archeological material are to report discoveries, which should be subject to confiscation if not declared. Nations should maintain high standards in excavations both by their own scholars and by investigators from other countries. Comparative research and international collaboration should be encouraged. A sample of sites ought to be preserved untouched for future research. Data should be shared, and publication of results should be prompt. Public education is encouraged. Excavators should be obliged to restore sites they dig and to conserve resulting material and data; nations should adopt rules for the assignment of material found and should suppress illicit trade in and clandestine excavations of archeological sites. During times of war, nations should try to protect sites and refrain from digging up other countries' antiquities during periods of occupation.

To a considerable extent, the United States has adhered to these principles, with one major caveat. Considering the sanctity of private property rights in this country, it is not surprising that UNESCO's recommendations about requiring people to report finds and confiscating stuff not declared have fallen on deaf ears. For the most part, U.S. archeological laws and regulations apply only on federal and federally administered tribal trust lands, and to situations in which the U.S. government provides nonfederal parties with some kind of assistance or permits.

Long before there was a UNESCO, the United States enacted the *Antiquities Act of 1906*[41] to protect sites on federal and tribal lands. By the 1970s, this statute had come to be thought inadequate—and had been declared "unconstitutionally vague."[42] Archeologists launched a new legislative initiative that resulted in the *Archeological Resources Protection Act*.

The Archeological Resources Protection Act (ARPA)

ARPA regulates access to "archeological resources" on federal and Indian lands. Uniform regulations issued cooperatively by the Department of the Interior, the Department of Agriculture, the Tennessee Valley Authority, and the Department of Defense[43] govern ARPA implementation.

ARPA's regulations define "archeological resource" as "any material remains of human life or activities which are at least 100 years of age, and which are of archeological interest."[44]

"Of archeological interest" means "capable of providing scientific or humanistic understandings of past human behavior, cultural adaptation, and related topics."[45]

The definition of "material remains" is similarly broad, encompassing everything from architecture to waste products.

ARPA forbids anyone from excavating or removing an archeological resource from federal or Indian land without a permit from the responsible land managing agency. It also forbids the sale, purchase, exchange, transport, or receipt of any resource removed in violation of ARPA or any similar legal provision. Violators face fines and jail sentences if convicted, plus confiscation of what they've dug up and what they've dug it up with (including vehicles, boats, etc.).

ARPA has been ably addressed by other writers.[46] Any cultural resource manager who expects to deal with ARPA or its violations should carefully study what these authors have to say. Training in ARPA enforcement is available from NPS and the Federal Law Enforcement Training Center (FLETC). There's been quite a bit of ARPA prosecution since the law was enacted, and there are now law enforcement officers and prosecutors who specialize in it. Cultural resource managers have important roles to play in ARPA administration, but we need to be careful not to go beyond our competence. Crime scene investigation is a specialized field in its own right, and ARPA investigators don't need well-intentioned amateurs mucking up their evidence. Some ARPA violators are armed and dangerous. If you see what you think is an ARPA violation in progress, take notes and report what you've seen to the authorities, but don't try to intervene.

Whether ARPA is a wise statute is debatable, though it's not debated much in professional archeological circles. Some avocational archeologists and most artifact collectors and dealers have less enthusiastic views of the law than do most professionals, for obvious and sometimes not-so-obvious reasons. One of the latter is a question about whether criminalization is the best way to deter destructive behavior. Another is justified unhappiness about lumping recreational artifact collectors, commercial diggers, and manifestly deranged vandals in a single outlaw category.[47] But whether one likes it or not (and professional archeologists, almost to a person, do), ARPA is the law of the land, and there's a body of practice that's developed around it in which a cultural resource manager who's so inclined can become expert.

If you're in a land-managing agency and want to be sure ARPA is implemented, you should obviously get to know your law enforcement personnel and work out how to support one another—

who's going to do what in preventing and responding to violations. Finding out that violations are occurring may be a daunting task; it's a big country out there. There's an increasing amount of relatively low-cost surveillance and detection technology available, though, and working with your law enforcement people may help make it available. There may be volunteers who can help monitor site conditions, too; quite a few states and agencies have volunteer site-steward programs. My own recommendation, too—though it's anathema to some people—is to get to know your local artifact collecting community. See who you might be able to enlist as an ally in monitoring sites for damage and turning in vandals. But you'll have to go part way to communicate with collectors, and that may be tricky to do even if you're inclined to be open-minded about their activities. Collecting artifacts from federal or Indian land is illegal under ARPA, and there's only so far you can go in cooperating with people who—however well-intentioned and sensible—are criminals in the eyes of the law.

For those *not* working for land-management agencies, ARPA is relevant because its permitting standards apply to any archeological work we want to do on federal or Indian land under section 106, NEPA, or another authority. The standards are not terribly onerous, though they can be interpreted in needlessly draconian ways and can be silly if carried to extremes. The permittee must meet professional qualifications,[48] but this doesn't mean, as it's occasionally construed, that every individual on the permittee's team has to meet them. Recovered material and data must be housed in an institution that meets specified standards.[49] The work must be done for scholarly and/or preservation reasons.[50] The recovered resources remain the property of the United States in perpetuity and can be disposed of only when they've lost archeological interest and hence become non-resources[51]—ironically, archeological resources are about the only kind of resource that the government can never sell or give away.

You may be told that federal agency employees and contractors don't need ARPA permits. In fact, they do, but their contracts and position descriptions are construed to be their permits. Such documents must, of course, meet the standards that ARPA and its regulations set forth.[52]

If a federal agency issues an ARPA permit and does nothing else, it doesn't have to go through section 106 review,[53] but if it's providing any other form of entitlement or assistance (funding, trucks, shovels, etc.) then it does need to do section 106. The kind of thing that is subject to section 106 review—putting in roads, cutting trees, and the like—isn't construed to be excavation and removal of archeological resources, so it doesn't require ARPA permits, but, of course, it is subject to other permit requirements and the environmental reviews that go along with them.[54]

Indian tribes with possible interests in resources to which a permit pertains must be notified by the relevant land manager and given an opportunity to consult about the work. Where the work will be done on tribal land, the tribe has to give its permission. Under NAGPRA, of course, the agency responsible for issuing the permit must make a real effort to consult with, not just notify, culturally affiliated tribes.

Archeologists in the 1970s weren't concerned only about people digging up archeological resources on public land. There were also all those federal, federally assisted, and federally licensed projects that were wasting sites on lands both public and private. To deal with these, archeologists turned to another oldish law, the Reservoir Salvage Act of 1960, and sought to bring it up to date.

The Archeological Data Preservation Act/Archeological and Historic Preservation Act of 1974

When the Corps of Engineers came home from World War II, Congress assigned it the job of building dams in the Missouri River drainage, and later elsewhere in the nation, for flood control and power generation. Recognizing that the reservoirs behind these dams would inundate thousands of archeological sites, NPS and the Smithsonian Institution set up the Missouri River Basin Program, later the River Basin Salvage Program. The purpose of the program was to do rapid salvage excavations of archeological sites before they were swallowed up by the rising waters.

By 1960 the Smithsonian had pulled out of the program, but Congress, in the Reservoir Salvage Act, gave NPS the authority to seek appropriations for it. For the next decade and a half, NPS supported the bulk of archeological salvage in the country on a few million dollars a year. But only reservoirs qualified for salvage; FHWA began to fund salvage on the Interstate Highway System in the 1960s, but it was a pale shadow of NPS's program. A few other projects had salvage components, but as federal involvement in agriculture, urban renewal, and other land modifying programs increased during the Eisenhower and Kennedy administrations, federally supported archeological destruction became rampant.

It was during this period, of course, and in response to the same stimuli, that the NHPA was created, but few archeologists recognized its potential. Instead we focused on amending the Reservoir Salvage Act to broaden its scope and increase its funding. The result, after five years of work led by Arkansas's redoubtable Bob McGimsey, was the "Moss-Bennett Act" (so called after its sponsors). Never given a formal title by Congress, Moss-Bennett came to be known as the Archeological Data Preservation Act of 1974 (ADPA) or the Archeological and Historic Preservation Act (AHPA), and by several other names.[55]

ADPA does three major things. First, it directs all agencies to report to the secretary of the interior whenever any of their projects may cause the loss of "significant scientific, prehistorical, historical, or archeological data." Second, it gives them the choice of recovering threatened data themselves or asking Interior to do it for them, and third, it authorizes them to transfer up to 1 percent of the cost of a project to Interior to support salvage if they request that Interior do it. Interior, of course, is represented by NPS.

ADPA today is something of an anachronism, since it is largely redundant with section 106 review. As a result, it's honored in the breach with one significant exception. It is often used as an authority for the conduct of salvage and, less frequently, for the transfer of funds to NPS to do salvage, when agencies discover archeological sites after section 106 review has been completed. It is also one of the authorities that NPS uses to justify producing an annual report to Congress on the status of the national archeological program.

ADPA could have a life of its own. In theory it applies to things other than National Register eligible properties. Its reference to "scientific, prehistorical, historical, or archeological data" gives it a scope that is both broader and narrower than NHPA. Narrower in that it doesn't relate to many kinds of historically and culturally significant properties—most buildings, for example, and traditional cultural properties—that are significant for more than the information they contain. Broader because scientific, prehistorical, historical, and archeological data are present in more than properties eligible for the National Register. On the whole, though, the scope of ADPA is taken to be narrower than that of NHPA, and it's used—when used at all—to justify funding data recovery from National Register eligible archeological sites.

ADPA is also responsible for the abiding myth that an agency can spend only the equivalent of 1 percent of its project cost on archeology or on all of historic preservation—and for the opposing myth that agencies are obligated to turn over 1 percent of project costs to archeologists. In fact, what the law does is to *authorize the transfer* of up to 1 percent to NPS (with provisions for waiving the limit where necessary). An agency can spend as much or as little as it wants (or as the consulting parties under section 106 decide) on data recovery if it funds the work itself rather than going through NPS. And ADPA by no means creates a 1 percent entitlement for archeology.

Most cultural resource managers will encounter ADPA in two contexts, if at all. If you're in a federal agency, every year you may be called upon to contribute data for NPS's annual report to Congress. You may also find occasion to transfer money to NPS to do data recovery in discovery situations. Be sure to remember that ADPA is not a substitute for section 106 review. If you discover something during a project, you need to follow the discovery provisions of 36 CFR 800, and you can invoke those provisions only if you've completed section 106 review on the project. ADPA simply gives you a mechanism for carrying out the plan you develop for handling discoveries under the section 106 regulations.

If you're an archeologist, or someone else interested in data, and you don't think the consulting parties under section 106 have done a sufficient job of providing for the recovery of such data from a threatened site, ADPA is an authority you can cite when trying to get them to do better. And it doesn't have to be a National Register eligible site or even an archeological site. A source of archeologically-historically important data, like the paleoenvironmental data in a desert pack rat midden, ought to be of concern under ADPA. Perhaps unfortunately, though, no one ever seems to use ADPA as a litigation tool.

The Curation Regulations

36 CFR 79, *Curation of Federally-Owned and Administered Archeological Collections*, is an NPS regulation, applicable government-wide, that governs the "curation" of federally owned archeological material and data. "Curation" as used by archeologists and museum people means caring for artifacts and data in a curatorial facility. The regulations, which NPS was authorized to issue under NHPA, ADPA, and ARPA, establishes standards for facilities that house federal collections and procedures by which federal agencies are to ensure that their collections are properly housed in such facilities.

36 CFR 79 is important because when we do archeological excavations for federal agencies, we need to be sure that the resulting data and materials are properly housed in institutions that meet the regulatory standards. This can be a costly, time-consuming effort, but it's clearly worthwhile. There's not much point in doing data recovery if we're not going to take care of the data and the stuff in which it resides.

On the other hand, there's a certain amount of irony in the strict standards imposed by Part 79—and indirectly by ARPA, which specifies that federal collections (except material repatriated under NAGPRA) must remain the property of the federal government. As a former federal preservation officer once pointed out in a speech in the spectacular New York Custom House (an NHL), GSA has the authority to sell a building like the Custom House as long as it's standing, but if it demolishes it and then digs up its fragments, it has to keep them in perpetuity.

Agencies have not been terribly vigorous in ensuring compliance with Part 79, in part because it's been hard to find institutions that met them. In some areas conditions have improved; new facilities have been built, old ones upgraded, and arrangements have been made to care for collections in an orderly manner. In much of the country, however, things are getting worse. Institutions are filling up and deciding that they can't keep federal collections, or they are charging increasingly steep fees for doing so. Fee structures are difficult to figure out, because when an institution accepts stuff, it usually, theoretically, does so in perpetuity, and perpetuity is a long, long time for which to budget.

Michael K. "Sonny" Trimble at the St. Louis District of the Corps of Engineers has spearheaded efforts by the corps to document the condition of federal collections. Their condition has usually turned out to be abysmal, regardless of who has held them. The corps has established a "Mandatory Center of Expertise" in curation at St. Louis and has generally taken the lead in interagency efforts to bring the curation crisis under control,[56] but there is a long, long way to go.

Moving on, let's look at the law pertaining to one particular kind of archeological site that's been singled out by Congress for special attention: the submerged remains of wrecked watercraft.

Shipwrecks

I might as well acknowledge that I'm prejudiced about shipwrecks—or to be a bit more gentle, I have some definite opinions, which diverge from those of mainstream CRM. My biases will show in this discussion; I can't help it. The best I can do is to try to be explicit about it.

Shipwrecks are a charismatic kind of cultural resource, and they're surrounded by mystique. Some contain treasure, and a lot more of them are assumed to. They are often hard to get to and dangerous. Their exploration often requires fancy, high-tech gear. They lie in an unusual, often beautiful, fragile, environment that's unfriendly to air breathers. They almost invariably are where they are because of some human tragedy, which may be expressed in their physical characteristics or in historical or oral historical data about them. Finally, each represents a parcel of stuff that was snatched out of the terrestrial world in a single event. As a result, each represents—as archeologists are fond of saying—a "time capsule" reflecting its times and the society that launched it on the waves.

So perhaps it's no wonder that maritime archeologists view shipwrecks as nearly religious objects.

Another result of being where they are, and what they are, is that human access to shipwrecks traditionally is governed by admiralty law, an esoteric body of theory and practice dealing with the regulation of ships at sea. Grounded (as it were) on the fact that a ship represents a considerable financial investment that should not lightly be given up to nature, admiralty law encourages the salvage of shipwrecks, and it has traditionally paid little attention to historic and archeological values. Under admiralty law a salvager can "arrest" a wreck and obtain exclusive salvage rights to it, with only such controls as the admiralty court chooses to impose. Where a salvager arrests a historic wreck, the court will sometimes require the salvager to salvage the wreck using archeological controls, sometimes not. Since archeological controls tend to increase the time and money that must be invested in salvage (though they arguably also increase the value of the products), salvagers have at best a mixed record of accepting such controls. This has led to some fairly egregious examples of shipwreck destruction by salvagers. This in turn has caused maritime archeologists to view salvagers pretty much as the devil incarnate. Maritime archeologists are prone to categorically deny the possibility that commercial salvage and good archeology can ever, conceivably, comfortably cohabit. While this view tends to have experience on its side, it's experience that's been shaped by archeologists as well as by salvagers. Maritime and historical archeologists have strongly discouraged one another from participating in commercial salvage ventures, thus leaving the salvagers to their own devices.

In any event, dissatisfaction with admiralty law and with the conflicts between admiralty law and the laws of certain coastal states (notably Texas) that tried to impose draconian controls on commercial salvage, led archeologists in the 1980s to promote passage of a new federal law. After much negotiation, this statute was enacted as the Abandoned Shipwrecks Act of 1988 (ASA).[57]

The Abandoned Shipwrecks Act (ASA)

To be covered by ASA and guidelines for its implementation issued by NPS,[58] a wreck has to be that of a vessel, including its cargo, whether intact or scattered, that has been "abandoned"— that is:

> to which title voluntarily has been given up by the owner with the intent of never claiming a right or interest in the future and without vesting ownership in any other person.[59]

For this reason U.S. Naval vessels are not covered—the navy never gives up the ship. Similarly, vessels of the Confederate Navy are not covered; they passed to the U.S. government when the Confederacy surrendered and are now administered by GSA. For that matter, all warships are entitled to sovereign immunity from the act and remain the property of the nations in whose names they are commissioned.[60] If you're not a nation with a warship, however, you don't have to sign a paper to "voluntarily" abandon your ship; if you don't take action to mark and remove it after it goes down, you are taken to have abandoned it.[61]

The wreck also has to be on or in submerged lands of the United States, as defined in the Submerged Lands Act,[62] and it has to meet one of two other tests. Either it has to be on the National Register or determined eligible for it, or it has to be "embedded" in the sea bottom or coral.

ASA asserts U.S. ownership of all wrecks meeting these criteria, thus removing them from the purview of the admiralty courts. It then transfers title over to the states within whose waters they lie, except in the case of submerged public lands—that is, lands administered by the United States or to which the United States holds fee title, with some exceptions—and Indian lands (in this case meaning lands held in trust for Indian tribes and individuals).

It is up to the states to manage wrecks and access to them, with attention to the nonbinding NPS guidelines.

So, if you want or need to do something with a shipwreck, you first need to find out if it's on public or Indian land. If not, then find out if it's a warship; if so you have its commissioning government or its successor to deal with. If not, and it's on the submerged lands of the United States, then you deal with the state.

There's a myth that the ASA forbids the commercial salvage of shipwrecks. It doesn't; in fact, it assumes that both public and private sector salvage *will* occur. The NPS guidelines do their best to discourage salvage by going into great detail about the controls that should be applied to it,[63] but the bottom line is that, subject to state regulation, commercial salvage is permitted. Of course, states regulate salvage to varying degrees, and there *are* states where it is effectively forbidden.

The Sunken Military Craft Act[64]

Though the navy has always held that it retains control of all its sunken commissioned ships and aircraft, not every case on the subject brought to court has gone the navy's way, so in 2005 Congress clarified the matter by enacting the Sunken Military Craft Act (SMCA). This act asserts federal ownership in perpetuity of all sunken military craft and prescribes penalties for salvaging or otherwise messing up such a craft without a permit from the secretary of the relevant military department.

The UNESCO Convention

Late in 2001, after lengthy and acrimonious debate, the United Nations Educational, Scientific and Cultural Organization (UNESCO) adopted a *Convention on the Protection of the Underwater Cultural Heritage*.[65] The convention, which is binding on states parties—that is, national governments that ratify it—would effectively prohibit commercial salvage of shipwrecks wherever a state party has control over such work. The United States—wisely, in my opinion—has not ratified the convention, so it doesn't now apply to U.S. waters or activities over which the United States has control, but it could in the future and presumably would supersede the more flexible provisions of the ASA.

Other Laws

The excavation of shipwrecks may be subject to legal requirements other than those of the ASA or SMCA. Wrecks on public and Indian land are subject to ARPA, and any federal permit to work on a wreck is subject to review under NEPA and (except for ARPA permits) section 106. It's not uncommon for a salvager, whether public sector or private, to need a permit from the Corps of Engineers (under section 10 of the Rivers and Harbors Act or section 404 of the Clean Water Act) to discharge dredged material. In such a case, the salvager is subject both to state requirements under ASA and its own laws and the terms of the section 106 agreement the Corps works out with the salvager, the SHPO, the ACHP, and other interested parties.

Cultural resource managers deal with shipwrecks as public servants responsible for managing them or for managing access to them and as contractors for public and private sector interests. It's in the latter role—as contractors for commercial salvagers—that one swims into turbulent water. The archeological community gives a very cold shoulder to those who have truck with salvagers; they are regarded as flirting (at least) with the devil. To punish such people and the salvagers for whom they work, organizations like the Society for Historical Archeology won't let them give papers at their meetings. No doubt many commercial salvagers tremble in their wet suits over this. If you want to work with a commercial salvager, there's no law against it except the UNESCO Convention where it applies, and no reason why you can't do perfectly good research, but you're likely to become a pariah, so be forewarned.

Out of This World

They're not exactly "of the land," on this planet anyway, but it's worth knowing that a small coterie of archeologists and historians, mostly in the U.S. Southwest and in Australia, are pressing for laws of some kind to protect cultural resources—essentially historic properties and artifacts, though one author refers to them as "landscape"—on other planetary and subplanetary bodies and in space itself.[66] Resources commonly mentioned are the landing sites of early probes and landers on the moon and Mars, once-occupied sites like Tranquility Base on the moon, and industrial objects in orbit like the International Space Station. No one I know of is promoting laws to protect big black slabs of extragalactic origin, but perhaps it wouldn't hurt to be prepared. One of the most serious efforts afoot is aimed at getting Tranquility Base placed on the World Heritage List,[67] ostensibly to protect it from the depredations of space tourists. This initiative is complicated by U.S. rules for nominating a place to the list, which require it first to become a U.S. National Historic Landmark. Expressing a comforting concern for international opinion, the U.S. Department of State has thus far rejected NHL listing, understandably arguing that other nations would see such listing as a territorial claim in contravention of the Outer Space Treaty of 1967.[68]

Notes

1. See www.nps.gov/history/hps/hli/index.htm (accessed December 31, 2007).

2. See www.nps.gov/history/hps/abpp/ (accessed December 31, 2007).

3. In *The Secretary of the Interior's Standards for the Treatment of Historic Properties with Guidelines for the Treatment of Cultural Landscapes* www.nps.gov/history/hps/hli/landscape_guidelines/index.htm. Also see NPS Preservation Brief 36, *Protecting Cultural Landscapes*, by Charles A. Birmbaum, ASLA, NPS 1994, www.oldhouseweb.com/gardening/Detailed/718.shtml, National Register Bulletin 18 on designed landscapes (www.nps.gov/nr/publications/bulletins/nrb18/), and Bulletin 30 on rural historic (vernacular) landscapes www.nps.gov/nr/publications/bulletins/nrb30/) (all accessed December 31, 2007).

4. *Guidelines for the Treatment of Cultural Landscapes*, 4.

5. See www.nps.gov/history/heritageareas/ (accessed December 31, 2007).

6. See http://portal.unesco.org/en/ev.php-URL_ID=13067&URL_DO=DO_TOPIC&URL_SECTION=201.html (accessed December 30, 2007).

7. See www.environment.fhwa.dot.gov/strmlng/newsletters/may05nl.asp (accessed December 31, 2007). The same practical result could have been achieved without violating the integrity of the eligibility concept as the exemption does and with much more room for creative "streamlining," by categorically recognizing the Interstate system as eligible and then stipulating how it would be managed.

8. See www.wildhorseandburro.blm.gov/92-195.htm (accessed December 31, 2007).

9. For details see T. F. King, "Creatures and Culture: Some Implications of Dugong v. Rumsfeld," *International Journal of Cultural Property* 13 (2) (2006): 235–40.

10. See www.crossingworlds.com/articles/hopiwater.html (accessed January 1, 2008).

11. See www.sacredland.org/historical_sites_pages/supporting/zuni_salt_lake_saved.html (accessed January 1, 2008).

12. See T. F. King, "Considering the Cultural Importance of Natural Landscapes in NEPA Review: The Mushgigagamongsebe Example," *Environmental Practice* 5 (4) (2003): 298–301, htp://journals.cambridge.org/action/display Abstract;jsessionid=E7B9B01D6AD35C73CAD36C07814481B7.tomcat1?fromPage =online&aid=331346 (accessed January1, 2008).

13. Executive Order 13007, *Indian Sacred Sites*, May 24, 1996.

14. By May 24, 1997; most agencies submitted something; some have updated their reports and procedures since.

15. See www.welcomehome.org/rainbow/nfs-regs/rfra-act.html (accessed December 31, 2007).

16. See www.nationalmemorialregistry.com/ (accessed December 31, 2007) for a national registry of such memorials, which has nothing to do with the National Register of Historic Places.

17. See Thomas F. King, "What's Really Wrong With NAGPRA," in *Thinking About Cultural Resource Management: Essays from the Edge* (Walnut Creek, CA: AltaMira Press, 2002), 103–11.

18. For more detailed treatment of NAGPRA issues, see David Hurst Thomas and Sarah Colley, *Skull Wars: Kennewick Man, Archaeology, and the Battle for Native American Identity*, ed. Sherry Hutt (New York: Basic Books, 2002) *Archeological Resource Protection* Washington, DC: Preservation Press, 1992); Kathleen S. Fine-Dare, *Grave Injustice: The American Indian Repatriation Movement and NAGPRA* (Lincoln: University of Nebraska Press, 2002).

19. H. Marcus Price III, *Disputing the Dead: U.S. Law on Aboriginal Remains and Grave Goods* (Columbia: University of Missouri Press, 1991).

20. As illustrated by the case of Kennewick Man, a 9,500-year old skeleton whose discovery on the Columbia River touched off a bitter legal battle, ending (subject to appeal) in the decision that the Corps of Engineers, which controlled the land where the bones were found, could not demonstrate their connection to any living tribe and therefore was not in a position to repatriate them under NAGPRA. See Thomas and Colley, *Skull Wars*, for background, and the decision in *Bonnichsen et al. v. U.S.*, Civil No. 96-1481JE, District of Oregon.

21. 43 CFR 10.9-14.

22. For more discussion of collections management issues, see Miriam Clavir, *Preserving What is Valued: Museums, Conservation, and First Nations* (Vancouver: University of British Columbia Press, 2002).

23. See Niccolo Caldararo, Lee Davis, Peter Palmer, and Janet Waddington, eds, "The Contamination of Museum Materials and the Repatriation Process for Native California: Proceedings of a Working Conference at the San Francisco State University, 29 September to 1 October 2000," Collection Forum 16:1&2, Society for the Preservation of Natural History Collections, 2001; see http://bss.sfsu.edu/calstudies/arttest/sum.htm (accessed January 2, 2008).

24. 43 CFR 10.2(f)(2); the definition goes on to include dependent Indian communities and lands administered for the benefit of Native Hawaiians.

25. 43 CFR 10.2(f)(2).

26. ARPA's own "consultation" provision essentially provided only for notification.

27. Section 3(d) applies to tribal land, too, but practically speaking, you notify the tribe and do what you're told.

28. 25 U.S.C. 3002(d).

29. At 43 CFR 10.3.

30. 43 CFR 10.3(c)(1).

31. 43 CFR 10.3(c)(1).

32. 43 CFR 10.3(c)(1).

33. 43 CFR 10.3(c)(1).

34. 43 CFR 10.5(b)(3).

35. 43 CFR 10.5(d).

36. 43 CFR 10.5(d).

37. 43 CFR 10.5(e).

38. 43 CFR 10.5(e).

39. Section 3(c) of the statute and 43 CFR 10.3(b)(2).

40. See www.unesco.org/culture/laws/archaeological/html_eng/page1.shtml or www.icomos.org/unesco/delhi56.html (both accessed December 31, 2007).

41. See www.nps.gov/history/local-law/anti1906.htm (accessed January 1, 2008).

42. A handy short historical discussion can be found at www.nps.gov/archeology/TOOLS/permits/legislative.htm (accessed January 1, 2008).

43. 43 CFR 7 (Interior), 36 CFR 296 (Agriculture), 18 CFR 1312 (TVA), and 32 CFR 229 (Defense).

44. 43 CFR 7.3(a) (using Interior's regulations; all others are identical).

45. 43 CFR 7.3(b).

46. See Sherry Hutt, ed., *Archeological Resource Protection* (Washington, DC: Preservation Press, 1992).

47. A study I did in 1991 under contract with the Society for American Archaeology, which looked into the attitudes of artifact collectors and suggested that it might be simpleminded to castigate them all as lawbreaking scoundrels has never been published (the contract unaccountably was allowed to lapse) but can be gotten from the author at tfking106@aol.com (Thomas F. King, *Looters or Lovers: Studying the Non-Archeological Uses of Archeological Sites*, Manuscript report: CEHP for Society for American Archaeology and National Park Service, Washington, DC, 1991); see also King, *Thinking About Cultural Resource Management*, 164–69.

48. 43 CFR 7.8(a)(1).

49. 43 CFR 7.8(a)(6); see also 36 CFR 79.

50. 43 CFR 7.8(a)(2).

51. 43 CFR 7.6(a)(5).

52. 43 CFR 7.5(c).

53. 43 CFR 7.12.

54. 43 CFR 7.5(b)(1).

55. Although I had a role in the NPS decision to call it the AHPA, I think ADPA is more accurate; the subject of the law is archeological, historic, and scientific data, and it has little or nothing to do with historic preservation.

56. Corps guidance on the subject is found in Suzanne Griset and Marc Kodack, *Guidelines for the Field Collection of Archaeological Materials and Standard Operating Procedures for Curating Department of Defense Archaeological Collections* (U.S. Army Corps of Engineers, St. Louis District, 1999); http://acra-crm.org/DoDCollectionGuide.pdf (accessed January 2, 2008). Examples of situation reports by the corps are M. K. Trimble and C. B. Pulliam, *An Archaeological Curation-Needs Assessment for the U.S. Army Corps of Engineers, Mobile District* (U.S. Army Corps of Engineers, St. Louis District, 1994); A. E. Halpin and K. L. Holland, *An Archeological Curation-Needs Assessment for the U.S. Navy, Engineering Field Activities, West and Northwest, Naval Facilities Engineering Command* (U.S. Army Corps of Engineers, St. Louis District, 1997); and R. L. Siemons and D. Sanders, *Assessment of Potential Archaeological Collections Facility Sites at Eaker Air Force Base, Blytheville, Arkansas* (U.S. Army Corps of Engineers, St. Louis District, 1998); and R. L. Seimons, et al., *Assessment of Potential Archaeological Collec-*

tions Facility Sites at Edwards Air Force Base (U.S. Army Corps of Engineers, St. Louis District, 1998). National Park Service guidance includes S. Terry Childs and Eileen Corcoran, "Managing Archaeological Collections: Technical Assistance," Archeology and Ethnography Program, www.cr.nps.gov/aad/collections (accessed January 2, 2008). See also www.cr.nps.gov/museum/publications/handbook.html (accessed January 2, 2008).

57. 43 U.S.C. 2101-2106.

58. NPS 1990b.

59. NPS 1990b:50120.

60. NPS 1990b:50121.

61. NPS 1990b:50120.

62. 43 U.S.C. 1301.

63. See National Park Service, "Abandoned Shipwreck Guidelines," 44 *Federal Register* 50116-45.

64. 10 USC 113 Note, 2005, www.nps.gov/archeology/submerged/intro.htm (accessed January 2, 2008).

65. UNESCO, *Convention on the Protection of the Underwater Cultural Heritage*, General Conference of UNESCO meeting at its 31st session in Paris October 15 to November 3, 2001, http://portal.unesco.org/en/ev.php-URL_ID=13520&URL_DO=DO_TOPIC&URL_SECTION=201.html (accessed January 2, 2008).

66. See for instance Alice Gorman, "The Cultural Landscape of Interplanetary Space," *Journal of Social Archaeology* 5 (1) (2005): 85–107; http://jsa.sagepub.com/cgi/content/abstract/5/1/85 (accessed December 31, 2007).

67. See Lunar Legacy Project, http://spacegrant.nmsu.edu/lunarlegacies/ (accessed December 31, 2007).

68. See www.state.gov/t/ac/trt/5181.htm (accessed December 31, 2007).

7

"Intangible" and Portable Cultural Resources

"Intangibles"

The "intangible cultural heritage" means the practices, representations, expressions, knowledge, skills—as well as the instruments, objects, artifacts and cultural spaces associated therewith—that communities, groups and, in some cases, individuals recognize as part of their cultural heritage. This intangible cultural heritage, transmitted from generation to generation, is constantly recreated by communities and groups in response to their environment, their interaction with nature and their history, and provides them with a sense of identity and continuity, thus promoting respect for cultural diversity and human creativity.

Thus says UNESCO's 2003 *Convention for the Safeguarding of the Intangible Cultural Heritage*, which goes on to say that this intangible heritage is manifested in

oral traditions and expressions, including language as a vehicle of the intangible cultural heritage; performing arts; social practices, rituals and festive events; knowledge and practices concerning nature and the universe, and traditional craftsmanship.[1]

As mentioned in chapter 1, "cultural heritage" means roughly the same thing as "cultural resource." The UNESCO convention reminds us that cultural resources are not all physical, material things; many of them are in our heads.

Personally, I dislike the "tangible/intangible" dichotomy; I think it's a false one. Even if you don't want to consider how much empty space there is in physical objects at the atomic level and below, it's obvious that the values with which we invest tangible things are never themselves tangible; they are made up of thoughts and feelings. They are in our heads. Arguably, everything cultural is intangible.

But the fact remains that, in the United States at least (and pretty much everywhere else in the world), the less tangible, less material aspects of culture—to which most people probably feel most attached—are the least explicitly treated in law. The social institutions, ways of life, belief systems that give communities and neighborhoods and social groups their identities are not the subjects of specific laws, executive orders, rules, or regulations. This is probably because they're so soft and squishy, so hard to define explicitly—though few would deny their importance.

When they are not entirely wrapped up in quantification, social impact assessment (SIA) practitioners sometimes deal with this kind of cultural resource. The *Guidelines and Principles for Social Impact Assessment* defines the very subject of SIA as:

> the ways in which people live, work, play, relate to one another, organize to meet their needs and generally cope as members of society, (as well as) the norms, values, and beliefs that guide and rationalize their cognition of themselves and their society.[2]

In other words, the social and cultural dimensions of the environment, which may or may not be related to such things as land, buildings, and neighborhoods.

Imagine that we're involved in providing satellite television service to remote villages in Alaska. The satellite dishes will sit on chunks of ground, and so do the houses of the people who'll watch the TV, but we've missed the major cultural impact of providing the service if all we do is avoid plopping the dishes down on archeological sites. The major impact of bringing Hollywood's latest fare to small, kin-based societies in the arctic is on their family structure, their values, their forms of interaction. These are all "cultural resources"; they are resources on which people rely for at least psychological sustenance, and often physical sustenance as well, but they have only incidental property referents. This is the kind of resource with which social impact assessment (SIA) is supposed to deal, and it's a kind of resource that people can feel very strongly about.

Most study of impacts on this kind of resource is done under the broad umbrella of the National Environmental Policy Act (NEPA), though sometimes laws dealing with specific programs are more directive. The Magnuson Fishery Conservation and Management Act,[3] for example, requires that the economic and social impacts of limiting access to fisheries be considered. The Outer Continental Shelf Lands Act[4] requires analysis of the impacts of resource development activities on "the physical, social, and economic components, conditions and factors which interactively determine the state, condition, and quality of living conditions, employment, and health."

A concern about "intangible" aspects of culture is also expressed in the American Folklife Preservation Act,[5] which created the American Folklife Center to "preserve and present American folklife." However, the AFPA only authorizes the *collection and presentation* of information about folklife; it doesn't have a NEPA-like or section 106-ish requirement that agencies consider folklife in planning, so folklife matters tend to remain marginal to the impact assessment enterprises we usually associate with cultural resource management.

In 1980, in an amendment to NHPA, Congress directed the American Folklife Center and NPS to prepare a report on "preserving and conserving the intangible elements of our cultural heritage such as arts, skills, folklife, and folkways."[6] The result was a report recommending, among other things, that the federal government:

> indicate the full range of cultural resources included under the protection of the law by defining cultural and historic resources to include historic properties, folklife, and related traditional lifeways.[7]

For want of a clear and well-organized constituency, this never happened, and it's probably a good thing. Legally associating folklife and folkways with historic properties probably would have resulted in something like a National Register of Folklife Resources. This, I think, would have been an utter disaster. We have enough trouble with a National Register of Historic Places without trying to divide up and register something as fluid and dynamic as folklife.

The 2003 UNESCO convention was a brave international effort to highlight the importance of cultural-resources-beyond-physical-things. On the Web site that UNESCO maintains to inform the world about the convention, we're told that "States Parties [i.e., nations that ratify the convention] shall take the necessary measures to ensure the safeguarding of their intangible heritage," in the context of which they are to "endeavor to ensure the widest possible participation of communities, groups and, where appropriate, individuals, that create, maintain and transmit such heritage, and to involve them actively in its management."[8] The convention doesn't commit its signatories to doing anything in particular to effect such safeguarding, however, and what it does do—creating an international register—is probably counterproductive. The United States is not among the convention's signatories.

So in the United States, impacts on sociocultural institutions, ways of life, and similar soft social factors are considered haphazardly in NEPA-based environmental review and occasionally under other authorities, usually under the rubric of social impact assessment. There are guidelines for SIA under NEPA,[9] but none is in the form of regulation or other official government direction.

The Guidelines and Principles for SIA

The closest thing we have to official direction is something I've cited several times already, the *Guidelines and Principles for Social Impact Assessment*.[10] The *Guidelines and Principles* were prepared by an Interorganizational Committee on Guidelines and Principles for Social Impact Assessment in 1993; the committee was made up of representatives of the Rural Sociology Society, the American Psychological Association, the American Sociological Association, the American Anthropological Association, the Society for Applied Anthropology, the Agricultural Economics Association, and the International Association for Impact Assessment. The *Guidelines and Principles* have been published in a number of venues, and both the National Marine Fisheries Administration and the National

Oceanic and Atmospheric Administration have put them up on the Web.[11]

I described the *Principles* in chapter 2. The *Guidelines* are more extensive and are usefully organized around the steps in the NEPA process, as follows:[12]

1. *Public Involvement—Develop an effective public involvement plan to involve all potentially affected publics.* This guideline goes on to discuss ways to do this, many of which we've touched on already. It stresses that public meetings by themselves are inadequate and recommends surveys as a first step in developing an ongoing public involvement program.

2. *Identification of Alternatives—Describe the proposed action or policy change and reasonable alternatives.* This guideline goes on to recommend collecting information on each step involved in each alternative—typically planning, implementation or construction, operation and maintenance, and decommissioning or abandonment. With respect to each stage and alternative, information should be developed on population characteristics, community and institutional structures, political and social resources, individual and family changes, and community resources.

3. *Baseline Conditions—Describe the relevant human environment/area of influence and baseline conditions.* The *Guidelines* recommend baseline studies of human relationships with the biophysical environment, historical background, political and social resources, culture, attitudes, social-psychological conditions, and population characteristics.

4. *Scoping—After obtaining a technical understanding of the proposal, identify the full range of probable social impacts that will be addressed based on discussion or interviews with numbers of all potentially affected.* Scoping, this guideline says, should include *reviews of the existing social science literature, public scoping, public surveys, and public participation techniques. It is important for the views of affected people to be taken into consideration. Ideally, all affected people or groups contribute to the selection of the variables assessed.*

5. *Projection of Estimated Effects—Investigate the probable impacts.* The *Guidelines* list a series of methods for use in predicting effects. The comparative method compares the proposed project with previous similar projects and their effects. The "straight-line trend" method projects change into the future based on existing trends. The "population multiplier method" links change in population size to changes in other variables. Scenarios are used to construct hypothetical futures and consider their implications. Expert testimony obviously employs expert advice. Computer modeling can be applied to a variety of other models. Finally, one can calculate "futures foregone," for example, what will be given up in terms of future land uses or social benefits if this river valley is flooded or that railroad is built?

6. *Predicting Responses to Impacts—Determine the significance of the identified social impacts.* The *Guidelines* note that this is "a difficult assessment task often avoided," but it is obviously important. Since SIA is about human responses to environmental change, it's necessary to figure out what these responses will actually be. So the proposed action will increase property tax rates. Will this actually drive out low-income families, or will they stay because of comparably higher property values? Comparison with previous like cases and interviews with affected groups can provide the basis for this sort of prediction.

7. *Indirect and Cumulative Impacts—Estimate subsequent impacts and cumulative impacts.* The *Guidelines* acknowledge that such impacts are "difficult to estimate precisely" but stress the importance of trying to predict them.

8. *Changes in Alternatives—Recommend new or changed alternatives and estimate or project their consequences.* The *Guidelines* don't promote just the passive collection and presentation of data. The impact assessor is supposed to provide feedback to planners, including recommendations about how to deal with sociocultural change and effects.

9. *Mitigation—Develop a mitigation plan.* The *Guidelines* discuss mitigation in some detail, promoting the well-known hierarchy of priorities ranging from avoiding adverse effect al-

together through compensation for unavoidable adverse effects.

10. *Monitoring—Develop a monitoring program.* The *Guidelines* here encourage full participation by the affected community in getting mitigation and monitoring plans in writing so they can be enforced.

However—

The *Guidelines and Principles* provide common sense advice about how the sociocultural aspects of the environment should be dealt with in environmental review. Unfortunately, though, they aren't very thoroughly attended to in many SIA studies. As discussed in chapter 2, SIA is often warped into "Socioeconomic Impact Assessment," and emphasizes economic and other easily quantifiable variables to the exclusion of all else. This doesn't need to be the case—indeed the *Guidelines and Principles* point in quite another direction—but it often *is* the case. This sort of narrowing of SIA's focus, coupled with a narrow equation of "cultural resource management" with section 106 review, allows much of the cultural environment to fall through the cracks between quantifiable economics and land-based historic properties.

Atmospherics

Hovering somewhere between the kinds of land resources we discussed in chapter 6 and the really intangible, in-the-head resources with which SIA deals lie culturally significant atmospheric elements—the air, the wind, the sky. Concerned about light pollution, heritage advocates in New Mexico have identified the night sky as one of the state's most endangered cultural resources, and are vigorously seeking its preservation.[13] The International Dark Sky Association[14] spreads a similar message worldwide.

At lower altitudes, wind patterns can be seen as having cultural value. People fighting a power line proposed over Wa'ahila Ridge on O'ahu in Hawaii told me that one of their major concerns was what the wires would do to the sound of the wind through the trees, said to be an important element in hula training. Although initially dismissed as not eligible for the National Register on the familiar grounds of having no archeological features, the ridge was listed by the National Trust for Historic Preservation in 1997 as one of the nation's eleven most endangered historic places;[15] the power line eventually was denied local permits. I suspect that the cultural significance of atmospheric elements is often an issue in struggles over historic sites and landscapes and perhaps urban historic districts; it is just not often articulated. In some cases people may be more concerned about the atmospherics than about the places per se; they focus on the places because they're the handle the law affords them.

Religious Practices

The First Amendment to the Constitution includes two clauses concerning religious practice, known as the "establishment clause" and the "free exercise clause." The first says that Congress will make no law respecting "establishment of religion"—in other words, the government will not give preference to one religion over another. The second says that Congress will make no law prohibiting anyone from freely exercising religious choice.

Under the free exercise clause, the federal government should do nothing to impede the exercise of Indian tribal religions, but in fact, it has done a lot. During some periods in history—including rather recent history—tribes have literally been forbidden to practice traditional religions. Military force has been used to suppress religious practices like the Ghost Dance and the Sun Dance. Christian missionaries have been encouraged to operate on Indian reservations and virtually ran some of them in the past. Students at schools run by the Bureau of Indian Affairs (BIA) used to be prohibited from engaging in traditional cultural activities, including religion. In recent times the use of peyote in traditional religious activities has been restricted. Starting in the late 1970s, the government began taking action to reverse such restrictions.

AIRFA

Recognizing the inequity of its past performance, in 1978 Congress passed what came to be known as the American Indian Religious Freedom Act (AIRFA).[16] AIRFA is a joint resolution of Congress, expressing as policy that the United States will respect and protect the inherent right of Indian tribes to the free exercise of their traditional religions.

AIRFA doesn't actually tell agencies to do anything or to refrain from doing anything. But the policy it sets forth has been cited repeatedly in court. Generally the courts have held that under AIRFA, agencies should consult with tribes about anything that might affect their religious practices. The agency doesn't have to accede to a tribe's wishes, but it has to find out what they are and consider them. What the agency does or doesn't do, of course, is constrained by the First Amendment; it can neither establish religion nor prohibit its free exercise.

AIRFA doesn't focus only on religious *places*, though it is clearly relevant to how agencies consider such impacts under NEPA and section 106. It addresses impacts on the *practice* of traditional religions. So under AIRFA an agency should consider, and consult about, the impacts of its actions on things like plant and animal gathering for religious purposes and on worship in places that are *not* historically rooted traditional cultural properties, as well as places that *are*.

Religious Freedom Restoration Act (RFRA)

The Religious Freedom Restoration Act (RFRA) requires that what's referred to as "strict scrutiny" be applied when a court— and by extension, an agency that doesn't want a court to overturn its decisions—decides whether government action violates the free exercise clause of the First Amendment. Assuming an individual or group—not just an Indian tribe but any citizen or group of citizens—has a sincere religious belief, and a federal agency action will "substantially burden" practices driven by that belief, then RFRA says that the agency can take its action only if it can demonstrate two things. First, the action must further a "compelling state interest," and second, it must do so in a manner that's "least burdensome" to the practice of religion.

That's obviously a rather strict standard, and again, it applies to government actions potentially affecting *anyone's* religious practices. Getting back to tribal practices, though—under RFRA in 2007 the Ninth Circuit Court of Appeals ruled in another case[17] involving the Arizona Snowbowl on the San Francisco Peaks (see chapter 5) that using treated sewage effluent to create faux snow on the Peaks would substantially burden the practice of tribal religions, and hence it could not be done unless it could be shown to further a compelling state interest—a tall order, under the circumstances.

Religious Practices and the GO Road

We left the GO Road in chapter 4, with the Forest Service having decided to go ahead with the road through the National Register eligible Helkau Historic District, despite the objections of the tribes, the SHPO, and the ACHP. We asked the questions: What do you suppose the ACHP's position was on the Forest Service's compliance with section 106, and what do you suppose the Court decided?

The ACHP said that the Forest Service had complied with section 106 and testified in court to this effect. Section 106 doesn't require agencies to follow the ACHP's recommendations, only to take effects into account and give the ACHP a reasonable opportunity to comment. The Forest Service had done both things, in accordance with the regulations.

The District Court threw out the section 106 charge, as well as charges of violating NEPA and other statutes. It concluded that the Forest Service had consulted with the tribes, so AIRFA wasn't an issue. The First Amendment, however, *was* a problem. The court held that to build the road through the district would violate the free exercise clause, by prohibiting the tribes from freely exercising their religions. The case was appealed, and the Ninth Circuit Court of Appeals upheld the decision.

The government appealed the case to the Supreme Court, which considered it and reversed.[18] The Supreme Court found, first, that constructing the road through the district wouldn't prohibit the tribes from exercising their freedom of religion. They could still go up there and pray, they'd just have to dodge the trucks. The Court went on to hold that even if the rights of the tribes *were* inhibited, the government had a "compelling interest" in opening up the timber reserves of the interior.

Those who like to see the glass as half full for the tribes, rather than half empty, note that the Court expressed sympathy and respect for the tribal position and said that the Forest Service was right to make efforts to mitigate its impacts. The bottom line, though, is that harvesting timber was held to be superior to tribal religious practice and that running huge trucks through a sacred site was found not to keep people from practicing their religion. A troublesome decision, to say the least.

So when push comes to shove, the First Amendment by itself offers thin support for the practice of traditional Native American religion. Taken together, though, the whole corpus of federal civil rights, religious freedom, treaty and trust, environmental, and cultural resource law can make it very much in an agency's interests to pay close attention to such practices and try to give them wide berth. In the GO Road case, by the time the Supreme Court reversed and remanded the Appeals Court's decision, the timber land that once had been slated for logging had been designated "wilderness" and couldn't be logged, and the mills on the coast that would have turned its trees into lumber had mostly gone belly-up. Congress then capped things by prohibiting the Forest Service from ever completing the road. So the tribal religious practitioners now have a nice road to their sacred site. And the Forest Service in California, to its great credit, learned an important lesson, and now—in contrast with some other Forest Service regions—has an exemplary program of cooperative forest management and cultural resource management with the tribes of the area.[19]

Environmental Justice and Cultural Resources

During the 1980s, it became apparent—particularly to residents—that things like toxic waste storage facilities and public facilities tended to be built in neighborhoods and communities where most of the residents were minorities or didn't make much money. This probably occurred because property there could be obtained cheaply and the residents didn't make much fuss—or if they did, they didn't use the decision-making systems well enough to have much impact. They could seldom afford good lawyers.

Whatever the reason, low-income and minority communities were taking it in the chin when it came to environmental impacts. Representatives of such populations began to make noise about it, and the environmental justice (EJ) movement was born.

EJ is based on a simple principle: that people shouldn't suffer disproportionate environmental impacts because of their ethnicity or income.

EJ entered the environmental impact assessment game informally when practitioners began to address inequitable impacts, occasionally, in EISs, EAs, and similar studies. When the Interorganizational Committee on Social Impact Assessment issued its *Guidelines and Principles for Social Impact Assessment* in 1993, one of its principles was that social impact assessors should "analyze impact equity."[20] But EJ became a formal part of environmental impact assessment when President Clinton issued Executive Order 12898 in 1994.[21]

Executive Order 12898

The executive order directs each federal agency to:

> make achieving environmental justice part of its mission by identifying and addressing, as appropriate, disproportionately high and adverse human health or environmental effects of its programs, policies, and activities on minority populations and low-income populations.

Minority populations and low-income populations—whether just minority, just low-income, or both—have come to be referred to by many EIA practitioners as "EJ populations" or "EJ communities." The executive order goes on to tell each agency to:

> conduct its programs, policies, and activities that substantially affect human health or the environment, in a manner that ensures that such programs, policies, and activities do not have the effect of excluding persons (including populations) from participation in, denying persons (including populations) the benefits of, or subjecting persons (including populations) to discrimination under, such programs, policies, and activities, because of their race, color, or national origin.

Further, it tells agencies to collect and analyze data on the comparative health and environmental risks borne by EJ populations vis-à-vis the rest of the population and to remove barriers to participation by such populations in review of agency documents, public hearings, and other public participation activities.

In case this direction wasn't clear enough, the president followed up with a memorandum[22] directing agencies to analyze environmental effects on EJ communities as part of their NEPA studies and to mitigate "significant and adverse effects" on such communities "whenever feasible." The memorandum underscored the need to "provide opportunities for community input in the NEPA process" and to "ensure that the public, including minority and low-income community, has adequate access to public information."

Executive Order 12898, like other executive orders, does not provide an independent basis for litigation—in other words, it can't be enforced in court by itself. However, like all other executive orders, it is grounded in statutory law—in this case environmental law, civil rights law, and administrative law dealing with public information and participation. These laws *do* provide bases for legal action.

The Environmental Protection Agency (EPA) and the Justice Department followed up on EO 12898 and the presidential memorandum by issuing guidance to agencies and creating EJ units of their own. Until about 2001, EPA was quite active prior to in lobbying agencies to integrate EJ into their environmental analyses; in the last few years it has understandably been less aggressive, but retains a responsibility for EJ coordination within the federal establishment.

EJ and Cultural Resources

What does EJ mean for cultural resource management? Consider a hypothetical example (but one based on a real case).

Out in the great State of Washafornia, there's a hilltop that's much like any other hilltop, except that about fifteen years ago, members of a local Indian community set up a sweat lodge there. They have sweats there every Friday night, with a fire, singing, drumming, and discussion of spiritual subjects, life lessons, and so on. The community is not a federally recognized tribe. It has no treaty rights. The site is not an archeological site; no sweat lodge (nor anything else) stood on the site until fifteen years ago. The Washafornia Department of Transportation (WashDOT) wants to build a highway through the hill. What are its responsibilities?

The sweat lodge is not old enough to be eligible for the National Register (one might make an "exceptional significance" argument for it, but good luck), so section 106 isn't an issue. The community isn't a federally recognized tribe and the land isn't federal, so Executive Order 13007 doesn't come into play. But the community is a minority community, and it's quite probably low-income as well. So under EO 12898, WashDOT had better look closely at its impacts on the hilltop as part of its contribution to FHWA's NEPA analysis.

Is the impact on the community "high and adverse"? Is it "disproportionate"? As usual, it depends, and as part of their NEPA analysis WashDOT and FHWA need to consider what it depends on. They'll need to consider what role the sweat lodge plays in the life of the community—is it one of a dozen or the only one? If it's one of a dozen, are all twelve equally important? How does the community's use of this one compare with the ways it uses the other eleven? And does anybody else in the area have sweat lodges (in which case the impacts might not be "disproportionate" if WashDOT was knocking some of them out, too), or is it only the group that has one? In short, the impact may or may not be high, adverse, or disproportionate, but to find out, WashDOT has to analyze the role the sweat lodge plays in the culture of the community.

Unlike NHPA, EJ is not concerned only with physical places on the land. Suppose, for example, that a community of Vietnamese Americans harvests mushrooms on the Kindling National Forest, and the Kindling plans a fungicide program to wipe out the dread Fir Fungus. Or the residents of an African American neighborhood fish for carp in Round Rock Reservoir, and the Corps of Engineers wants to raise the reservoir level, potentially affecting fish habitats. Whether or not the impacts of these actions turn out to be high, adverse, and disproportionate, the National Forest and the Corps have some analysis to do and that analysis has to address sociocultural issues.

The Urge to Quantify

As we've discussed, there's a tendency in social impact assessment (SIA) under NEPA to focus analysis on quantifiable variables. This tendency has influenced how some people—including such authoritative entities as CEQ and EPA—have approached EJ analyses. Practice in EJ analysis is prey to the notion that one determines whether there may be an EJ problem and, hence, whether one has anything to analyze, by looking at census data to determine whether lots of low-income or minority people live in the area. If they do, then you may have a problem, and you'd better address it; if they don't, then you're in the clear. There's also a tendency to analyze impacts and community values as independent variables; you analyze air quality in terms of parts per million of stuff in the atmosphere; if you're going to degrade air quality in an area where lots of low-income or minority people live, and if you're not going to degrade it as much in other areas, then you do an EJ analysis.

What's wrong with this? Well, first consider that impacts don't necessarily occur only where people live.

Almost nobody lives on the Kindling National Forest; those few who do are either Forest Service employees (mostly nonminorities, and however they may feel about it, not terribly low-income) or the owners of swank hunting cabins on inholdings. So census data won't indicate the potential for any EJ issues. But the spiritual leaders of the Motomac Tribe travel for days from their homes on the Barerock Reservation to the high country on the Kindling to seek visions. A reduction in air quality on the Kindling very well may affect the Motomacs' ability to pursue their vision seeking or to breathe while doing so. The Motomac at least would probably define this as a high and adverse impact, and it's disproportionate because nobody but the Motomac are carrying out spiritual activities in the high country. But this impact isn't going to be detected if nobody initiates EJ analysis because census data don't indicate a resident EJ population.[23]

Viewing environmental impacts and EJ as independent variables is also a problem. An air quality expert, or the standards of the Washafornia Quality of Air Commission (WQAC), may indicate that discharging 0.0001 parts per million of gold dust into the atmosphere presents no human health or environmental problems. Ergo, the discharge of such a level of dust by the Family Jewel

Mine can't have any impacts on anybody, low-income or minority or not. But suppose those Motomac religious practitioners up there on the Kindling NF believe that they must look for their visions in the hills across the valley from their prayer stations, and suppose further that they think 0.0001 ppm of gold dust in the air will get in the way. Now, maybe they're nuts, or maybe they're not, but it is hardly consistent with the spirit of the executive order—which after all stresses the importance of involving low-income and minority people in analysis and decision making—not even to examine the issue because WQAC in its Olympian wisdom doesn't think any impacts will occur.[24]

Executive Order 12898 challenges cultural resource managers to identify and deal with disproportionate impacts on those aspects of the environment valued for cultural reasons by EJ populations. How can we do this?

CEQ has provided guidelines for the integration of EJ compliance into NEPA analyses.[25] Let's look at them from a cultural resources standpoint.

CEQ's Six Principles and Cultural Resources

CEQ's guidance outlines six principles that should guide NEPA review so that EJ issues are considered. Somewhat abridged and paraphrased, the first of these says to:

- Consider the human composition of the affected area, to determine whether minority populations, low-income populations, or Indian tribes are present . . . and if so whether there may be disproportionately high and adverse . . . effects on (such) populations.

What does "human composition" mean? In cultural terms, surely it means both the resident population and people who use or visit the affected area. And surely in determining what the affected area is, an analyst should try to ascertain the views of those affected, in ways that exhibit some level of cultural sensitivity.

- Consider not only direct impacts on the health and environmental quality of low-income populations and minority populations, but indirect, multiple, and cumulative effects as well, including effects that are not within the agency's control or subject to agency discretion.

The actual language of the guidance is more complicated than that, but that's the gist. Important direction: an agency should look not only at whether its particular project will poison the community, but whether it will contribute to a pattern of poisoning involving multiple sources. In a more explicitly cultural example, an agency should be concerned not only about whether its particular project is going to drive the Cambodian farmers out of the valley or the Jamaicans out of the neighborhood, but whether its project is part of a pattern of development that will have this effect.

- Recognize that the cultural, social, occupational, historical, and economic characteristics of a low-income community or a minority community may amplify the environmental effects of an action. Such a population may be more sensitive to such effects, and less resilient in adapting to them, than another community.

Here, too, I've paraphrased a considerably more complex piece of direction—one that's particularly important from a cultural resource standpoint. It should be the business of cultural resource managers to help agencies be sensitive to such characteristics.

- Implement effective public participation strategies that seek to overcome linguistic, cultural, institutional, geographic and other barriers to meaningful participation, and that include active outreach.

Consider this direction with reference to a case like *Pueblo of Sandia v. United States*. Think about the fact that a Native American community's traditional cultural practitioners may not have the money or free time to attend public meetings, and they may not get much out of them or contribute much to them if they do attend. How can we make participation in environmental impact assessment possible for traditional cultural leaders in a low-income or minority community? It depends, of course, but cultural resource managers should play large roles in helping an agency reach out to such people.

- Assure early and meaningful community representation in the process of NEPA analysis and review, recognizing that there may be diverse constituencies within a given community and seeking complete representation.

Often the political leadership of an EJ community is made up of people who interact easily with the dominant society because they've adopted much of that society's value system. It's with this leadership that a government agency can most comfortably deal. CEQ is telling agencies to do better than that—they've got to seek "complete representation." Locating and assisting elements of a group that may not participate readily, or that may be discouraged from it by the group's leadership, should be a job for cultural resource managers, among others.

- Where Indian tribes may be involved, make sure that interactions with tribes are consistent with the government-to-government relationship between the United States and tribal governments, the U.S. government's trust responsibility to tribes, and any pertinent treaty rights.

Where a tribe is involved, seeking "complete" representation has to be done in the context of government-to-government consultation. If the tribal government says "talk with us, and ignore those wacky traditionalists," the agency has to do the former, but not the latter; the traditionalists are, after all, American citizens who are entitled to be heard. Helping an agency walk the narrow line between government-to-government consultation and openness to citizen participation can be an important job for a cultural resource manager.

EJ and NEPA Review

Some kind of EJ analysis should be part of every NEPA review—not just EIS-level analyses. In screening a project to see if it's a legitimate categorical exclusion—that is, if no "extraordinary circumstances" exist that could drive it out of the CATEX category, you need to consider circumstances that could produce disproportionately high and adverse impacts on EJ communities. The same, of course, goes for the analyses leading to EAs and EISs.

Scoping

In formal scoping for an EIS, and in the less formal scoping usually done for an EA, an agency should ask itself, its research data and consultants, other knowledgeable parties, and the potentially affected community about whether impacts on EJ groups may occur. The composition of the *resident* community can be determined using Bureau of the Census (BOC) data and information from local social service agencies. The CEQ guidance says that low-income populations should be identified with reference to the annual statistical poverty thresholds from the BOC Current Population Reports, Series P-60 on Income and Poverty, and that:

> Minority populations should be identified where either: (a) the minority population of the affected area exceeds 50 percent or (b) the minority population percentage of the affected area is meaningfully greater than the minority population percentage in the general population or other appropriate unit of geographic analysis.[26]

"Minority," by the way, is defined as:

> Individuals who are members of the following population groups: American Indian or Alaskan Native; Asian or Pacific Islander, Black, not of Hispanic origin; or Hispanic.

People who use the affected area but don't live there may be harder to identify, since they don't appear in census data pertinent to the defined affected area. CEQ makes a bow toward identifying such groups, but isn't very explicit and doesn't give any direction about how to do it:

> In identifying minority communities, agencies may consider as a community either a group of individuals living in geographic proximity to one another, or a geographically dispersed/transient set of

individuals (such as migrant workers or Native Americans), where either type of group experiences common conditions of environmental exposure or effect.[27]

Anthropologists, sociologists, and others who've researched the social and cultural characteristics of an area can be particularly helpful in identifying populations that may not be easily identifiable from census data. Scoping should certainly include consulting such specialists, both within and outside the interdisciplinary team doing the scoping, as well as knowledgeable community organizations.

Public participation is a critical part of scoping, a key technique for identifying affected populations, and a context in which a cultural resource manager's knowledge of cultural issues can be important. EPA has produced detailed guidelines that list ways to promote effective participation, including translation of significant documents, use of facilities and locations that are local, convenient, and accessible, and tailoring meeting sizes and formats to the community or population. Scheduling meetings to avoid conflict with work schedules and community social events may be important.[28]

The agency ought to use its cultural resource management or social impact assessment expertise to learn about the EJ community's communication styles and principles and design its public participation program with these in mind. People obviously won't participate if they feel they're being asked to do so in an inappropriate or offensive manner.

Establishing the Affected Environment

The shape, size, and character of the affected environment[29] always varies depending on the resources and impact type being considered. For EJ purposes, you need to think about where the proposed action could have impacts of any kind—physical, social, cultural, health—on people and their valued environments and make sure these areas are included in the analysis.

The CEQ guidance reminds us that:

The impacts within minority populations, low income populations, or Indian tribes may be different from impacts on the general population due to a community's distinct cultural practices.

For example, data on different patterns of living, such as subsistence fish, vegetation, or wildlife consumption and the use of well water in rural communities may be relevant to the analysis.[30]

This is CEQ's most explicit acknowledgment of the fact that where one lives isn't the only indicator of where one may be affected. The places where a community fishes, gathers, hunts, or draws water may be relevant—as may the areas where its people carry out other cultural and religious activities.

Environmental Assessments

As discussed in chapter 2, an EA examines the intensity of a project's environmental consequences, in their relevant contexts, in order to measure their significance and determine whether an EIS is necessary.

The interests of potentially affected EJ communities make up one of the contexts within which the intensity of impacts must be considered; the regulations explicitly identify "affected interests" as such a context.[31] In this context, an EA needs to consider questions like the following:[32]

- Does the proposed action have the potential to affect the health or safety of an EJ community? If so, how?
- Could the action affect unique environmental characteristics valued by an EJ community, such as farmlands, recreation areas, traditional cultural properties and other historic places, and culturally valued neighborhoods or businesses?
- Is the action controversial in the eyes of an EJ community on environmental grounds, or are there reasons for it to become controversial if the community comes to understand it?
- Are there uncertain or unknown risks to the community, for instance, ill-defined potential social or economic changes in the character of a neighborhood or rural area?
- May the action set precedents for similar actions in the potentially affected EJ community, or in other similar communities?
- May the action contribute to a pattern of cumulative impact on a community—for example, changes in the community's

ethnic makeup, loss of culturally important habitat, or the erosion of traditional values?

- Is the action likely to affect historic properties or other lands of cultural value to an EJ community?
- Could the action result in violation of a federal, state, Indian tribal, or local law—AIRFA, for instance—designed to protect an EJ populations from disproportionate impacts?

The NEPA regulations at 40 CFR 1508.14 say that economic or social effects by themselves aren't enough to require preparation of an EIS. But if such effects are disproportionate and adverse, and linked to one of the measures of intensity listed above, then they *may* indicate the need for a higher level of analysis, perhaps including preparation of an EIS.

For example, suppose a federal construction project in a city will drive up property tax rates so high that low-income homeowners or businesspeople won't be able to remain in town. Under section 1508.14 this might not require the responsible agency to prepare an EIS, unless the socioeconomic effect of displacement by rising property taxes was related to something like exposure to toxic materials or impacts on historic properties, even if the socioeconomic effect fell disproportionately on the low-income or minority community. It *would* be necessary to include measures to mitigate socioeconomic impacts in the FONSI, though, and to ensure that mitigation was completed. Where socioeconomic effects are disproportionate and related to one or more other effects on the environment, then an EIS may be necessary unless acceptable mitigation measures can be developed and included in the FONSI.

Environmental Impact Statements

Of course, what goes for an EA goes for an EIS, too. EJ issues should be thoroughly and understandably addressed, in consultation with potentially affected communities. The CEQ guidance says that:

> Where a potential environmental justice issue has been identified . . . , the agency should state clearly . . . whether, in light of all the facts and circumstances, a disproportionately high and ad-

verse . . . impact on minority populations, low income populations, or Indian tribe is likely to result from the proposed action
and any alternatives. This statement should be supported by sufficient information for the public to understand the rationale for
the conclusion. The underlying analysis should be presented as
concisely as possible using language that is understandable to the
public and that minimizes use of acronyms or jargon.[33]

Cultural resource managers should have a lot to say about how
an affected community can be helped to participate in the EIS (or
EA) analysis and about how information should be presented so it
will be understandable. Preliminary information and findings
should be shared with potentially affected communities, in a manner sensitive to cultural differences and modes of communication.

Alternatives

The CEQ guidance says that:

agencies should encourage the members of the communities that
may suffer a disproportionately high and adverse . . . effect . . . to
help develop and comment on possible alternatives to the proposed agency action as early as possible in the process.[34]

This important guidance presents another context in which cultural resource management practice can be fruitfully employed.
Many cultural resource managers who work in section 106 review
are familiar with the consultation and negotiation that take place
there, often in cross-cultural contexts. This familiarity with dispute
resolution can be usefully applied to encouraging EJ communities
to work with agencies in exploring alternatives. Helping an EJ
community not only understand what environmental impacts a
project may have, but work to define impacts and explore alternatives to avoid them is a truly satisfying kind of practice.[35]

Mitigation of Adverse Effects

Mitigation measures should, of course, be developed in consultation with EJ communities and groups and should provide for

their ongoing participation as such measures are carried out. CEQ reminds agencies to "carefully consider community views in developing and implementing mitigation strategies."[36]

What might some mitigation measures be? As always, it depends, but here are some examples from one of my own experiences—mediating an environmental dispute over a proposed airport in Micronesia:

- Relocating aircraft warning lights to reduce impact on a sacred mountain;
- Redesigning a dredge area to permit continued access to reef resources;
- Developing a moorage place for village boats;
- Establishing an adjudication panel to settle disputes over land and natural resources;
- Creating a fund to support a village agricultural cooperative;
- Accelerating sewerage service construction to make up for lost over-water sanitation facilities;
- Permitting temporary access to over-water facilities across the construction site;
- Control of noise and dust impacts; and
- Archeological data recovery carried out by the villages.[37]

Record of Decision

CEQ recommends that agencies distribute their RODs to affected communities, designing such documents to explain impacts, decisions, and mitigation measures:

in non-technical, plain language for limited-English speakers. Agencies should also consider translating documents into languages other than English where appropriate and practical.[38]

So, in a nutshell, Executive Order 12898 provides strong direction to agencies to consider cultural, along with other, kinds of impacts on EJ communities and populations, including Indian tribes. Cultural resource managers have important roles to play in EJ analysis—particularly, I think, in helping to balance the tendency by some other environmental practitioners to deal only with easily quantifiable variables and to treat affected communities as sources of data rather than as collaborators in impact analysis.

Portable Cultural Resources

That many portable objects and documents are important cultural resources ought to be a no-brainer, and for those who don't routinely think of themselves as "cultural resource managers," it is. Such resources are in trouble. In 2005 the organization Heritage Preservation[39] released the results of a comprehensive sample survey of "collections held in the public trust" in the United States—collections, that is, of artifacts, art, literature, natural history specimens, digital information—in the form of a "heritage health index." Unsurprisingly to anyone who works with such collections, the index documented a pretty sickly condition. High percentages of such collections' contents need preservation work, while the condition of about 30 percent is simply not known.[40] And that clause, "held in the public trust," is a telling one; the index study addressed only collections held by museums, libraries, and similar institutions. Material in private hands, and languishing in storerooms, attics, and basements, is another matter entirely.

Depending on your perspective, portable cultural resources either seem to get a lot of consideration in federal law or are hardly considered at all. On the one hand, the federal government invests substantially (though to judge from the heritage health index, not nearly enough) in the Smithsonian Institution, the Library of Congress, and—through grants and contracts—innumerable other libraries and museums around the country and overseas that house such resources. And laws like the Native American Graves Protection and Repatriation Act (NAGPRA) and the Archaeological Resources Protection Act (ARPA) are in part designed to keep people from walking away with such things when they're buried in or lying on federal or tribal lands. On the other hand, portable cultural resources are customarily understood to be ineligible for the National Register of Historic Places, and I can't recall ever seeing documents or artifacts addressed in an environmental assessment or impact statement under the National Environmental Policy Act (NEPA). There are understandable reasons for this; National Register staff, for example, say that portable things aren't eligible for the Register because they don't need to be; we can preserve them in museums and libraries. But there's some ambivalence in this answer—enough that when the National Historic Preservation Act (NHPA) was amended in 1980 to include a definition of "historic property," it included "artifacts, records, and material remains related to such a property." [41] And because the National Register wasn't very comfortable with that definition, the Department of the Interior persuaded the Advisory Council on Historic Preservation to define the same term in its section 106 regulations to include only those artifacts, records, and remains that are "located within such properties."[42] It's ironic that in its 2007 preservation summit report, the ACHP recommended improving collections care through "collaboration between the historic preservation community and the broader cultural heritage community," without noting that its own regulations stand in the way of such collaboration by denying the relationship Congress itself had noted between historic properties and portable cultural resources.

But there are some laws and regulations that are specific to portable cultural resources, and a responsible CRM practitioner ought to know about them. Generally speaking, one set of authorities deals (or fails to deal) with artifacts, while the other addresses documents.

Artifacts

In chapter 6 we discussed the Archaeological Resources Protection Act (ARPA) as it relates to taking care of archeological sites on federal and tribal land. But ARPA is substantially about artifacts, not sites. Certainly a major reason for not wanting people to dig up artifacts is that it messes up the sites and disturbs the record that archeologists study, but there's a considerable element of material possessiveness behind the law. The artifacts are federal or tribal property and making off with them is theft. Much of the police work involved in ARPA enforcement involves tracking down people who have taken artifacts from federal and tribal land,[43] and most prosecutions—under ARPA and for the theft of government property—have sought or followed return of artifacts to the government or a tribe. NAGPRA is also substantially about controlling the ownership of those artifacts that are Native American cultural items. Such items constitute something of a special case in that the law favors their repatriation to tribes regardless of what the tribes are going to do with them. Laws like ARPA, however, are clearly based on the assumption that artifacts should be in public ownership, in museums.

The same assumption underlies UNESCO's 1970 *Convention on the Means of Prohibiting and Preventing the Illicit Import, Export and Transfer of Ownership of Cultural Property*,[44] its 1964 recommendation on the same subject,[45] and the closely related 1995 UNIDROIT Convention on Stolen or Illegally Exported Cultural Objects.[46] The 1970 convention—which covers not only archeological artifacts but collections of fauna, flora, and minerals, documents, art objects, ethnographic specimens, and a wide range of other material, defines as a nation's "cultural heritage" those things either found in the country or obtained legally elsewhere. States parties are to set up government services to advance preservation, conservation, and archeology and inevitably to maintain an inventory. They are to issue certificates for licit—and forbid illicit—exportation. Infringements are to be penalized, and states parties are to cooperate with one another in enforcement. The UNIDROIT Convention adds detail about how cultural objects are to be restituted to their legal owners and provides for an overseeing committee. The United States is a party to the 1970 convention, and enforcement actions are not entirely uncommon. I'm not aware of any evidence that these conventions have been at all effective in controlling international trafficking in antiquities or anything else, but UNESCO seems quite bullish on them, and most archeologists accept them without question as good and necessary.

There is no overall U.S. law dealing with the preservation of historic objects that are neither "archaeological resources" as defined under ARPA nor "Native American cultural items" as defined under NAGPRA. Some agencies have policies and procedures aimed at protecting such objects, however. For example, in the navy the preservation of historic objects is coordinated by the Office of the Navy Historian, who reports to the chief of naval operations (CNO). OPNAVINST 5730.13 directs naval units to re-port "items of historical interest" to the historian. The historian's own instruction, tersely titled NAVHISTCENCUAINST 11100.1, identifies items of historical interest as those associated with com-bat, capture, achievement, notable events, technical uniqueness or significance, heroism, humane efforts, human interest, and spon-sorship of unit activities by others. The historian's tiny staff works with naval units to identify objects of interest and arranges for them to be cared for. Most other large agencies have programs that are more or less similar, but aside from selective efforts by the Smithsonian Institution there is no government-wide program to manage historical objects and no general-purpose government re-quirement to do so.

For the cultural resource manager, this means being knowl-edgeable about the collections management policies and proce-dures of your agency or client and doing the best you can with them.

Historical Documents

Historically and culturally important documents—as represented by the Library of Congress—were the first kind of cultural resource in which Congress invested legislation and money. Today two statutes with government-wide application deal with this type of resource.

The Federal Records Act

The Federal Records Act (FRA) [47] isn't ordinarily thought of as a cultural resource management statute. Certainly, though, histori-cal documents are cultural resources, and the FRA is intended to make sure that such resources, when produced by or in the pos-session of the federal government, are properly managed.

The FRA is also one of the few—really the only—cultural re-source law that carries fines and jail sentences with it. Violation of the FRA can put a federal official in jail for up to three years and saddle him or her with a fine of two thousand dollars, or both. However, the FRA is routinely violated by federal agencies—

including such ostensibly historically oriented agencies as NPS and the ACHP.

The FRA covers all kinds of records—books, papers, maps, photographs, "machine-readable" material, and other documentary materials—as long as they're made or received by a federal agency in the transaction of the agency's business. Its central purpose is to preserve evidence of the government's organization, functions, policies, decisions, operations, and activities, as well as basic historical and other information.

FRA implementation is overseen by the National Archives and Records Administration (NARA), which has an extensive set of regulations.[48] At their core, these regulations require agencies to establish internal procedures for compliance, set up retention and disposal schedules, and manage their records accordingly. Agencies do this, although compliance on paper and in reality are rather different things. The navy, for example, has FRA procedures in the form of its *Records Disposal Manual* that total about a thousand pages,[49] but when I was hired in the late 1990s to do a CRM class for a closing navy base whose personnel had found lots of old files stuffed away in its odd corners, nobody on the base seemed to have heard of the procedures, and everyone seemed rather awestruck to learn that they existed. I also found that the navy's whole records management program was supervised by one rather beleaguered-seeming lieutenant at the Washington Navy Yard. And that's the navy—a highly organized, by-the-book sort of operation. I think it's safe to say that the FRA is often honored in the breach.

The navy's *Records Disposal Manual* can give us an example of how FRA is supposed to work. It divides the world of records up into a host of categories, and for each of these it prescribes "retention standards." Here are some examples:

- Naval Reserve Officer and Enlisted Strength Reports: Destroy when two years old or when purpose is served, whichever is earlier.
- Correspondence, messages, and reports pertaining to personnel casualty incidents: Permanent. Transfer to WNRC when three years old, offer to NARA when twenty-five years old.

- Routine monthly weather observations from naval units: Transfer monthly to Fleet Numerical Meteorology and Oceanography Detachment (FLENUMMETOCDET), Asheville, North Carolina, for periodic transfer to the National Climatic Center.
- Captured documents: Permanent. Transfer to NARA after intelligence evaluation or twenty-five years after cessation of hostilities, whichever is later.

There are hundreds of such categories, each with its own standard. Some standards, like the first one quoted above, provide for prompt destruction of records that nobody thinks will have historical value. Others provide for temporary retention, others for retention forever. Permanent records are typically retired by the operational office or unit to an agency management center and eventually to NARA for management by the National Archives at a NARA-approved repository or a Federal Records Center.

What does this mean for the cultural resource manager? If you're in an agency, you're probably producing records that may themselves become historical, and you ought to manage them according to your agency's FRA procedures. So you'll need to find out what these procedures are. There should be somebody in the organization—probably a clerk—who carries the title of records management officer. This person should be able to advise you.

You may find, however, that your FRA procedures don't provide for your particular kind of record to be preserved in perpetuity, and you may want it to be. If that's the case you're going to have to look to other authorities,[50] or find a way to sneak a copy to some permanent repository—which may be a problem if you work for the navy or the CIA or even the Department of Energy.

If you're a contractor, or an agency employee, or staff to an SHPO, a local government, a tribe, or a local organization, you may encounter situations where records are threatened by some kind of proposed action. In the navy base instance I mentioned, the base—a high-tech weapons testing facility—was closing and would be transferred out of federal ownership. Base personnel found piles and piles of old lab notebooks, files on experiments, and the like stuffed in lockers, under lab benches, and so forth. What to do with them?

In theory, the thing to do in a case like this is to find out what the agency's records management policy is and dispose of the records in accordance with it. But if the records are old, and the people who produced them have passed on to other jobs or to the big cubicle in the sky, more research may be required. It may be hard to figure out what categories to assign things to. To be in compliance with the FRA, agencies ought to think about and budget for this kind of thing just like they think about and budget for doing section 106 review or cleaning up toxic wastes, but my impression is that this doesn't often happen, and a lot of important records go into the dumpster as a result. There's a well-known horror story about the Forest Service, when its headquarters moved from the main Agriculture Building in Washington to the old Auditor's Building across the street. Supposedly, a lot of records from the days of Gifford Pinchot, who started the service back in Teddy Roosevelt's administration, wound up in a dumpster, where they were luckily rescued by a collector of historical documents—who then sold them back to the Forest Service. At about the same time, the Department of Veterans' Affairs dumped a great bunch of old veterans' files—really old ones, with a lot of papers signed by a long-ago president named Lincoln—which made quite a splash in the records-collecting community. Don't let this happen to you; someday somebody's going to jail for this sort of thing.

Besides whoever is responsible for records management in your agency or your client's agency, NARA has regional archives whose staff can be consulted, and it puts out various publications about records management.[51]

Section 112 of NHPA

Section 112 of NHPA also addresses records—in this case, records of historic preservation work and its results.

> Each Federal agency that is responsible for the protection of historic resources, including archeological resources pursuant to this Act or any other law shall ensure . . .
>   Records and other data, including data produced by historical research and archeological surveys and excavations are permanently maintained in appropriate data bases and made available

to potential users pursuant to such regulations as the Secretary shall promulgate.[52]

The records we're talking about here include things like archeological survey reports and drawings or photographs of historic buildings, oral histories collected during a survey or mitigation program, documents and photographs found in the course of such work—the cache of old photos in the closet of the house that's going to be rehabilitated, the letters from the Spanish-American War soldier in the trunk in the attic.

The responsibility imposed by NHPA operates separately from that imposed by FRA, but the two should be coordinated. Under NHPA, records of historic preservation work are always permanent records and should be managed accordingly under FRA. In carrying out or contracting for historic preservation work—and other kinds of cultural resource management work, too, though the responsibility to do so isn't as clearly established—a cultural resource manager should make sure that permanent retention of records is provided for.

Permanent retention, of course, means finding a place that will care for the records and putting them there, often providing for conservation treatment, usually paying for long-term maintenance, and for making them available for research. Although they may or may not be strictly applicable, depending on how "federal" the collection is, the curation regulations at 36 CFR 79 provide good guidance in what's needed.

The Clara Barton Problem

In the mid-1990s, an incident happened in Washington, D.C., that illustrates a gap in protection of cultural resources, through which important artifacts and documents can fall. The General Services Administration had inherited a building from another, recently disestablished federal agency, and proposed to demolish it. The building had been constructed before the Civil War, but it had long since lost its architectural integrity through replacement of its facades, so it was determined not eligible for the National Register. Hence, no further review was required under section 106.

As the building was being prepared for demolition, a contractor's employee pried open a long-closed door and found a room whose walls were covered with old wallpaper and that contained a lot of old furniture, plus plaster that had fallen from the ceiling. Papers were sticking down between the lathes off which the plaster had fallen. Curious, the demolition specialist climbed into the crawl space above the room and found it full of papers that had fallen out of some burst-open boxes. He picked up a board lying on the rafters and dusted it off. It was a signboard announcing the presence of the Missing Veterans' Office, under the direction of Miss Clara Barton. He very responsibly turned the sign in, and it wound up with NPS historians who scoured the room and confirmed that it had indeed been where the founder of the American Red Cross had operated a program to help grieving families locate the resting places of lost Union soldiers. Apparently Barton, or others helping her, had simply locked the door and walked away when she got better digs in 1865, and the room hadn't been opened since. Obviously the room and its contents are of great historical interest and interpretive value; the building now is being preserved and restored.

The only reason the signboard was turned over in the first place was that its discoverer was a personal friend of the superintendent of a nearby unit of the National Park system. Otherwise, it might well have been lost, together with the documents and the room.

The documents, which may turn out to be of considerable historical interest, were not federal records (except by virtue of their unknowing acquisition by GSA), so there was no reliable way they could have been managed under FRA. Neither they nor the signboard were strictly archeological resources, so they weren't managed under ARPA or 36 CFR 79. Most important, they weren't detected during the identification phase of the section 106 process, which focused on the character of the building, not its contents.

To guard against future Bartonesque situations, GSA rather red-facedly issued guidance to its field offices calling for identification and management of documents and artifacts under FRA, NHPA, and particularly ADPA.[53] Perhaps this will help, but it's no substitute for a government-wide effort.

We need a systematic approach to identifying and preserving documents and objects that are not of an archeological nature, and we don't have it. A responsible cultural resource manager should be on the lookout for such materials, though, and not be limited by the specifications of the National Register and other federal institutions.

Notes

1. UNESCO, Convention for the Safeguarding of the Intangible Cultural Heritage, Paris, October 17, 2003, www.unesco.org/culture/ich/index.php?pg=00006 (accessed January 1, 2008).

2. Interorganizational Committee, *Guidelines and Principles: NOAA 1994*, 1, www.nmfs.noaa.gov/sfa/social_impact_guide.htm (accessed January 2, 2008).

3. 18 U.S.C. 1801 et seq.

4. 43 U.S.C. 1331 et seq.

5. 20 U.S.C. 2101.

6. 16 U.S.C. 470a note.

7. Ormond H. Loomis, *Cultural Conservation: The Protection of Cultural Heritage in the United States* (Washington, DC: American Folklife Center and National Park Service, 1983), 74.

8. UNESCO Web site, www.unesco.org/culture/ich/index.php?pg=00012 (accessed December 27, 2007).

9. cf. Kristi Branch et al., *Guide to Social Impact Assessment* (Boulder, CO: Westview Press, 1983); Rabel J. Burdge et al., *A Conceptual Approach to Social Impact Assessment* (Madison, WI: Social Ecology Press, 1994); Kurt Finsterbusch and C. P. Wolf, *Methodology of Social Impact Assessment*, 2nd ed. (Stroudsburg, PA: Hutchinson Ross, 1981); C. Nicolas Taylor, D. Hobson Bryan, and Colin C. Goodrich, *Social Assessment: Theory, Process and Techniques* (New Zealand: Lincoln University, 1990), *Guidelines and Principles*.

10. For an excellent critique and suggested improvements on the *Guidelines and Principles* see Frank Vanclay, "International Principles for Social Impact Assessment," *Impact Assessment and Project Appraisal* 21 (1) (2003): 5–12.

11. *Guidelines and Principles.*

12. *Guidelines and Principles*, 11–18.

13. For instance, see www.nmheritage.org/sky/news.php (accessed January 1, 2008).

14. See www.darksky.org/mc/page.do (accessed January 1, 2008).

15. See www.nationaltrust.org/11Most/list.asp?i=129 (accessed January 1, 2008).

16. American Indian Religious Freedom Act, a.k.a. American Indian Freedom of Religion Act, 42 U.S.C. 1996.

17. *Navajo Nation et al. v. U.S. Forest Service et al.*, 506 F.3d 717, Nos. 06-15371, 06-15436, 06-15455; see www.ca9.uscourts.gov/ca9/newopinions.nsf/64C37FB597BF2F848825729C0058BFE8/$file/0615371.pdf?openelement (accessed December 26, 2007).

18. *Lyng v. Northwest Indian Cemetery Protective Association*, 108 S. Ct. 1319 (1988).

19. See, for instance, U.S.D.A. Forest Service, "Working Together: California Indians and the Forest Service," Accomplishment Report 2000. Vallejo, CA: Pacific Southwest Region, USDA Forest Service.

20. *Guidelines and Principles*, 18.

21. Executive Order 12898, *Federal Actions to Address Environmental Justice in Minority Populations and Low-Income Populations*, February 11, 1994.

22. Presidential memorandum accompanying Executive Order 12898, February 11, 1994.

23. To its credit, as of 2003 EPA guidance on EJ analysis directed attention to "areas of interest that are culturally or economically important for ancestral reasons to populations not physically represented in the assessment" (*EJ Tool for Analysis*, USEPA, n.d.). In 2007, however, this "tool" has disappeared from EPA's Web site.

24. This kind of difference of opinion, though with respect to water quality, is at the heart of disputes over the impacts of mining on the Mushgigagamongsebe Historic District in Wisconsin and the Zuni Salt Lake in New Mexico and the impacts of observatory expansion on Mauna Kea in Hawai'i.

25. CEQ (Council on Environmental Quality), *Environmental Justice Guidance Under the National Environmental Policy Act*, December 10, 1997, Washington, DC, www.nepa.gov/nepa/regs/ej/justice.pdf (accessed January 2, 2008).

26. CEQ, *Environmental Justice Guidance*, 19.

27. CEQ, *Environmental Justice Guidance*, 19.

28. U.S. Environmental Protection Agency, *The Model Plan for Public Participation*, EPA-300-K-96-003; Washington DC, 1996, www.epa.gov/compliance/resources/publications/ej/model_public_part_plan.pdf (accessed January 2, 2008).

29. Or Area of Potential Effects (APE) in section 106 terms.

30. CEQ, *Environmental Justice Guidance*, 12.

31. 40 CFR 1508.27(a).

32. Based on 40 CFR 1508.27(b).

33. CEQ, *Environmental Justice Guidance*, 13.

34. CEQ, *Environmental Justice Guidance*, 13.

35. See, for instance, Patricia L. Parker and Thomas F. King, "Intercultural Mediation at Truk International Airport," in *Anthropological Praxis: Translating Knowledge into Action*, eds. Robert M. Wulff and Shirley J. Fiske (Boulder, CO: Westview Press, 1987).

36. CEQ, *Environmental Justice Guidance*, 14.

37. Parker and King, "Intercultural Mediation."

38. CEQ, *Environmental Justice Guidance*, 14.

39. See www.heritagepreservation.org/ (accessed January 6, 2008).

40. See www.heritagepreservation.org/HHI/full.html; the study was carried out in cooperation with the Institute of Museum and Library Services, www.imls.gov/ (accessed January 6, 2008).

41. NHPA Sec. 301(5), 16 USC 470w-Definitions(5).

42. 36 CFR 800.16(l)(1); My attribution of this language to the Department of the Interior is based on personal experience as one of the drafters of the ACHP regulations in the mid-1980s.

43. See www.nps.gov/archeology/PUBS/TECHBR/tch11C.htm; and Robert D. Hicks, "Time Crime: Protecting the Past for Future Generations," *FBI Law Enforcement Bulletin,* July 1, 1997, www.fbi.gov/publications/leb/1997/july971.htm (both accessed January 1, 2008).

44. See portal.unesco.org/en/ev.php-URL_ID=13039&URL_DO=DO_TOPIC&URL_SECTION=201.html (accessed January 1, 2008).

45. See www.unesco.org/culture/laws/illicit/html_eng/page1.shtml (accessed December 30, 2007).

46. See www.unidroit.org/english/conventions/1995culturalproperty/1995 culturalproperty-e.htm (accessed January 1, 2008).

47. 44 U.S.C. 2101-2118, 2301-2308, 2501-2506, 2901-2909, 3101-3106, 3301-3324.

48. 36 CFR 1222-1238.

49. SECNAVINST 5212.5C, which stands for Secretary of the Navy Instruction #5212.5C.

50. Like section 112 of NHPA; see below.

51. NARA (National Archives and Records Administration), *NARA and the Disposal of Federal Records. Laws and Authorities and their Implementation. A Report of the Committee on Authorities and Program Alternatives,* Washington DC, 1989; NARA, *Disposal of Federal Records,* Washington, DC, 1992.

52. NHPA section 112(a)(2).

53. General Services Administration Environmental Fact Sheet: Recommendations for Considering Historical Objects and Documents in Environmental Project Review, Washington, DC, 1997.

8

Comprehensive CRM?

In the preceding chapters we've hacked and slashed our way through a thicket of laws, executive orders, regulations, standards, and guidelines that are intended to structure the practice of cultural resource management in the United States. In reality, however, they don't give much structure. Most CRM practitioners grope around in whatever small segments of the thicket relate to their particular areas of academic training. Archeologists do archeology, historians do history, and architectural historians do the history of architecture, driven mostly by section 106 of the National Historic Preservation Act (NHPA). Historical architects do historic architecture, under NHPA, the Public Buildings Cooperative Use Act (PBCUA) and the tax code. Indian tribes and museums argue over collections under the Native American Graves Protection and Repatriation Act (NAGPRA), and so on. Nobody really works with and tries to maintain the whole cultural environment and that environment accordingly suffers.

There are two reasons for this, I think. One is that beyond the vagaries of the National Environmental Policy Act (NEPA) there is no law that deals comprehensively with cultural resources. The other is that no one is trained to deal with them; instead we are trained in much narrower areas of practice—even when we're ostensibly learning about "CRM."

In this chapter we'll consider ways to practice a more responsible, comprehensive sort of CRM—one that doesn't ignore huge pieces of the cultural environment. I see two such ways—short of changing the law, for which see the next chapter. One way is to conduct impact analysis with all the cultural resource laws in mind—a challenging but not utterly impossible feat. Another—useful only in limited situations—is to develop and implement comprehensive plans.

Let's begin by returning to the closest thing we have to a law that mandates comprehensive cultural (and natural) resource impact analysis—NEPA. It never actually happens, but let's imagine how a NEPA analysis might address the whole cultural environment in preparing environmental assessments (EAs), environmental impact statements (EISs), findings of no significant impact (FONSIs), records of decision (RODs) and in screening categorically excluded (CX) projects. I hope this brief outline will be helpful to those who plan and prepare scopes of work for NEPA studies, though I'm not going to hold my breath in anticipation.

Comprehensive Cultural Resource Impact Assessment

Ideally, assessing impacts on cultural resources should be a coordinated, holistic process that addresses all legal and regulatory requirements in the context of NEPA compliance. Combining the requirements of all CRM laws, executive orders, and regulations produces the following steps.

1. Scoping
When scoping a NEPA analysis of any kind, consider what's needed to address cultural resources. Things to consider include:

- Does the action require review under section 106? If so, we need to initiate review by identifying consulting parties, coordinating with other legal requirements, and figuring out how to involve the public.
- What is the area of potential effects (APE), and what does background research and consultation with interested parties tell us about it?
- Is it likely that the action will unearth ancestral graves or Native American cultural items on federal or tribal land? If so, we need to begin consultation with tribes or Native Hawai-

ian groups about developing a NAGPRA plan of action (POA) for managing such discoveries.

- Does background research and consultation indicate that issues exist with *Native American sacred sites* (per Executive Order 13007) or *religious practices* (under the American Indian Religious Freedom Act and/or the Religious Freedom Restoration Act), with *shipwrecks* (under the Abandoned Shipwrecks Act), the cultural concerns of *low-income and minority populations* (per Executive Order 12898), *historical documents* (per the Federal Records Act), *historical, scientific, or archeological data* (per Archaeological Data Preservation Act), or any other aspects of the environment to which people attach cultural value (per NEPA itself)? If so, we need to structure our analysis to characterize these cultural resources and figure out what effects the action we're reviewing may have on them.

2. Identifying Effects on Cultural Resources

Among the things the NEPA analysis should do is to identify and assess the likely effects of all project alternatives on all relevant kinds of cultural resources—historic properties, Native American graves and cultural items, archeological, historical, and scientific data, religious practices, Indian sacred sites, cultural aspects of the natural environment, community cultural norms, values, and beliefs, and historical documents and artifacts.

Like other environmental impact assessment work, cultural resource studies should be interdisciplinary. Specialists commonly needed in identification include planners, historians, architectural historians, landscape historians, archeologists, cultural anthropologists, sociologists, and experts in consultation and negotiation. Sometimes one person may combine multiple specialties.

The actual work of analysis may include a wide range of activities, such as:

- Finding and consulting stakeholders;
- Background literature research;
- Field surveys to identify and characterize cultural landscapes, historic districts, buildings, structures and sites, archeological resources, traditional cultural places, cultur-

ally important plants, animals, and natural resources, and historically or culturally important artifacts and documents;
- Ascertaining the likelihood of encountering Native American graves or cultural items; and
- Characterizing potential impacts on living sociocultural systems.

3. Exploring Alternatives and Mitigation Measures

Since the cultural aspects of the environment involve human perceptions and beliefs, alternative approaches to the proposed action, and possible ways to mitigate the adverse effects of each such alternative, have to be developed in consultation with stakeholders. Consultation means informing people, seeking their thoughts, and negotiation aimed at achieving agreement. If agreement is reached, it should be memorialized and referenced in the documents produced by the NEPA analysis, in ways that are consistent with the relevant cultural resource laws and regulations. If agreement isn't reached, this should be explained in the NEPA documents, and compliance with the relevant cultural resource laws should be completed.

The section 106 regulations[1] permit NEPA analyses and documents to substitute for standard section 106 review, provided the agency notifies the relevant SHPO(s) and/or THPO(s) and the Advisory Council on Historic Preservation that it intends such substitution, and the NEPA analysis includes identification, evaluation, and consultation about historic properties and impacts. Mitigation measures can be described in an EA or EIS and provided to the SHPO/THPO and ACHP (as well as other interested parties) for review in lieu of a section 106 MOA; assuming no objection within the NEPA review period, the measures proposed can be referenced in the FONSI or ROD and implemented, in lieu of executing and implementing a section 106 memorandum of agreement or finding of no adverse effect. This approach can (theoretically) simplify historic preservation impact review. It can also—more important, I think—make it easier to coordinate managing impacts on historic properties with the management of impacts on other types of cultural resources and the cultural environment generally.

4. Implementing Alternatives and Mitigation

Alternatives and measures to mitigate impacts are no good if they're not implemented. So it's important to make specific arrangements for implementing the alternatives and mitigation measures agreed upon or selected. It's also important to monitor progress. Documents like FONSIs and RODs can be used to lay out implementation and monitoring systems. Of course, so can section 106 memoranda of agreement and NAGPRA plans of action, if they're produced.

Comprehensive Cultural Resource Management Plans

Back in chapter 5 we discussed historic preservation plans, developed and used by federal agencies, SHPOs, and local governments under a variety of names and acronyms. Some such plans are called "cultural resource management plans," but I have yet to see one that deals with all kinds of cultural resources. Most are strictly about historic buildings and archeological sites; some refer to cultural landscapes, Native American graves and cultural items, or traditional cultural places.

Is a truly comprehensive cultural resource management plan imaginable? Let's try to imagine what would go into one. What follows is based mostly on studies I participated in around the turn of the century for the Department of Defense and the navy.[2&3]

What's the Purpose of a CRMP?

A CRMP is supposed to be a tool for use in carrying out the mission of whatever agency or facility is involved, in a manner that's consistent with the cultural resource laws and the national policy of environmental stewardship. To be useful, a CRMP has to help advance that mission or at least not get unnecessarily in its way. It has to be consistent with other plans, such as operating plans, natural resource management plans, and recreation plans.

A CRMP should help avoid surprises; it should make management of cultural resources a predictable enterprise. To do this, the CRMP ought to address all the cultural resource types that may be affected or managed by whatever entity—military base, park, wildlife refuge—the CRMP applies to. It's the things the plan doesn't cover that are likely to generate nasty surprises. If the plan doesn't deal with all kinds of cultural resource, it should be explicit about what it does and doesn't address, and why. If it doesn't cover the full range of cultural resources, it probably shouldn't be called a CRMP; to do so can generate a false sense of security that everything is under control when it really isn't. Call the plan what it is—an archeological plan, a historic preservation plan, whatever.

A CRMP should be based on full understanding of the applicable laws. For example, if NAGPRA applies, there are distinct limitations on what the CRMP can provide for with respect to Native American cultural items.

Intangible cultural resources—ways of life, cultural traditions, beliefs—though they are not the subjects of much specific law, ought to be given early and thorough attention. They're important in their own rights, and they may be what makes places and other physical things significant. And respecting them can build support for the CRMP that won't be there if it's only about what interests historians and archeologists.

What Should Be in a CRMP?

The CRMP should include both *proactive* and *reactive* elements. An example of a proactive element is the adaptive use of historic buildings or providing access to a gathering site by Native American medicine people. An example of a reactive element is a procedure for stabilizing eroding archeological sites or a system to ensure that planned land-use changes are reviewed for impacts on cultural resources.

The CRMP should include procedures—such as review procedures or the application of standards—to minimize damage to cultural resources and procedures to promote their proper use. If it specifies tasks to be accomplished, it should set realistic goals and targets.

The CRMP should provide for ready access—for instance, through a geographic information system (GIS)—to such pertinent information as survey data, standards and guidelines, and points of contact.

If all cultural resources haven't been identified (and they almost never have been), the CRMP should provide for ongoing identification, coordinated with mission needs. If data aren't complete (and they almost never are), there needs to be a procedure to ensure that this doesn't lead to decisions that unnecessarily damage cultural resources and enrage other stakeholders. Don't pretend that the data are adequate if they're not, but don't expect the mission to be put on hold until adequate data are acquired.

Planning and Management Contexts

The CRMP needs to address contexts, but historical contexts in the NPS sense are a lot less important than planning contexts or management contexts. How does the agency or facility or land management system work? How are decisions made? What ground rules have to be followed, considering the mission? The CRMP is supposed to support that mission while ensuring that good cultural resource management is done. If the mission of a hydroelectric project is to produce X amount of electricity, there is no point in designing a CRMP that requires drawdown of its reservoir to a point at which only Y amount can be produced. If the management system is decentralized, it will be fruitless to design a CRMP that requires a centralized system. The CRMP needs to work within the management philosophy of the entity to which it applies, or be designed to improve the philosophy. And it needs to relate efficiently to existing systems like the processes by which planning and budgetary decisions are made.

Resource Types

If you want a CRMP that's truly comprehensive, you need to think through the types of cultural resources to which it's going to apply or that may be affected. Are there buildings or groups of buildings that are or may be eligible for the National Register? Landscapes? Archeological sites? Traditional cultural properties of various kinds? What about human remains, funerary items, sacred items, and cultural patrimony? Are there likely to be archeological sites to deal with? Bodies of historical data like archives, collections of artifacts, oral history sources? Places or things containing scientific data relevant to history or prehistory —geomorphological data, paleoclimatic data, data on historical land use? Native American spiritual places, traditional use areas, and other traditionally important places? What about places that tribes or Native Hawaiian groups think are important in their traditions and traditional beliefs? The fact that there may not be tribes or Native Hawaiian groups on-site or in the immediate vicinity doesn't matter; you can bet that if they're not, they've been relocated someplace else, and they may still have serious concerns about the area.[4] And don't forget traditional ways of life, culturally valued view sheds, places of cultural association, other valued places, traditional social institutions, culturally important socioeconomic institutions that may be affected?

I am not saying that all these resource types have to be managed in every case. Quite the opposite. The planner needs to figure out whether there's a realistic likelihood of each type being an issue. If so, the plan ought to address them; if not, it's a waste of time and money to do so.

It's vital to be clear about the resource types the plan will focus on—what they are and why they, and not others, are the focus of attention. But it's also important not to get so hung up on defining them, describing them, studying them, fondly contemplating them, that one doesn't get on to the job of planning how the entity's mission can be carried out without unnecessarily screwing them up. That's the purpose of the plan, and it needs to be always kept in mind.

Inventory of Resources

There's often a tacit assumption that you need to identify and record—"inventory"—all your cultural resources (however defined) before you can plan to deal with them. This is simple-minded, to say nothing of impossible. We need to know something about our resources, certainly; we don't want to invest money planning for archeological site protection if there aren't any archeological sites. But we don't necessarily need to know very much. We need to know what *kinds* of resources we have to deal with, and we need a system for compiling data on them, maintaining the security of the data, and making the data available for planning actions that might affect the resources. How much we need to know depends on the circumstances—maybe a lot, in areas where there's lots going on that can affect things, maybe not much at all in areas where nothing much is happening.

Whatever kind of inventory we have or develop, the plan needs to include a way of accessing it. But if the plan itself begins to look like an inventory, you have a problem. If for no other reason, it's a problem if the guy planning the next project has to wade through four hundred pages of resource descriptions before (maybe) getting some guidance about how to take care of them.

Stakeholders

The CRMP needs to identify stakeholders, and they need to be involved both in its creation and in its implementation. The agency that wants the CRMP is obviously a stakeholder. In addition:

- Indian tribes may be very important stakeholders because of the special rights they may have under treaty and because of the government-to-government relationship that exists between them and the U.S. government. They sometimes don't like to be called "stakeholders," because that implies (they think) that they are no more special than everybody else. They *are* special; they're sovereign governments with which the U.S. government has to relate in special ways, but nevertheless, they hold a stake in the outcome and operation of the CRMP. And nonfederally recognized tribes, though not sovereigns, need to be involved as well; they just don't have the same kind of authority as recognized tribes.
- Regulators such as the SHPO, the ACHP, and EPA may have important roles to play.
- Local residents are obviously stakeholders, and if they constitute a minority or low-income community, their interests require special consideration under Executive Order 12898.
- Property owners naturally have stakes in what happens to their land or community, and there may be a variety of legitimate special interest groups such as land rights groups, environmental groups, and historic preservation groups.

Identifying and Resolving Conflicts

The central reason for a CRMP is to address and resolve conflicts between the mission and cultural resources. Conflicts usually fall into two categories:

Action Planning Conflicts

For some reason, our planning for specific actions like road building, building renovation, or military training doesn't fully consider cultural resources. Maybe it's because of some sort of institutional failure—management just doesn't care about this sort of thing. Or maybe it's a lack of data—we don't know what we may be getting into when we plan something in this or that location, and we don't have a ready way of finding out—or even of knowing that not knowing is a problem. Or maybe we do consider them, but we haven't yet figured out a way to keep them from causing problems.

Ongoing Management Problems

We may have archeological sites eroding into the reservoir. We may have a problem with vandalism, or with unauthorized artifact collecting, or plant harvesting. We may have a tribe that wants unfettered access to a piece of land to carry out subsistence fishing where we normally hold live-fire exercises. And we may have clashes over cultural values—for example, between the tribe's cultural authorities who don't want to talk about deeply spiritual matters, and our planners who say, "If you won't tell us where your sacred sites are, how can we manage them?"

The CRMP needs to define these conflicts and problems as a basis for solving them.

What to Do About the Conflicts?

This is where the rubber meets the road. The CRMP should analyze and answer questions like:

What's Practical?

Are there management system changes that will help? Are they do-able? Can we establish partnerships with other stakeholders? Should we? Would better stakeholder involvement help? Do we need more data, more study of specific matters, before we can figure out what to do? Are there specific, short-term management actions we can take (providing access, capping the archeological site)?

What's Legal?

The laws—NHPA, NAGPRA, and the rest—establish standards (of greater or lesser specificity) that must be met. Sometimes these are not as rigorous as people think they are, but you need to talk with your lawyers and with other knowledgeable people to determine just what can be legally done. For example, if NAGPRA applies, we can't just negotiate a reburial agreement with a tribe and go rebury bodies; we have to go through the steps set forth in the NAGPRA regulations for establishing title and carrying out repatriation.

Make it Usable

Make sure that your CRMP is tied in with other plans, other operating systems, other standard procedures. Make sure it's available to those who need it.

Make your CRMP easy to use by those who will use it. It should be compatible with the software and operating system that people routinely use in their work. There's no use designing something for a Mac if everybody is on PCs, and vice versa. Text should be written in plain English (unless users preferentially use another language), and graphics should be liberally employed.

Plan for training. The CRMP will not work if people aren't trained to use it. Training should be explicitly provided for, built into plan implementation, and repeated at regular intervals. If key personnel change regularly, there should be a system for briefing them on the plan and how it works, before they have to start using or relying on it.

Plan for periodic review and updating. No plan is good forever; things change, people change, systems change. Provide for
regular assessments or program audits and for multiparty status
assessments, involving all stakeholders.

Scoping is the Key

Just as you "scope" an environmental impact statement (EIS),
you need to scope your CRMP. You need to think about the issues the CRMP should address, and you need to coordinate your
thinking with the thinking of others, including people and
groups outside the organization—regulators like the SHPO and
such other stakeholders as Indian tribes and local communities.
You need to integrate your work with what's going on elsewhere
in the organization—for example, natural resource planning and
recreation planning.

Three Rules of Thumb

A CRMP shouldn't be very long. It may refer to, relate to all
kinds of lengthy bodies of data—databases, research documents—
but those shouldn't be in the plan. Keep the plan short, keep it to
the point, keep it focused on what it's supposed to accomplish (see
below).

A CRMP isn't a research document. It's probably based on research, and it certainly may refer to things like research designs for
archeological sites or a scholarly study of local sociology or architecture, but its main purpose is not to support research. If you find
your CRMP becoming heavy with text about what happened here
during the Middle Archaic period, or the Tin Rush, stop; think
about what you're doing and how you expect this plan to be used.
Rework it so it can be used, so people are tempted to use it. Put the
research stuff in appendixes, in accessible databases, anywhere but
in the plan.

Be careful in your selection of people to do the CRMP. You
don't necessarily want a professionally qualified archeologist or
architectural historian or historian in charge, though all may be important members of the planning team. The person in charge, or at
least a person with influence over how the plan is structured,

should be somebody who knows about the entity to which the plan pertains—its mission, its character, its existing planning and management systems. Maybe even a planner.

What Do You Do With a CRMP?

The hardheaded rationale for doing a CRMP is to simplify and rationalize one's compliance with the cultural resource laws and regulations, in the real-world environment to which the CRMP applies. Making this happen requires engaging with the laws and regulations, constructing a relationship between them and the CRMP. Section 106 regulations provide a structured way to do this, via a program alternative like an agency's own section 106 regulations, an advisory council program comment, or most commonly, a programmatic agreement (PA). A PA may be executed before a CRMP is done and set the plan standards with respect to historic properties. In such a case, the PA needs to provide for review and acceptance of the plan by the SHPO, ACHP, and other key parties. Or the PA can be done after the plan is complete, and simply endorse it: as long as we follow the plan, we're in compliance with section 106.[5] In much the same way, an agency can prepare a programmatic EIS or EA under NEPA, considering the environmental impacts of all actions carried out consistent with the plan. Under NAGPRA an agency can enter into a comprehensive agreement (CA) with a tribe or tribes about how Native American cultural items will be managed; such an agreement could refer to elements in a CRMP. The other cultural resource laws don't have similar provisions, but they certainly don't discourage designing things like CRMPs to structure compliance. A properly prepared plan—done in consultation with all the pertinent stakeholders and reflecting or providing for compliance with all the pertinent laws and executive orders—should demonstrate that the agency or facility is meeting its legal obligations. This can be important to management if the agency or facility gets reviewed for environmental compliance under an internal or external environmental audit system (as required by ISO 14000), and, of course, it can do an agency good in court.

The advantage to making your plan the subject of a section 106 PA is that it can permit the plan to substitute an efficient way of dealing with historic properties for the standard section 106 process, which is often *not* very efficient. For example, if your military installation contains a lot of old buildings that have to be maintained and periodically renovated, you might specify in your CRMP that specific methods will be employed in conducting routine maintenance and renovation—perhaps some variant on the *Secretary of the Interior's Standards for Rehabilitation*, or perhaps something entirely different.[6] If you do a PA, you can specify in it that as long as these methods are employed, there's no need for standard section 106 review of routine maintenance and renovation work. If you don't have a PA, you can't create this kind of efficiency improvement—or at least, if you do, you won't be in compliance with section 106. To be in compliance, you'll still have to run every maintenance and renovation project through the standard section 106 review process.[7]

An interesting but as yet (to my knowledge) untested possibility under the section 106 regulations lies in the provision for substituting NEPA compliance for the standard section 106 process, provided standards of consultation, identification, and adverse effect resolution are met.[8] This could be a very good way to simplify section 106 review in the context of an overall CRMP; make the CRMP the subject of NEPA review, involve the necessary parties under 106 in consultation on its creation, resolve any conflicts with them during review of the draft EA or EIS, and then put the plan in place. This could be especially helpful in cases where there are multiple types of cultural resources to deal with, some of them subject to the provisions of section 106, others not.

Who Prepares a CRMP?

Unfortunately but inevitably, most agencies and regulated non-federal parties like hydroelectric project operators get what they think to be CRMPs prepared by contracting for them. Those who get the contracts—indeed, those toward whose qualifications scopes of work and requests for proposals tend to be biased—are drawn from one of the following pools of talent:

- "CRM" contractors staffed mostly by archeologists and architectural historians, usually with a very thin knowledge of and little interest in the agency's or facility's mission and management systems; or

- "Environmental planning" contractors who know little about either mission and management systems or cultural resources.

CRM contractors will typically deliver a product that is very heavy on research into the history, prehistory, and historic properties of the area, with little said about other types of cultural resources and sometimes even less said about how to prosecute the entity's mission in a culturally responsible manner. Management recommendations tend to be tired replays of the standard section 106 process, the *Secretary of the Interior's Standards for Rehabilitation*, or someone's exotic notion of what these standard forms of impact control comprise. Environmental planning firms tend to obtain contracts for multiple plans and establish standardized systems for cranking them out, which are applied to all plans without much attention to the particularities of mission and resources. They then hire or subcontract with "cultural resource" specialists who perform in their usual manner within the environmental contractor's specified structure. The results are "plans" unworthy of the name and of the money spent to produce them.

Preparation of a CRMP ought to be overseen by someone who knows the entity to which the plan is to relate—not just as a contracting officer's technical representative but as a key member of the planning team, with the authority to structure the way the CRMP will be developed and the issues it will address. Generally that means someone within the organization of the installation, forest, park, local government, or other entity that's going to get and use the plan. The composition of the planning team should be established through scoping. Obviously the people doing the work vis-à-vis different resource types and different procedural approaches need to be professionally qualified to do the work, but simply hiring qualified architectural historians and archeologists isn't going to get you a good plan. Having the planning supervised by someone who cares about the mission, and also cares about the management of resources and the rule of law, just may.

CRMPs in Other Countries

Although as we discussed in chapter 5, most U.S. cultural resource management and environmental impact laws apply only in more or less domestic contexts, there are reasons that CRMPs and things like CRMPs are developed by U.S. governmental and private interests in other countries. First, of course, most other countries have environmental laws, and often cultural resource management laws, of their own.[9] The effectiveness of these laws varies widely. In Latin American countries, for example, there are severe prohibitions on messing about with *el patrimonio nacional*, but these often don't seem to apply to governmental projects.

U.S. military forces abroad theoretically adhere to the Overseas Environmental Baseline Guidance Document (OEBGD) and, hence, follow either the host country's environmental laws or the pertinent U.S. laws, whichever are more stringent (see chapter 5). So U.S. military installations in other countries should have Integrated Cultural Resource Management Plans (ICRMPs) just like their domestic equivalents, and at least some of them do, addressing the host nation's cultural resource laws as understood by the installations.[10]

The various international pronouncements on cultural resource matters—notably UNESCO conventions and recommendations—mentioned throughout this book provide some guidance to both governmental and nongovernmental U.S. organizations operating in other countries. The UNESCO *Convention for the Safeguarding of the Intangible Cultural Heritage*,[11] *Recommendation Concerning the Safeguarding and Contemporary Role of Historic Areas*,[12] and *Recommendation Concerning the Safeguarding of the Beauty and Character of Landscapes and Sites*[13] might be particularly relevant to cultural resource management planning, and the U.N. *Declaration on the Rights of Indigenous Peoples*[14] ought to be attended to when such plans relate to the interests of indigenous groups. The fact that the United States did not officially support this declaration might impede a government agency in following it—at least for awhile—but it should nevertheless be recognized as a statement of the international community's expectations.

Many private corporations and some government agencies have their environmental protection programs certified as meeting appropriate standards under ISO 14000[15]—a standard established by the International Organization on Standards, with which agencies and companies comply voluntarily. Some national governments look to ISO certification as a means of exerting environmental controls over corporations operating within their boundaries; some stockholder groups are looking to it as a way of ensuring corporate responsibility toward the environment, and some companies and agencies see it as an important demonstration of such responsibility and hence as a marketing tool. ISO 14000 is an entirely process-oriented standard, but some of the processes it espouses, like having systems in place to attend to the environmental concerns of those around one's place of business, can have useful implications for cultural resource management—both internationally and in the domestic context. A program specifying how a corporation, installation, or agency operating in any country will meet ISO 14000 standards with respect to the cultural environment would in essence be a CRMP, but I'm not aware of anyone who has made that connection, and I don't know that it would be useful to do so.

So . . .

A CRMP—in domestic and international contexts, and whether required by law or not—can be a useful tool for coordinated, practical compliance with the whole range of cultural resource management legal requirements and best practices. To do a good one, you need to plan the plan, based on solid, thoughtful scoping, with the involvement of all key internal and external stakeholders. The CRMP should deal with all kinds of cultural resources and all pertinent laws or explain precisely which ones are not dealt with and why. Although you need to know about the resource types that have to be dealt with, defining them—à la historic contexts—should not be the primary focus of the plan. The plan should be sensitive to the mission of the agency or facility and relate effectively to internal management and decision-making systems. It should serve as the basis for demonstrating compliance with pertinent laws such as section 106 and NAGPRA or their equivalents in other countries, and for complying with these authorities in a cost-effective, time-effective manner. It should be prepared by qualified people, under the supervision of somebody who can keep his or her eye on the prize of achieving a plan that actually helps manage resources, and effect the mission. It should be developed in culturally sensitive consultation with stakeholders, particularly local indigenous and other groups. Unfortunately, things that pass for CRMPs seldom meet all these standards, so good examples are very thin on the ground.

Notes

1. 36 CFR 800.8(c).
2. CEHP, *Principles of Cultural Resource Management Planning in the Department of Defense* (Washington, DC: Legacy Resource Management Program, Department of Defense, 1993); *Historic and Archeological Resource Protection Planning Guidelines* NAVFACENGCOM Code 150RH (Alexandria, VA: Department of the Navy, 1997).
3. For generally consistent, more official, guidance, see ACHP (Advisory Council on Historic Preservation) and FERC (Federal Energy Regulatory Commission), *Guidelines for the Development of Historic Properties Management Plans for FERC Hydroelectric Projects*, Washington, DC, jointly issued May 20, 2002.
4. In the southeast, for example, agencies trying to do a good job of compliance with environmental and cultural resource laws have to consult with tribes that were relocated to Oklahoma in the 1830s along the Trail of Tears. The sins of the fathers—President Andrew Jackson and his cohort—are visited upon their progeny.
5. The U.S. Army, in its direction on the preparation of Integrated Cultural Resource Management Plans (ICRMPs), actually specifies that "NHPA PAs and MOAs shall not refer to or implement an ICRMP (AR-200-4, Sec. 2-3.b(4)). This is about as wrong-headed a piece of guidance as I've seen in federal regulation and leads to ICRMPs that quite systematically lead army installations into noncompliance with NHPA.
6. Even that they'll all be demolished, though expect some argument about that.
7. This seemingly self-evident principle seems to be lost on some of the most active "cultural resource planning" specialists currently in business—the preparers of ICRMPs for the army and other military services. Army ICRMPs I've reviewed routinely prescribe Standard Operating Procedures for treatment of various types of historic property and in those procedures fail to provide for standard section 106 review. But, of course, under AR 200-4, as noted above, there's no PA that makes these deviations from the regulations legal. Such a plan, then, directs those who implement it to break the law. This seems a silly way to conduct government business, even if you are the agency with most of the guns.
8. 36 CFR 800.8(c).

9. See Robert Stipe, ed., *Historic Preservation in Foreign Countries* (Washington, DC: U.S. Committee of the International Council on Monuments and Sites, 1982; supplement 1986); Rex L. Wilson, ed., *Rescue Archeology: Proceedings of the Second New World Conference on Rescue Archeology* (Dallas: Southern Methodist University Press, 1987); Rex L. Wilson and Gloria Loyola, eds., *Rescue Archeology: Papers from the First New World Conference on Rescue Archeology* (Washington, DC: Preservation Press, 1981); Thomas F. King and Samuel E. Stuelson, *Preservation Laws and Policies*, in UNESCO online Encyclopedia of Life Support Systems, www.eolss.net/ (accessed December 27, 2007; subscription required).

10. See https://portal.navfac.navy.mil/pls/portal/docs/PAGE/NAVFAC/ NAVFAC_WW_PP/NAVFAC_NAVFACFE_PP/TAB34276/CH%2012_ HISTORIC%20%26%20CULTURAL%20_2006_.PDF (accessed January 11, 2008) for an example of the national "operating standards" under which ICRMPs in other countries are supposed to be prepared.

11. UNESCO, *Convention for the Safeguarding of the Intangible Cultural Heritage*, Paris, October 17, 2003, www.unesco.org/culture/ich/index.php?pg=00006 (accessed January 1, 2008).

12. UNESCO, *Convention on the Means of Prohibiting and Preventing the Illicit Import, Export and Transfer of Ownership of Cultural Property* (New York: UNESCO, 1976).

13. UNESCO, *Recommendation Concerning the Safeguarding of the Beauty and Character of Landscapes and Sites* (New York: UNESCO, 1962).

14. United Nations, *United Nations Declaration on the Rights of Indigenous Peoples*, Adopted by the General Assembly September 13, 2007. See www.un.org/esa/ socdev/unpfii/en/declaration.html, (accessed December 24, 2007).

15. International Organization on Standards, *Environmental Management Systems: 14000 Series*, 1995, http://ems-hsms.com//Implementation/ISO14K/ iso14k_index.htm (accessed January 3, 2008); Don Sayre, *Inside ISO 14000: The Competitive Advantage of Environmental Management* (Delray Beach, FL: St. Lucie Press, 1996).

9

Working With CRM

Being a Cultural Resource Manager

If you've dipped into this book either on your own or as part of a class, and you're not already doing cultural resource management in some way that's satisfactory to you, you may be wondering whether there's a future for you in the field. Let's look at some possibilities.

Working in an Action Agency

You may work, or be interested in working, in an agency that actually does things—funds highway construction, builds dams, assists farmers, manages land, fights wars. If you get into such an agency, you'll probably work in an "environmental shop"—the office or division or department that is responsible for project review under NEPA and some of the other authorities we've discussed in this book. Or you may be in a "cultural resource shop," that focuses mostly on the care and feeding of historic buildings and/or archeological sites, and occasionally more—in the context of project review and sometimes in that of long-term management. More rarely you may be in a "social assessment shop" concerned with social and economic impacts, perhaps at both project and policy levels. Another possibility is employment in a "Native American shop," focusing on your agency's government-to-government relationship with tribes, and perhaps handling treaty rights issues as well as Native American cultural resources per se. Or you may be on a staff that deals with several of these kinds of things.

In any of these contexts, and irrespective of the professional specialization you bring to the job, if you're a new employee you'll have things to learn as quickly as you can, and attitude adjustments to make, if you're going to be happy in your work.

You'll need to respect the agency's mission and priorities. This may not come easy. You probably—I hope—have commitments to environmental protection, to doing right by cultural resources, and to public responsibility. You may even be a bit starry-eyed about these things. You may be a very ethical archeologist or historical architect who believes in protecting the resource over all else. Finding yourself in the company of a bunch of engineers devoted to, say, efficient transportation may be something of a shock. You may be used to thinking of the agency that's now your employer as a rapist of the world and of your colleagues as dangerous deadheads.

You have to adjust those attitudes. Don't lose them completely; they're probably not entirely incorrect. Just keep them encapsulated, and give your agency and your colleagues a chance. Recognize that, for all its warts, your agency is doing something that at least a segment of the public thinks is in its interests. You may not like a particular policy or project—that's fine, but if you can't accept the idea that your agency overall has a worthwhile mission, you ought not to be working for it.

You need to learn your agency's internal procedures. How are decisions made? How does paperwork move? How does the budget process work? How does the agency relate to others? To Congress? To other agencies? To the public? What are the limits of your agency's power, and the scope of its authorities? Don't expect your agency to ram something down the throats of those who receive its assistance if your agency just doesn't relate to its customers that way. Think of some other way to get them to swallow it.

You ought to learn something about what your colleagues do—particularly colleagues who perform other aspects of cultural resource management or related kinds of management. What does the social impact assessment guy do? What are the concerns of the wildlife manager? The handicap accessibility specialist? At the very least, showing respect for what they do will help you garner their assistance and support, and if you help look out for their interests, they just may return the favor.

But be careful about becoming *too* much a team player. Your job (probably) is to make sure that cultural resources of some kind are given a fair shake as your agency goes about its mission. You have an obligation to the public to do this; if the public weren't interested in doing right by cultural resources, you wouldn't have a job. Your job is not to help your agency or your agency's clients or customers, ignore cultural resources or the interests of the public, or run roughshod over them. Maintaining balance between respect for your agency's mission and your own integrity may be a challenge, but that's why they pay you the big bucks.

Working in a Review Agency

In a review agency like the Advisory Council on Historic Preservation or the Council on Environmental Quality, or on a state or tribal historic preservation officer's project review staff, you need many of the same attitudes and skills as in an action agency. You need to know something about, and respect, the missions and operations of the agencies whose actions you review, as well as those of your own agency. Balanced with this, you need a commitment to the public interest and tolerance for a diversity of publics. You're going to be on the firing line, expected by people to help them represent their interests against agencies they feel are doing them wrong, or doing wrong by things they think are important— even sacred. It can be tough, but it's imperative that you be seen by everyone as fair and unbiased.

Of course, you'll need to know the laws and regulations that drive your agency's work and you ought to know how far you can flex them and how. You should also be able to work with laws and regulations other than your own, with which your laws and regulations interact—or ought to. If you're doing section 106 review you ought to know about NEPA and NAGPRA, and the Clean Water Act if you interact with the Corps of Engineers.

And more than people in some other jobs, you'll need to get familiar with the specializations of your colleagues. You may be an urban planner, but you're not necessarily going to be able to call on your friendly neighborhood architectural historian or archeologist when you're faced with a problem involving their specialties. You need to know something about them yourself—and know your limitations, when to ask for help.

Getting formal training in negotiation, mediation, and other forms of alternative dispute resolution (ADR) is a really good idea. You'll often be a middleperson between an agency and an affected community or affected interests. Most of us fly by the seats of our pants in such situations, but there's a better way. Take some classes, get some hands-on guided experience, tap the expertise that's out there in the world of ADR.

Working in Local Government

Historic preservation specialists in local government typically are employed as staff to design review commissions, in planning agencies, in housing agencies, and occasionally in city archeology programs. Social impact specialists may be found in planning, housing, and social services agencies. Other kinds of cultural resource management jobs may be in local museums, libraries, and educational institutions. Depending on your position, you may need to know a lot about the secretary of the interior's *Standards for Rehabilitation* or about federal authorities like NEPA and NHPA—or these may not be particularly important to you at all. You'll certainly have local ordinances and standards to deal with and probably state enabling rules and the rules of various funding agencies like HUD. And if you intend to live long and prosper in your work, you'll learn your way around the local political system.

Working in a Regulated Industry

Large public utility companies, hydropower companies, pipeline companies, mining companies—all kinds of private companies that need licenses or assistance from the federal government and therefore are subject to agency regulation—have staffs to help them help the regulatory agencies comply with cultural resource and environmental laws. The smaller, less well-heeled companies, of course, do not, relying instead on contractors when they need help with specific projects.

Working in a large regulated industry is similar to working in an agency; you'll probably be in some kind of NEPA shop or planning shop, or maybe an office that coordinates work with regulatory agencies. And as in an agency, it's important to get a handle on your employer's mission and seek ways to balance the needs of that mission with the public interest in CRM. It's different from working in an agency in that you have a responsibility to your company's stockholders, customers, corporate structure, and bottom line. You really *are* part of your company's team, expected to help advance its interests. If you've a taste for this kind of work, you'll have to figure out how to handle its ethical challenges. You'll need to be careful in your relationships with peers in other companies and in the regulatory agencies; if you're in a hydropower company you have to get along with FERC's cultural resource staff, even if you disagree with them, but you need to be careful not to lose sight of your company's interests, or to transgress the sometimes exotic rules that law or agency policy may impose.

Contracting

A cultural resource contractor, to a considerable extent, needs to know, learn, and do all of the above, in varying degrees depending on what kinds of contract work she or he does. In addition, the more you can learn about business, the better—budgets, safety and health requirements, workers' compensation, marketing, proposal writing, how to read the *Commerce Business Daily*. But it's not enough just to know—say—archeology plus business, as a lot of contractors seem to think. You need to know the laws, the rules, the regulations, the agency procedures, and the range of disciplines whose practice may be necessary to give a client full service. Contractors, more than anyone else, have to be generalists.

Contractors also have to be ready for anything. Today you may be working in the desert, looking for archeological sites in the path of a pipeline. Tomorrow you may be assessing the visual impacts of a power line on an urban neighborhood, coordinating a meeting with affected property owners, or driving out to a reservation to meet with an Indian tribe. Your range of activities probably won't actually be quite that broad, at least until you rise to a fairly high level in the corporate structure, but you can't expect to specialize as narrowly as you might in, say, an academic job. You may really want to be the world's leading authority on shotgun houses in East Carolina, xylophone music in the Great Basin, or the technology of chert tool production, but you're going to have to be ready to deal with a whole lot of other kinds of things, places, and activities.

Contractors also walk an ethical knife edge that may be even sharper than the one trod by agency and industry employees. The contracting firm makes its living by serving clients, and its clients understandably want their contractors to be on board with them, parts of their team. In the last decade or so, it has seemed (to me, at least) that contracting firms have become pretty blasé about this; it's just understood that if you're a contractor for Gigabyte Corporation, your job is to make sure that no lousy cultural or environmental resources get in the way of Gigabyte's project plans. That may be a good business plan, but it vitiates the purposes of the environmental and cultural resource laws and deprecates the public interest. I'd like to think, too, that in the long run it's not in Gigabyte's best interests; that what your client needs is honest, complete, unbiased advice about creative ways to comply with the law and serve the public interest, rather than help in trashing them. I'm not sure that's really true, but I do think—hope—that you'll sleep better at night if you don't sell your soul entirely to your client's perceived bottom line. At the same time, though, if you expect to remain employed and help your company keep getting contracts, you can't look down your nose at the client's interests. It may be that the life of a CRM or environmental contractor in the United States has come to be compromised beyond tolerance—or beyond what society ought to tolerate in its own self-interest. More about that later. Suffice to say that it can be hard to keep the term "ethical contractor" from being an oxymoron.

Advocacy

Finally, you may be able to work in an advocacy organization that promotes some aspect of cultural resource management—in the National Trust for Historic Preservation, perhaps, or in some national, state, or local environmental group. Or you might work in a law firm that serves advocacy groups. In such a job you can have the satisfaction—unique in the CRM world—of not having to balance conflicting interests very much; you're *expected* to be partisan.

But even in this kind of role, an understanding of the points of view of the agencies, organizations, and professional specialists with which and with whom you deal is important—if for no other reason than to know the enemy.

In General . . .

So, some general advice for those who may want to work in CRM:

Learn more than one specialty. It's fine to be the expert landscape historian, but you'd better know about some specializations if you're going to work well in an interdisciplinary team, and in an environment where your employer, client, reviewer, or enemy is interested in and responsible for things other than landscapes.

Look beyond your own responsibilities. If you're in an SHPO office, your primary, if not sole, emphasis is going to be on dealing with places that are eligible for the National Register. That's fine, but don't forget that there may be other cultural resource types out there. Don't let people believe that if they'll just take care of what you're responsible for, they will have covered the cultural resource ground. Even if you can't help them deal with historical documents or contemporary cultural institutions, keep them in mind and be prepared to suggest sources of information and expertise.

Learn the laws, regulations, rules of practice. Don't accept them as God-given; if you think something's wrong with them, say so, and work to fix it, but don't scorn them as a bunch of bureaucratic fol-de-rol. They're why get you paid and you disrespect them at your peril. And think about the function of the laws and rules, not just their forms. The fact that your agency or company customarily writes NEPA documents or does landscape surveys in a particular way doesn't necessarily mean the law requires that they be done that way; there may be creative ways of doing them better, and you ought to be alert to them.

Distinguish between the real rules and the phony ones. Your firm or your agency may be very comfortable doing or insisting on Phase

IA(4)(x) surveys as the unvarying way of complying with section 106, but that's not what the regulations provide for. You may have to do Phase IA(4)(x) surveys as a matter of policy or because everybody expects you to, or you may do them because you want to, but understand that it's not a regulatory requirement. It's the *real* requirements you need to be sure are met, not the phony ones.

Don't be a purist. If you come into CRM believing that it's a sin ever to knock down a historic building or muck up an archeological site for any reason other than research, or that human communities should never change, or that local values should always prevail, you're going to be disillusioned. And when this happens, it can do terrible things to your soul. Some of the most crass, dishonest, disreputable people I know in CRM came into the field as true believers. When they found they couldn't make the world entirely safe for roadside commercial architecture or cultural landscapes or whatever, their belief systems fell in on themselves like stars spiraling into a black hole. Don't let this happen to you. Maintain perspective; understand that your piece of CRM is only one piece that has to be balanced with others, and that all of CRM is just one piece of public policy. And your business is promoting good public policy, not your own values or professional interests.

Remember the public. CRM is supposed to be a service to the public. The buildings and sites don't care whether they're preserved, and cultural values are intangible abstractions. We're working for the public, even if we're not officially identified as public servants. Learn to pay attention to what people say, how they interact. Get some training in how to work with the public—not as a public relations specialist, but as someone who tries to help people express their concerns and get them attended to. Listen to the conch, the voice of the people.

Professional Standards

Unfortunately, in my opinion, such formal standards as there are for the jobs you're likely to get don't encourage any of the things I've just recommended. In fact, they do quite the opposite, encouraging narrow specialization and dodging both practicalities and public responsibility.

The primary standards employed in the historic preservation part of CRM are the secretary of the interior's *Professional Qualifications Standards*, published back in 1983 as part of the *Secretary's Standards and Guidelines for Archeology and Historic Preservation.*[1] At the time they were written, there was a good deal of concern in the historic preservation world about inadequate practice, and a lot of it was voiced by architectural historians who didn't want archeologists to talk about buildings, archeologists who didn't want architectural historians to opine about stuff in the ground, and historians who just wanted some respect. So the *Standards* are all about what it takes to be an archeologist, an architectural historian, a historical architect, an architect, a historian. In other words, they're particularizing; they don't encourage interdisciplinary practice. They specify that to be recognized as an archeologist, or whatever, you have to have an advanced degree in the field and a certain number of years in its performance; in some cases experience can substitute for education, in others it can't.[2] All well and good as long as one is interested in being a qualified archeologist, historian, or other such specialist, but if one wants to be a qualified cultural resource manager, there's no joy to be found in the *Standards*. And the *Standards* don't require knowledge of the laws, regulations, and procedures that guide CRM practice—the 106 regulations, for example, or procedures for consultation, or principles of public accountability. As a result, neither those seeking to hire CRM practitioners nor those seeking jobs are encouraged to think about them.

Shortly after the *Standards* were issued, NPS made them mandatory for SHPO staffs and review boards.[3] In theory they remained, and remain, optional for contractors and agency employees—the latter have to meet Office of Personnel Management (OPM) standards, which are looser and more flexible, though no more relevant—but they are widely recommended and used and are often cited as though the regulations for SHPO personnel applied to everyone doing CRM.

In the 1992 amendments to NHPA, the continuing quest for quality control was reflected in section 112, requiring that (1) "all actions taken by employees or contractors" of federal agencies dealing with historic resources "meet professional standards under regulations developed by the Secretary" (of the Interior) in consultation with a range of interested parties; and that (2) "agency personnel or contractors responsible for historic resources shall meet qualifications standards established by the Office of Personnel Management in consultation with the Secretary (of the Interior) and appropriate professional societies of the disciplines involved." There was some hope that the broad consultation the law called for would lead to more interesting, flexible, interdisciplinary standards, but it was not to be. As section 112 was being codified, then-vice president Gore launched his "reinvention of government" campaign, featuring the wholesale discard of things like professional qualifications standards. OPM wasn't about to launch a drive to develop *new* standards, no matter what Congress had told it to do. NPS said it would try to shoehorn professional qualifications into the performance standards that section 112 directed it to produce. The result would have probably been a rather tired tweaking of the old 1983 *Standards*, but in any event it didn't happen. NPS began to consult with professional societies, who predictably couldn't agree with NPS on much of anything, and the whole initiative drifted off into oblivion.

Needing to do *something* in response to the amendments, NPS re-issued the 1983 *Standards* in 1993,[4] without specifying that they had anything to do with section 112. Their precise status vis-à-vis section 112 remains ambiguous, though they obviously are not the standards that Congress directed either NPS or OPM to prepare in detailed consultation with all kinds of parties.

The other standards often cited as requisites for CRM practice are even narrower than those of the secretary. These are the standards for archeologists administered by the Registry of Professional Archeologists (RPA),[5] a certification body maintained by a consortium of national archeological organizations. One can become a certified, registered archeologist, provided one has the appropriate education and experience and agrees to adhere to a code of ethics and professional performance. Which is fine if one wants to be or hire an archeologist, but irrelevant to a CRM that's more than archeology. Luckily, RPA certification is not required by any federal law, though there are some states and counties that have (unwisely in my opinion) made it more or less mandatory. So I suppose I should say to ignore everything you've just read about being flexible, understanding multiple disciplines, paying attention to the public. But I won't. If you work in the historic preservation part of CRM you're going to have to meet the *Secretary's Standards* for something or other, but that doesn't have to constrain your practice; you *can* be more than an archeologist or a historian. You just aren't likely to get much encouragement from your employers or regulators. If you're not in historic preservation you don't have the *Standards* to worry about, but given how historic preservation dominates CRM, you may not have a job, either.

Learning CRM

In this chapter and elsewhere I've nattered about the fact that students bound for careers in CRM don't actually get educated in its practice. People learn to be historians, archeologists, architectural historians, folklorists, and then they learn by the seats of their pants how to apply the skills they've learned—and many that they've not learned—to the CRM practice they stumble into when they finish graduate school.

So how do you learn to work in CRM? Everyone in my generation learned on the job, and it's easy to recommend doing the same. Just finish your graduate work in your specialty, whatever it is—because lack of a graduate degree will limit your options—and plunge into the workforce.

There are serious downsides to this approach, however. The worst, I think, is that what you learn on the job is how things are done right now, right here. This is the way we've always done it; this is the way it's done in this state, this agency, this company. If you ever want to work anyplace else, do things differently, if you ever want to consider alternative ways of doing CRM, the narrow base of your on-the-job training is likely to limit you.

For people in generations younger than my own there are alternatives. There are academic CRM programs, usually offering masters' degrees or certificates. But there's no real yardstick against which to measure the quality of such programs; you're on your own in judging which one is right for you. And I for one am skeptical. I've been told that there are good CRM graduate pro-

grams around the country, and there may be. But the young people I see coming into the CRM work force—often very smart, dedicated, creative, hard-working young people—do not seem any
better prepared for work in the field than the members of my generation were.

What to do? Here are some suggestions about what I think a
person ought to learn in order to practice well in CRM. If you can
get it all in an academic institution, fine, but if not, I'd suggest a
combination of formal class work and self-education that somehow, to some extent, exposes you to most of or all the following areas of study.

Learn About the CRM Disciplines

A range of disciplinary specialists get involved in CRM, and a
practitioner needs to have a handle on what each discipline does.
Through class work, short courses online or elsewhere, or just
through reading, you should dip into such disciplines as architectural history, historical architecture, folklife studies, cultural geography, landscape history, anthropology, archeology, and perhaps
museology. You're not trying to become expert in them all, but to
get a general feeling for their core concepts and practices and to
know when and how to call in a specialist.

Learn About Consultation

As we've seen, many if not most of the cultural resource laws—
NHPA, AIRFA, NAGPRA, to throw out just a few acronyms—
emphasize consultation among concerned parties. It follows that
students of CRM ought to spend serious time learning how to consult. Many universities and colleges, including community colleges, offer coursework and special training in alternative dispute
resolution (ADR)—techniques of resolving conflicts that are alternatives to litigation. It's generally the "softer" of these techniques
that get practiced in CRM—negotiation, facilitation, mediation, as
opposed to things like binding arbitration. If you can't get formal
training, at least read up on the subject, and look for opportunities
to watch a skillful ADR practitioner at work or to get hands-on
experience.[6] If you expect to work with Indian tribes or other

non–Euro American groups, be sure to spend some time learning about cross-cultural dispute resolution, which has its own peculiar charms.[7]

Learn About Cultural Diversity in Practice

CRM students need to learn about cultural variability in belief and behavior, not just in an abstract academic way but in practical terms. How does a group's belief that cultural information must be kept secret affect an analyst's ability to define the cultural content of an environment or the impacts of a project? How do we balance respect for a traditional society's definition of sex roles with Euro-American notions of gender equality? What can we do when compensation for impacts on the cultural environment begins to look to the unsympathetic eye like extortion? Some kind of training in ethnographic sensitivity is needed, with emphasis on practical applications.

Learn About Laws, Regulations, and Policy

Students need to know not only that laws like NHPA and NAGPRA exist; they need to understand *why* they exist, how they have evolved, and they need an accurate appreciation for what they actually require. Not only the federal laws; you ought to examine state and local law as well, to say nothing of relevant international law and policy. It would be interesting to design courses or study programs built around bundles of related or similar laws and regulations, looking at their histories, their content, and how they have been interpreted by courts.

It's very important, I think, that students should come to understand the laws as dynamic phenomena that can be influenced by citizen action. I think it's appalling that no CRM educational program (as far as I know) assigns students to review the *Federal Register* to find, analyze, and comment on relevant pieces of current rulemaking and see how the responsible agencies react. Agencies could use input from the academic community, and if academics won't provide that input, and train their students to, they have only themselves to blame when the rules wind up saying things they don't like. But the *Federal Register* is freely available online, so you can dip into it on your own.

Learn How an Agency Works

Pick an agency—any agency—and try to figure out how it integrates CRM into its mission, or doesn't. If it doesn't, figure out why it doesn't, whether it ought to, and if it should but isn't, how it gets away with it. If it does have a CRM program, see how it's organized, what range of resources it pays attention to, how it works. Decide whether you think it's doing a good job, and think about how it could be improved—within the context of the agency's mission.

Internships

See if you can arrange an internship—or better, several different internships—in action agencies, regulatory agencies, maybe with Indian tribes or intertribal organizations, in consulting firms, to get hands-on experience and get an appreciation of the frustrations that people face in the workplace. Write up your experiences and observations.

Thesis or Dissertation

If your college or university has a thesis or dissertation requirement—or even if it doesn't—consider analyzing a CRM-related subject. Here are a few I'd consider if I had a thesis to write:

- How do practices and underlying theories or assumptions about CRM (whatever it may be called) vary among nations and cultural traditions—for example, between North America and China?
- How have common management practices such as registration of historic properties or rehabilitation and restoration evolved over the years? How may they evolve in the future?
- What do people in different walks of life want to preserve and manage? What can the governmental and nongovernmental sectors do to address interests in different aspects of the cultural environment?

- How can we ensure proper consideration of the cultural values of low-income groups, minority groups, indigenous communities, and others who have difficulty participating in "mainstream" decision making?
- What are the relationships between cultural and natural heritage management? When there are conflicts between managing natural resources and respecting cultural values, how can they be resolved? How can the cultural significance of natural phenomena be appropriately respected?
- How can CRM be more effectively related to environmental and social impact assessment?
- What are the CRM implications of such phenomena as globalization and global warming? How can cultural resource managers address these implications?
- What can be done to manage impacts on cultural resources in times of war, terrorism, and natural disaster?
- Are there more creative, effective ways than we are currently employing to deal with commercial markets in antiquities, ethnic arts, and natural medicinal and pharmaceutical products?

Things Not Recommended

It's very common for historic preservation educational programs today to assign students to prepare the forms for nominating a place to the National Register of Historic Places. This isn't necessarily a bad thing to do, but it's really just a piece of academic research; it's not cultural resource management. Another common assignment—or at least, something that a lot of people in CRM firms argue ought to be an assignment—is studying requests for proposals (RFPs) in the *Commerce Business Daily*, and otherwise becoming familiar with the world of budgets and contracts. I don't see this as a bad thing to spend some time with, either, but it seems to me that this truly can be picked up on the job, if you get into a job that needs this kind of skill. What it comes down to, I suppose, is that it seems to me that an education in CRM ought to focus on the big issues in the field and the aspects of practice that have serious intellectual content. The clerical work is important, but I think it's a lot less problematical for someone to learn by the seat of his pants how to nominate things to the National Register or respond to an RFP than it is to learn architectural history or consultation methods that way.

The Future of CRM

As one of my classes on some aspect of CRM winds down, I'm often asked to prognosticate about the future. Though this book is no more about the future than it is about the past, a few comments on the former may be a good way to bring it to a close.

I would be remiss if I failed to note that in October 2006 the ACHP convened the Preserve America Summit in New Orleans to examine the condition of the historic preservation part of CRM. The report of the conference came out in 2007.[8] Like every other such manifesto, the summit report recommended a "comprehensive inventory" of historic properties, but with even less sophistication than the average UNESCO recommendation it imagined that such an inventory could somehow be "completed." It proposed to "promote cultural diversity" in historic property identification by nominating a more diverse range of places to the National Register; it is not clear what this is supposed to accomplish or who is supposed to do it. It suggested a committee to promote better responses to disasters and wanted the Department of the Interior to provide guidance in improving security in historic buildings without damaging their character. It sought collaboration with "the broader cultural heritage communities" to conserve "cultural collections"—museum objects and works of art. It recommended that the National Park Service disseminate historic preservation and interpretation skills and technologies, and it proposed to share knowledge with communities in various ways. It asked NPS and others to spread the word about the economic and other benefits of preservation, and, of course, it promoted education. Helpfully, it recommends a reengagement with the international historic preservation community, but with typical American hubris it suggests that the United States should exercise "leadership" there. After almost a decade of not even being a team player, it is a bit much for this country to pretend to a leadership role.

Virtually all these things have, of course, been proposed before—notably in the National Historic Preservation Act—and I doubt that their new iteration will do anything but justify more conferences.

So what's to say about the future of CRM? It probably reflects some limitation of mind, but I can't help thinking about CRM practice in dialectic terms, and I can't help being pretty obvious about which side of each dialectic I come down on. This may be as good a way as any to organize a brief foray into the future.

Interdisciplinary or Not?

After over forty years of practice, we still have little effective communication among even the disciplines that make up the historic preservation aspect of CRM. Architectural historians and historical architects can still talk about "historic properties" when they mean "historic buildings," while archeologists remain uncomfortable being regarded as historic preservation practitioners at all. Most SHPOs and even NPS continue to bifurcate their programs into "aboveground" and "belowground" categories, and things that aren't quite either—cultural landscapes, traditional cultural properties, districts whose significance doesn't lie in their architecture or archeology—are left to catch as catch can. CRM continues to be narrowly interpreted as applied archeology or some sort of historic preservation. Whichever historic preservation practitioner is assigned the CRM label in preparation of an EIS or EA seldom has anything to do with the people doing SIA, who tend to be economists or sociologists bedazzled with number crunching. Is this just the way things somehow have to be? Maybe so. Would it be better to have a truly interdisciplinary practice? Maybe not. I think it would be, however, and I think that if we don't develop in this direction we'll soon become irrelevant, as broader and more effective ways of addressing the cultural environment and cultural identity develop in areas of practice that don't align themselves with CRM.

Flexible or Inflexible Procedures?

My frequent use of the words "it depends" in this book reflects my observation and conviction that there's little that's black and white in the world of CRM—if there is anywhere. We need flexible, creative approaches to the management of cultural resources and impacts on them. Will we get them? I don't know, but I'm not sanguine.

- What do we do to identify historic properties in the state of Washafornia? A Phase I survey following the SHPO's guidelines. Why? Because that's the way we do it.
- How do we determine whether we're going to have disproportionate impacts on a minority population? Look at the census. Why? Because it's "scientific."
- Can we use a treasure salvager to help recover this shipwreck? No. Why not? Because salvagers are evil.

Inflexibility is comfortable; nobody has to think.

Can the urge toward inflexibility be counteracted? I don't know, but history is full of lessons about what happens to social and biological entities that fail to flex.

Process or Outcome?

As I've suggested elsewhere, good process is vital, and if you're interested in balanced policy you can find pleasure in a process that works, that's fair, that's efficient, regardless of the substantive outcome. But there's danger in finding too much comfort in process. Not only that one will stop caring about the results altogether, but in getting so enamored of a *particular* process, a *particular* set of procedures, that we cannot or will not consider alternative ways to achieve the purposes for which the procedures were created.

We may believe that we can't consider the effects of the project until we've determined the eligibility of each potentially affected property for the National Register. Why not, we may be asked, if we can clearly achieve the purposes of section 106 without investing time and money in evaluation? Because, we reply, the regulations say that you *first* do identification, *then* evaluation, and *then* effect determination. Those are the *rules*.

We encourage people to think of such rules as immutable, and we select for employment those who are comfortable with immutable rules and don't care much about outcomes—or who have become too jaded to care much about anything. Can we achieve a more outcomes-oriented system without sacrificing fair process? I don't know. Should we try? I think we should.

Professionals or Publics

For whom do we try to deal with impacts on cultural resources? However much we may puff out our chests and pontificate about doing things "for the resource," it's a safe assumption that old buildings, archeological sites, and even living human social institutions in the abstract don't greatly care what happens to them. It's *people* who care, so the question really comes down to, For which groups of people do we concern ourselves with impacts on cultural resources? Are we concerned primarily about the interests of professional specialists or about the public in all its permutations?

Archeologists, historians, and others will protest that professionals are, after all, trying to preserve things for generations yet unborn, and they represent a longer view than that of the contemporary self-seeking multitude. There's truth in that, I think, and it ought to be respected, but it can be carried too far.

Out on the flat plains of southern Illinois there's a little town called Mark that grew up around a surface mine. The mine tailings formed a big heap at the edge of town that people called "the Gob Pile." The Gob Pile was the only geographic relief for miles around, and it became a familiar and appreciated local landmark. People would go to the top of the Gob Pile to look out over the world and doubtless to have beer parties and neck and look at the stars and do all the other things that people do in special places. When it came time to reclaim the old mine site, the question arose as to whether the Gob Pile was eligible for the National Register—and hence whether its preservation would have to be considered—or whether it could be pushed back into the mine without further ado. The keeper of the Register ended up evaluating it and found that since it really wasn't a very good representative of historic mining technology, it wasn't eligible.

Was this to the point? Was the major reason for considering saving the Gob Pile its possible importance to students of mining technology or was it its obvious importance to the people who lived around it, who identified with it, in whose local culture it played a role?

This sort of thing happens all the time in the historic preservation side of CRM—we don't really know, we haven't really settled on, why old things may be worth saving. Certainly a place that can tell us a lot about early mining technology is worth saving in some form, if only in that of documentation, but is a place that figures in a community's sense of identity not at least equally worthy?

Comprehensive or Particular?

Are we moving toward the kind of comprehensive, interdisciplinary, public-oriented CRM that this book espouses? Should we? I obviously think we should; indeed I think we *must* if we aren't to get swept off into some corner of frivolous public policy and left to decay. But that doesn't mean we *will*. We can instead sip our sherry or chug our beers and age gracefully among our like-minded, culturally and professionally homogenous peers, debating fine points of historical, archeological, or sociological theory and practice, and expressing mild frustration with the fact that our colleagues in academia don't respect us as we think they should. Absent some event that shakes us up and forces change, that's probably exactly what we'll do; it's very human.

Who Do We Work For?

It may be a reflection of who's been running the country for the last eight years (2001–2008), but it seems to me that the practices of both CRM and environmental impact assessment (EIA) have been becoming steadily more crass. A decade ago, I seem to recall, people doing EIA and CRM were prone to pious characterizations of themselves as working for the environment or for "the resource." Today it seems widely accepted that the smart CRM or EIA practitioner is a hardheaded business person, concerned primarily with the financial bottom line. And since those providing the financing are almost always the proponents of environment-changing projects, giving priority to the bottom line inevitably means advancing proponents' interests.

I don't miss the pieties, but I worry, and I think we all should worry, about ostensibly practicing in the public interest but really working as part of an employer's or client's planning team, trying to advance the very projects whose impacts we are supposed to be assessing.

A colleague to whom I fretted about this said she didn't think it was a problem, because in the long run a client's interests are in having good work done. If one does a bad job of assessing impacts on cultural resources or the environment, there will be surprises when the project goes forward and something pops up. Thus, she argued, a CRM or EIA practitioner serves a client well only by doing high-quality work and by being honest about the impacts a client's project may have. That sounds good, but I don't buy it. There are too many subtle ways to bias the results of an impact analysis, often without even knowing one is doing so.

Some agencies do third-party impact analyses, charging project proponents for the work but managing contracts themselves; the CRM or EIA practitioner reports to and is overseen by the agency rather than directly by the proponent. This seems—superficially at least—like a superior system, but I have heard responsible and thoughtful colleagues complain about it, precisely because it distances them from the proponents' plans and keeps them from helping proponents make mid-course corrections that would save cultural resources.

We need to address this problem, I think, in our own self-interest if for no nobler reason. If our work doesn't provide the public and its officials with reliable information and advice about cultural resources and environmental impacts, there is no earthly reason the taxpayers should continue paying for it.

When I was in graduate school we were all enamored of Thomas Kuhn's *Structure of Scientific Revolutions.*[9] Kuhn demonstrated—to our satisfaction at the time, anyway—that science is not characterized by slow, steady growth. Rather, we have long periods of "normal science" in which everybody does pretty much the same thing and doesn't much question their assumptions, punctuated by paradigm shifts that shake people up and stimulate exploration in new directions. What we now call CRM was born out of set of paradigm shifts in the 1960s and 1970s when people in those "social sciences and environmental design arts" that NEPA alludes to began to consider a new relationship between human society and its environment. Historic preservationists began looking beyond the preservation of landmarks and house museums, archeologists began looking beyond salvage, and anthropologists, sociologists, and other social scientists began to apply their skills and knowledge outside academia. CRM practitioners have all settled into our own kind of normal science in the last couple of decades, I think—into a dispersed scattering of normal science practices, actually. Are we due for a paradigm shift? It would be nice to think so, but who knows?

It depends.

Notes

1. 48 *Federal Register* 44716-42; the professional qualifications standards are on pages 44738–39.

2. I should acknowledge that I wrote an early version of the standards for archeologists, as part of a soon-dead regulation implementing the ADPA; I like to think it was better than what eventually was promulgated, but maybe not. It was a different world back then, and as a once-popular song put it, I was so much older.

3. 36 CFR 61, Appendix A.

4. See www2.cr.nps.gov/laws/ProfQual83.htm (accessed July 26, 2003).

5. See www.rpanet.org/ for information (accessed July 26, 2003).

6. See, for instance, Nicolas Dorochoff, *Negotiation Basics for Cultural Resource Managers* (Walnut Creek, CA: Left Coast Press, 2007).

7. See, for instance, Raymond Cohen, *Negotiating Across Cultures* (Washington, DC: U.S. Institute of Peace Press, 2002).

8. ACHP, *The Preserve America Summit: Charting a Future Course for the National Historic Preservation Program*, Washington, DC, 2007, www.preserveamerica.gov/docs/Summit_Report_full_LR.pdf (accessed January 6, 2008).

9. Thomas Kuhn, *The Structure of Scientific Revolutions* (Chicago: University of Chicago Press, 1962).

Appendix 1:
Acronyms and Abbreviations

ACHP	Advisory Council on Historic Preservation
ACR	Association for Conflict Resolution
ADPA	Archeological Data Protection Act (aka Archeological and Historic Preservation Act
ADR	Alternative (to litigation) Dispute Resolution
AFC	American Folklife Center
AFPA	American Folklife Preservation Act
AIRFA	American Indian Religious Freedom Act
APE	Area of Potential Effect
ARPA	Archeological Resources Protection Act
ASA	Abandoned Shipwrecks Act
BIA	Bureau of Indian Affairs
BLM	Bureau of Land Management
BOC	Bureau of the Census
BOR	Bureau of Reclamation
CA	Comprehensive Agreement (under NAGPRA)
CATEX	Categorical Exclusion under NEPA (Also CX or CatEx)
CBA	Central business area or centralized business area
CDBG	Community Development Block Grant
CEHP	Conservation, Environment, and Historic Preservation, a Washington, D.C.–based consulting firm

CEQ	Council on Environmental Quality
CERCLA	Comprehensive Environmental Response, Compensation, and Liability Act
CFR	Code of Federal Regulations
Cir	Circuit (court of appeals, in legal citations)
Clovis	Early (ca. 12,000 years ago) archeological complex
CNAE	Conditional No Adverse Effect Determination under section 106
CNO	Chief of Naval Operations
COE	Corps of Engineers (U.S. Army)
Council:	Depending on context: Advisory Council on Historic Preservation or Council on Environmental Quality
CRM	Cultural Resource Management
CRMP	Cultural Resource (or Resources) Management Plan
CX	Categorical Exclusion under NEPA (also CATEX or CatEx)
DEIS	Draft EIS
DoD	Department of Defense
DoT	Department of Transportation
EA	Environmental Assessment under NEPA
EIS	Environmental Impact Statement under NEPA
EJ	Environmental Justice (See Executive Order 12898)
EO	Executive Order
EPA	Environmental Protection Agency
EQA	Environmental Quality Advisory (in GSA)
FACA	Federal Advisory Committees Act
Facade	Face of a building or structure
FEIS	Final EIS
FEMA	Federal Emergency Management Agency
FERC	Federal Energy Regulatory Commission
FHWA	Federal Highway Administration
FLETC	Federal Law Enforcement Training Center
FLPMA	Federal Land Policy and Management Act

FNSI	Finding of No Significant Impact under NEPA (also FONSI)
FONSI	Finding of No Significant Impact under NEPA (also FNSI)
FPO	Federal Preservation Officer
FR	*Federal Register*: Really boring daily publication of regulations, notices, etc., by U.S. federal government
FRA	Federal Records Act
GIS	Geographic Information System
GSA	General Services Administration
HABS	Historic American Buildings Survey (NPS)
HAER	Historic American Engineering Record (NPS)
HALS	Historic American Landscapes Survey (NPS)
HBPP	Historic Building Preservation Plan (GSA)
HSA	Historic Sites Act of 1935
HSR	Historic Structures Report
HUD	Department of Housing and Urban Development
ICRMP	Integrated Cultural Resource Management Plan (DOD)
IECR	Institute for Environmental Conflict Resolution
Ironfront	Building with front facade of cast iron
ISO	International Standards Organization; also Greek for "balance"
kV	Kilovolt
LDS	Latter Day Saints (churches)
MFASAQHE	Major Federal Action Significantly Affecting the Quality of the Human Environment
MFONSI	Mitigated FONSI under NEPA
MOA	Memorandum of Agreement under Section 106
Muntin	Divider between lights in a window
NAGPRA	Native American Graves Protection and Repatriation Act
NARA	National Archives and Records Administration
NCAI	National Congress of American Indians
NCSHPO	National Congress of State Historic Preservation Officers

NEPA	National Environmental Policy Act
NFMA	National Forest Management Act
NHL	National Historic Landmark under Historic Sites Act
NHPA	National Historic Preservation Act of 1966, as amended
NOAA	National Oceanic and Atmospheric Administration
NOI	Notice of Intent (to prepare an EIS)
NPI	National Preservation Institute, a Washington, D.C.–based nonprofit educational and consulting organization
NPS	National Park Service
OAHP	Office of Archeology and Historic Preservation (NPS, defunct)
OEBGD	Overseas Environmental Baseline Guidance Document (DoD)
OPNAVINST	Naval Operations Instruction
PA	Programmatic Agreement under section 106
PBCUA	Public Buildings Cooperative Use Act
PMP	Proactive Maintenance Plan (Corps of Engineers)
POA	Plan of Action under NAGPRA
ppm	Parts per million
REA	Rural Electrification Administration (defunct)
Rehab	Rehabilitate (a building, structure, or part thereof)
RFRA	Religious Freedom Restoration Act
ROD	Record of Decision under NEPA
RP3	Resource Protection Planning Process (NPS)
Scope	What an analysis will contain. Verb: to figure out what the scope of an analysis should be
SECNAVINST	Secretary of the Navy Instruction
Section 106	Section of NHPA that directs agencies to consider the effects of their actions on historic properties
SEPA	State Environmental Policy Act (or "Little NEPA")
SHPO	State Historic Preservation Officer
SIA	Social Impact Assessment

TCP	Traditional Cultural Property or Place
THPO	Tribal Historic Preservation Officer
UNESCO	United Nations Educational, Scientific, and Cultural Organization
USC	United States Code
WNRC	Washington Naval Records Center

Appendix 2:
Frequently Used Terms

Advisory Council on Historic Preservation (ACHP): An independent federal agency that advises the president and Congress on historic preservation matters and oversees the review of projects under section 106 of the National Historic Preservation Act (NHPA). See chapters 1, 4.

Council on Environmental Quality (CEQ): Part of the Executive Office of the president, CEQ advises on environmental matters, prepares studies and assessments, and oversees implementation of the National Environmental Policy Act (NEPA). See chapters 1, 2.

Cultural resource: As used in this book, any resource (i.e., thing that is useful for something) that is of a cultural character—generally tied up with some community's identity. Examples are social institutions, historic places and cultural sites, artifacts, documents, and traditional ways of life. Others define the term much more narrowly, often to mean only archeological sites or historic properties. Semi-synonyms include heritage and patrimony.

Cultural resource management (CRM): The management both of cultural resources and of effects on them that may result from activities of the contemporary world. See chapters 1, 8, 9.

Historic property: Any district, site, building, structure or object included in or eligible for inclusion in the National Register of Historic Places.[1] See chapter 3.

Indian tribe: Can mean different things to different people and in different contexts. Federally recognized Indian tribes are those the federal government recognizes formally as sovereign entities with which it has a government-to-government relationship and for which, in many but not all cases, it holds resources in trust. Other tribes are not federally recognized—because they never have made peace with the federal government, because they were virtually wiped out by Euro-Americans, or because their formal status was terminated during one of our spasmodic seizures of passion for the American melting pot—but still have real tribal roots. See chapter 1.

National Park Service (NPS): A bureau of the Department of the Interior whose primary function is to manage the National Park System. NPS also has external programs that relate to cultural resource management—particularly in historic preservation—beyond the lands it manages. See chapters 1, 3, 4, 5, 6.

National Register of Historic Places (National Register): A list, maintained by NPS, of districts, sites, buildings, structures, and objects, each determined by NPS to be of historic, cultural, architectural, archeological, or engineering significance at the national, state, or local level. See chapter 3.

Preservation (or historic preservation): According to NHPA, includes identification, evaluation, recordation, documentation, curation, acquisition, protection, management, rehabilitation, restoration, stabilization, maintenance, research, interpretation, conservation, and education and training regarding the foregoing activities or any combination of the foregoing activities.[2] According to the *Secretary of the Interior's Standards for the Treatment of Historic Properties*,[3] preservation means the act or process of applying measures necessary to sustain the existing form, integrity, and materials of a historic property.

Significance: Under NEPA, the seriousness of a potential impact, measured in terms of context and intensity. See chapter 2. Under NHPA, the historical, cultural, archeological, architectural, or engineering importance of a property. See chapters 3, 4.

Social impacts: Impacts of a project, program, or activity on people's ways of life, shared beliefs, customs, values, and language, the character and cohesion of their community, their political systems, their access to and control of environmental and other resources, their health, well-being, rights, fears, and aspirations.[4] See chapters 2, 7.

Social impact assessment (SIA): An assessment of the social impacts of a project, program, or activity.[5] See chapters 2, 7.

Socioeconomic impact assessment: Often confused with social impact assessment. An assessment that focuses on economic and sometimes other easily quantifiable indicators of social impact. See chapter 2.

Sociocultural: Pertaining to human culture and society, as in "the sociocultural environment."

State Historic Preservation Officer (SHPO): The state official, designated by the governor, who carries out the functions ascribed to the SHPO by NHPA.[6] SHPOs receive and administer matching grants from NPS to support their work and pass through to others. They identify historic properties and nominate them to the National Register. They maintain inventories, do plans, and consult with others about historic preservation. See chapters 1, 3, 4, 5.

Traditional cultural property or traditional cultural place (TCP): A place that is valued by a community for the role it plays in sustaining the community's cultural identity. Generally figures in important community traditions or socioculturally important activities. May be eligible for inclusion in the National Register.[7] See chapters 1, 3, 4, 6, 7.

Tribal Historic Preservation Officer (THPO): The official of a federally recognized Indian tribe that oversees the tribe's historic preservation program, particularly where the tribe has been approved by NPS to carry out all or some of the functions of the SHPO within the external boundaries of its reservation. See chapter 1.

Notes

1. 16 U.S.C. 470w(5).
2. 6 U.S.C. 470w(8).
3. NPS, "Standards for Preservation," *Secretary's Standards for Treatment of Historic Properties* (Washington, DC: Preservation Assistance Office, Government Printing Office, 1992).
4. See Frank Vanclay, "International Principles for Social Impact Assessment," *Impact Assessment and Project Appraisal* 21 (1) (2003): 8, for a more expansive definition. Also see NOAA, *Guidelines and Principles for Social Impact Assessment*, 1994, 1.
5. NOAA, Guidelines and Principles, 1.
6. 16 U.S.C. 470a(3).
7. See Thomas F. King, and Patricia Parker, *Guidelines for Evaluating and Documenting Traditional Cultural Properties* (Washington, DC: National Park Service, 1990, rev. 1992 and 1998).

Appendix 3: Laws, Executive Orders, and Regulations

We've discussed a lot of legal tools in this book; this appendix summarizes them and briefly discusses how they're dealt with—or not—by federal agencies and others.

It's convenient to divide the legal authorities up by subject—the kinds of resources or situations they apply to, so that's what I've done, beginning with the most general and proceeding toward the particular.

Authorities that Deal with All Types of Cultural Resources

The National Environmental Policy Act—NEPA—is the broadest authority, articulating national policy on environmental protection and requiring agencies to analyze and control the effects of their actions on the environment. The procedural core of NEPA is its requirement for a detailed analysis of actions "significantly affecting the quality of the human environment." Among the variables that the NEPA regulations (40 CFR 1500-1508) identify as comprising significant impacts are impacts on cultural resources in general, as well as specific cultural resource types like historic properties and scientific resources (40 CFR 1508.27(b)(3) and (8)). In any event, since the human environment obviously includes sociocultural elements, NEPA logically requires agencies to be concerned with

376 / Appendix 3

their impacts on all kinds of cultural resources—as well as on the whole panoply of natural resources. This is not to say that all agencies do a very good job of considering impacts on the full range of resources—only that in theory, they should.

NEPA is probably the best understood of the legal authorities, in that most agencies have staff dedicated to NEPA compliance, there's a large body of practitioners, and there are several organizations and journals that focus on NEPA practice. NEPA is widely misunderstood, though—and abused—as a mere process of documentation, justifying decisions made and impacts tolerated on the environment. That's not what it's supposed to be; it's supposed to be an honest, open, analysis of impacts, leading to decisions that balance environmental protection—including cultural resource protection—with other public values.

Executive Order 12898 also deals with all kinds of resources, but in a particular socioeconomic context. This executive order deals with environmental justice (EJ)—preventing the levying of disproportionate adverse environmental impacts on low-income and minority populations. The executive order is implemented in the context of NEPA analyses, and it requires consideration of all kinds of impacts on all aspects of the environment, provided they are relevant to low-income or minority populations. It's particularly important for CRM because it promotes culturally sensitive outreach and public participation in environmental review, and because sociocultural impacts are often among those that low-income and minority groups are concerned about.

Executive Order 12072 in theory causes the consideration of cultural resources of all kinds in the context of urban centers. This executive order directs agencies to give priority to siting their activities in central business areas (CBA). Important for CRM, it requires that the positive and negative cultural effects of such sitings be considered. This executive order provides a legal rationale for some social impact assessments, typically absorbed into NEPA analyses.

Executive Order 13352, on "facilitating cooperative conservation," tells federal agencies to cooperate and collaborate with state and local governments, tribes, and private-sector interests to promote conservation. It could and should push agencies to be more sensitive to the sociocultural interests of such ostensible collaborators, but there seems to be little evidence that it has had this effect.

Historic Preservation Authorities

*The National Historic Preservation Act—NHPA—*is the best-known authority dealing with historic properties, including archeological resources and many traditional cultural properties. Actually the best-known part of NHPA is section 106, which requires agencies to consider the effects of their actions on historic properties. There are many other sections of NHPA, however, some of which have impacts on federal agencies and recipients of federal assistance and permits. In general, NHPA requires agencies to identify and manage historic properties under their jurisdiction or control; to consider doing things that will advance the purposes of the act and avoid, if possible, doing things contrary to its purposes; to consult and cooperate with others in carrying out historic preservation activities, and to consider the effects of their actions—including permit and assistance actions—on historic properties following a regulation issued by the ACHP (36 CFR 800). NHPA also spells out the roles and functions of the ACHP, the SHPO, and the THPO.

The Historic Sites Act (HSA) of 1935 was a seedbed from which NHPA sprang. Rather narrow in its actual provisions, it was politically important because it established NPS as the government's paramount historic preservation advocate. The HSA authorized NPS to identify, register, describe, document, and acquire full or partial title to historic properties determined to be nationally significant in the interpretation and commemoration of the nation's history. It had no regulatory provisions, and it didn't actually require NPS or anyone else to do much of anything. NPS promoted its passage, however, and seized the authority it gave to create what are today the National Historic Landmarks (NHL) and Historic American Buildings Survey (HABS) programs. Together with archeological elements of NPS that grew out of the River Basin Salvage programs of the 1950s and 1960s, these provided the organizational and theoretical frameworks within which the post-NHPA national historic preservation program grew.

Executive Order 11593, issued by President Richard Nixon in 1972, directed federal agencies to nominate all historic properties under their jurisdiction or control to the National Register of Historic Places by mid-1974. More important, it directed them to treat properties eligible for the Register as though they were already included, and it directed NPS to publish guidance as to how determinations of eligibility were to be made. Since nobody met the deadline for nominations, and since the order's provisions have all been absorbed by amendment into NHPA itself in some way or other, EO 11593 today is a sort of historical oddity, but it was very important in its time.

Executive Order 13006 complements both NHPA and Executive Order 12072. It requires agencies to give priority consideration to using historic buildings in historic districts in CBAs. This executive order has been incorporated by reference into section 110(a)(1) of NHPA.

Executive Order 13287, issued in 2003, directs federal agencies to review their programs for compliance with sections 110 and 111 of NHPA and report findings periodically to the ACHP and NPS. It also directs them to seek partnerships with others to advance the interests of preservation through continued use and reuse, particularly economic use involving heritage tourism.

Section 4(f) of the Department of Transportation Act prohibits any agency of the Department of Transportation (DOT)—for example, the Federal Highway Administration (FHWA), the Federal Aviation Administration (FAA), and the Federal Railroad Administration (FRA)—from implementing a transportation project that uses a historic property (or a park or wildlife refuge) unless there is "no prudent and feasible alternative" to doing so and all possible planning is carried out to minimize harm. Section 4(f) has been the subject of a tremendous body of litigation, and section 4(f) analyses—typically carried out in tandem with NEPA analyses—are a major preoccupation of DOT agencies.

The federal tax code contains provisions—which change often, given the highly political nature of tax law—encouraging the preservation and rehabilitation of income-producing historic structures. Generally speaking, the owner of an income-producing historic structure (e.g., a historic hotel) can claim a credit against his or her federal income tax based on the costs incurred in rehabilitating the structure in accordance with standards issued by NPS (the *Secretary of the Interior's Standards for Rehabilitation*). Virtually every session of Congress sees battles over the shape of these provisions—notably over the size of the credit, how actively the claimant of a credit must participate in the rehabilitation project upon which the claim for credit is based, and over extending the credit to nonincome producing residential structures. Some states have their own parallel tax provisions.

Archeological Authorities

The Antiquities Act of 1906, the nation's earliest historic preservation law, prohibits the unauthorized excavation, removal, or defacement of "objects of antiquity" on public lands. It also authorized the president to withdraw land from multiple use status for purposes of creating national monuments. The prohibition on removal of "objects of antiquity" was declared "fatally vague" by courts in the 1970s, leading to enactment of . . .

The Archeological Resources Protection Act (ARPA), which prohibits the unauthorized excavation, removal, or damage of archeological resources on federal and Indian lands. "Archeological resource" is comprehensively defined to include archeological sites, structural remains, artifacts, bones, debris—everything including the kitchen sink, provided it's at least one hundred years old. ARPA provides stiff penalties for violators and spells out permit requirements. These are elaborated upon in uniform regulations issued jointly by the Departments of the Interior, Agriculture, and Defense and the Tennessee Valley Authority. Interior's regulations apply to all agencies that are not Agriculture or Defense, except for TVA.

The Archeological Data Preservation Act of 1974, a.k.a. the Moss-Bennett Act, after its authors, and the Archeological and Historic Preservation Act, amended the Reservoir Salvage Act of 1960, which authorized NPS to fund salvage archeology in Corps of Engineers reservoirs. The 1974 act applied to all agencies and all kinds of projects, directing the agencies themselves to pay attention to their impacts on archeological, historical, and scientific data. It also directed them either to fund the recovery of such data themselves or to assist NPS in doing so, and authorized transfer of up to 1 percent of the cost of a project to NPS to defray its expenses.

The Abandoned Shipwrecks Act (ASA) deals with a particular class of archeological site—the shipwreck. Designed to remove shipwrecks from the purview of the admiralty courts, which were perceived to be too sympathetic to commercial salvagers, ASA asserts U.S. ownership of all abandoned wrecks in its waters and then transfers control of them to the states. NPS issued guidelines for implementing ASA, which are advisory only; the states call the shots on shipwreck management—except with regard to commissioned naval vessels, which enjoy sovereign immunity from the statute. The *Sunken Military Craft Act* governs ownership of sunken U.S. military ships and aircraft.

The Curation Regulations (36 CFR 79), though issued by NPS, are applicable government-wide under the authority of NHPA and ARPA. They establish standards for curation facilities that care for federally owned artifacts, other archeological specimens, and related documents, all of which are supposed to be retained in perpetuity.

Native American Cultural Resource Authorities

In a way, the archeological authorities are Native American cultural resource authorities as well, since all archeological resources over about five hundred years old in the United States (and many that are younger) are of Native American origin. But there are several legal authorities that deal more explicitly with Native American resources—and with a broader range of resources than just archeological sites.

And the range of things a Native American group is concerned about, and that an agency may need to consult with the group about, may be broader still. Don't ever assume that a Native American group is interested only in cultural resources, or that such resources are all you need to consult with the group about. The group may have economic concerns, social concerns, educational concerns, concerns about health and safety and sanitation and crime that go way beyond even a broad definition of "cultural resource," and the group has the right—particularly if it's a federally recognized tribe—to be consulted about all of them.

That said, here are the major legal authorities that address various types of Native American cultural resources—and sometimes more.

The American Indian Religious Freedom Act—AIRFA—is a joint resolution of Congress declaring that the U.S. government will protect the inherent rights of Indian tribes to free exercise of their traditional religions. AIRFA has been taken to require agencies to consult with tribes—but not necessarily accede to their requests—when any action is contemplated that might affect the practice of traditional religions. Note that the "resource" involved here is the practice of religion itself. The places and physical paraphernalia needed for religious practice are among the elements to be considered, but AIRFA deals with the broader, less tangible resource of religious practice itself.

Executive Order 13007 deals with Indian sacred sites on federal and Indian land. It calls on agencies to avoid physical damage to such sites and to avoid interfering with access to them by tribal religious practitioners. Although this executive order is concerned with physical places, a "sacred site" need not be a historic property; the scope of Executive Order 13007 is different from that of NHPA.

The Native American Graves Protection and Repatriation Act—NAGPRA—requires that federal agencies and museums that have received federal funds repatriate Native American ancestral human remains and cultural items to tribes that can show genetic or cultural affiliation with such remains and items. It also regulates excavation of such remains and items on federal and Indian land and provides for a minimum thirty-day hold on earthmoving activities that cause the inadvertent discovery of such remains and items. NPS regulations, applicable to all agencies, are at 43 CFR 10.

Federally recognized tribes may also claim some degree of protection for cultural resources of interest to them under the terms of treaties, the general interpretation that a right not explicitly relinquished in a treaty is retained, and the general legal requirement that the U.S. government respect tribal sovereignty and exercise a trust responsibility toward tribes.

Historical Documents Authorities

The Federal Records Act (FRA), and its very extensive implementing regulations, deals with how federal agencies are to manage their records—largely for the purpose of ensuring that historically important records aren't lost. Agencies are required to establish and implement their own FRA records retention and disposal procedures, approved by the National Archives and Records Administration (NARA), and to have personnel assigned to ensure that records are managed in accordance with such procedures. FRA is about the only cultural resource authority for which violation is punishable by fines and prison sentences, though this does not seem to deter many agencies—including, amusingly enough, NPS and the ACHP—from routinely ignoring it.

Section 112 of NHPA also deals with records, but only with records resulting from the conduct of historic preservation activities–archeological survey and excavation reports, architectural documentation of historic buildings, oral historical and ethnographic material relating to historic properties. It requires agencies to ensure that such documents are preserved in perpetuity.

Land Management Authorities

Finally, most major land management agencies have some kind of "organic" legislation that establishes policy direction for the way they manage the land and resources under their charge, including cultural resources. Examples are the *National Forest Management Act* (NFMA), which governs the Forest Service, and the *Federal Land Policy and Management Act* (FLPMA), which governs the Bureau of Land Management. Agency organic laws contain important direction to agencies about how they are to carry out their management activities, and they usually contain helpful procedures by which concerned members of the public can appeal agency decisions up the chain of command.

Appendix 4: Model Section 106 Memorandum of Agreement

Besides illustrating the standard form of an MOA, this hypothetical model tries to show how one could be prepared at an early stage in planning, when multiple alternatives are under consideration—improving coordination with NEPA and addressing effects while there's still time to do something about them.

Reports and appendixes referred to are for illustrative purposes only and are not actually included. For annotated, downloadable MOA stipulations and formats, go to www.npi.org and click on "Tools for Cultural Resource Managers."

MEMORANDUM OF AGREEMENT
AMONG THE NATIONAL BUILDING SERVICE,
THE NORTH NORWICH STATE HISTORIC
PRESERVATION OFFICER, AND THE
CITY OF FEATHERBERG
REGARDING CONSTRUCTION OF THE
GOVERNMENT LOGISTICS INVESTIGATION
BUREAU REGIONAL ABORATORY

WHEREAS the National Building Service (NBS) proposes to provide a new regional laboratory for the Government Logistics Investigation Bureau (GLIB) in the City of Featherberg; and

WHEREAS NBS has agreed to assume lead agency status in review of the proposed laboratory project (Laboratory Project) under Section 106 of the National Historic Preservation Act, 16 U.S.C. § 470 (NHPA) and its implementing regulations (36 CFR Part 800) on behalf of itself and GLIB, as represented in the document entitled "Lead Agency Assignment, Featherberg Laboratory Project," executed by GLIB and NBS on March 15, 2009; and

WHEREAS NBS is considering three optional sites for the laboratory (plus a no-project alternative) the *Parking Structure Site*, the *Burned Block Site*, and the *Weatherbeat Warehouse Site*, as described in the document entitled "Preliminary Identification of Feasible Alternatives, Featherberg Laboratory Project" by Kungbutaie Consultants, Ltd. (Kungbutaie), dated April 1, 2010 (Preliminary ID Report); and

WHEREAS NBS has established the laboratory's area of potential effects, as defined at 36 CFR § 800.16(d), to be:
a) For the *Parking Structure Site*, the construction site, the utility and road rights-of-way, and the vacant land within ¼ mile of the site, where induced development may occur, plus the upper slopes of Grassy Knob where visual effects may occur (See Preliminary ID Report at Figure III.4);
b) For the *Burned Block Site*, the construction site and the neighborhoods bordering the site on all sides for approximately eight (8) city blocks, where visual, economic, and social effects may occur (See Preliminary ID Report at Figure III.5);
c) For the *Weatherbeat Warehouse Site*, the Weatherbeat Warehouse, which would be renovated as the main Laboratory building, plus the proposed new construction sites and the complex of early twentieth century warehouses of which the Weatherbeat Warehouse is a part (See Preliminary ID Report at Figure III.6);
d) For the *No Project Alternative*, the site of the existing Laboratory at 793 Mudd Street and the land between the Laboratory and the Bigslow River (See illustration of the existing toxic waste plume in the Preliminary ID Report at Figure I.3); and

WHEREAS NBS has determined that the Laboratory Project may have adverse effects on districts, sites, buildings, structures, and/or objects eligible for inclusion in the National Register of Historic Places (historic properties), and has so notified the Advisory Council on Historic Preservation (ACHP) in accordance with 36 CFR 800.6(a)(1); and

WHEREAS NBS has conducted studies and consulted with the parties listed in Appendix I, "Parties Consulted During Scoping, Featherberg Laboratory Project" Kungbutaie, 2/14/2009, on the basis of which it has projected the distribution and character of historic properties subject to effect by each alternative (See Preliminary ID Report Chapter V); and

WHEREAS likely historic properties subject to potential effects include, but are not limited to, Grassy Knob, the Red Rooster Neighborhood, the warehouse complex, and several possible archeological sites (See Preliminary ID report Chapter V);

WHEREAS NBS has consulted with the North Norwich State Historic Preservation Officer (SHPO) and the City of Featherberg (City) in accordance with 36 CFR 800.6(a), and has involved the public in accordance with 36 CFR 800.6(a)(4) and its "Public Participation Plan, Featherberg Laboratory Project" (Kunbutaie, 6/2/2008); and

WHEREAS pursuant to Section 101(d)(6)(B) of NHPA, the American Indian Religious Freedom Act, and the Native American Graves Protection and Repatriation Act (NAGPRA), NBS has invited the Wimok Indian Tribe (Tribe) to consult and to concur in this Memorandum of Agreement (MOA); and

WHEREAS NBS, the SHPO and the City have invited GLIB, the Bigslow River Planning Authority, the Featherberg Association for Architectural Heritage (FAAH), the Featherberg Archeological Society (FAS), and the Red Rooster Neighborhood Commission (Red Rooster) to consult and to concur in this MOA; and

WHEREAS NBS intends to use this MOA to address applicable requirements of NHPA Section 110(a)(1), the Archeological Data Preservation Act (16 U.S.C. 469-469c: ADPA), and Executive Orders

13006 and 13007 (See "Memorandum to the File: Featherberg Laboratory Project Compliance with Historic Preservation Requirements," 4/1/2009);

NOW, THEREFORE, NBS, the North Norwich SHPO, and the City agree that should NBS elect to proceed with the Laboratory Project using any of the alternatives listed above, NBS will ensure that the following stipulations are implemented in order to take into account the effects of the undertaking on historic properties, and that these stipulations shall govern the undertaking and all of its parts until this Agreement expires or is terminated.

Stipulations

I. *Priority Consideration.* Pursuant to Executive Order 13006, NBS shall give priority consideration to adaptive use of the Weatherbeat Warehouse. Should the Weatherbeat Warehouse not be NBS' preferred alternative, NBS will consult with and explain its rationale to the parties to this MOA before issuing its draft Environmental Impact Statement (DEIS), and explain its decision in the DEIS.

II. *Weatherbeat Warehouse.* Should the Weatherbeat Warehouse become the preferred alternative, NBS shall ensure that the following stipulations are implemented:

A. *Review of Documents.* No demolition or site preparation work shall occur until the following documents have been reviewed by the City, NBS, and SHPO.

1. Drawings identifying all known or anticipated historic fabric, and documents detailing how such fabric will be treated during site preparation.

2. An interim report on archeological investigations as of the date of the submittal, including a plan of action for treating archeological resources (if any) that may be disturbed.

B. *Interim Protection.* NBS shall ensure that the Weatherbeat Warehouse is secured and protected from vandalism, fire, and weather damage during the period it is unoccupied, following *Preservation Brief #31, Mothballing Historic Buildings* (Department of the Interior, National Park Service, 1993).

III. *Parking Structure Site.* Should the Parking Structure Site become the preferred alternative, NBS shall ensure that the following stipulations are implemented:

A. *Archeology*

1. NBS will ensure that the construction site, utility and road rights-of-way, and any other areas subject to physical disturbance are subjected to archeological study following a plan developed in consultation with the SHPO, the Tribe, and FAS, and submitted in draft to the same parties for at least thirty (30) days review and comment or objection. The study shall address the possible existence of an ancestral Wimok village site and the 19th century Six Corners neighborhood (See Preliminary ID Report, Chapter V). The study shall be conducted in consultation with, and if they so desire with participation by, the Tribe and FAS.

2. Should the study indicate the existence of archeological resources, NBS in consultation with the SHPO, the Tribe, and FAS shall determine whether and how they will be treated. Any treatment involving excavation shall be in accordance with the Plan of Action to be developed by NBS pursuant to the regulations implementing NAGPRA (43 CFR 10). NBS shall afford the SHPO, Tribe, and FAS at least thirty (30) days to review and comment on, or object to, its decision about treatment of archeological resources.

3. Any plan to avoid impacts on archeological resources shall meet the "Standards for Avoidance," set forth in "Technical Standards: Featherberg Laboratory Project Historic Preservation" (Kungbutaie 6/3/09), attached hereto as Appendix I.

4. Any archeological data recovery plan shall meet the "Standards for Archeological Data Recovery, Featherberg Laboratory Project" set forth in the same "Technical Standards" (Appendix I).

5. Having determined a course of action pursuant to Stipulation III.A.2, and subject to dispute resolution under Stipulation VI.E, NBS will implement the selected course of action.

B. *Growth Inducement*

1. NBS will conduct background study including sample field investigation on the vacant land within 1/4 mile of the construction site, to determine the likelihood that archeological resources are present and if so to define their approximate extent. NBS shall develop the scope of work for the study in consultation with the Tribe, SHPO, City, and FAS.

2. Should the study indicate that significant archeological resources may be present, NBS will consult with the City, the Tribe, the SHPO and FAS to ascertain what steps the City may take to protect such resources from development, and encourage the City to take such steps.

C. *Visual Impacts*

1. NBS will consult with the Tribe concerning the possible visual impacts of the Laboratory Project on traditional use of Grassy Knob, and will seek agreement with the Tribe on measures to mitigate such impacts, subject to Stipulation VI.E.

2. Should NBS's agreement with the Tribe, or any supporting documents, reveal the nature of the Tribe's use of Grassy Knob, NBS will endeavor to protect this information in accordance with NHPA Section 304.

3. Mitigation measures may include, but are not limited to:

a) Design of the laboratory buildings to control siting, massing, color, and placement on the land;
b) Controls on the season in which construction occurs;
c) Vegetative barriers; and
d) Compensatory actions such as purchase of easements for future tribal access to Grassy Knob.

D. *Parking Structure Demolition.* In consultation with FAS, NBS will ensure that demolition of the existing parking structure is monitored to test the local tradition that the body of Jimmy Hoffa is embedded in one of the supporting concrete pylons.

IV. *Burned Block Site.* Should NBS consider the Burned Block its preferred alternative, NBS shall ensure that the following stipulations are implemented:

A. *Archeology*

1. Coordinated with the identification of toxic and hazardous wastes (if any) associated with the burned out residential block, NBS will ensure that the site is subjected to archeological study following a study plan developed in consultation with the SHPO, the City, the Tribe, and FAS, and submitted in draft to the SHPO, City, Tribe and FAS for at least thirty (30) days review and comment. The study shall explicitly address the possible existence of the mid-19th century Muntinmasher's Window Factory (See Preliminary ID Report, Chapter V), and the archeological significance, if any, of the burned out residential block. The study shall be conducted in consultation with, and should they so desire with active participation by, the City, Tribe and FAS.

2. Should the study indicate the existence of archeological resources, NBS in consultation with the SHPO, the Tribe, and FAS shall determine whether and how they will be treated. Any treatment involving excavation shall be in accordance with the Plan of Action to be developed by NBS pursuant to the regulations implementing NAGPRA (43 CFR 10). NBS shall afford the SHPO, Tribe, and FAS at least thirty (30) days to review and comment on, or object to, its decision about treatment of archeological resources.

3. Any plan to avoid impacts on archeological resources shall meet the "Standards for Avoidance," set forth in "Technical Standards: Featherberg Laboratory Project Historic Preservation" (Kungbutaie 6/3/09), attached hereto as Appendix I.

4. Any archeological data recovery plan shall meet the "Standards for Archeological Data Recovery, Featherberg Laboratory Project" set forth in the same "Technical Standards" (Appendix I).

5. Having determined a course of action pursuant to Stipulation IV.A.2, and subject to dispute resolution under Stipulation VI.E, NBS will implement the selected course of action.

B. *Visual and Social Effects*

1. NBS will analyze the laboratory's possible visual and social (including economic) effects on the Red Rooster neighborhood and other residences and commercial buildings 45 years old or older within the area of potential effect, in consultation with the City, Red Rooster, and residents of the area. NBS will ask Red Rooster and the City to assist NBS in consulting with residents. In accordance with Executive Order 12898, consultation will accommodate the special needs of the Hispanic and Orthodox Jewish residents, as well as the needs of disabled persons.

2. Subject to Stipulation VI.E, NBS will seek agreement with the City, Red Rooster, and other concerned residents regarding means of mitigating adverse visual or social (including economic) effects on the Red Rooster neighborhood and surrounding residential neighborhoods.

3. Measures selected may include, but are not limited to:

a) Design of the laboratory buildings, including siting, massing, color, scale, and fenestration, to harmonize with the character of surrounding structures, taking into account the guidelines for new construction in the Secretary of the Interior's Standards for Rehabilitation and Guidelines for Rehabilitating Historic Buildings ("Rehabilitation Standards").
b) Educating laboratory employees about the cultural and architectural features of the neighborhoods, and encouraging respect for such features by anyone planning to relocate to the neighborhoods.
c) Encouraging businesses and homeowners to conduct any new construction or rehabilitation in a manner consistent with the Rehabilitation Standards.
d) Creation of a revolving fund to assist local businesspeople and homeowners in maintaining their properties.
e) Purchase of development rights.

f) City property tax controls to minimize financial impacts on local businesses and homeowners.

V. *Existing Laboratory Site.* Whichever alternative, NBS will provide all its data on the historic preservation implications of the "no project" alternative to GLIB for use in GLIB's compliance with environmental and historic preservation authorities in remediating toxic wastes at the existing Laboratory site.

VI. *Administration*

A. *Review of Submittals*

Whenever any signatory or concurring party to this MOA is given the opportunity to review documents, that party shall have thirty (30) calendar days for such review. Failure of such party to provide comments may be taken to indicate that party's approval of the document.

B. *Professional Supervision*

NBS shall ensure that all preservation treatment of historic buildings is carried out by or under the supervision of a person or persons meeting at a minimum the *Secretary of the Interior's Professional Qualifications Standards for Historic Architecture* (48 FR 44739), and that all archaeological activities are carried out by or under the direct supervision of a person or persons meeting at a minimum the *Secretary of the Interior's Professional Qualifications Standards for Archeology* (48 FR 44739). However, nothing in this stipulation may be interpreted to bar NBS or any agent or contractor of NBS from using the properly supervised services of employees and volunteers who do not meet the above standards.

C. *Alterations to Project Documents*

NBS shall not alter any plan, scope of work, or other document that has been reviewed and commented on pursuant to this MOA, except to finalize documents commented on in draft, without first affording the other parties to this MOA the opportunity to review the proposed change and determine whether it requires that this MOA be amended. If one or more of the parties determines that an amendment is needed, the parties to this MOA shall consult in accordance with 36 CFR 800.6(c)(7) to consider such an amendment.

D. *Annual Report and Review*

1. On or before December 5 of each year until NBS, the City, and the SHPO agree in writing that the terms of this MOA have been fulfilled, NBS shall prepare and provide an annual report to all signatory and concurring parties to this MOA, to any party invited to concur who has declined to do so, and to any other individual or group that so requests, detailing how the applicable terms of this MOA are being implemented.

2. NBS shall ensure that the annual report is made available for public inspection, that interested members of the public are made aware of its availability, and that interested members of the public are invited to provide comments to the ACHP and SHPO as well as to NBS and the City.

3. The SHPO and City shall review the annual report and provide comments to NBS. Other parties to this MOA may review and comment on the annual report at their discretion.

4. At the request of any signatory or concurring party to this MOA, a meeting or meetings shall be held to facilitate review and comment, to resolve questions, or to resolve adverse comments. Requests for such a meeting by parties invited to concur who have declined to do so, and from other interested parties, will be considered by the parties to this MOA.

5. Based on this review, NBS, the SHPO, and the City shall determine whether this MOA shall continue in force, be amended, or be terminated.

E. *Resolving Objections*

1. Should any party to this MOA object to any action carried out or proposed with respect to development of the Laboratory or imple-

mentation of this MOA, NBS shall consult with the objecting party to resolve the objection. If after initiating such consultation NBS determines that the objection cannot be resolved through consultation, NBS shall forward all documentation relevant to the objection to the ACHP, including NBS's proposed response to the objection, with the expectation that within thirty (30) days after receipt of all pertinent documentation, the ACHP shall exercise one of the following options:

a) Advise NBS that the ACHP concurs in NBS's proposed final decision, whereupon NBS will respond to the objection accordingly;
b) Provide NBS with recommendations, which NBS shall take into account in reaching a final decision regarding its response to the objection; or
c) Notify NBS that the objection will be referred for comment pursuant to 36 CFR § 800.7(c), and proceed to refer the objection and comment. The resulting comment shall be taken into account by NBS in accordance with 36 CFR § 800.7(c)(4) and §110(1) of NHPA.

2. Should the ACHP not exercise one of the above options within thirty (30) days after receipt of all pertinent documentation, NBS may assume the ACHP's concurrence in its proposed response to the objection.

3. NBS shall take into account any ACHP recommendation or comment provided in accordance with this stipulation with reference only to the subject of the objection; NBS's responsibility shall remain unchanged to ensure that all provisions of this MOA that are not the subjects of the objection are carried out.

4. At any time during implementation of the measures stipulated in this MOA, should an objection pertaining to this MOA be raised by a member of the public, NBS shall notify the parties to this MOA and take the objection into account, consulting with the objector and, should the objector so request, with any of the parties to this MOA to resolve the objection.

F. *Amendments*

Any party to this MOA may propose to NBS that the MOA be amended, whereupon NBS shall consult with the other parties to

394 / Appendix 4

this MOA to consider such an amendment. 36 CFR § 800.6(c)(7) shall govern the execution of any such amendment.

G. *Termination*

1. If NBS determines that it cannot ensure implementation of the terms of this MOA, or if the SHPO, City, or ACHP determines that the MOA is not being properly implemented, NBS, the SHPO, the City, or the ACHP may propose to the other parties to this MOA that it be terminated.

2. The party proposing to terminate this MOA shall so notify all parties to this MOA, explaining the reasons for termination and affording them at least thirty (30) days to consult in accordance with 36 CFR 800.6(c)(8) and seek alternatives to termination.

3. Should such consultation fail and the MOA be terminated, NBS shall either:
a) Consult in accordance with 36 CFR § 800.6(b)(2) to develop a new MOA; or
b) Request the comments of the ACHP pursuant to 36 CFR § 800.7(a)(1).

4. If the terms of this MOA have not been implemented by January 1, 2013, unless it has been amended to extend its life this MOA shall be considered null and void. In such case NBS, if it chooses to continue with its participation in the project, shall re-initiate its review in accordance with 36 CFR 800.

Execution of this MOA by NBS, the City, and the SHPO, and its submission by NBS to the ACHP in accordance with 36 CFR 800.6(b)(1)(iv), shall evidence that NBS has afforded the ACHP an opportunity to comment on the Laboratory Project and its effects on historic properties, and that NBS has taken into account the effects of the Laboratory Project on historic properties.

NATIONAL BUILDING SERVICE

By: _____
    Date:_____
NORTH NORWICH STATE HISTORIC PRESERVATION OFFICER

By: _____
    Date:_____
CITY OF FEATHERBERG

By: _____
    Date:_____
CONCUR:
GOVERNMENT LOGISTICS INVESTIGATION BUREAU

By: _____
    Date:_____
WIMOK INDIAN TRIBE

By: _____
    Date:_____
BIGSLOW RIVER PLANNING AUTHORITY

By: _____
    Date:_____
FEATHERBERG ASSOCIATION FOR ARCHITECTURAL
  HERITAGE

By: _____
    Date:_____
FEATHERBERG ARCHEOLOGICAL SOCIETY

By: _____
    Date:_____

RED ROOSTER NEIGHBORHOOD COMMISSION

By: _____
    Date:_____

Appendix 5:
Model NAGPRA Plan of Action

The model follows NAGPRA regulations as closely as I could make it. It illustrates just how complicated a POA can be if it actually meets the regulatory requirements. None of the tribes or other parties given in it are real, and I've not drafted any of the lengthy appendixes referred to in the text.

PLAN OF ACTION
TREATMENT OF NATIVE AMERICAN CULTURAL ITEMS
DURING CONSTRUCTION OF THE LIGHTGAS PIPELINE
WITHIN THE STATE OF UTAZONA

I. Background

A. Pursuant to 43 CFR 10.5(a), the Bureau of Range Management (BRM), assisted by the Lightgas Transportation Company (LTC), has determined that:

1. There are no known lineal descendants of specific Native Americans whose remains or cultural items are likely to be disturbed by construction of the Lightgas Pipeline (pipeline);

2. The three alternative routes for the pipeline within the State of Utazona cross the aboriginal lands of the following Indian tribes:

a) Alternative A: Yavajo and Malagansett;
b) Alternative B: Loomatilla, Tunipa, and Yavajo; and
c) Alternative C: Loomatilla and Malagansett.

3. Each of the above tribes is likely to be culturally affiliated with human remains, funerary objects, sacred objects, or objects of cultural patrimony discovered within its aboriginal lands in connection with construction of the pipeline in Utazona. In addition, the Chippesaw, whose ancestors are said to have occupied eastern Utazona before the coming of the Tunipa, may be culturally affiliated with Native American cultural items from eastern Utazona.

4. The Southern Skyute have a demonstrated cultural relationship with human remains and other cultural items associated with their passage across Utazona in 1879 along the "Trail of Hardship," which crosses the Alternative A and C rights-of-way near the City of Flatrock.

B. Pursuant to 43 CFR 10.3(c)(1) and 43 CFR 10.5(b)(1), BRM notified the governments of the six above tribes (the tribes) of the plans for the pipeline, providing them with the information required by 43 CFR 10.3(c)(1), and proposed consultation.

C. Pursuant to 43 CFR 10.3(b)(2) and 43 CFR 10.5(b)(2) and (3), BRM and LTC consulted with the tribes and their traditional religious leaders, providing them with the information required by 43 CFR 10.5(c) and requesting the information required by 43 CFR 10.5(d).

D. Pursuant to 43 CFR 10.3(b)(4), proof of BRM's and LTC's consultation with tribes is provided in Appendix C-7 ("Native American Consultation") of the draft Environmental Impact Statement dated July 31, 2007, and entitled "Draft Environmental Impact Statement: Lightgas Pipeline."

E. Based on BRM's program of identification and consultation, and pursuant to 43 CFR 10.5(e), BRM and LTC have developed the Plan of Action set forth in Section II.

F. Pursuant to 43 CFR 10.3(c)(3), BRM and LTC have coordinated consultation with tribes and development of the Plan of Action with review of the pipeline under Section 106 of the National Historic Preservation Act, and propose that the following Plan of Action be included by reference in the Memorandum of Agreement (MOA) being developed pursuant to Section 106 and its implementing regulations (36 CFR 800), which MOA shall be made consistent with this Plan of Action's applicable terms.

II. Plan of Action

BRM will ensure that the following Plan of Action (POA) is implemented:

A. Pursuant to 43 CFR 10.3(b)(1), LTC will contract for all excavation and treatment of Native American cultural items, as defined below, to be carried out by or under the direct supervision of persons holding permits issued in accordance with the Archeological Resources Protection Act (ARPA) (16 U.S.C. 470aa et seq.) and its implementing regulations. Such a permit may take the form of a contract, provided the terms of such contract meet the requirements of ARPA's regulations. BRM employees meeting the professional standards set forth in ARPA's regulations shall be understood to hold ARPA permits when engaged in their professional duties.

B. Pursuant to 43 CFR 10.3(b)(3), BRM and LTC will ensure that disposition of any Native American cultural items is as specified in paragraph J below.

C. Based on BRM's and LPG's consultation with tribes, and pursuant to 43 CFR 10.5(e)(1), BRM and LTC shall consider the following as Native American cultural items:

1. Human remains not obviously of non-Native American origin.

2. Associated funerary objects, that is, objects placed intentionally with human remains and still physically associated with such remains. The location of objects within grave fill or in immediate

proximity to human remains shall be understood to indicate intentional placement with human remains.

3. Unassociated funerary objects, that is, objects intentionally placed with human remains but whose association has been disturbed. Types of objects typically placed with human remains in Yavajo, Malagansett, Loomatilla, Tunipa, Chippesaw, and Southern Skyute cultural practice are listed in the report entitled "Typical Funerary Objects, Sacred Objects, and Cultural Patrimony of the Yavajo, Malagansett, Loomatilla, Tunipa, Chippesaw, and Southern Skyute," prepared by Backdirt Consultants, Inc., in consultation with the tribes and dated June 1, 2007 (Appendix A).

4. Sacred objects, that is, classes of objects identified by Yavajo, Malagansett, Loomatilla, Tunipa, Chippesaw, and Southern Skyute religious leaders as needed in the practice of traditional tribal religions (See Appendix A).

5. Objects of cultural patrimony, that is, classes of items having ongoing historical, traditional, or cultural importance central to the Yavajo, Malagansett, Loomatilla, Tunipa, Chippesaw, and/or Southern Skyute tribes, as distinct from items that could be owned and alienated by individual tribal members (See Appendix A).

D. BRM shall determine custody of Native American cultural items as follows:

1. Should Alternative A, which crosses the Loomatilla Reservation, be selected for the Pipeline, the Loomatilla tribe shall have custody of any such items found within the external boundaries of that reservation. No other tribal lands are crossed by any of the alternatives.

2. For Native American cultural items found beyond the boundaries of the Loomatilla Reservation, BRM will determine custody based on the findings of the report entitled "Cultural Affiliation with Lands along the Alternative Routes of the Proposed Lightgas Pipeline," prepared by Backdirt Consultants, Inc., in consultation with the tribes and dated May 1, 2007 (Appendix B).

E. BRM and LTC shall treat, care for, and handle Native American cultural items as follows:

1. Treatment, care, and handling of Native American cultural items found during archeological data recovery at specific, pre-identified sites shall follow the data recovery plan for the specific site, as prepared, reviewed, and finalized in accordance with the Memorandum of Agreement executed pursuant to Section 106 of the National Historic Preservation Act (MOA), subject to paragraph II.G-J.

2. Native American cultural items found during archeological monitoring shall be treated, cared for, and handled as follows:

a) All pipeline-related ground disturbances shall be monitored by a monitoring team employed by LTC and accepted by BRM after consultation with the tribes.

b) Should an object that in the opinion of the monitoring team might be a Native American cultural item be found, LTC shall halt work that might disturb the item or items until the following procedures have been implemented:

(1) The monitoring team shall inspect each item and record it in place to the extent feasible, subject to paragraph II.H. If the team determines that the object is not a Native American cultural item, it shall so certify in writing, and construction may continue, subject to the terms of the MOA.

(2) Where the archeological monitoring team determines that an item is a Native American cultural item, LTC shall reroute construction to the extent feasible to leave the item or items in place and unharmed. The items shall be recorded in place by the monitoring team, and LTC will cover them with earth under the monitoring team's supervision.

(3) Where rerouting is not feasible, the monitoring team shall remove the item or items to a safe location and prepare it for reburial or repatriation. LTC may resume construction in the vicinity as

soon as the monitoring team certifies that the item or items have been properly and safely removed.

F. BRM and LTC shall ensure that recording and analysis of Native American cultural items is carried out as follows:

1. LTC shall record and analyze any Native American cultural items found during archeological data recovery at specific, pre-identified sites in accordance with the data recovery plan for the specific site, as prepared, reviewed, and finalized in accordance with the MOA, subject to paragraphs II.G-J.

2. LTC shall record and analyze any Native American cultural items found during monitoring following the procedures set forth in the document entitled "Archeological Monitoring Plan, Lightgas Pipeline," prepared by Backdirt Consultants, Inc., in consultation with the tribes and dated May 20, 2003 (Appendix C).

3. In no case shall LTC allow analysis of Native American cultural items to continue beyond one year after the date such items are recovered, without the express written concurrence of BRM and the tribe(s) affiliated with such items. Analysis of material other than Native American cultural items may continue over a longer period of time.

G. BRM and LTC shall maintain contact with the tribes throughout the conduct of archeological data recovery and monitoring, as follows:

1. As the U.S. Government's formal government-to-government contact with the tribe, the BRM Regional Manager shall ask the governing body of each tribe to designate an official point of contact (POC) with LTC.

2. LTC shall contact the POC during planning for any data recovery or monitoring on lands with which such tribe is affiliated, advise the POC of the work schedule, and invite the POC to participate in or observe the work.

3. Through the POC, LTC shall offer employment to tribal members on data recovery projects and monitoring teams, and shall make special efforts to employ tribal members on lands with which each tribe is affiliated.

4. Upon the identification of a possible Native American cultural item, LTC shall notify the POC, and invite the POC to observe and advise during treatment and handling of the item.

5. LTC may, at its discretion, compensate or reimburse the POC for the POC's assistance.

6. LTC shall provide the tribes with written reports on all work accomplished.

H. Should a tribe request to conduct ceremonies or other traditional activities with respect to a Native American cultural item or items, BRM and LTC will accommodate such request to the maximum extent allowable by considerations of health, safety, environmental protection, and the project schedule. BRM and LTC shall ensure that all Native American cultural items found during data recovery and monitoring are treated with respect, and that the following provisions are observed:

1. Malagansett sacred objects shall not be washed or otherwise cleaned.

2. No person under the age of eighteen (18) years shall be permitted to view or handle any Chippesaw sacred object.

3. Yavaho human remains and funerary objects shall be reburied by non-Yavajo persons, or by Yavajo persons who specifically volunteer to do so, as close to their location of recovery as is consistent with their continued safety.

4. Loomatilla human remains shall be delivered to the Loomatilla Elders' Council unwashed and without analysis beyond determination of age, sex, and major physical abnormalities and traumas.

I. BRM and LTC shall ensure that reports are prepared, meeting contemporary archeological standards, on each pre-planned data recovery project and on each monitoring program. In consultation with the tribes, BRM and LTC will ensure that reports cannot be readily used to facilitate the disturbance of any Native American cultural item without the permission of the affiliated tribe(s). LTC shall distribute reports to the tribes and to parties specified in the MOA.

J. Except in the case of items disposed of in accordance with paragraphs H.3 and H.4, BRM and LTC shall ensure that Native American cultural items are disposed of as follows:

1. LTC shall deliver all Native American cultural items to BRM. LTC shall ensure that all such items are appropriately labeled to designate the tribe with which each is affiliated.

2. Within one week after receiving a Native American cultural item, BRM shall contact the affiliated tribe's POC, and arrange to transfer the items to the tribe. BRM shall proceed to transfer the items, documenting the date, time, and place of such transfer and a description of the items transferred.

APPROVED:

REGIONAL MANAGER, BUREAU OF RANGE MANAGEMENT

Bibliography

ACHP (Advisory Council on Historic Preservation). 2006. *In a Spirit of Stewardship: A Report on Federal Historic Property Management*. Washington, DC.

———. 2007. *The Preserve America Summit: Charting a Future Course for the National Historic Preservation Program*. Washington, DC.

ACHP and FERC (Federal Energy Regulatory Commission). 2002. *Guidelines for the Development of Historic Properties Management Plans for FERC Hydroelectric Projects*. Jointly issued. Washington, DC.

Anzalone, Ronald. 1995. "Remarks for 'Public Benefit of Mitigation.'" Annual Meeting of the National Conference of State Historic Preservation Officers, Washington DC, March 27.

Beierle, Thomas C., and Jerry Cayford. 2002. *Democracy in Practice: Public Participation in Environmental Decisions*. Washington, DC: Resources for the Future (RFF).

Bickman, Leonard, and Debra J. Rog. 1997. *Handbook of Applied Social Research Methods*. Thousand Oaks, CA: Sage Publications.

Bogdanos, Matthew, and William Patrick. 2005. *Thieves of Baghdad*. New York: Bloomsbury.

Branch, Kristi, et al. 1983. *Guide to Social Impact Assessment*. Boulder, CO: Westview Press.

Burdge, Rabel J., ed. 2003. Special Issue on the Practice of Social Impact Assessment. *Impact Assessment and Project Appraisal* 2 (2).

Burdge, Rabel J., et al. 1998. *A Conceptual Approach to Social Impact Assessment*. Madison, WI: Social Ecology Press.

Caldararo, Niccolo, Lee Davis, Peter Palmer, and Janet Waddington, eds. 2001. "The Contamination of Museum Materials and the Repatriation Process for Native California: Proceedings of a Working Conference at the San Francisco State University, September 29 to October 1, 2000." Collection Forum 16:1&2, Society for the Preservation of Natural History Collections.

Canter, Larry W. 1996. *Environmental Impact Assessment*. 2nd ed. New York: McGraw-Hill.

Carroll, Matthew S., et al. 2002. "Social Assessment for the Wenatchee National Forest Wildfires of 1994: Targeted Analysis for the Leavenworth, Entiat, and Chelan Ranger Districts." Gen. Tech. Rep. PNW-GTR-479. Portland, OR: U.S. Department of Agriculture, Forest Service, Pacific Northwest Research Station. www.treesearch.fs.fed.us/pubs/2961 (accessed December 27, 2007).

Carson, Rachel. 1962. *Silent Spring*. Cambridge, MA: Houghton Mifflin.

CEHP. 1993. *Principles of Cultural Resource Management Planning in the Department of Defense*. Washington, DC: Legacy Resource Management Program, Department of Defense.

———. 1994a. *Cultural Resource Law and Department of Defense International Activities*. Interim Paper, January 12. Washington, DC.

———. 1994b. *Cultural Resource Law and Department of Defense International Activities*. Background Paper, March 1. Washington, DC.

———. 1997. *Historic and Archeological Resource Protection Planning Guidelines*. Department of the Navy, NAVFACENGCOM Code 150RH, Alexandria, VA.

CEQ (Council on Environmental Quality). 1997a. *Considering Cumulative Effects Under the National Environmental Policy Act*. January 19. Washington, DC.

———. 1997. *Guidelines for Addressing Environmental Justice Under NEPA*. December 10. Washington, DC.

———. 2007. *A Citizen's Guide to the NEPA: Having Your Voice Heard*. December. Washington, DC.

Childs, S. Terry, and Eileen Corcoran. n.d. "Managing Archaeological Collections: Technical Assistance." Archeology and Ethnography Program, National Park Service. www.cr.nps.gov/aad/collections

Clavir, Miriam. 2002. *Preserving What Is Valued: Museums, Conservation, and First Nations*. Vancouver: University of British Columbia Press.

Cohen, Raymond. 2002. *Negotiating Across Cultures*. Washington, DC: U.S. Institute of Peace Press.

Constantino, Cathy A., and Christina Sickles Merchant. 1995. *Designing Conflict Management Systems*. San Francisco: Jossey-Bass Publishers.

Derry, Anne, Ward E. Jandl, Carol D. Shull, and Jan Thorman. 1985. *Guidelines for Local Surveys: A Basis for Preservation Planning*. National Register Bulletin 24, first issued 1977, revised 1985 by Patricia L. Parker. Washington, DC: National Park Service.

DOD (Department of Defense). 1996. Environmental Conservation Program. DOD Instruction 4715.3.

DoE (Department of Energy). 1995. *Environmental Guidelines for Development of Cultural Resource Management Plans*. Washington, DC: Office of Environmental Policy and Assistance.

Dorochoff, Nicholas. 2007. *Negotiation Basics for Cultural Resource Managers*. Walnut Creek, CA: Left Coast Press.

EPA (Environmental Protection Agency). 1996. *The Model Plan for Public Participation*. EPA-300-K-96-003. Washington, DC.

——. n.d. *EJ Tool for Analysis.* Handout, EPA Environmental Justice Training, June 18. Greenbelt, MD.

Epperson, Terrence W. 1997. "The Politics of 'Race' and Cultural Identity at the African Burial Ground Excavations, New York City." *World Archaeological Bulletin* 7: 108–17.

Executive Memorandum on Government-to-Government Relations with Native American Tribal Governments. April 29, 1998. Washington, DC.

Executive Order no. 13007. 1996. *Indian Sacred Sites,* May 24. Washington, DC.

Executive Order no. 13175. 2000. *Consultation and Coordination with Indian Tribal Governments,* November 6, Washington, DC.

Executive Order no. 13287. 2003. *Preserve America.* March 3. Washington, DC.

Executive Order no. 13336. 2004a. *American Indian and Alaska Native Education.* April 30. Washington, DC.

Executive Order no. 13352. 2004b. *Facilitation of Cooperative Conservation.* July 23. Washington DC.

Fine-Dare, Kathleen S. 2002. *Grave Injustice: The American Indian Repatriation Movement and NAGPRA.* Lincoln: University of Nebraska Press.

Finsterbusch, Kurt, and C. P. Wolf. 1981. *Methodology of Social Impact Assessment.* 2nd ed. Stroudsburg, PA: Hutchinson Ross.

Fischer, Frank. 2000. *Citizens, Experts, and the Environment: The Politics of Local Knowledge.* Durham, NC: Duke University Press.

Fisher, Roger, and Scott Brown. 1988. *Getting Together: Building Relationships as We Negotiate.* New York: Penguin Books.

Fisher, Roger, and William Ury. 1981. *Getting to Yes.* New York: Penguin Books.

——. 1991. *Getting to Yes: Negotiating Agreement Without Giving In,* edited by Bruce Patton, 2nd ed. New York: Penguin Books.

Fitch, James Marsten. 1982. *Historic Preservation: Curatorial Management of the Built World.* New York: McGraw-Hill.

Forester, John. 1999. *The Deliberative Practitioner: Encouraging Participatory Planning Processes.* Cambridge, MA: MIT Press.

Forest Service, USDA. 2000. "Working Together: California Indians and the Forest Service." Accomplishment Report 2000. Vallejo, CA: Pacific Southwest Region, USDA Forest Service.

Freudenburg, William R. 1986. "Social Impact Assessment." *Annual Review of Sociology* 12: 451–78.

Fullilove, Mindy Thompson. 2004. *Root Shock: How Tearing Up City Neighborhoods Hurts America, and What We Can Do About It.* New York: Ballantine.

Georgia Tech. 1993. "HBPP Building Manager's Training Course." Syllabus, Georgia Tech Continuing Education and General Services Administration, Atlanta.

Glass, James A. 1990. *The Beginnings of a New National Historic Preservation Program, 1957 to 1969.* American Association for State and Local History, Nashville, TN, and National Conference of State Historic Preservation Officers, Washington, DC.

Gorman, Alice. 2005. "The Cultural Landscape of Interplanetary Space." *Journal of Social Archaeology* 5 (1): 85–107, http://jsa.sagepub.com/cgi/content/abstract/5/1/85 (accessed December 31, 2007).

Grimm, Lydia T. 1997. "Sacred Lands and the Establishment Clause: Indian Religious Practices on Federal Lands." *Natural Resources and Environment* 12 (1): 1–9, 78.

Griset, Suzannne, and Marc Kodack. 1999. *Guidelines for the Field Collection of Archaeological Materials and Standard Operating Procedures for Curating Department of Defense Archaeological Collections.* U.S. Army Corps of Engineers, St. Louis District.

GSA (General Services Administration). 1999. *NEPA Desk Guide.* Washington, DC: Public Buildings Service, www.gsa.gov/gsa/cm_attachments/GSA _DOCUMENT/NEPA_Desk_Guide_R2E-c-q-v_0Z5RDZ-i34K-pR.pdf (accessed December 24, 2007).

HABS/HAER (Historic American Buildings Survey/Historic American Engineering Record). 1990. *Secretary of the Interior's Standards and Guidelines for Architectural and Engineering Documentation.* Compiled by Caroline H. Russell, HABS/HAER, National Park Service. Washington, DC: HABS/HAER.www .cr.nps.gov/habshaer/pubs/sisgaed.pdf.

Halpin, A. E., and K. L. Holland. 1997. *An Archeological Curation-Needs Assessment for the U.S. Navy, Engineering Field Activities, West and Northwest, Naval Facilities Engineering Command.* U.S. Army Corps of Engineers, St. Louis District.

Herman, Helen Y. 2004. "Why is Paris Arguably the World's Most Beautiful City?" *Preservation in Print* 31 (5): 12–13.

Hester, Randolph T. 1987. "Subconscious Landscapes of the Heart." *Place* 2 (3): 10–22.

Hicks, Robert D. 1997. "Time Crime: Protecting the Past for Future Generations." *FBI Law Enforcement Bulletin,* July 1, www.fbi.gov/publications/leb/1997/ july971.htm (accessed January 1, 2008).

Hosmer, Charles B., Jr. 1965. *Presence of the Past: The History of the Preservation Movement in the United States Before Williamsburg.* New York: G.P. Putnam's Sons.

———. 1981. *Preservation Comes of Age: From Williamsburg to the National Trust, 1926–49.* 2 vols. Charlottesville: University of Virginia Press.

Hutt, Sherry, Elwood W. Jones, and Martin E. McAllister. 1992. *Archeological Resource Protection.* Washington, DC: Preservation Press.

Interorganizational Committee on Guidelines and Principles for Social Impact Assessment. 1993. "Guidelines and Principles for Social Impact Assessment." *Environmental Impact Assessment Review* 15 (1): 11–43.

ISO (International Organization for Standards). 1995. *Environmental Management Systems: 14000 Series.* Released by American National Standards Institute, ASQC, Milwaukee, WI. 532013005. www.iso14000.com/ (accessed July 26, 2003).

Johnson, Ronald W., and Michael G. Schene. 1987. *Cultural Resources Management.* Malabar, FL: Robert E. Krieger Publishing.

Judge, W. James, and Lynne Sebastian. 1988. *Quantifying the Present and Predicting the Past: Theory, Method, and Application of Archaeological Predictive Modeling.* Denver, CO: Bureau of Land Management, Department of the Interior.

Keller, J. Timothy, and Genevieve P. Keller. 1987. *How to Evaluate and Nominate Designed Historic Landscapes.* National Register Bulletin 18. National Register of Historic Places, National Park Service, Washington, DC.

King, Thomas F., and Patricia Parker. *Guidelines for Evaluating and Documenting Traditional Cultural Properties*. Washington, DC: National Park Service, 1990, rev. 1992 and 1998.

King, Thomas F. 1998. "How the Archeologists Stole Culture. A Gap in American Environmental Impact Assessment and How to Fill It." *Environmental Impact Assessment Review* 18 (2): 117–33.

———. 2001. *Federal Planning and Historic Places: The Section 106 Process*. Walnut Creek, CA: AltaMira Press.

———. 2002a. *Thinking About Cultural Resource Management: Essays From the Edge*. Walnut Creek, CA: AltaMira Press.

———. 2002b. "Cultural Resources in an Environmental Assessment under NEPA." *Environmental Practice* 4 (3): 137–44.

———. 2003a. "Considering the Cultural Importance of Natural Landscapes in NEPA Review: The Mushgigagamongsebe Example." *Environmental Practice* 5 (4): 298–301.

———. 2003b. *Places That Count: Traditional Cultural Properties in Cultural Resource Management*. Walnut Creek, CA: AltaMira Press.

———. 2006. "Creatures and Culture: Some Implications of Dugong v. Rumsfeld." *International Journal of Cultural Property* 13 (2): 235–40.

———. 2007. *Saving Places That Matter: A Citizens Guide to the National Historic Preservation Act*. Walnut Creek, CA: Left Coast Press.

King, Thomas F., and Patricia P. Hickman. 1973. *The Southern Santa Clara Valley: A General Plan for Archaeology*. San Felipe Archaeology I, San Francisco State University, A.E. Treganza Anthropology Museum, San Francisco.

———. 1977. "San Felipe: Designing a General Plan for Archaeology." In *Conservation Archaeology: A Guide for Cultural Resource Management Studies*. Edited by Michael B. Schiffer and George Gumerman. New York: Academic Press.

King, Thomas F., and Ethan Rafuse. 1994. *NEPA and the Cultural Environment: An Assessment of Effectiveness*. Washington, DC: CEHP for Council on Environmental Quality.

King, Thomas F., and Samuel E. Stuelson. 2001. "Preservation Laws and Policies." Available online (subscription required) at UNESCO *Encyclopedia of Life Support Systems*. www.eolss.net/ (accessed July 26, 2003).

Klesert, Anthony L., and Alan S. Downer. 1990. *Preservation on the Reservation: Native Americans, Native American Lands, and Archeology*. Navajo Nation Papers in Anthropology, no. 26. Navajo Nation Archeology Department, Window Rock, AZ.

Kritek, Phyllis Beck. 1994. *Negotiating at an Uneven Table*. San Francisco: Jossey-Bass Publishers.

Kuhn, Thomas. 1962. *The Structure of Scientific Revolutions*. Chicago: University of Chicago Press.

Lawrence, David P. 2003. *Environmental Impact Assessment: Practical Solutions to Recurrent Problems*. New York: John Wiley & Sons.

Lee, Antoinette J. 1987. "Discovering Old Cultures in the New World: The Role of Ethnicity." in *The American Mosaic*, edited by Robert Stipe and Antoinette J. Lee. Washington, DC: U.S. Committee for the International Council on Monuments and Sites (US/ICOMOS).

Lipe, W. D., and A. J. Lindsay Jr. 1974. *Proceedings of the 1974 Cultural Resource Management Conference.* Museum of Northern Arizona Technical Series No. 14, Flagstaff, AZ.

Loomis, Ormond H. 1983. *Cultural Conservation: The Protection of Cultural Heritage in the United States.* Washington, DC: American Folklife Center and National Park Service.

Lynch, Kevin. 1972. *What Time Is This Place?* Cambridge, MA: MIT Press.

McCarthy, John P. 1996. "Who Owns These Bones? Descendant Communities and Partnerships in the Excavation and Analysis of Historic Cemetery Sites in New York and Philadelphia." *Public Archaeology Review* 4 (2): 312.

McClelland, Linda Flint, J. Timothy Keller, Genevieve P. Keller, and Robert Z. Melnick. 1990. *Guidelines for Evaluating and Documenting Rural Historic Districts.* National Register Bulletin 30, National Register of Historic Places, National Park Service. Washington, DC.

Miller, Frederic M. 1990. *Arranging and Describing Archives and Manuscripts.* Chicago: Society of American Archivists.

Murtagh, William J. 1997. *Keeping Time: The History and Theory of Preservation in America.* Rev. ed. New York: John Wiley & Sons.

NARA (National Archives and Records Administration). 1989. *NARA and the Disposal of Federal Records. Laws and Authorities and Their Implementation. A Report of the Committee on Authorities and Program Alternatives.* Washington, DC.

———. 1992. *Disposal of Federal Records.* Washington, DC.

NASA (National Aeronautics and Space Administration). 2002. *Environmental Assessment for the Outrigger Telescopes Project, Mauna Kea Science Reserve, Island of Hawaii.* Washington, DC: NASA, Office of Space Science.

New Orleans, City of. 1968. *Vieux Carre Historic District Demonstration Study.* New Orleans: Bureau of Government Research for the City of New Orleans.

NOAA (National Oceanic and Atmospheric Administration). 1994. *Guidelines and Principles for Social Impact Assessment.* National Marine Fisheries Service; prepared by the Interorganizational Committee on Guidelines and Principles for Social Impact Assessment.

NPS (National Park Service). 1983. "Secretary of the Interior's Standards for Archeology and Historic Preservation," 48. *Federal Register* 44716-68.

———. 1983. "Secretary of the Interior's Standards for Architectural and Engineering Documentation," 48. *Federal Register* 44730-34.

———. 1988. "Guidelines for Federal Agency Responsibilities Under Section 110 of the National Historic Preservation Act," 53. *Federal Register* 4727-46. Annotated and republished by ACHP as "The Section 110 Guidelines." Superceded 1998.

———. 1990. "Abandoned Shipwreck Guidelines," 44. *Federal Register* 50116-45.

———. 1992. *The Secretary of the Interior's Standards for the Treatment of Historic Properties. Properties with Guidelines for Preserving, Rehabilitating, Restoring, and Reconstructing Historic Buildings.* Washington, DC: Preservation Assistance Division, Government Printing Office. Reissued 1995. www2.cr.nps.gov/tps/secstan1.htm.

———. 1998. "Secretary of the Interior's Standards and Guidelines for Federal Agency Historic Preservation Programs Under Section 110 of the National Historic Preservation Act," 63. *Federal Register* 20495-20508.

NRHP (National Register of Historic Places). 1991. *How to Apply the National Register Criteria for Evaluation.* National Register Bulletin 15. Washington, DC: National Park Service.

Odegaard, Nancy, et al. 1990. "Training in Collections Care and Maintenance." in *Archaeology and Ethnography.* Vol. 1. Washington, DC: National Institute for Conservation.

Parker, Patricia L. 1990. *Keepers of the Treasures: Protecting Historic Properties and Cultural Traditions on Indian Lands.* Report to Congress on Tribal Preservation Funding Needs, Interagency Resources Division. Washington, DC.

Parker, Patricia L., and Thomas F. King. 1978. "Intercultural Mediation at Truk International Airport." in *Anthropological Praxis: Translating Knowledge into Action.* Edited by Robert M. Wulff and Shirley J. Fiske. Boulder, CO: Westview Press.

———. 1990. *Guidelines for Evaluating and Documenting Traditional Cultural Properties.* National Register Bulletin 38, National Park Service, Washington, DC.

Price, H. Marcus, III. 1991. *Disputing the Dead: U.S. Law on Aboriginal Remains and Grave Goods.* Columbia: University of Missouri Press.

Rapoport, Amos. 1982. *The Meaning of the Built Environment: A Nonverbal Communications Approach.* Beverly Hills, CA: Sage Publications.

Rubenstein, David, Jerry Aroesty, and Charles Thompsen. 1992. *Two Shades of Green: Environmental Protection and Combat Training.* Santa Monica, CA: Rand National Defense Research Institute R-4220-A.

Rushlow, Frederick J., and Don Kermath. 1978. *Proactive Maintenance Planning for Historic Buildings.* USACERL Technical Report CRC-94/01. Champaign, IL: Construction Engineering Research Laboratories.

San Francisco (City and County of). 1972. *Urban Design Plan.* San Francisco: Department of City Planning.

Savage, Beth L., ed. 1996. *African American Historic Places.* Washington, DC: National Register of Historic Places.

Sayre, Don. 1996. *Inside ISO 14000: The Competitive Advantage of Environmental Management.* Delray Beach, FL: St. Lucie Press.

Schensul, Stephen L., Jean J. Schensul, and Margaret D. LeCompte. 1999. *Essential Ethnographic Methods.* Vol. 2, *The Ethnographer's Toolkit.* Walnut Creek, CA: AltaMira Press.

Siemons, R. L., and D. Sanders. 1998. *Assessment of Potential Archaeological Collections Facility Sites at Eaker Air Force Base, Blytheville, Arkansas.* U.S. Army Corps of Engineers, St. Louis District.

Siemons, R. L., et al. 1998. *Assessment of Potential Archaeological Collections Facility Sites at Edwards Air Force Base.* U.S. Army Corps of Engineers, St. Louis District.

Smith, Michael D. 2006. "Cumulative Impact Assessment Under the National Environmental Policy Act: An Analysis of Recent Case Law." *Environmental Practice* 8 (4): 228–40.

Stapp, Darby C., and Michael S. Burney. 2002. *Tribal Cultural Resource Management.* Walnut Creek, CA: AltaMira Press.

Stipe, Robert, ed. 1982. *Historic Preservation in Foreign Countries.* Washington, DC: U.S. Committee of the International Council on Monuments and Sites (Supplement 1986).

Stipe, Robert E., and Antoinette J. Lee, eds. 1987. *The American Mosaic: Preserving a Nation's Heritage.* U.S. Committee of the International Council on Monuments and Sites. Washington, DC: Preservation Press.

Susskind, Lawrence E., S. McKearnan, and J. Thomas-Larmer, Jr. eds. 1999. *The Consensus Building Handbook: A Comprehensive Guide to Reaching Agreement.* Thousand Oaks, CA: Sage.

Taylor, C. Nicholas, D. Hobson Bryan, and Colin C. Goodrich. 1990. *Social Assessment: Theory, Process and Techniques.* Lincoln University, New Zealand.

Thomas, David Hurst, and Sarah Colley. 2002. *Skull Wars: Kennewick Man, Archaeology, and the Battle for Native American Identity.* New York: Basic Books.

Thompson, J. G., and Gary Williams. 1992. "Social Assessment: Roles for Practitioners and the Need for Stronger Mandates." *Impact Assessment Bulletin* 10 (3):43–56.

Trimble, M. K., and C. B. Pulliam. 1994. *An Archaeological Curation-Needs Assessment for the U.S. Army Corps of Engineers, Mobile District.* U.S. Army Corps of Engineers, St. Louis District.

Tyler, Norman. 1999. *Historic Preservation: An Introduction to Its History, Principles, and Practice.* New York: W.W. Norton & Co.

UNESCO (United Nations Educational, Scientific, and Cultural Organization). 1962. *Recommendation Concerning the Safeguarding of the Beauty and Character of Landscapes and Sites.* New York: UNESCO.

———. 1976a. *Recommendation Concerning the Safeguarding and Contemporary Role of Historic Areas.* New York: UNESCO.

———. 1976b. *Convention on the Means of Prohibiting and Preventing the Illicit Import, Export and Transfer of Ownership of Cultural Property.* New York: UNESCO.

———. 2001. *Convention on the Protection of the Underwater Cultural Heritage.* New York: UNESCO.

———. 2003. *Convention for the Safeguarding of the Intangible Cultural Heritage.* New York: UNESCO.

United Nations General Assembly. 2007. *United Nations Declaration on the Rights of Indigenous Peoples.* New York: United Nations.

Ury, William. 1978. *Getting Past No.* New York: Bantam Books.

U.S. Conference of Mayors. 1967. *With Heritage So Rich.* New York: Random House.

Vanclay, Frank. 2003. "International Principles for Social Impact Assessment." *Impact Assessment and Project Appraisal* 21 (1): 5–12.

Warnow, Joan, et al. 1982. *Documentation of Postwar Physics.* 3 vols. New York: American Institute of Physics.

Wescott, Konnie, and R. Joe Brandon, eds. 2000. *Practical Applications of GIS for Archaeologists: A Predictive Modeling Toolkit.* London and New York: Taylor & Francis.

Wilkins, Hugh. 2003. "The Need for Subjectivity in EIA: Discourse as a Tool for Sustainable Development." *Environmental Impact Assessment Review* 23 (4): 401–14.

Wilkinson, Charles, ed. 1997. *Indian Tribes as Sovereign Governments*. American Indian Lawyer Training Program. Oakland, CA: AIRI Press.

Wilson, Rex L., ed. 1987. *Rescue Archeology: Proceedings of the Second New World Conference on Rescue Archeology*. Dallas: Southern Methodist University Press.

Wilson, Rex L., and Gloria Loyola, eds. 1981. *Rescue Archeology: Papers from the First New World Conference on Rescue Archeology*. Washington, DC: Preservation Press.

Wilson, Sherrill D. 1996. *Citations on the New York African Burial Ground: 1991–1996*. 3rd ed. Compiled by the Office of Public Education and Interpretation of the African Burial Ground, New York.

WRC/FEMA (Water Resource Council [defunct] and Federal Emergency Management Agency [successor]). 1978. "Floodplain Management: Guidelines for Implementing Executive Order 11988," 43. *Federal Register* 6030-55. February 10. See also 44 CFR 9. Further advice on EO 11988 available from FEMA at www.governmentguide.com/govsite.adp?bread=*Main*&url=http%3A//www.fema.gov/ (accessed January 25, 2003).

Index

landscapes and section 106, 252–53; discoveries and section 106, 186–89; eligibility for National Register and section 106, 139–54; emergencies and section 106, 189–90; enactment of, 18–19; extra-territorial application of section 106, 244–45; first cases under section 106, 20; folklife study under, 289; identification of historic properties under section 106, 123–39, 151–53, 184–86, 326; language of section 106, 19–20, 25, 89–90; linear resources and section 106, 254–55; memorandum of agreement (MOA) under section 106, 175–77, 180–83, 186–88, 222, 269–70, 326; NAGPRA and section 106, 267–70; National Historic Landmarks and section 106, 244; NEPA and section 106, 326; participants in review under section 106, 31–49; pre-emptive destruction and section 106, 198–99; problems with (summary) of section 106, 199–201; process summarized in section 106, 109–201; programmatic agreements under section 106, 191–198; reasonable and good faith effort standard under section 106, 129–31, 136–38; recordation and section 106, 229–31; regulations implementing under section 106, 25, 27, 30, 41, 48, 111–12, 116–17, 119, 146, 148, 151–52, 165, 190, 193, 229, 234–35, 237, 244, 264, 276, 312, 335–36, 351; rehabilitation/adaptive use and section 106, 222–23, 227
section 2 (purposes), 183–84; section 101(b)(3) SHPO responsibilities, 39–40; section 101(e)(3)(B), grants to tribes, others, 27; section 110, 26, 30, 48; section 110(a)(1), 224–25, 229; section 110(a)(2), 36, 149, 232–36, 238; section 110(b), 180, 229; section 110(d), 183; section 110(f), 244;

section 110(k), 198–99; section 110(l), 177–78; section 110 Guidelines, NPS, 180; section 111, 227; section 112, 317–18, 351–52, 382; section 301(7), 118; section 301(8), 210–11; section 402, 245, 256; section 4(f) of DOT Act and section 106, 241–44; SHPO roles under section 106, 25, 39–41, 115–16, 121–23, 129–38, 146–48, 154–55, 161, 164–65, 175–76, 194, 199–201; substitution of tribal procedures for section 106, 41; terminating consultation under section 106, 170, 175, 177–79; tribes and section 106, 27–29, 41–44; "undertaking" as review trigger in section 106, 110, 113, 115–21, 125, 128, 136, 155, 162, 187

National Mining Association v. Fowler, 120
National Park Service (NPS), 372; creation and early history of, 16–18, 110–11, 274–75; external programs, 37–38; roles in CRM, 36–41, 87–106, 180, 187, 209–37, 239–40, 244, 252–52, 262–64, 172, 277–80, 351–52, 372; Historic Preservation Fund matching grants, 24–26, 40; response to EO 11593, 21–22; response to NHPA enactment, 19–20
National Preservation Institute, 12
National Register of Historic Places, 372; animals/habitats and, 255–56; criteria, 90–97, 141; criteria considerations, 97–106; determining eligibility for, 146–154; keeper of, 87, 93, 95, 144–49, 152–53, 163, 241, 361; nomination to, 89, 149–53, 233–34; nomination regulations (36 CFR 60), 90, 98, 141; obsolete eligibility regulations (36 CFR 63) still extant, 203n43
National Rifle Association, 45
National Trust for Historic Preservation, 17, 19, 31, 39, 224–25, 294, 348

About the Author

Thomas F. King was a teenaged pothunter. Interested in archeology by age five, he dug into his first prehistoric site at age fourteen. By the time he completed undergraduate work in anthropology at San Francisco State University in 1968, he was supporting himself and his family as a field archeologist, working on "salvage archeology" projects—digging sites that were about to be destroyed by highways and reservoirs. By the late 1960s, he had become disenchanted with digging sites on the brink of destruction and had begun to wonder if there wasn't a better way to manage them. Thanks to Eric Barnes, a planning student colleague at San Francisco State University, King discovered the then shiny-new National Historic Preservation Act. King continued his archeological studies at UCLA and received his PhD from the University of California at Riverside in 1976, but he became increasingly involved in historic preservation and the evolving field of cultural resource management. In 1972 he was hired by the Agua Caliente Band of Cahuilla Indians in Palm Springs, California, who were trying to save Tahquitz Canyon, their traditional origin place, from a dam project; this launched him into continuing work with indigenous and other non-mainstream communities and with what now are called "traditional cultural properties."

King's career has included working as a private consultant in archeology and historic preservation, as an archeologist with the National Park Service, as chief of staff for the "State" Historic

Preservation Officer of the Trust Territory of the Pacific Islands, and as overseer of section 106 review with the Advisory Council on Historic Preservation. He is now in private practice as a consultant, teacher, facilitator/mediator, and writer in and around historic preservation, affiliated with SWCA Environmental Consultants (www.swca.com). He continues to dabble in archeology through the International Group for Historic Aircraft Recovery (www.tighar.org), in pursuit of Amelia Earhart on a remote Pacific island. He brings to his writings and teachings a substantial knowledge of archeology; a more general acquaintance with architectural history, historical architecture, and planning; experience in writing and implementing laws, regulations, and guidelines; and an appreciation for the concerns of indigenous and other minority communities and groups. This book is drawn from the many short courses in historic preservation and cultural resource management that he has taught for SWCA as well as for the National Preservation Institute, the Advisory Council, the University of Nevada, Reno, the General Services Administration, and various other agencies, state, and territorial governments, private firms, Indian tribes, and Native Hawaiian organizations.

King can be contacted at TFKing106@aol.com and welcomes comments, questions, and consulting business.

The first edition of this book (1998) was the first of King's books to be published by AltaMira Press. Others have followed, including:

Federal Projects and Historic Places: The Section 106 Process (2000)
Thinking About Cultural Resource Management: Essays From the Edge (2002)
Places that Count: Traditional Cultural Properties in Cultural Resource Management (2003)
Amelia Earhart's Shoes (With R. Jacobson, K. Burns, and K. Spading) (2001, 2004)